# The Cultural Industries

What are the 'cultural industries'? What role do they play in contemporary society? How are they changing?

Combining a political economy approach with the best aspects of cultural studies, sociology, communication studies and social theory, this book provides an overview of the key debates surrounding the cultural industries.

*The Cultural Industries*
- considers both the entertainment and the information sectors
- combines analysis of the contemporary scene with a long-range historical perspective
- uses a range of examples drawn from Europe, North America and beyond.

Hesmondhalgh's clearly-written text not only represents an important intervention in research on cultural production, but also provides students of cultural studies, communication and media with an invaluable introduction to the area.

**David Hesmondhalgh** is Lecturer in Sociology in the Faculty of Social Sciences, The Open University.

# The Cultural Industries

David Hesmondhalgh

SAGE Publications
London • Thousand Oaks • New Delhi

First published 2002 , Reprinted 2002

SAGE Publications Ltd
6 Bonhill Street
London EC2A 4PU

SAGE Publications Inc
2455 Teller Road
Thousand Oaks, California 91320

SAGE Publications India Pvt Ltd
32, M-Block Market
Greater Kailash – I
New Delhi 110 048

**British Library Cataloguing in Publication data**

A catalogue record for this book is available
from the British Library.

ISBN 0 7619 5452 X
ISBN 0 7619 5453 8 (pbk)

**Library of Congress Control Number 2001132946**

Typeset by Photoprint, Torquay, Devon
Printed in Great Britain by The Cromwell Press Ltd,
Trowbridge, Wiltshire

To Helen

Media conglomeration, blah blah blah

Things are more like they are now than they've ever been before.

Attributed to Dwight D. Eisenhower

# Contents

## PART TWO: CHANGE AND CONTINUITY IN THE CULTURAL INDUSTRIES

# Boxes, Tables and Figures

# My thanks to:

(in alphabetical order)

- All those people, too numerous to name here, who have given up valuable time to be interviewed by me over the last few years.
- At Sage, Julia Hall, for skilfully and patiently fostering this book; and Rosie Maynard, not only for her work but also for enduring my views on the cultural industries twice, once as a student at Goldsmiths and once as a publisher.
- Audiences at the following places for their comments on papers drawn from drafts of this book (and to those who invited me and/or facilitated my visits): The Centre for Mass Communication Research, Leicester University (Gillian Youngs); The Centre for Political Economy Research, University of Sheffield (Mike Kenny); The Manchester Institute for Popular Culture, Manchester Metropolitan University (Justin O'Connor); The Faculty of Humanities, Nottingham Trent University (Joanne Hollows); The Department of Culture and Communications, New York University (Jonathan Burston and Ted Magder); The 'Beyond the Great Divide' panel at the 3rd *Crossroads in Cultural Studies* conference, University of Birmingham; The UK Media, Communication and Cultural Studies Association annual conference, 2001; The Centre for Cultural Industries and Practices Research, Newcastle University, New South Wales (David Rowe); The School of Media, Communication and Culture, Murdoch University, Perth (Mark Gibson and, at Curtin, Jon Stratton).
- Claire Boffey (interlibrary loans) and various other helpful and friendly library staff at the Open University.
- Helen Steward, for her grace, calm, warmth and humour, in sharing the burdens and joys of bringing up children while both of us were (and are) working full time.
- Jonathan Burston, Aeron Davis and Des Freedman for teaching seminars on courses I taught on the cultural industries, and for providing me with valuable feedback. The structure of the book derives from the courses I taught in Media Sociology and Contemporary Issues in the Cultural Industries in the Department of Media and Communications at Goldsmiths College, University of London between 1995 and 1998.
- Julie Hesmondhalgh for her reports on life in the madness of the cultural industries, and for emergency doses of telephonic empathy.

♦ Kev Grant, for moments of insight.

♦ My Mum and Dad, Maureen and John Hesmondhalgh, for their incredible, loving support and all sorts of indispensable help; and Rosa and Joe's other grandparents, Ernie and Cathy Steward, for helping out with childcare crises, often at very short notice.

♦ Rosa and Joe, for pictures, stories, play, jokes, words, videos, shouts, screams, laughs and performances.

♦ Sophie Taysom for her efficient research assistance on all manner of things, from finding good sources to checking references; and Karen Ho for secretarial support.

♦ Students and colleagues at the workplaces where the ideas for this book were first worked out, tried out, fought over and rethought: Accrington and Rossendale College of Further Education; Eccles Sixth Form College, Salford; Department of Media and Communications, Goldsmiths College, University of London; Communication, Culture and Media Subject Group, Coventry University School of Art and Design; and most recently, the Faculty of Social Sciences at the Open University.

♦ The following for support and encouragement over the years, even if they had no direct input into this book (and therefore, like everyone else listed here, can't be blamed for its shortcomings): Georgie Born, James Curran, Simon Frith, Christine Geraghty, Dave Laing, Dave Morley, Will Straw, John Street, Tim Wall.

♦ The following friends and colleagues for their invaluable and perceptive comments on various draft chapters: Elizabeth Barnett, Jonathan Burston, Nick Couldry, Teresa Gowan, Tim Jordan, Keith Negus, Chad Raphael and Jason Toynbee. Nick and Jonathan's encouragement was crucial at a stage when I was having serious doubts. Jason read the whole book in rough draft form. He contributed in untold ways to the ideas here in conversations, comments and brilliant asides. I don't know what I would have done without him as a supportive friend and reader.

♦ The following friends, plus other unnamed ones, for discussion of politics, creativity and/or culture – and preferably all three at the same time: Alev Adil, Dave Archer, Les Back, Bill Brewer, Clare Buntic (and the Oxford–Swindon axis), Graham Caveney, Patrick Costello, Mark Edmondson, Cathy Gough, Dai Griffiths, Tanika Gupta, Mark Haddon, Mike Kenny, Caspar Melville, Polly Radcliffe, Mark Rawlinson, Nilly Sarkar, Dave Swann, Steve Swann, Fran Tonkiss, the sisters Vermond, Tim Ward, Rick Wojcik.

♦ The wonderful staff of Balliol College Day Nursery, Oxford.

♦ Those involved in the Goldsmiths/University of Stockholm Media and Communications exchange, 1995–8, especially Michael Forsman, Johan Fornäs and Hillevi Ganetz.

♦ Tony Bennett and the Sociology discipline at the Open University, for the opportunity to work as a research fellow between Autumn 1999 and Spring 2001. This enabled me to spend two to three days a week working on this book during that period, and I'm very grateful for this.

No animals were harmed in the making of this book.

# Introduction: Change and Continuity, Power and Creativity

Nearly all commentators accept that the cultural industries have undergone remarkable transformation since the early 1980s. Here are some of the major changes I intend to deal with in what follows.

♦ The cultural industries have moved closer to the centre of the economic action in many countries and across much of the world. Cultural-industry companies can no longer be seen as secondary to the 'real' economy, where durable, 'useful' goods are manufactured. Indeed, some of these companies (Disney, Rupert Murdoch's News Corporation) are amongst the most highly valued and discussed businesses in the world.

♦ The ownership and organisation of the cultural industries have changed radically. The largest companies no longer specialise in a particular cultural industry, such as film, publishing, television or recording; they now operate across a number of different cultural industries. These conglomerates compete with each other, but more than ever before they are connected in complex webs of alliance, partnership and joint venture.

♦ Yet there are also more and more small and medium-sized companies in the business of culture and there are increasingly complex relationships between large, medium and small cultural companies.

♦ Cultural products increasingly circulate across national borders. Images, sounds and narratives are borrowed and adapted from other places on an unprecedented scale, producing new hybrids but also, for some, reaffirming the value of cultural authenticity. The long-standing domination of cultural trade by the USA may be diminishing.

♦ There has been a remarkable proliferation of new communication technologies, and of new applications of existing technologies.

♦ The way that the cultural industries conceive of their audiences is changing. There is greater emphasis on audience research, marketing and on addressing 'niche' audiences.

♦ Cultural policy and regulation have undergone significant shifts. Long-standing traditions of public ownership and regulation have been dismantled. Important policy decisions are increasingly carried out at an international level.

♦ There has been a huge boom in the amount of money that businesses spend on advertising. This has helped to fuel the spectacular growth of the cultural industries.

♦ The cultural tastes and habits of audiences have become more complex. The production and consumption of cultural texts, and the turnover of tastes and fashions, has quickened.

♦ Texts (in my view, the best collective name for cultural 'works' of all kinds: the programmes, films, records, books, comics, images, magazines, newspapers, etc. produced by the cultural industries) have undergone radical transformation. There is an increasing penetration of promotional and advertising material into previously protected realms, especially in European television, but also across a wide range of other cultural industries. There is more and more product of all kinds, across a wider range of genres, across a wider range of forms of cultural activity. Various forms of cultural authority are increasingly questioned and satirised.

But to what extent do such changes in the cultural industries really represent major, epochal shifts in the way that culture is produced and consumed? After all, alongside these changes, there are many important continuities, which might be obscured by an overemphasis on change. For example: television continues to play a huge role, as a source of information and entertainment, in people's lives; stars continue to be the main mechanism via which cultural-industry companies promote their products; the USA is still thought of, across the globe, as the world centre for popular culture. Because continuities such as these are entangled with the above changes, I refer throughout what follows to *patterns of change/ continuity in the cultural industries*. This issue – the interweaving of change and continuity – is the central theme of this book.

## Why do the cultural industries matter?

### The cultural industries make and circulate texts

More than other types of production, the cultural industries are involved in the making and circulating of products – that is, texts – that have an influence on our understanding of the world. Debates about the nature and extent of this influence comprise, in the words of a valuable survey of the concept, 'the contested core of media research' (Corner 2000: 376). The best contributions to such debates suggest the complex, negotiated and often indirect nature of media influence, but of one thing there can be no doubt: the media do have an influence. We are influenced by informational texts, such as newspapers, broadcast news programmes, documentaries and analytical books. But we are also influenced by entertainment. Films, TV serials, comics, music, video games and so on provide us with recurring representations of the world and thus act as a kind of reporting. But just as crucially, they draw on and help to constitute our inner, private lives: our fantasies, emotions and identities. What is more, the sheer amount of time that we spend absorbing the texts produced by the cultural industries, however distractedly we might do so, makes the cultural industries a powerful factor in our lives.

So studying the cultural industries might help us to understand how such texts take the form they do, and how these texts have come to play such a central role in contemporary societies. Importantly, most texts that we consume are circulated by powerful corporations. These corporations, like all businesses, have an interest in making profits. They want to support conditions in which businesses in general – especially their own – can make big profits. This raises a crucial issue: do the cultural industries ultimately serve the interests of their owners and their executives, and those of their political and business allies?

Simplistic answers to this vital question must be avoided. Throughout this book, I argue for a view of the cultural industries and the texts they produce as *complex, ambivalent and contested*. (Some of the most important and influential analyses of the cultural industries have downplayed these aspects – see Chapter 1). In societies where the cultural industries are big business, cultural-industry companies tend to support conditions in which large companies and their political allies can make money: conditions where there is constant demand for new products, minimal regulation by

the state outside of general competition law, relative political and economic stability, workforces that are willing to work hard and so on. Yet in
contemporary societies, many of the texts produced and disseminated by
the cultural industries do not simply support such conditions. They very
often (not just occasionally) tend to orient their audiences towards ways of
thinking that do not coincide with the interests of capitalism, or of structured domination by men over women, or institutional racism. (I address
this issue further in Chapter 2.)

If this is true, why does it happen? Partly for the simple economic
reason that cultural companies have to compete with each other, as well as
maintain general conditions in which to do business, and so they attempt
to outstrip each other to satisfy audience desires for the shocking, the
profane and the rebellious. But it is also because of social and cultural
factors deeply embedded in many societies, regarding what we expect
of art and entertainment. This takes us to a second argument for the
importance of the subject of this book, and into a domain that has been
neglected in academic and public debate in recent years.

## The cultural industries manage and circulate creativity

The cultural industries are concerned fundamentally with the management and selling of a particular kind of work. Since the Renaissance, and
especially since the Romantic Movement of the nineteenth century, there
has been a widespread tendency to think of 'art' as the highest form of
human creativity. Sociologists and Marxists have argued in response that
artistic work is not so different from other kinds of labour, in that both are
oriented towards the production of objects or experiences (see Wolff, 1993:
Chapter 1 for a good summary of these debates). This view is important in
countering the idea that 'artists' are different from the rest of us, that they
are involved in some mystically special form of creativity. Nevertheless,
there is something distinctive about that area of human creativity that has
often been called 'art'. The invention and/or performance of stories, songs,
images, poems, jokes and so on, in no matter what technological form,
involves a particular type of creativity – the manipulation of symbols for
the purposes of entertainment, information and perhaps even enlightenment. Instead of the term 'art', with all its connotations of individual
genius and of a higher calling, I want to use the more cumbersome term
***symbolic creativity***.[1] And instead of the term 'artists', I prefer the phrase

---

1 My use of the term is borrowed from Willis (1990), but I differ from him in focusing on industrialised symbolic creativity, whereas he is concerned with the creativity of young people as consumers.
Throughout this book, I use bold italics to denote key concepts, bold to highlight key phrases and
italics for titles and ordinary emphasis.

*symbol creators* for those who make up, interpret or rework stories, songs, images, etc.[2]

Symbol creators have been pretty much ignored in recent thinking about the cultural industries, because of an understandable but excessive reaction against the fetishisation of their work as extraordinary. In media and cultural studies, this has taken the form of an emphasis on the creativity of audiences, of those who do not in general work professionally as symbol creators. But a number of recent writers have started to put symbol creators back in the picture (e.g., Born, 1993a, 1993b; McRobbie, 1998; Toynbee, 2000). After all, symbol creators are the primary workers in the making of texts. Texts, by definition, would not exist without them, however much they rely on industrial systems for the reproduction, distribution, marketing and remuneration of their work. This does not mean that we should romantically celebrate the work of all musicians, authors, film-makers and so on. Ultimately my interest in symbolic creativity derives, like that of Born, McRobbie and Toynbee, from a sense that symbolic creativity *can* enrich people's lives – even though it often doesn't.

Other traditions of study have focused on great traditions of especially talented or feted symbol creators, at times hardly referring to the means by which authors, musicians, etc. reached their audiences. Some such studies amount to a pious and complacent celebration of the achievements of western civilisation (Clark, 1969). The work of Raymond Williams (1981) and Pierre Bourdieu (1993), amongst others, suggests better ways of historicising symbolic creativity, by showing how such creativity has been a more or less permanent presence in human history but how its management and circulation have taken radically different forms in different societies. In Europe, for example, systems of patronage gave way in the nineteenth century to the organisation of symbolic creativity around the market. It was at this point that the cultural industries began to emerge. From the early twentieth century, this market organisation began to take a new, complex form (see Chapter 2). Examining changes in the cultural industries allows us to think about how symbolic creativity has been organised and circulated in our own lifetimes and, crucially in this book, how this might be changing.

Here again, I have to emphasise the fundamentally *ambivalent* nature of the cultural industries. The way the cultural industries organise and circulate symbolic creativity reflects the extreme inequalities and injustices (along class, gender, ethnic and other lines) apparent in contemporary

---

2 In the sense in which I am using the term, journalists and others dealing in the more information-oriented parts of the cultural industries are also symbol creators. Studies of journalism have a long and noble history of focusing attention on key symbol creators: i.e., journalists.

capitalist societies. There are vast inequalities in access to the cultural industries. Those who do gain access are often treated shabbily; and many people who want to create texts struggle to earn a living. There are great pressures to produce certain kinds of texts rather than others, and it is hard to come across information about the existence of organisations and texts that attempt to do things differently. Some types of text are made much more available than others. These are bleak features of the cultural-industry landscape. Yet because original and distinctive symbolic creativity is at a premium, the cultural industries can never quite control it. Owners and executives are forced to make concessions to symbol creators by granting them far more autonomy (self-determination) than they would to most other workers. This helps to produce the ambivalence in texts referred to earlier.

Cultural-industry companies face another difficulty too. They have to find audiences for the texts that symbol creators produce. Usually, this is not a matter of finding the greatest possible mass audience for a product. Different groups of people tend to have different tastes, so much of the work of cultural-industry companies attempts to match texts to audiences, to find appropriate ways of circulating texts to those audiences, and to make audiences aware of the existence of texts. As we shall see, this is a risky business. Many texts fail, even those that companies expect to succeed. The upshot of these processes is that cultural-industry companies keep a much tighter grip on the *circulation* of texts than they do on their production.

The importance of ***the social relations of symbolic creativity*** helps to explain the fact that the main focus of this book is on patterns of change/continuity in the cultural industries, as opposed to, say, change/continuity in the texts produced by those industries, or in how audiences understand texts. As I should have made clear by now, I am interested not only in the cultural industries as systems of production, but as systems of production in relation to texts. But all writers, given their limited time and energy, must make decisions about where to concentrate their attention; and rather than focusing on the texts themselves, and then working backwards from there to the industries, my primary interest in this book is in the cultural industries.

### The cultural industries are agents of economic, social and cultural change

A third and final reason why it is important to examine change and continuity in the cultural industries is that they are increasingly important sources of wealth and employment in many economies. This is significant in itself of course. But it also has implications for how we understand the relationships between culture, society and economy.

Many of the most important debates in social science of the last 30 years have concerned what we might call theories of transition. Have we moved from industrial societies to post-industrial or information societies, based on a much greater emphasis than before on knowledge? This was a line of thought initiated in the 1960s and 1970s by the work of, amongst others, Daniel Bell (e.g., 1974) and maintained by writers such as Manuel Castells (e.g., 1989, 1996) in the 1980s and 1990s. Have we moved from societies best characterised as 'modern', because of their increasing ephemerality, fragmentedness and flux, to a situation better characterised as 'post-modern', where these features become so accentuated that rationality and meaning seem to break down (Harvey, 1989; Lyotard, 1984)? In a recent version of such debates, a number of recent commentators (most notably Castells, 1996; Lash and Urry, 1994) have suggested that symbolic creativity and/or information is increasingly central to social and economic life. The implication of this, drawn out more fully by Lash and Urry than by Castells, is that the cultural industries therefore increasingly provide a model for transformations in other industries. Others claim that the cultural industries themselves are becoming more like other industries and losing their distinctiveness as an economic sector (Padioleau, 1987). And of course the internet has fuelled these debates.

These academic debates are echoed by business analysts, who place increasing emphasis on firms' non-tangible assets, especially the value of these businesses' brand names (see Wolf, 1999 for a popularising version). Brands can only be made valuable through massive amounts of work on how product names and logos are represented and circulated. Cultural-industry companies such as Disney, because they are considered so experienced in developing brands (in a sense, every film, every star, every book is something like a brand) are often named alongside companies such as Nike and more traditional firms such as Coca-Cola as leaders in this field. If the cultural industries are playing a central part in these supposed transitions – to the information society, to an entertainment or an experience economy, or to economies based on signs and meaning – it is surprising how rarely systematic, historically-informed analysis of changes in these industries has been carried out by those involved in such debates. Such an analysis may help to cast light on these various notions, and on whether they exaggerate change at the expense of continuity.

## Outline of the argument

Two questions seem to me to be of particular importance in relation to patterns of change/continuity in the cultural industries, both involving a set of important subsidiary questions. First, **how might we *explain* them**?

What were the forces driving change and ensuring continuity? Which groups of people have made the key decisions in bringing about new patterns of change and continuity? What interests did they represent?

Second, **how might we *assess* change and continuity**? This involves two aspects: measuring change, and evaluating it. Which phenomena represent fundamental transformations in cultural production and consumption and which are merely superficial changes? What political and ethical principles can we draw on to think about what is right and wrong in the way that the cultural industries are structured, governed and organised in the late twentieth century and at the beginning of the twenty-first?

The rest of the Introduction lays out the working definition of the cultural industries I am using in this book; it explains the etymology of the term and my reason for preferring it over other alternatives; and it outlines the distinctive features of the cultural industries. These distinctive features are important for the argument in the rest of the book, because they help to explain changes and continuities in the way that the cultural industries are structured, organised and regulated.

Chapter 1 prepares the ground for assessment and explanation by considering **the main approaches that have been taken to the cultural industries**. It argues for an approach based on a particular type of political economy account, associated with the mainly European cultural industries tradition (rather than with a distinctive US tradition often equated with political economy). I recognise the important contributions of sociology of culture and liberal-pluralist communication studies to studies of the cultural industries, while highlighting some of their limitations. I argue that the best contributions from cultural studies are compatible with the best political economy approaches.

Chapter 2 deals with how we might **assess** patterns of change/continuity in the cultural industries. I begin with a historical overview of changing forms of cultural production, drawing on the work of Raymond Williams, and provide a brief sketch of the form that became dominant from the middle of the twentieth century onwards: what, adapting Williams, I call **the complex professional era of cultural production**. A key objective of the book is to assess whether the changes of the 1980s and 1990s have seen the emergence of a completely new era of cultural production; or whether these changes represent shifts *within* the complex professional stage, and therefore relatively limited (though still potentially significant) transformations. This involves a 'measurement' of change/continuity.

The second part of the chapter then outlines **a framework for evaluating the cultural industries**, based on: access to the means of cultural production; the treatment of creativity in cultural-industry organisations; rewards and conditions for symbolic creativity; ownership, control and the serving of class (and related) interests; and what kinds of texts tend to get produced. This in turn has important implications for how we think about the difference between fundamental and superficial changes in the cultural industries.

Chapter 3 discusses how we might **explain** change, assessing the rival claims of approaches that emphasise economic, political, technological and sociocultural factors. It begins the story of recent change/continuity in the cultural industries, by looking at how a number of such factors interacted to produce an economic and cultural crisis in western societies in the late 1960s and 1970s. I argue that this crisis initiated many of the key changes discussed in the book. The Long Downturn in advanced industrial econ-omies from the late 1960s onwards is a vital context for understanding even very recent developments – as is the 1990s boom in some of those same economies. Such general contexts are necessary but insufficient to explain patterns of change/continuity in the cultural industries, however. We also need to examine the specific organisational and economic dynamics of the cultural industries themselves. In particular, I argue, we need to see the management of creativity and the matching of texts to audiences, discussed above, as being the fundamental problems facing cultural businesses, problems that are partially but never entirely resolved.

The four core chapters of the book then focus on four key types of change/continuity. Chapter 4 on **government communications policy** argues that governments and businesses in advanced industrial countries responded to the downturn in capitalism in the 1970s by beginning to look away from traditional manufacturing industries and towards new sectors, in order to restore profit and productivity levels. The cultural industries were one of the key sectors they turned to; telecommunications and computers were others. My account analyses how governments changed their communications policies in the 1980s and 1990s to encourage the development of the commercial cultural industries by privatising public corporations and 'loosening' the regulation of media and culture. The story of this privatisation and 'deregulation' will be familiar to some readers. My account is different from existing ones, though, because of its international emphasis, and its attempt to periodise change. There were four overlapping waves of change in the communications policies of national governments:

- the first in the USA in the 1980s
- the second in other advanced industrial countries from the mid-1980s to the mid-1990s
- the third in transitional and mixed societies after 1989
- the fourth, which continues today, across all these regions/polities, concerning the convergence of the cultural industries with telecom-munications and computers sectors.

These changes in government communications policy, which swept the world during this period, have been extremely important in fuelling the changes discussed in the following chapters.

In Chapter 5, I examine **industrial and organisational changes/ continuities**. In the Long Downturn, cultural-industry businesses looked to various forms of company structure and organisational strategy to compete effectively with each other, and with firms in other sectors. Cultural industries were already prone to domination by a few, powerful companies but this intensified in the 1980s and 1990s. There were important changes in the conglomerates which dominated the production and distribution of cultural goods and services. Independents continued to proliferate – and go bust. New relationships between conglomerates and such independents came into being. All this concerns industrial and market structure, but in line with the emphasis in earlier chapters on the management and organisation of creative work in the cultural industries, the chapter proposes that organisational changes and continuities are vitally important too. Perennial questions of how to control risk and manage creativity were being answered in new and important ways in the 1980s and 1990s, notably an increasing focus on marketing and market research. There were also significant changes in the terms and conditions of cultural work. But did such changes represent a fundamental shift in the social relations of cultural production?

One of the most important ways in which firms tried to compete in the new business environment created by the Long Downturn and by various sociocultural changes of the period was by internationalising their operations, and the consequences of this for the cultural industries are assessed in Chapter 6. **Internationalisation** in the cultural industries has helped lead to a much greater complexity of international flows of culture, but it has also meant the increasing global presence of vast corporations. So the chapter asks whether we should think of the new state of play in the cultural industries, internationally, as a new stage of cultural imperialism, or as a sign of a new global interconnectedness with democratising possibilities (and the chapter also questions whether this dualism between imperialism and interconnectedness is an adequate way of addressing the most important issues).

Cultural-industry businesses also attempted to compete by introducing, and using, **new communication technologies**. Chapter 7 focuses on what is generally agreed to be the key technological development of the last 20 years, **digitalisation**. Has digitalisation brought about a fundamental shift in the cultural industries? Unlike some other approaches, I attempt to break down the term by looking at very different examples and applications of digital technology in the cultural industries. As in much of the rest of the book, I focus on implications for cultural work, especially in looking at digital music technologies and the impact of desktop publishing on the magazine publishing industry. But I am also concerned with impacts on creativity, diversity and innovation. Particularly significant are the rise of the internet and multichannel television. Digitalisation is often said to be about to change the way that cultural production is organised and experienced. In particular, talk of convergence between the cultural industries, telecommunications and computers is now commonplace to the point of being humdrum. How can we assess the effects of the internet and digital television so far? To what extent have these innovations altered, in any significant way, the power relations that have generally prevailed in the cultural industries?

Chapter 8 deals with the effects of all these patterns of change/continuity, at the point at which the cultural industries arguably have their most profound effects on social and cultural life: **texts**. In what significant ways have cultural texts and their consumption by audiences changed (or not) during the 1980s and 1990s? And in what ways has this then had reciprocal effects on the institutions, organisation and economics of the cultural industries? I deal with three particularly important but tricky issues in assessing texts: diversity, quality, and the extent to which texts serve the interests of cultural-industry businesses and their political allies.

Finally, a concluding chapter summarises the arguments of the book, and outlines its importance for understanding changing relationships of power and social justice in relation to cultural production.

## Matters of definition

The term, 'the cultural industries', is surrounded by difficulties of definition. If we define culture, in the broadest anthropological sense, as a ' "whole way of life" of a distinct people or other social group' (Williams, 1981: 11), it is possible to argue that all industries are cultural industries in that they are involved in the production and consumption of culture. For by this definition, the clothes we wear, the furniture in our houses and workplaces, the cars, buses and trains we use for transport, the food and drink we guzzle are all part of our culture and they are nearly all produced industrially, for profit.

In fact the term 'cultural industries' has tended to be used in a much more restricted way than this, based implicitly on a definition of culture as 'the *signifying system* through which necessarily (though among other means) a social order is communicated, reproduced, experienced and explored' (Williams, 1981: 13, original emphasis). To put this a little more simply, the cultural industries have usually been thought of as those institutions (mainly profit-making companies, but also state organisations and non-profit organisations) which are most directly involved in **the production of social meaning**. So nearly all definitions of the cultural industries would include television (including cable and satellite), radio, the cinema, newspaper, magazine and book publishing, the music recording and publishing industries, advertising and the performing arts. These are all activities the primary aim of which is to communicate to an audience, to create texts.

All cultural artefacts are texts in the very broad sense that they are open to interpretation. Cars signify, and most cars involve significant design and marketing inputs. However, the primary aim of nearly all cars is not meaning, but transport. What defines a text, then, is a matter of degree, a question of balance between its functional and communicative aspects (see Hirsch, 1990/1972 for a similar argument). Texts (songs, narratives, performances) are heavy on signification and tend to be light on functionality and they are created with this communicative goal primarily in mind. Box 0.1 presents the core cultural industries that are the main focus of this book. They are the core cultural industries because **they deal with the industrial production and circulation of texts**.

---

### Box 0.1 The core cultural industries

The following industries are centrally concerned with the industrial production and dissemination of texts and they therefore constitute what I want to call **the core cultural industries** for the purposes of this book:

♦ Advertising and marketing: compared with other cultural industries, advertisements tend to have a greater functional element; they are intended to sell other products. Nevertheless, advertising is very much centred on the creation of texts, and crucially requires the work of symbol creators
♦ Broadcasting: the radio and television industries, including their newer cable, satellite and digital forms
♦ Film industries: this includes the dissemination of films on video, DVD and other formats, and on television
♦ The internet industry, including website creation, portal providers
♦ The music industries: recording (which of course includes the recording of sounds other than music, but is for the most part centred on music) publishing (which is about much more than the printing of sheet music; it is about the ownership and control of the rights to musical works) and live performance
♦ Print and electronic publishing, including books, CD-ROMs, on-line databases, information services, magazines and newspapers
♦ Video and computer games

All these core cultural industries interact and interconnect with each other in complex ways. They form, in many respects, a linked production system. They are the main competitors with each other for (Garnham, 1990: 158):

♦ a limited pool of disposable consumer income
♦ a limited pool of advertising revenue
♦ a limited amount of consumption time
♦ skilled creative and technical labour

There is another set of cultural industries, which I will call 'peripheral'. These are important industries, and the term 'peripheral' is in no way intended to marginalise the creativity of those involved in such work. As in the core cultural industries, they are centrally concerned with the production of texts. But the reproduction of these symbols uses semi-industrial or non-industrial methods. Theatre, for example, has only recently begun to take on what might be called industrial forms of production and reproduction (see Chapter 5). The making, exhibition and sale of art works (paintings, installations, sculptures) generates enormous amounts of money and commentary each year, but there is no reproduction stage here. The art prints industry meanwhile limits reproduction artificially, and uses laborious methods, in order to add value to the prints. I refer in passing to some of these industries but, in order to make this book readable – and writable – I have focused on the core cultural industries listed in the box.

As with all definitions of complex phenomena, there are a number of very important borderline cases.

♦ *Sport*: Industries such as football (soccer) and baseball arrange for the performance of live spectacles, which are in many respects very like the live entertainment sector of the cultural industries. People pay to be entertained in real time in the co-presence of talented (or not-that-talented, depending on which team you support) performers. But there are significant differences even from live entertainment in the cultural industries. Sport is fundamentally competitive, whereas symbol making isn't. Texts tend to be more scripted or scored than sport, which is essentially improvised around a set of competitive rules.[3]

♦ *Consumer electronics/cultural-industry hardware*: Making television programmes is based on an intentional act of cultural communication and would be included as a cultural industry in almost all definitions. But does the making of television *sets* constitute a cultural industry? The consumer electronics industry develops and makes the machines through which we can experience these texts. Developments in consumer electronics are extremely important for understanding change and continuity in the cultural industries, because this provides the hardware on and through which texts are reproduced or transmitted (hi-fi, television sets, personal stereos, VCRs). These goods and others (fridges, microwave ovens) rely on the crucial input of designers, but they are not centred on the work of symbol creators, in the way that the core cultural industries are.

♦ *Software*: The software industry has some very important parallels with the cultural industries. Creative teams work together to try to

---

3 Thanks to Jason Toynbee for clarifying these differences for me.

create distinctive outcomes. But the actual presentation of the software does not take the form of a text. Its functional aspects – to carry out certain computerised tasks – outweigh the very important aesthetic dimensions of its design.

◆ *Fashion*: Fashion is a fascinating 'hybrid' of a cultural industry, in the sense that I use the term here, and a consumer goods industry. The high degree of balance between functionality and signification makes this a complex special case, made all the more interesting by distinctive forms of organisation (see McRobbie, 1998 for an important study).

I could go on for pages more, dealing with borderline cases, which share features with the cultural industries, but which are, I think, sufficiently different to merit separate treatment. I hope by now that my point will be clear: that I am focusing here on industries based upon the industrial production and circulation of texts, and which are centrally reliant on the work of symbol creators.

The term 'cultural industries' is clearly a contested, difficult one and, as I have implied, its problems derive from the difficulty of defining 'culture' (not to mention 'industry'). Given all these problems of definition, why not abandon the term 'cultural industries' altogether, in favour of an alternative? A number of possibilities spring to mind. It would be quite possible to write a book called 'the leisure industries' which would include sport and tourism, alongside what I call the cultural industries. A book on the 'information industries' might treat the cultural industries as just one example of the increasing prominence of information in contemporary economies, societies and cultures.[4] US business analysts increasingly use the term 'entertainment industries'. In Europe, the term 'creative industries' is increasingly popular in policy circles as a means of encompassing not only the heavily industrialised and commodified industries which I have called 'cultural industries' but also the more craft-based activities of jewellery making, fashion, furniture design and household objects and so on. Lastly, the cultural industries are often referred to interchangeably with the 'media industries', a term which has the benefit of being somewhat more precise – though the concept of mass media is not without its problems of definition either. Leisure, information, entertainment, creativity and media will all be addressed in this book, but I prefer the term 'cultural industries'. For it not only refers to a type of industrial activity, it also invokes a certain tradition of thinking about this activity, and about the relationship between culture and economics, texts and industry, meaning and function.

---

4 The term 'information industry' was in vogue during the late 1980s and 1990s (see Sadler, 1997 for an interesting analysis of the recording industry as an information industry) but even some of those who used it (e.g., Wasko, 1994) recognised that it marginalised entertainment.

## From The Culture Industry to the cultural industries

The term has its origins in a chapter (1977/1944) by two German-Jewish philosophers associated with the Frankfurt School of Critical Theory, Theodor Adorno and Max Horkheimer. Although the term may have been used before, The Culture Industry was part of the title of a chapter in their book, *Dialektik der Aufklarung* (*Dialectic of Enlightenment*) which they wrote in the USA in the 1940s, while in exile from Nazi Germany. The book was written out of a conviction that life in the capitalist democracy of the USA was, in its own way, as empty and superficial, if not quite as brutal and horrific, as life in the Germany they had fled. The Culture Industry was a concept intended to shock. Adorno and Horkheimer, like many other users of the term 'culture' in the nineteenth and twentieth centuries, equated culture in its ideal state with art, with special, exceptional forms of human creativity. For them, and for the tradition of Hegelian philosophy they were part of, art could act as a form of critique of the rest of life, and could provide a utopian vision of how a better life might be possible. But, in Adorno and Horkheimer's view, culture had almost entirely lost this capacity to act as utopian critique because it had become commodified, a thing to be bought and sold. Culture and Industry were supposed, in their view, to be opposites but in modern capitalist democracy, the two had collapsed together. Hence, The Culture Industry.

By the late 1960s, it was clear that culture, society and business were becoming more intertwined than ever, as transnational corporations invested in film, television and record companies, and as these forms took on ever greater social and political significance. Adorno, Horkheimer and other present and former members of the Frankfurt School became internationally prominent as left-wing students and intellectuals turned to their ideas to make sense of these changes. The term The Culture Industry became widely used in polemics against the perceived limitations of modern cultural life. The term was picked up by French sociologists (most notably Morin, 1962; Huet et al., 1978; Miège, 1979), and by activists and policy makers[5] and was converted to the term 'cultural industries'.

Why prefer the plural to the singular form? The distinction is revealing and surprisingly significant. The French 'cultural industries' sociologists rejected Adorno and Horkheimer's use of the singular term 'Culture Industry' because it suggested a 'unified field', where all the different forms of cultural production which co-exist in modern life are assumed to

---

5 Internationally, the term was disseminated in policy circles through the United Nations Educational, Scientific and Cultural Organization (UNESCO), based in Paris. UNESCO sponsored a large-scale comparative international programme on the cultural industries in 1979 and 1980, which culminated in a conference in Montreal, in June 1980, the proceedings of which were published in English as UNESCO (1982).

obey the same logic. They were concerned instead to show how *complex* the cultural industries are, and to identify the different logics at work in different types of cultural production; how, for example, the broadcasting industries operated in a very different way from the press, or from industries reliant on 'editorial' models of production, such as publishing, or the recording industry (see Miège, 1987). As a result, they preferred the plural term 'industries culturelles'.[6]

The cultural industries sociologists rejected the approach of Adorno and Horkheimer on other important grounds too, as the most important writer in this tradition, Bernard Miège (1989: 9–12), made clear in a foreword to a translated collection of his work.[7] First, they rejected Adorno and Horkheimer's nostalgic attachment to pre-industrial forms of cultural production. Following other critics of the Frankfurt School, including Adorno's friend and contemporary, Walter Benjamin, Miège argued that the introduction of industrialisation and new technologies into cultural production did indeed lead to increasing commodification, but that it also led to exciting new directions and innovations. The commodification of culture, then, was a much more *ambivalent* process than was allowed for by Adorno and Horkheimer's cultural pessimism. (As we shall see in the next chapter, this is an insight shared by some cultural studies approaches.) Second, rather than assuming that the process of commodification of culture has been a smooth, unresisted one, the cultural industries sociologists were concerned with the limited and incomplete nature of attempts to extend capitalism into the realm of culture. They saw the cultural industries, in other words, as *contested*, a zone of continuing struggle, whereas there is a constant sense in Adorno and Horkheimer that the battle has already been lost, that culture has been already subsumed by capital, and by an abstract system of 'instrumental reason'.

These modifications of Adorno and Horkheimer's Culture Industry thesis are real advances. The point here is not simply to show that two German intellectuals writing in the mid-century got it wrong. Adorno and Horkheimer are important, amongst other reasons, because they provided a version of a mode of thinking about culture that is still common today. Newspaper commentators can often be read or heard dismissing industrialised culture as debased. Writers, teachers and students often lapse into a pessimism similar to that of The Culture Industry chapter, even while they enjoy and feel enriched by many of the products of the cultural industries. Adorno and Horkheimer provide the fullest and most intel-

---

6 Many writers (e.g., Lash and Urry, 1994 and Garnham, 2000 – though not Garnham, 1990) use the term 'culture industries'. The difference is trivial, but I prefer 'cultural industries' because it symbolises the move beyond the Frankfurt School approach.

7 This poorly edited translation forms the most important source in English of French sociological work on the cultural industries.

ligent version of the extreme pessimistic view of the industrialisation of culture. But for Miège and others, even this intelligent version of cultural pessimism is lacking. Abandoning extreme pessimism is not the same thing as complacently celebrating the cultural industries as they are. The key words, to repeat, are *complex, ambivalent and contested*. These terms drive my efforts to explain and to assess the cultural industries in what follows. Using the term 'cultural industries' signals an awareness of the problems of the industrialisation of culture, but a refusal to simplify assessment and explanation.

## Industries that make texts: the distinctive features

In the light of work by Miège and others, including most notably Garnham (1990), it is possible to outline the distinctive features of the cultural industries, as compared with other forms of capitalist production. These are summarised in Box 0.2. The first three features are the distinctive *problems* faced by the cultural industries; the next five features are the most common *responses*, or attempted solutions, undertaken by cultural-industry businesses. These distinctive features have important implications in the rest of the book. They help to explain recurring strategies of cultural-industry companies in terms of how they manage and organise cultural production. They indicate potential causes of change. They help us to understand the constraints facing those who want to work as symbol creators, or who want to set up their own independent and/or alternative cultural organisations.

### Box 0.2 Summary of distinctive features of the cultural industries

Problems:
Risky business
High production costs and low reproduction costs
Semi-public goods; the need to create scarcity

Responses:
Misses are offset against hits through a repertoire
Concentration, integration and co-opting publicity
Artificial scarcity
Formatting: stars, genres and serials
Loose control of symbol creators; tight control of distribution and marketing

### Risky business

All business is risky, but the cultural industries are a particularly risky business (the title of a book on the film industry by Prindle, 1993) because they are centred on the production of texts to be bought and sold. For Garnham, influenced by Bourdieu (1984), this risk derives from the fact that audiences use cultural commodities in highly volatile and unpredictable ways, often in order to express their difference from other people (Garnham, 1990: 161).[8] As a result, fashionable performers or styles, even if heavily marketed, can suddenly come to be perceived as outmoded, and other texts can become unexpectedly successful. These risks, which stem from consumption, from the ways in which audiences tend to use texts, are made worse by two further factors related to production. First, companies grant symbol creators a limited autonomy in the hope that the creators will come up with something original and distinctive enough to be a hit. But this means that cultural companies are engaged in a constant process of struggle to control what symbol creators are likely to come up with. Second, any particular cultural-industry company (company A) is reliant on other cultural industry companies (B, C, D and so on) to make audiences aware of the existence of a new product, or of the uses and pleasures which they might get from experiencing the product. Even if company A actually owns company B or F, they can't quite control the kind of publicity the text is likely to get, because it is difficult to predict how critics, journalists, radio and television producers and presenters, and so on are likely to evaluate texts.

These factors mean that cultural-industry companies face special problems of risk and unpredictability. Nearly 30,000 albums were released in the USA in 1998, of which fewer than 2 per cent sold more than 50,000 copies (Wolf, 1999: 89). Neuman (1991: 139) quotes a rule of thumb in publishing that 80 per cent of the income derives from 20 per cent of the published product. Bettig (1996: 102) claims that of the 350 or so films released each year in the USA at the time of his study, only ten or so will be box-office hits. Driver and Gillespie (1993: 191) report that only one-third to one-half of UK magazines break even; and only 25 per cent make a profit. According to figures cited by Moran (1997: 444), about 80 per cent of the 50,000 book titles published in the USA each year in the mid-1980s were financial failures.

### High production costs and low reproduction costs

Most cultural commodities have high fixed costs and low variable costs: a record can cost a lot to make, because of all the time and effort that has to go into composition, recording, mixing and editing to get the right sound for its makers and their intended audience. But once 'the first copy' is

---

8 Even if we do not think of the problem in this way, it is clear that consumption of texts is likely to be highly subjective and arational.

made, all subsequent copies are relatively cheap to reproduce. The important point here is the ratio between production and reproduction costs. Nails, for example, have a low design input, making the first copy cheapish to produce, and each further copy costs not much less. This produces a very different kind of market from that which prevails in the cultural industries. Cars are more like the texts that the cultural industries produce, but are still substantially different. The prototype of a car is extremely expensive, with enormous amounts of design and engineering input, but the costs of each new car built from the prototype are very expensive too, because of the materials and safety checks required. So even though fixed costs are high, the ratio of variable costs to fixed costs is relatively low. The much higher ratio of fixed costs to variable costs in the cultural industries means that big hits are extremely profitable. This is because, beyond the break-even point, the profit made from the sale of every extra unit can be considerable,[9] and can compensate for the inevitably high number of misses that comes about as a result of the volatile and unpredictable nature of demand. This leads to a very strong orientation towards 'audience maximisation' in the cultural industries (Garnham, 1990: 160).

### Semi-public goods

Cultural commodities are rarely destroyed in use. They tend to act like what economists call 'public goods' – goods where the act of consumption by one individual does not reduce the possibility of consumption by others. If I listen to a CD, that doesn't in any way alter your experience of it if I pass it on to you. The same could certainly not be said of my eating a pie. Using a car diminishes its value. What is more, the means of industrial reproduction of cultural goods are relatively low in cost. This means that firms have to achieve the scarcity that gives value to goods by limiting access to cultural goods and services by artificial means (see below).

### Misses are offset against hits through a repertoire

This extra emphasis on audience maximisation means that in the cultural industries, companies tend to offset misses against hits through 'over-production' (Hirsch, 1990/1972), through the attempt to put together a large catalogue or 'cultural repertoire' (Garnham, 1990: 161), or, to put it another way, by 'throwing mud' – or other similar substances – 'against

---

9 Clearly, those cultural industries which do not sell goods directly to customers, most notably broadcasting, work in different but related ways. Here the extra unit is of audiences, which are then 'sold' on to advertisers.

the wall' and seeing what sticks (Laing, 1985: 9; Negus, 1999: 34). If, as Garnham suggests, one record in every nine is a hit, and the other eight are misses, then a company issuing five records is less likely to have the hits which will keep the company afloat than the company which has a repertoire or catalogue of 50 record releases. This is one of the pressures towards greater size for cultural companies; though there are counter-vailing tendencies which favour smaller companies.

### Concentration, integration and co-opting publicity

Cultural-industry companies deal with risk and the need to ensure audience maximisation by using strategies that are also apparent in other sectors:

- Horizontal integration: they buy up other companies in the same sector so that there will be less competition for audiences and audience time.
- Vertical integration: they buy up other companies involved in different stages of the process of production and circulation. A company might buy 'downstream', such as when a company involved in making films buys a video distributor; or 'upstream', when a company involved in distribution or transmission (such as a cable television company) buys a programme-maker.
- Internationalisation: by buying and partnering other companies abroad, corporations can sell massive amounts of extra copies of a product they have already paid to produce (though they will have to pay new marketing costs of course).
- Multisector and multimedia integration: they buy into other related areas of cultural-industry production, to ensure cross-promotion.
- Also important is the attempt to 'co-opt' (Hirsch, 1990/1972) critics, DJs and various other people responsible for publicising texts, by socialising with them, sending them gifts, press releases and so on.

Such forms of integration have led to the formation of bigger and more powerful companies. Nearly all major industries, from aluminium to biochemicals to clothing, are dominated by large companies. There is only limited evidence that the cultural industries have higher degrees of industry concentration than other industries. Arguably, though, the consequences of not succeeding in growth and integration are greater in the cultural industries than elsewhere, because there is a very high rate of failure of smaller companies. This in turn is explained by the fact that small cultural companies are unable to spread risk across a repertoire. And crucially, the consequences of this size and power are unique to the cultural industries, because of the ability of the goods they produce – texts

– to have an influence on our thinking about their operations, about all other industries, and indeed potentially about all aspects of life.

### Artificial scarcity

Garnham (1990: 38–9, 161) identifies a number of ways in which scarcity is achieved. Primary amongst them is vertical integration. The ownership of distribution and retail channels allows companies to control release schedules, and to ensure the adequate availability of goods. But just as important are: advertising, which limits the relative importance for profits of the *sale* of cultural goods; copyright, which aims to prevent people from freely copying texts; and limiting access to the means of reproduction, so that copying is not easy.

### Formatting: stars, genres and serials

Another way for cultural-industry companies to cope with the high levels of risk in the sector is to minimise the danger of misses, through 'formatting' their cultural products (Ryan, 1992). One major means of formatting is *the star system*: by associating the names of star writers, performers and so on, with texts. This involves considerable marketing efforts, in order to break a writer or performer as a new star, or to ensure the continuation of the star's aura. This type of formatting is reserved for privileged texts which cultural-industry companies hope will become big hits. The importance of the star system can be indicated by the following statistic. Of the 126 movies that made more than US$100 million at the US box office in the 1990s, 41 starred one or more of just seven actors: Tom Hanks, Julia Roberts, Robin Williams, Jim Carrey, Tom Cruise, Arnold Schwarzenegger, and Bruce Willis (Standard & Poor's *Movies and Home Entertainment Industry Survey*, 11 May 2000: 14).

   Another crucial means of formatting is the use of *genre*, such as 'horror film', 'hip hop album', 'literary novel'. Genre terms operate as labels, not unlike brand names, which suggest to audiences the kinds of pleasure which can be attained through experiencing the product. The terms might not be universally understood, and might not even be explicitly used: the important thing is that a type of cultural product is suggested, associated with particular uses and pleasures. Many cultural products promoted and publicised primarily via genre also carry author names, but until the author becomes a star, genre is paramount. Finally, *the serial* remains an important type of formatting, where authorship and genre are still often significant, but less so. This has been an important aspect of publishing, in popular fiction, comics and so on, but it is also to be found in films, and even in records (such as the huge-selling compilations of the most popular music in the UK, *Now That's What I Call Music*, which is issued four times a year; *Now 54* is the most recent at the time of writing).

### Loose control of symbol creators; tight control of distribution and marketing

In discussing symbol creators earlier, I pointed out that symbol creators are granted considerable autonomy within the process of production – far more, in fact, than most workers in other forms of industry. There are cultural reasons for this: long-standing assumptions about the ethical desirability of creative autonomy, which derive from the romantic conception of symbolic creativity, and traditions of free speech. But there are also economic/organisational reasons. Managers assume that major hits and the creation of new genre, star and series brands require originality. Symbol creators are usually overseen from a certain distance by 'creative managers' (Ryan, 1992), such as editors or television producers, who act as intermediaries between the creators and the commercial imperatives of the company. Those symbol creators who become stars – whereby their names come to be understood as promises of certain experiences – are rewarded enormously; but most creative workers exist in a vast reservoir of under-used and underresourced talent, picking up work here and there. In many cases, production will actually take place under the auspices of a separate, independent company. Such 'independents' – often in fact tied to larger companies through financing, licensing and distribution deals – are to be found in abundance in the cultural industries, mainly because symbol creators and audiences are suspicious of the bureaucratic control of creativity, again reflecting ingrained cultural assumptions about art. In order to control the risks associated with managing creativity, senior managers exert much tighter control over reproduction, distribution and marketing – what I will call *circulation* – in many cases through vertical integration.

◆  ◆  ◆

I have placed a great deal of emphasis in the above discussion on *uncertainty*. It is important to realise, however, that across the cultural industries as a whole, this risk is successfully negotiated by the larger companies. Television profits have traditionally run at a rate of 20 per cent of sales, according to Neuman (1991: 136). Compaine (1982: 34, cited by Neuman, 1991: 136) claims that profits from motion pictures tend to run at 33 to 100 per cent higher than the US average. Dale (1997: 20) samples figures from 1992 showing the following profit margins (operating income divided by sales) in different industries: cable, 20 per cent; broadcast television, nearly 17.5 per cent; the press and books, around 12 per cent; music, network television and magazines, just under 10 per cent; and film and advertising agencies, in the high single digits. However, profits are highly variable, depending on the degree of competition within and across industries. Profits in the film industry fell from an average of 15 per cent in the 1970s to about 10 per cent in the early 1980s, then to around 5–6 per cent in the late 1980s, before making a recovery in the early 1990s (Dale, 1997: 20).[10] However, the success of the largest companies does not alter the fact that cultural-industry companies were responding in specific ways to perceived difficulties of making profits.

## Author to reader

I outlined at the beginning of this Introduction why I think the cultural industries matter: the power they have to influence people; the varied ways in which they manage the work of symbol creators; and their role in bringing about more general industrial, social and cultural change. Relating the fundamental concerns of the book to my own personal background may help to make them more concrete. This will help to provide context for the particular approach I take to the cultural industries, the approach developed in the next three chapters.

As a teenager, I was infuriated by what I perceived as the lies and distortions of television, and of the ultraconservative newspapers my parents read (typically for a certain section of the Northern English, working class/lower middle class). *The Daily Mail* and *The Sunday Express* seemed constantly to be attacking anyone who was trying to achieve social justice in Britain in the late 1970s: trade unions, feminists, anti-racist activists. They wrote as if the British role in Northern Ireland was one of making peace between tribal factions; at fifteen, I knew enough about Irish history to find this difficult to accept. And these newspapers were decidedly lukewarm in their condemnation of far-right neo-Nazi groups, whose graffiti was all over the town where I grew up, directed at the British South Asian community there. It seemed to me right from my teens that the cultural industries had a role in maintaining power relations, and in distorting people's understanding of them.

My other main relationship to the media and popular culture was as a fan, and a fan I remain. Even if some media seemed to take a stance against everything I stood for, there was plenty of exciting, interesting and funny popular culture around. I still find this the case today, and so I cannot accept the version of the cultural industries to be found in some writing on the subject: as a monstrous system for the maintenance of conformity. In the late 1970s and early 1980s, the musical genre of punk seemed to me to embody the most remarkable creative energy. Suddenly, the emotional range of my small record collection was massively expanded:

10 My thanks to John Downey for pointing me in the direction of Dale's figures.

music could be shocking or coolly detached; intelligent or belligerent; hilarious or deadly serious. Punk musicians were always talking about the music industry, and were arguing that it could be changed, to make creativity more possible, and to make sure that more of the money went to those creating.

My sense of the importance (and ambivalence) of media and popular culture eventually led me to a career in teaching, where I was fortunate enough to meet dozens of students who were prepared to share their perspectives with me. My love of American popular culture (particularly classic and Movie Brat Hollywood cinema, black music and Jewish comedy) and my fascinated loathing for the US government's role in global geo-politics took me to the USA for a postgraduate degree. Teaching and learning provided the impulse to write this book, but it's also informed by my experience, over the last few years, of researching and writing about the cultural industries. There is an assumption amongst many academics that the most prestigious books will necessarily be more or less incomprehensible to students. I've worked hard to make this book interesting for other teachers and researchers, but I've also endeavoured to make it accessible for students, by explaining difficult concepts as they arise, and by trying to get across why I think the issues I'm dealing with matter. I've had to assume some knowledge of and interest in the topic, but I've tried not to assume too much.

# PART ONE
# ANALYTICAL FRAMEWORKS

# 1  Approaches to Culture

How have researchers approached the cultural industries? My aim here is to examine which research traditions provide the most useful tools for addressing the central themes of this book – explaining and assessing patterns of change/continuity in the cultural industries since the late 1970s. The search is for approaches that address the fundamental issues outlined in the second section of the Introduction (Why do the cultural industries matter?). We need approaches that are sensitive to the potential power of the cultural industries, as makers of texts, as systems for the management and marketing of creative work, and as agents of change. I'll begin with two traditions of analysis which promise, at first sight, to make major contributions to such an analysis, but which are in fact compromised by their lack of attention to such issues of power.

## Cultural economics

Cultural economics is the branch of economics devoted specifically to culture and to the arts. Since it developed in its modern form in the nineteenth century, economics has been dominated by the *neoclassical conception* of its assumptions and goals. Neoclassical economics is not concerned with determining human needs and rights, nor with intervening in questions of social justice; instead it focuses on how human wants might be most efficiently satisfied. Even though its language and procedures are often very specialist and esoteric, neoclassical economics claims to be a practical social science, aimed at understanding how and under what conditions markets best function. It equates the well-being of people with their ability to maximise their satisfactions. It provides methods of calculating how such satisfaction might be maximised, thus showing its roots in utilitarianism, the philosophy of happiness maximisation (see Mosco, 1995: 47–8). Given our concerns, as outlined in the Introduction, with the way that public and everyday life are affected by the products of the cultural industries, such a bracketing of questions concerning ethics and justice is limiting, to say the least. The equation of human happiness with the optimising of economic satisfactions, an assumption that many cultural economics writers inherit from neoclassical economics, provides a poor basis on which to proceed in assessing the cultural industries. There are other striking features of the literature of cultural economics that make its paucity for our present purposes even clearer. Much of the literature (for example, much of the work anthologised in Towse, 1997) is concerned not with those industries which produce the culture which most of us consume, but with the peripheral cultural industries. The major debate which founded the field concerned whether the performing arts (mainly theatre) were doomed to difficulties because of rising labour costs (Baumol and Bowen, 1966). Countless articles have been produced on the art market. These are important areas of human life and attempts by economists to understand their markets should not be dismissed. But the neglect of important cultural industries such as popular music and television within mainstream cultural economics is remarkable.[1]

In recent years, however, there have been signs of a more flexible approach from mainstream economics towards questions of culture, and an increasing concern with the core cultural industries. Mainstream economics was never entirely dominated by the neoclassical tradition: institutional economics, for example, provided a more sociological approach to organisational power. While the neoclassical conception is still dominant, certain assumptions are increasingly questioned from within the paradigm. There is less uncritical use of ahistorical and asocial concepts, for example (see Fine, 1999). Some of the best of the more recent mainstream work seeks to provide explanations of recurring problems and inequities

---

1 Discussion of broadcasting was for many years confined mainly to the issue of whether broadcasting should be subsidised, given its status as a public good (see Peacock Report, 1986).

in cultural production and consumption (Caves, 2000) and is oriented towards influencing public cultural policy. Increasingly, cultural economics has been influenced by debates in other areas discussed below, such as debates in political economy approaches about the domination by the USA of the international cultural industries (e.g., Hoskins et al., 1997) and about the special problems surrounding concentration and conglomeration in the cultural industries (e.g., Congdon et al., 1995). I will draw on some of this work later in the book. Nevertheless, the limitations of mainstream cultural economics are profound, in terms of its failure to address the issues of power that I am concerned with in this book. In particular, mainstream economics is completely uninterested in the relationships between economic organisations and issues of textual meaning. As we shall see, this relationship is at the heart of an alternative set of approaches to economics and culture, usually labelled political economy.

## Liberal-pluralist communication studies

From the 1930s onwards, researchers began to investigate mass communication media using sociological methods. By the 1950s in the USA there was an established tradition of communication studies. The subject continues to thrive today, and has spread to Europe and elsewhere. For many years, the dominant concern of this field was the 'effects' of media messages on audiences, with a tendency to conceive of those effects as limited and difficult to prove (see Lowery and DeFleur, 1995). This tradition was strongly influenced by behaviourism, the belief that society is best understood by observation of outward behaviour of individuals, rather than by efforts to understand (in psychology or philosophy) mental processes and events or (in sociology) issues of social power and status. What is more, analysis of consumption of messages was cut off from any consideration of cultural production and organisation.

However, more recent work in liberal-pluralist communication studies has been much more concerned with the issues of power and social justice in relation to cultural production that are the fundamental concerns of this book. An important tradition looks at the way that the impact of the media has transformed political communication. This often puts strong emphasis on the dangers for a society of the way that democratic processes are increasingly run via the broadcast and press media. Jay Blumler and Michael Gurevitch (1995), for example, have written convincingly about a 'crisis of civic communication', and of the difficulties of sustaining participatory citizenship in a society where most people get their knowledge of politics from television. Other writers in this tradition have attempted to develop normative models to assess how well (and how badly) the mass media perform in fostering democracy (e.g., McQuail, 1992). The work of the Euromedia Research Group (e.g., 1997; McQuail and Siune, 1998) and its individual associates (e.g., the prolific Jeremy Tunstall, cited throughout this book) has provided important information about changes in cultural policy and in cultural-industry organisations. Throughout these strands of communication studies and sociological work, there is an important concern, from an ultimately liberal-pluralist political perspective, with how the cultural industries affect democratic processes and public life.

In spite of the strengths of such work, there are real limitations in the liberal-pluralist communication studies tradition. First, and most important, it fails to offer any systematic account of how the cultural industries relate to more general economic, political and sociocultural processes. This derives from the problems of liberal-pluralism as a form of politics: structured forms of inequality and power are downplayed, in favour of an implicitly optimistic notion of society as a level playing ground, where different interest groups fight for their interests.

Second, liberal-pluralist communication studies tends to conceive the relationship between culture and society primarily in terms of formal democratic procedure. What ultimately counts is information: the idea that participating citizens should be given the tools to make rational decisions about the proper functioning of democratic institutions. Information about citizenship and democratic procedure are indeed important. But we live in societies where we are increasingly saturated in entertainment. It is not enough to dismiss the pleasures of entertainment as a distraction from 'real' politics. We need to rethink how the massive presence of entertainment in people's everyday lives affects not only our notions of how democracy works, but also how we think about other aspects of human life, including ourselves as feeling, emotional beings. I shall suggest later in this chapter that certain strands of cultural and media theory – in particular, cultural studies approaches – might provide some pointers in the right direction for thinking about these matters. But liberal-pluralist communication studies have, on the whole, been somewhat hostile to such innovations in thinking.

## Political economy approaches

Political economy approaches have a great deal more to offer than cultural economics and liberal-pluralist communication studies in terms of analysing power in relation to cultural production. Political economy is a general term for an entire tradition of economic analysis at odds with mainstream economics, in that it places much greater emphasis on ethical and normative questions. The term is claimed not only by those on the political left who are critical of the sidelining of questions of power and conflict in mainstream economics. There are strong conservative traditions too. So some writers use the term **critical political economy** to distinguish their perspective from the work of conservative classical theorists such as Adam Smith and David Ricardo, and their twentieth-century heirs.[2]

Critical political economy approaches to culture (or media or communications – the terms are often used indiscriminately in labelling this tradition) developed in the late 1960s amongst academic sociologists and political scientists concerned by the increasing role of private businesses in cultural production. Critical political economy approaches to culture are often misunderstood, simplified or dismissed. Because such approaches are so heavily critical of media and cultural corporations and their allies in government, it is no surprise that many media institutions are dismissive or hostile. More surprising perhaps is the animosity of many elsewhere on the political left to political economies.

One common misunderstanding is to see political economy approaches as a version of orthodox cultural economics. In fact, political economies explicitly aim at challenging the lack of an ethical perspective in the neo-classical paradigm. Peter Golding and Graham Murdock (2000: 72–3) distinguish critical political economy approaches to the media from mainstream economics approaches in four respects:

- Critical political economy approaches to the media are **holistic**, seeing the economy as interrelated with political, social and cultural life, rather than as a separate domain.
- They are **historical**, paying close attention to long-term changes in the role of state, corporations and the media in culture.
- They are 'centrally concerned with **the balance between private enterprise and public intervention**' (p. 73).
- Finally, 'and perhaps most importantly of all', they go beyond 'technical issues of efficiency to **engage with basic moral questions of justice, equity and the public good**' (p. 73).

These go some way towards defining political economy approaches, and they certainly clarify their difference from cultural economics, but two further features will help to clarify the distinctiveness of this area of study.

- Critical political economy approaches **see the fact that culture is produced and consumed under capitalism as a fundamental issue in explaining inequalities of power, prestige and profit**. This emphasis in political economy work on capitalism and its negative effects

---

2 See Mosco (1995: 22–69) for a detailed and informative analysis of political economy approaches in general, as a background to understanding the political economy of communication.

should make it clear that although you don't have to be a Marxist to work here, it helps.

♦ A major area of contribution from political economy approaches to the study of the cultural industries has been to put on to the intellectual agenda debates about **the extent to which the cultural industries serve the interests of the wealthy and powerful**. As a result, a central theme in political economy approaches has been the ownership and control of the cultural industries (see Chapters 2 and 5). Does ownership of the cultural industries by the wealthy and powerful ultimately, through their control of cultural-industry organisations, lead to the circulation of texts which serve the interests of these wealthy and powerful owners and their governmental and business allies? This has been such an important debate that some writers, teachers and students tend, wrongly, to equate political economy approaches with the view that cultural-industry organisations do indeed serve the interests of their owners in this way, when in fact many political economy writers are concerned precisely with addressing the difficulties and complexities surrounding this issue.

## Which political economy?

It should be clear that the focus within political economy approaches on ethical and political issues in relation to culture mean that they will have important contributions to make to this study, given the concerns outlined in the Introduction. However, certain versions of the political economy of culture provide much more scope for understanding what drives change/continuity in the cultural industries than others. At this point, it is important to delineate political economy more carefully. This will also help us to counter some simplifications and misunderstandings surrounding the term.

Proponents and opponents of political economy of culture often portray the field as a single unified approach. Vincent Mosco (1995: 82–134) has provided a detailed account of the differences between the kinds of political economy work developed in three geographical and political settings: North America, Europe and 'The Third World', that is, developing countries in Asia, Latin America and Africa. I will deal with important work from this last bloc, on cultural dependency and media imperialism, in Chapter 6. But here I want to build on Mosco's useful division by discussing the tensions between two particular strands of North American and European political economy approaches:

♦ A tradition within North American political economy work, exemplified in the work of Herbert Schiller, Noam Chomsky, Edward Herman and Robert McChesney. This **Schiller–McChesney tradition** has been extremely important in cataloguing and documenting the growth in wealth and power of the cultural industries, and their links with political and business allies.

◆ The **cultural industries approach**, initiated in Europe by Bernard Miège (1989) and Nicholas Garnham (1990), amongst others, and continued by other European writers and by writers based in other continents (Straw, 1990; Ryan, 1992; Aksoy and Robins, 1992; Driver and Gillespie, 1993; Toynbee, 2000).[3]

In the Introduction, I referred to the work of Bernard Miège, who helped to popularise the plural term 'cultural industries' (as opposed to Adorno and Horkheimer's singular 'Culture Industry') as an example of an approach that allowed for complexity, contestation and ambivalence in the study of culture.[4] As my praise for Miège's work there suggests, I think that the cultural industries approach has more to offer in terms of assessing and explaining change/continuity in the cultural industries than the Schiller–McChesney tradition. In my view, the cultural industries approach is better at dealing with:

## Contradiction

The Schiller–McChesney tradition emphasises strategic uses of power. There is no doubt that such strategic uses of power by businesses are common, and it is wrong to dismiss the approach of Schiller and others as 'conspiracy theory' (an accusation sometimes levelled at political economy approaches in general). But in emphasising concerted strategy, this tradition underestimates the contradictions in the system. The cultural industries approach's emphasis on problems and contradictions, on the partial and incomplete process of commodifying culture, provides a more accurate picture of cultural production. It allows for contradiction *within* industrial, commercial cultural production, rather than assuming a simplistic polarity *between* corporations and non-profit 'alternative' producers, as in the Schiller–McChesney tradition.

---

3 This division leaves out many important contributions to critical political economy work, such as those of James Curran, Peter Golding, Armand Mattelart, Vincent Mosco and Graham Murdock. The best work of these writers shares many of the major strengths of the cultural industries approach, while pursuing distinctive agendas.

4 Some teachers and students tend to equate the cultural pessimism of Adorno and Horkheimer and some of their Frankfurt School colleagues with political economy, defining one by the other. But, as we saw in the Introduction, Miège founds his particular approach on a critique of Adorno and Horkheimer. For many in the Schiller–McChesney tradition, the theoretical concerns of the Frankfurt School seem to be more or less irrelevant.

### The specific conditions of cultural industries

The cultural industries approach's greater ability to deal with contradiction stems from another important advantage: its ability to combine an interest in the macro level of relations between general economy and cultural industries (which is an important concern in the Schiller–McChesney tradition) with an analysis of what distinguishes industrial cultural production from other forms of industrial production (which isn't). It was work within the cultural industries approach that provided the breakdown of the specific conditions of cultural production laid out in the Introduction.

### Tensions between production and consumption

Although as its name suggests, the cultural industries approach focuses on the supply side – on cultural production and circulation and their social and political contexts – it does not ignore the activity of audiences, a charge often levelled at political economy approaches and at certain versions of media sociology. Instead, the cultural industries approach sees the business of cultural production as complex, ambivalent and contested largely because of certain problems derived from the nature of the audiences for cultural texts. Production and consumption are not seen as separate entities, but as different moments in a single process. The connections and tensions between production and consumption are more or less ignored in the Schiller–McChesney tradition.

### Symbol creators

In my view, the processes of concentration, conglomeration and integration relentlessly catalogued by the Schiller–McChesney tradition are extremely important. But Schiller, McChesney and others rarely comment on how such issues of market structure affect the *organisation* of cultural production and the making of texts on an ordinary, everyday level. The cultural industries approach puts symbol creators – the personnel responsible for the creative input in texts, such as writers, directors, producers, performers – in the picture, whereas they are almost completely absent from the Schiller–McChesney tradition. The cultural industries approach has emphasised the conditions facing cultural workers as a result of these processes.[5] Its attention to this important issue makes the cultural industries approach better equipped to assess the degree to which cultural production is organised in a socially just manner (see Chapter 2).

---

5 Miège (1989), Garnham (1990) and Ryan (1992) were for many years very unusual in paying serious attention to this issue. More recently, cultural studies writers such as McRobbie (1998) and Ross (1998) have begun to address these questions.

### Information and entertainment

In the Schiller–McChesney tradition, as in liberal-pluralist communication studies, the primary concern is with information media. The cultural industries approach has been more successful in the difficult task of addressing both information and entertainment.

### Historical variations in the social relations of cultural production

Finally, both approaches are concerned very much with history (see, e.g., McChesney, 1993) but the cultural industries approach is often more sensitive than the Schiller–McChesney tradition to historical variations in the social relations of cultural production and consumption, a concern that some of its writers derive from Raymond Williams' interventions in the historical sociology of culture (see Chapter 2).

## Sociology of culture: the production of culture perspective

On the basis of my arguments above, and in the Introduction to this book, it should be clear by now that I find critical political economy approaches to culture useful, especially the cultural industries approach. But even within the cultural industries approach, which is much more interested in the organisational dynamics of cultural production than the Schiller–McChesney tradition, there has been a lack of empirical attention to what happens in cultural-industry *organisations*.

A certain tradition of work in the sociology of culture, primarily based in the USA, and drawing on Weberian and interactionist traditions of analysis, the 'production of culture' perspective, has important contributions to make in this respect. One of the most valuable contributions of this perspective is its enrichment of our notions of creativity. Instead of understanding culture as the product of supremely talented individuals, writers such as Howard Becker (1982) and Richard Peterson (1976) have helped to make it clear that creative cultural and artistic work is the product of collaboration and a complex division of labour.

Particularly useful in this literature is the work of Peterson and Berger (1971), Hirsch (1990/1972) and DiMaggio (1977) on the distinctive characteristics of the cultural industries. Here there is important concordance with work in the cultural industries approach on the distinctive strategies of companies that produce texts. Hirsch's work, for example, informed my outline of the distinctive features of the cultural industries in the Introduction.

The work of the US sociologists, developed in parallel to that of the French cultural industries writers already mentioned, was groundbreaking, but it is only when it is synthesised into a more comprehensive vision of how cultural production and consumption fit into wider economic, political and cultural contexts that an analysis of specific conditions of cultural production really produces its explanatory pay-off. The cultural industries are treated by the US organisational sociologists as isolated systems, cut off from political and sociocultural conflict. Issues of power and domination are sidelined. The conditions of creative workers are hardly registered, other than the admittedly important fact that they are granted more autonomy than workers in other industries. The world of the rip-off, the shady deal, the disparity between the glass skyscrapers of the multinational entertainment corporation and the struggle for young artists and musicians to stay afloat financially are scarcely considered. As with communication studies, I think these problems derive from the liberal-pluralist political perspective ultimately underlying the work of these writers. There is undoubtedly a democratising impulse to be detected here. The aim is to demystify creativity and to understand and question hierarchies of taste and value. There is a strong emphasis, particularly in the work of Becker, on the resourcefulness of people in their everyday lives. While this is a valuable counter to easy, glib assumptions about our powerlessness in the face of giant cultural-industry corporations, the production of culture perspective often seems reluctant to consider the existence of these institutions and their consequences. As a result, questions concerning whose interests tend to be served by the various legal, technological, market and organisational factors which the 'production of culture' sociologists draw attention to are marginalised. There is no way of answering such questions in advance of an analysis. But the 'production of culture' sociologists appear uninterested in even asking such questions.

## Radical media sociology/media studies

Empirical studies of cultural-industry organisations that are more attuned to issues of power can be found in radical media sociology and media studies. I mean 'radical' here in the sense that that these approaches see pernicious forms of power and inequality as rooted in the very structure of contemporary societies, rather than as the result of correctable aberrations, as in liberal-pluralist perspectives. From the early 1970s onwards, radical media sociology in the USA and the emergent discipline of media studies in Europe provided approaches which were complementary to the political economy work which was developing in parallel with them, from the early 1970s onwards. Some of the most important US work grew out of a Weberian sociological tradition, and concentrated on how news programmes did not simply report reality, but reflected the imperatives of news organisations (e.g., Tuchman, 1978; Gans, 1979). According to this perspective, journalists worked autonomously of owners, but their work was structured by bureaucratic requirements and routines. These routines ultimately produced texts that failed adequately to address existing power relations. The thrust of such work was echoed in important British studies of news (e.g., Schlesinger, 1978). Studies of entertainment were rarer, but at their best, provided real insight into cultural-industry dynamics. Todd Gitlin's book *Inside Prime Time* (1983) for example, showed through interviews with television executives and through reconstructions of the histories of these organisations, how the commercial imperatives of the networks resulted in tremendous conservatism.

Because it is compatible with critical political economy approaches to culture, such work has often been confused with political economy. But critical political economies attempt an overall understanding of the place of cultural production within contemporary capitalism. Few of the writers usually associated with political economies of culture have made empirical work on cultural-industry organisations central to their work. The great benefit of such radical media sociology is that, at its best, it links dynamics of power in the cultural industries to questions of meaning, to questions regarding the kinds of texts that are produced by cultural-industry organisations.

## The problem of meaning: thinking about texts

So far I have been addressing which approaches to the cultural industries most adequately deal with questions of power in relation to cultural-industry organisations. But how do these various approaches think about meaning? Liberal-pluralist communication studies has, for the most part, operated with a deficient view of texts. There is a branch of this tradition which analyses cultural outcomes, using the methods of quantitative content analysis. The aim is to produce an objective, verifiable measure of meaning. As John Fiske (1990: 137) points out, 'this can be a useful check to the more subjective, selective way in which we normally receive messages'. But there is a notion of content as *message* in the effects research which has dominated this tradition. A considerably more complex notion of *meaning* needs to be put into operation, which recognises polysemy – the ability for texts to be interpreted in a (limited) number of ways. This requires consideration of questions of form, as well as of content (in practice, the two are never really separate; the one always affects the other).

While liberal-pluralist communication studies has generally had a seriously limited understanding of texts as 'content' or 'messages', the production of culture perspective, at least until recently (see Peterson,

1997) often chose to ignore the issue of textual meaning. Richard A. Peterson, for example, in outlining the production of culture perspective, was frank in admitting the approach's lack of interest in the form and content of cultural artefacts, but he claimed that an interest in production can complement such concerns (1976: 10). This suggests that the study of production has no effect on the study of texts, that the two are separate, autonomous domains of analysis. The challenge of the cultural industries, though, if my arguments in the Introduction are correct, is to think through these relationships, rather than ignore them. We need to think, for example, about how historical transformations in the way that culture is produced and consumed relate to changes in texts.

There is a serious lack of attention to textual analysis and meaning amongst writers drawn to political economy approaches to culture. For all its strengths, the work of Miège barely mentions the question of textual meaning. Many of the essays in Garnham's *Capitalism and Communication* attack the tendency within media studies to 'privilege the text' and to 'focus on questions of representation and ideology' (Garnham, 1990: 1).[6] Golding and Murdock claim that 'analysing the way that meaning is made and re-made through the concrete activities of producers and consumers is . . . essential to the perspective we are proposing here' (2000: 74) but it is revealing that they do not make any reference to such studies. In the Schiller–McChesney tradition, the underlying assumption is that most texts produced by the cultural industries are conformist and conservative. But no systematic evidence is marshalled to support this assumption; indeed, the assumption is rarely made explicit.

## Cultural studies approaches

On the other side, supposedly, of an intellectual and political divide from the approaches just discussed, stands cultural studies. This is a diverse and fragmented field of study, but at its core is **the attempt to examine and rethink culture by considering its relationship to social power**. There has been remarkable hostility towards this interdisciplinary field from many of the approaches discussed above. And in turn some cultural studies writers have been extremely negative about the above approaches, including political economy and radical media sociology. Yet cultural studies approaches, at their best, have much to offer in terms of aiding our understanding of meaning and cultural value, in ways that can help fill the gaps left by the lacks in approaches to the cultural industries. What have been the main achievements of cultural studies in this respect?

---

6 Garnham's *Emancipation, the Media and Modernity* (2000) addresses the study of texts and of symbolic forms in much greater detail than did his work in the 1980s and 1990s.

First, cultural studies has argued convincingly that **ordinary, everyday culture needs to be taken seriously**. This has meant questioning hierarchical ways of understanding culture to be found in public debate and in the more established humanities and social science disciplines. Cultural studies resists this focus on consecrated, 'high culture' texts, but it does not necessarily 'celebrate' popular culture in an uncritical way.[7] It insists that we need to think broadly about all the different elements in a culture in relation to each other, rather than decide in advance which parts need to be analysed and which do not. This broader conception of culture has an international dimension too. As cultural studies has become internationalised in the 1980s and 1990s, writers originally from outside the Euro-American cosmopolitan heartlands, including diasporic intellectuals such as Edward Said (1994) and Gayatri Spivak (1988) have created a space for thinking about culture in ways which recognise the complex legacy of colonialism in matters of culture. Because of this, the best cultural studies approaches can be seen as a considerable improvement on the often dismissive attitude to popular and non-western culture to be found in some political economy and liberal-pluralist communication studies work. The best cultural studies work has achieved in-depth, serious consideration of a much wider range of cultural experience than had been recognised in other traditions of writing about culture. Other, anthropological and sociological approaches (including empirical sociology of culture) had this democratising impulse but cultural studies deals more fully with questions of symbolic power.

Second, **cultural studies has provided considerable refinement of what we might mean by that difficult term culture**. In particular, it has provided powerful criticisms of essentialist notions of culture which see the culture of a particular place and/or people as 'one, shared culture' (Hall, 1994: 323) as a bounded, fixed thing, rather than as a complex space, where many different influences combine and conflict. Again, work by writers outside the Euro-American metropolitan centre, and by migrants from former colonies to such centres, has been important in developing this understanding. Such challenges to traditional ways of thinking about culture have important implications in what follows. Through its richer understanding of the concept of culture, cultural studies has greatly advanced thinking about the politics of texts. Political economy writers and their allies in media studies and radical media sociology have been much concerned with the question of whose interests might be served by the texts produced by the cultural industries. But cultural studies has

---

7 Although there are of course writers working within the field who might lapse into such 'uncritical cultural populism' (McGuigan, 1992) at times.

extended this conception of interests beyond economic and political interests to include a strong sense of the politics involved in issues of recognition and identity. It has pointed out how certain texts, while seemingly innocent, serve (further) to exclude and marginalise the relatively powerless.

Third, **cultural studies has raised vital political questions about 'who speaks?', about who has the authority to make pronouncements on culture**. Importantly, these questions are applied with equal vigour to those who seek to criticise capitalism, patriarchy, heterosexism, white supremacy, imperialism and so on, as to those who defend these structures. Throughout the best cultural studies writing, there is a relentless probing of authority in culture. Anthropologists working in cultural studies, for example, have scrutinised the apparent objectivity of the traditional ethnographer who observes the culture of indigenous, 'primitive' peoples from a relatively privileged position (see Clifford, 1988). In some respects, this echoes the questioning of positivism and objectivism in the 'interpretative turn' in social thought over the last thirty years. At its worst, it involves a naïve constructivism and a suspicion of anyone's right to say anything at all about any less powerful social group. But emergent disciplines such as black studies, queer studies and women's studies have brought new voices into cultural studies and have raised serious and important questions about the politics of speaking from one particular subject position (say, white, private-school educated, male) about the cultural practices of others.

Fourth, **cultural studies has forefronted issues of textuality, subjectivity, identity, discourse and pleasure in relation to culture**. It has enormously enriched our understanding of how judgements of cultural value might relate to the politics of social identity, especially class, gender, ethnicity and sexuality. This is not just a matter of saying that taste is a product of social background (which is the approach that empirical sociology of culture has tended to take). Cultural studies explores the complex ways in which systems of aesthetic value feed into cultural power. Whose voices are heard within a culture and whose voices are marginalised? Which (and whose) forms of pleasure are sanctioned and which/whose are felt to be facile, banal, or even dangerous? These are questions about discourse – about the way that meanings and texts circulate in society. They also concern subjectivity and identity, and the often irrational and unconscious processes by which we become who we are. These questions, sidelined in many of the approaches to the cultural industries discussed above, have been investigated with great vigour by cultural studies writers, who have pointed out that the most dismissed and reviled forms of culture are still those consumed by relatively powerless groups in society. Feminist work on such forms as soaps (Geraghty, 1991) and women's magazines (Hermes, 1995) has been extremely important in this respect.

A final note on this subject. Some important cultural studies work has been devoted to empirical studies of the ways in which members of television audiences interact with television. In fact, although much commentary was devoted to such studies in the 1980s and early 1990s, there weren't that many of them (the most discussed were Ang, 1985 and Morley, 1986). Few major studies in this vein have appeared in recent years (Gillespie, 1995 and Mankekar, 1999 are two). The tendency in cultural studies has been instead towards theoretical work on conceptions of culture and on questions of cultural identity. While much of this work has been valuable, the irony is that there has not been enough empirical study of consumption and reception in cultural studies, rather than too much.

## Beyond cultural studies versus political economy . . . and the rest

In the respects discussed above, and others too, cultural studies has made an enormous contribution to our understanding of culture and power. Given its interest in questioning existing power relations, you would expect a vigorous backlash from conservatives who find issues of social justice unproblematic or unchangeable. But cultural studies has also been attacked by potential liberal and radical allies. The strongest attacks on cultural studies have often come from fellow leftists in political economy and radical media sociology, who often accuse it of secret complicity with conservatism (e.g., Gitlin, 1998; Miller and Philo, 2000; and others). But cultural studies has given as good as it has got. And again, the main targets have been potential allies on the political left.

Perhaps because of these spats between fellow radicals with different interpretations of how to address and combat social inequality, the idea has sprung up that the field of the study of the media and popular culture is evenly divided between two camps: political economy and cultural studies. This idea is reproduced not only in published books and articles but in countless everyday references in seminar rooms, conference bars and so on, along the lines of 'political economy does X, cultural studies does Y'. Even when some writers claim that they want to move beyond the split, they then proceed to attack, from a position strongly identified with one camp, a caricatured version of the other, thus maintaining the myth (e.g., Grossberg, 1995).

But **political economy versus cultural studies is neither an accurate nor useful way to characterise approaches to the media and popular culture**. It simplifies a whole web of disagreements and conflicts between the various different approaches discussed in this chapter down to two players. The issue, then, is not cultural studies versus political economy, as if the field of enquiry was divided neatly between two approaches. Nor is it cultural studies, characterised in whatever caricatured way the writer fancies, versus the rest. The real goal is to find a way of understanding tensions between a whole number of approaches to culture. And in the present context, the key issue is how to synthesise the best aspects of the various approaches already outlined, in order to produce a fruitful account of change and continuity in the cultural industries. In this section, I outline my perspective on the most important controversies between the relevant approaches.

### Production versus consumption

Political economy is often used as a shorthand term for 'studies of production', ignoring the huge differences between attitudes to production taken by mainstream cultural economics, media sociology, empirical sociology of culture, etc. and sidelining the importance of consumption in the best political economy approaches. Similarly, cultural studies is often treated in caricatured descriptions as if it consists almost entirely of empirical studies of audiences, when far more such studies have taken place within liberal-pluralist communication studies.

The very fact that I have chosen to concentrate on the cultural industries in this book – for the reasons outlined in the Introduction – suggests that I will be mainly drawing here on those approaches oriented towards the understanding of the dynamics of cultural production and of regulation/ policy: political economy approaches, some contributions within cultural economics, radical media sociology and empirical sociology of culture. Production and regulation are only two aspects of the 'circuit of culture' (see Figure 1.1).

I make no apology for focusing on production and regulation more than other points in the circuit. Such choices are inevitable, given the boundaries of time and energy we all work within. But even if the emphasis here is on these aspects of the circuit, we still need to think about them *in relation to* the other dimensions represented: consumption, identity and texts. As I argued above, cultural studies has important contributions to make to a fuller understanding of textual meaning and cultural value, as do a number of other approaches. But there remain very real difficulties in synthesising analysis of industries, organisations and texts.

### Texts, information and entertainment

Cultural studies is sometimes accused by advocates of other approaches of being overly concerned with issues of textual meaning. In fact, although cultural studies has contributed in important ways to developing theories

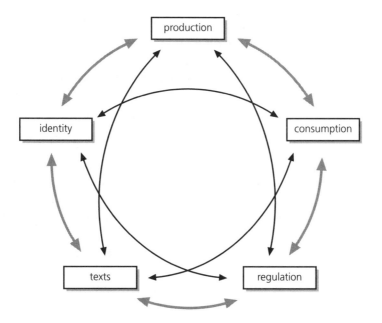

The figure, adapted from the Open University book series, *Culture, Media and Identities*, draws attention to the interconnectedness of the various aspects of culture. Ideally analyses would take account of all these different moments, but in practice this is impossible, even in focusing on a limited phenomenon. The idea of the circuit owes much to an article by Richard Johnson (1986/7), who in turn was drawing on Marx's writings on the links between production and consumption.

**Figure 1.1   The circuit of culture (du Gay et al., 1997)**

of how meaning and identity relate to issues of social power, in its most developed forms it has been relatively little concerned with matters of textual interpretation and evaluation. Help in developing textual analysis is at hand in the form of a number of approaches oriented primarily to the study of texts, such as critical discourse analysis (Fairclough, 1995), aesthetic theory (Carroll, 1998; Frith, 1996), social semiotics (Van Leeuwen, 1999), critical musicology (Walser, 1993) not to mention good criticism (Reynolds and Press, 1995). The focus in such studies tends not to be on the revelation of complex meanings which the great artist is able to transmit into his work, as in some traditional forms of humanities study, but on the *unintentional complexity* of cultural texts.

Political economy, radical media sociology and liberal-pluralist communication studies, meanwhile, have been much more concerned with informational texts such as news and current affairs, and with the extent to which the cultural industries provide the informational resources citizens need to act against injustice and abuse of power. But these approaches have enormously emphasised informational content over form, and have tended to value cognitive and rational modes of thought over the aesthetic, the emotional and the affective (see McGuigan, 1998 for a similar argument). Judged as a whole, these approaches, for all their strengths, can perhaps be fairly accused of treating entertainment as merely a *distraction*, a diversion from what it sees as the most desirable goal of mass communication: the activism of the concerned, rational, participatory citizen. The best forms of textual analysis and cultural studies help to counter this bias.

## Questions of epistemology

The myth of political economy versus cultural studies overemphasises conflicts between the two sets of approaches, and downplays their common differences with other approaches. Some versions of cultural studies and political economy have more in common with each other in terms of being concerned with grounding their understanding in a theory of cultural power than they do with some more empirically-oriented studies (empirical sociology of culture, liberal-pluralist communication studies). Nevertheless, there are serious theoretical and epistemological tensions between political economy and cultural studies. Put crudely, political economy writers tend towards realism in questions of epistemology: the 'assumption that there is a material world external to our cognitive processes which possesses specific properties ultimately accessible to our understanding' (Garnham, 1990: 3). This view is crucially linked to the view that we can achieve objective knowledge of that independent reality. Cultural studies writers take a variety of more constructivist and subjectivist epistemological paths, in some cases aiming to gain greater objectivity through recognition of the effect of the observer on the observed (see Couldry, 2000b: 12–14 on feminist epistemology); in other cases, there is a radical scepticism about truth-claims. This is especially true in post-structuralist and postmodernist approaches. Once again, though, this is not just a case of political economy versus cultural studies. The radical constructivist, postmodernist wing of cultural studies is at odds with *all* the approaches to the cultural industries outlined in the first few sections of this chapter, not just political economy. The positivism of communication studies and sociology of culture is just as far from the critical-realist position of political economy as is postmodern cultural studies.

## Politics

The very idea of the split between political economy and cultural studies is based on a false political dichotomy. Cultural studies derives much of its inspiration from the tendency in political activism and thinking since the early 1970s to focus on issues of social identity, such as gender, ethnicity and sexuality, as opposed to issues of economics, and the redistribution of resources.[8] For some, this concern with social identity is a retreat from the project of building coalitions to resist the economic and political forces that bring about oppression in the first place. This is why some political economy writers, as mentioned above, think that cultural studies is implicitly conservative: their view is that it misunderstands power (e.g., Garnham, 1990). But it is not just political economy writers who take this position. Writers in radical media sociology (such as Gitlin, 1998; Miller and Philo, 2000) often share this perspective and many within communication studies and empirical sociology of culture might well agree. Again, the whole idea of political economy versus cultural studies is crudely inaccurate.

Important issues are reflected in some of these responses to cultural studies. Building a politics only around the oppression and injustice faced by the group to which you feel you belong risks abandoning any notion of solidarity and empathy with others. But little positive purpose is served by the unthinking polemics of some radical commentators. Rather than engaging in a dialogue with important new ways of thinking about politics and culture, and finding common cause against neoconservatism, such radical commentators often seem more interested in mounting sectarian attacks. The objects of their scorn are often writers who, in fact, are concerned precisely with building such coalitions of marginalised peoples, but only on the basis that such groups are granted recognition within the institutions of the left.

These questions are vital in the context of the cultural industries because of the dual role of these industries as systems of production and as producers of texts. If we want to criticise the forms of culture produced by the cultural industries, and the way that they produce them, then we need to take account of both the politics of *redistribution*, focused on issues of political economy, and the politics of *recognition*, focused on questions of cultural identity (Fraser, 1997).

## Questions of determination and reductionism

A criticism commonly advanced, within cultural studies but also within communication studies and empirical sociology of culture, against some kinds of political-economic analysis is their supposed *reductionism*: that they attribute complex cultural events and processes, such as the form of the Hollywood film industry, or the nature of television soap operas, or the development of television as a medium of communication, to a single political-economic cause, such as the interests of the social class which controls the means of production; or to the requirement within capitalism

---

8 See Hall (1992) for an account of cultural studies which portrays it as a reaction from the left against certain forms of Marxism, especially those influenced by Stalinism.

for owners and executives to make profits. There are indeed such reductionist accounts, which fail to do justice to the complex interplay of factors involved in culture.[9] But the fact that some political-economic accounts are reductionist is no argument against political-economic analysis per se. A necessary concept here is ***determination*** in its non-reductionist sense of setting limits and exerting pressures, rather than in the sense of an external force or forces which leads inevitably to something happening (see Williams, 1977: 83–9 for an exposition of this distinction). A good analysis will set processes of economic determination alongside other processes and pressures in culture and think about how they interact. Other factors which it will be important to stress in examining a cultural moment, phenomenon or process are: the role of institutions in the legal and political realm; the forms of discourse, language and representation available at a particular time; and the beliefs, fantasies, values and desires characteristic of different groups of people. Of course, not all accounts will be able to do justice all of the time to the complex mixture of forces at play. Which elements are emphasised will depend 'upon our own subjective purposes, upon the knowledge we think we can assume on the part of our audience, or on the identification of some new piece of the historical jigsaw to which we wish to draw our readers' attention' (Rigby, 1998: xiii). Such eclecticism need not involve the abandonment of political and ethical priorities and concerns, however. The 'subjective purposes' which Rigby draws attention to might, for example, include the identification of particular pressure points for achieving social change. Nor need pluralism of method mean adopting a relativist ethics and a liberal-pluralist model of politics, whereby present systems of democracy are assumed to function more or less effectively.

Too much time has been spent trying to resolve a set of debates couched in impossibly abstract terms. We should abandon tortuous arguments about what Marx intended to say, and over whether he has been misinterpreted. Instead, we need to think hard about the complex interplay of determinations in any situation, in order to understand how difficult social change might be to achieve, and where it might be possible.[10] If it is true that debates about economic determination and reductionism have produced the most significant tensions between political economy and other

---

9 Whether Marxism itself is inherently reductionist is an enormously difficult area of debate, which there is no space to address here. See Rigby (1998) for a view that Marxism is not necessarily reductionist, but where it avoids reductionism it ends up with a pluralism which makes it indistinguishable from pluralist sociology.

10 A number of prominent neo-Marxist cultural studies writers have continued to emphasise the importance of determination by multiple factors (overdetermination) while still talking about determination by the economic in the last instance (e.g., Grossberg, 1995). But it is difficult to find much explicit address of political-economic factors, other than invocations of the term 'capitalism', in much of the cultural studies literature.

approaches, an eclectic methodology, allied to a radical social-democratic recognition of the existence of structures of power, inequality and injustice might provide the possibility of greater convergence. The more pragmatic option advocated here involves identifying particular moments where economic factors are strongly determinant, and moments where other factors, such as those listed above, need to be stressed more. This, as we shall see, will be a crucial aspect of Chapter 3, on explaining change and continuity in the cultural industries.

◆ ◆ ◆

In this chapter, I have concentrated on identifying the achievements and pinpointing the limitations of the main approaches relevant to study of the cultural industries, in terms of the issues identified in the Introduction as central to the book as a whole. I have also attempted to move beyond the idea that the field of study of media and popular culture is split between political economy and cultural studies approaches. My aim here is an overall strategy which might be described as **a particular type of political economy approach, informed by certain aspects of empirical sociology of culture, communication studies and cultural studies**. How this overall approach can be mobilised to produce a framework for assessing and explaining change and continuity in the cultural industries is the subject of the next two chapters.

## Further reading

As this chapter has commented on much of the most relevant literature on the cultural industries, I will confine myself to discussing overviews here.

### General overviews of the field of media, communications and popular culture:

Various chapters by Curran (e.g., 1996; 2000) are remarkable in their range, synthesising approaches from political economy, communication studies and sociology of culture, while being attentive to the interventions of cultural studies. McQuail (2000) is the leading overview of the field of mass communication from the point of view of liberal-pluralist communication studies. Mattelart and Mattelart's *Theories of Communication* (1998) puts much Anglo-American work to shame for its parochialism. The Schiller–McChesney tradition has shown less interest in theory and more in public activism; but Dan Schiller's *Theorizing Communication* (1997) tells the story of the development of communication research in a distinctive and refreshing way. The best textbook in my view is by Croteau and Hoynes (1997).

### Overviews of specific approaches:

The best book-length overview of the political economy approach is Vincent Mosco's excellent *The Political Economy of Communication* (1995), even if its tracing of academic genealogies is sometimes perhaps a little too detailed. It includes good discussion of the limitations of mainstream, orthodox economics, as does Garnham (2000). Peter Golding and Graham Murdock have provided a series of important statements on critical political economy approaches to media and culture, beginning with an essay in 1974 (Murdock and Golding, 1974), and an overview of the changing communications field in 1977 (Murdock and Golding, 1977). In 1991, they published a substantially new version of the latter essay, which has since been revised twice, in 1996 and 2000 (see Golding and Murdock, 2000). Changes in the political economy approach can be traced across these five essays. The best overview of cultural studies approaches I know is Nick Couldry's *Inside Culture* (Couldry, 2000b), which covers a remarkable international range. Amongst the dozens of anthologies, During (1993) stands out. Morley and Chen (1996) provide a valuable anthology of Stuart Hall's writings, plus interesting commentary on them by leading cultural studies writers.

# 2   Assessing the Cultural Industries

The purpose of this chapter is to provide a framework that will allow for the assessment of changes and continuities in the cultural industries in the rest of the book. The notion of assessment here has two elements. First, it involves **measuring** change. But what yardstick can we use to measure change against? In the first part of the chapter, I lay out a large-scale map of the distinctive features of the cultural industries in the late twentieth century. The rest of the book then asks: in what ways has this picture undergone transformation in the 1980s and 1990s? Do the changes since the late 1970s, some of which were listed at the beginning of the Introduction, represent fundamental alterations of this landscape, or are they merely surface changes, underpinned by continuity? The second element of assessment involves **evaluating** change and in the second part of the chapter, I outline a framework for evaluating change and continuity in the cultural industries.

## From patronage to market to cultural industries

One way into a picture of the cultural industries in the period before the changes discussed in this book is provided by Raymond Williams (1981:

38–56) in his account of the history of cultural institutions. Williams focuses on three *eras* in the development of cultural production, and he names each after the main *form* of social relations between symbol creators and wider society prevailing at the time.

♦ *Patronage*: This term refers to a variety of systems prevalent in the west from the middle ages until the nineteenth century. Poets, painters, musicians and others would, for example, be 'retained' by aristocrats, or protected and supported by them. Such systems were dominant until the early nineteenth century, and can still be found today.

♦ *Market professional*: From the early nineteenth century onwards, however, 'artistic works' were increasingly offered for sale, and were bought in order to be owned. Symbolic creativity, in other words, increasingly came to be organised as a *market*. Under this system, more and more work was sold not directly to the public but indirectly, via intermediaries: either distributors such as booksellers, or 'productive intermediaries' (Williams, 1981: 45) such as publishers. This made for a much more complex division of labour in cultural production than before. By the late nineteenth century and throughout the early twentieth century, both distributive and productive intermediaries were becoming much more highly capitalised, as leisure time and disposable income expanded in industrialised countries. Successful symbol creators achieved 'a form of professional independence' (Williams, 1981: 48), and were increasingly paid by royalties.

♦ *Corporate professional*: Finally, from the early twentieth century, but expanding enormously after 1950, there was a new phase which Williams calls 'corporate professional'. Commissioning of works became professionalised and more organised. Increasing numbers of people became direct employees of cultural companies, on retainers and contracts. Alongside older forms such as writing books, performing music and acting out plays, new media technologies appeared, most notably radio, film and television, sometimes including and altering these old forms, sometimes producing entirely new ones (such as the drama serial or the situation comedy). Alongside direct sales, advertising became an important new means of making money for creative work, and an increasingly important cultural form in itself. This was, in other words, the period in which the cultural industries boomed. It was this period which the Frankfurt School was trying – and largely failing – to interpret.

I wish Williams hadn't used the term 'corporate' in this context. To the modern ear, it sounds as though the chief issue is the rise of large private companies. Important as large companies are in cultural production in the late twentieth century, Williams in fact intends the term in an older sense:

'a number of people in a unified group'. To avoid such confusion, I want to use a modified term, *complex professional*, to label this form – and stage or era – of cultural production. I prefer the word 'complex' because one of the most important features of this era was the increasing complexity of the division of labour involved in making texts. The term refers to social relations between symbol creators and patrons or businesses, but it also describes *an era of cultural production*, encompassing associated issues of company ownership and structure, cultural policy and regulation, and communication technologies. So the term reflects my – and Williams' – focus on the social relations of symbolic creativity, but it refers to a whole set of conditions of cultural production.

It is important to understand the nature of the historical transitions from era to era that Williams outlines. The complex professional form was that which dominated cultural production from the 1950s onwards. But market professional and even patronage-based forms of cultural production continued to exist alongside the features of this dominant form, along with non-market forms of cultural institution, such as state broadcasting companies. We can think of the cultural industries from the 1950s onwards as being composed of three different types of form, each corresponding to terms developed by Williams (1977: 121–7) to refer to the historical variability of any period under examination in an 'epochal' analysis (that is, analysis of a particular time).

- The complex professional form was the *dominant* way in which production was organised, and that is why it gives its name to the whole era.
- Patronage and market professional forms, dominant in previous eras, continued to exist in *residual* form.
- State broadcasting had emerged in the 1920s and 1930s and continued to expand across the world with the spread of television in the 1960s. It was an *emergent* form within the complex professional form.

So I use the term complex professional to describe the whole era of cultural production from the 1950s onwards, but in fact it refers to a mix of different forms.

In the next section, I will outline in more detail the distinctive features of the cultural industries in the complex professional era of cultural production. The idea of the complex professional era of cultural production is important to the argument of the book as a whole. If Williams is right, and the complex professional form represented a new era in cultural production from the mid-twentieth century onwards, then one way of differentiating fundamental transformations from superficial changes in the cultural industries (so that continuity can be recognised) is to ask the following question: **Have the 1980s and 1990s seen the emergence of a** completely new era of cultural production, including new social relations between symbol creators and society; or do the changes represent shifts within the complex professional era? This is a refined version of the central question of the book, outlined in the Introduction.

## The complex professional era of cultural production

In this section, I outline the main characteristics of the complex professional era. Each set of characteristics generates questions to be answered in the book. These questions are summarised in Box 2.1.

---

### Box 2.1  Guiding questions for 'measuring' change in the cultural industries

 ◆ To what extent have the dynamics of the distinctive organisational form of the cultural industries changed since the late 1970s?
 ◆ To what extent have the cultural labour market and systems of reward for cultural workers changed since the 1970s?
 ◆ To what extent have changes in conglomeration and integration led to recognisably new and distinct forms of ownership and structure during the 1980s and 1990s?
 ◆ Have the US cultural industries retained their international dominance? Have the spatial relations of international cultural flows changed sufficiently for us to speak of a new era in cultural production and circulation?
 ◆ What have been the key technological, sociocultural and policy changes affecting changes in the cultural industries?

---

### The organisation of production in the cultural industries

In a neglected contribution to the cultural industries approach, Bill Ryan (1992) examines the organisational dimensions of the cultural industries in detail, and I'll draw on his account below. Whereas the creative stage of making cultural products used to be carried out primarily by individuals, in the era of the complex professional form of cultural production, it is nearly always carried out by a 'project team' (Ryan, 1992: 124–34). Within this team, various people play the following roles. (Sometimes the same person can span more than one role.) Adapting from Ryan's discussion, I will give examples from five particular cultural industries: books, film, magazines, recording and television.

 ◆ *Primary creative personnel* such as musicians, screenwriters and directors, magazine journalists and authors (symbol creators). This category also includes 'technicians' who have come to take a creative role, such as sound mixers who, as record producers, have become increasingly important in the music industry (see Kealy, 1990/1974).

♦ *Technical craft workers* are expected to perform a technically-oriented set of tasks efficiently, such as sound engineers, camera operators, copyeditors, floor managers, typesetters, page designers. Of course, creativity is involved here, but not the conception of ideas that will be the basis of the finished text.

♦ *Creative managers* act as brokers or mediators between, on the one hand, the interests of owners and executives, who have to be primarily interested in profit (or at the very least, prestige) and those of creative personnel, who will want to build their reputation by producing original, innovative and/or accomplished works. Important examples are: Artists and repertoire (A&R) personnel in the recording industry, commissioning editors in the books industry, editors of magazines, and producers in the film industry. I find Ryan's concept of the creative manager much clearer than Miège's term 'editeur' or DiMaggio's 'broker' (1977) for more or less the same role. To add to the confusion, 'editeur' is translated as 'producer' in Miège (1987). The most confusing term of all is 'cultural intermediaries' – see Box 2.2 for an explanation of problems in the way this term has been used (and therefore of why I avoid it here).

♦ *Owners and executives* who have the power to hire and fire personnel, and set the general direction of company policy, but who will have a limited role in the conception and development of particular texts, except in rare cases such as the film industry, where 'executive producers' may be credited.

---

### Box 2.2   Cultural intermediaries and creative managers

'Cultural intermediaries' is one of the most confusing terms in the cultural-industries lexicon. It has been widely used in recent debates about changing relations between culture and society (e.g., Featherstone, 1991) but also in studies of cultural-industry organisations (e.g., Negus, 1992; Nixon, 1997). Its use derives from the discussion of the new petite bourgeoisie and the new bourgeoisie in Pierre Bourdieu's *Distinction*. For Bourdieu, at the core of the new petite bourgeoisie, a new social class with distinctive tastes and cultural practices, are 'all the occupations involving presentation and representation (sales, marketing, advertising, public relations, fashion, decoration and so forth) and in all the institutions providing symbolic goods and services' (Bourdieu, 1984: 359). This is important in understanding the development of the cultural industries, not only because the expansion of the cultural industries feeds the expansion of this social class, which has its own distinctive cultural practices, but also because this class constitutes a major new audience for certain cultural texts.

Bourdieu seems to have intended the term 'new cultural intermediaries' to refer to a particular type of new petit bourgeois profession, associated with cultural commentary in the mass media: 'the most typical of whom are the producers of cultural programmes on TV and radio or the critics of 'quality' newspapers and magazines and

*(continued)*

all the writer-journalists and journalist-writers' (Bourdieu, 1984: 325). Presumably, the 'old' cultural intermediaries were those who acted as critics and experts on serious, legitimate culture in the pre-mass media age. Both new and old cultural intermediaries, I assume, are thus named because they 'mediate' between producers and consumers. But Featherstone (1991) seems to have misunderstood the term. In the context of an interesting discussion of the new petite bourgeoisie as generators of a new consumer culture, based on a general interest in style, he says that 'Bourdieu analyses the new petite bourgeoisie, the cultural intermediaries, who provide symbolic goods and services' (1991: 89). So Featherstone equates the new petite bourgeoisie with a small sub-set of that social class, the (new) cultural intermediaries. Negus (1992) and Nixon (1997) appear to have inherited the confusion about the term. Negus (1992: 46), citing Featherstone, says that he will analyse recording industry personnel as cultural intermediaries. His intention is to argue that recording industry personnel contribute to the 'words, sounds and images of pop' and he seems to be using the term 'intermediary' to refer to this added contribution, which takes place between musician and audience. But in Bourdieu's sense of the term, it is critics that act as cultural intermediaries in the recording industry.

Nixon, meanwhile, makes an interesting point about advertising practitioners as members of the new petite bourgeoisie, marked by 'the ambition to establish authority over particular areas of symbolic production' (1997: 216). But like Featherstone, Nixon conflates cultural intermediaries with the new petite bourgeoisie as a whole: for example, he presents the famous passage from Bourdieu, quoted above, about the new petite bourgeoisie being concerned with representation and symbolic goods as if it were an analysis of the 'social make-up of cultural intermediaries' (1997: 211). In fact, Nixon seems to see all advertising practitioners as cultural intermediaries (1997: 216). By this point in its history, the term is being used to refer very generally to those involved in the production of symbols, of texts.

All these writers are making useful efforts to make connections between changes in cultural production and consumption and more general sociocultural changes. Bourdieu's analysis of the new petite bourgeoisie is potentially fruitful, especially with the modifications helpfully suggested by Nixon (1997: 216–7). My point is not the pedantic one that Featherstone, Negus and Nixon have been untrue to Bourdieu's intentions. It is that the term 'cultural intermediaries' has become confusing and unhelpful through its wide range of uses. Ryan's analysis and his term 'creative manager' seems to me to capture the role of the A&R and marketing personnel discussed by Negus much better than the confusing term 'cultural intermediary'. As for the creative practitioners discussed by Nixon, they might best be described as symbol creators. Or even as creative practitioners.

Box 2.3 adapts Ryan's analysis (1992) of the stages in making and circulating texts, and the division of labour within each stage. The stages themselves are not unique to the cultural industries: many industries involve the conception of an idea, its execution and reproduction of an object, followed by their circulation. But what happens within each stage, and the relations between the stages, reflects the distinctiveness of the cultural industries. The project teams involved in creation and conception **are given a large degree of autonomy**. At the time that the cultural industries were developing in the early- and mid-twentieth century, such creative autonomy was rare in other industries. So one of the defining features of the complex professional era of cultural production is this unusual degree of autonomy, which is carried over from preceding eras where artists, authors and composers worked independently of businesses. But it perhaps bears re-emphasising that this is by no means complete autonomy: it is carried out under the supervision of creative managers.

---

### Box 2.3  'Stages' of cultural production

Note: these stages do not necessarily follow one on the other, as in a factory production line. They overlap, interact and sometimes conflict.

*Creation*
- Conception: design, realisation, interpretation; writing of screenplays and treatments, composition and improvisation of songs, etc.
- Execution: performance in recording studios, on film and television sets.
- Transcription on to a final master: involving editing (film, books and magazines), mixing (music, film).[1]

*Reproduction*
- Duplication in the form of printing, copying of CDs from a master recording, making multiple copies of a film from a negative (there is no equivalent in television). The text now takes the form that the audience will experience.

*Circulation*
- Marketing: including advertising and packaging (each of which has its own processes of conception and reproduction) but also aspects which might take place alongside conception or between transcription and reproduction of the main text, such as market research.
- Publicity: involving trying to ensure that other organisations provide publicity for the commodity
- Distribution and wholesaling (or the broadcast of a television programme).

*Retailing/exhibition/broadcast*

*Source*: adapted from Ryan (1992)

---

**This point about creative autonomy is absolutely crucial for an understanding of the cultural industries in the late twentieth century.** It shows that the metaphor of the traditional factory production line, often used in critiques of industrial cultural production, entirely misses the point (a

---

1 Ryan includes this in the reproduction stage but, although these tasks might be undertaken by skilled, technical professionals, they will often be carried out under the supervision of creative personnel, as this is a vital part of the creative stage.

point also made by Negus, 1992: 46). Because of the history of attitudes towards symbolic creativity discussed in the introduction, factory-style production is widely felt to be inimical to the kinds of creativity necessary to make profits. Even in the Hollywood studio system, which developed at the beginning of the complex professional era, and which exerted very tight control over the conception and execution of films compared with the control over these stages in other cultural industries, there was still considerable autonomy for screenwriters and directors, within certain formats and genres.

Crucially, companies in the business of cultural production exert much stricter control over the other stages of making texts after the creation stage (see Box 2.3): reproduction and circulation.[2] The reproduction stage is heavily industrial, is often and increasingly reliant on technically complex electronic systems, and is strictly controlled, especially in terms of when master copies of films, books, records, etc. are *scheduled* to be copied and released, or when a programme is scheduled to be broadcast. In terms of circulation, a very few superstars may have some bargaining power about which works get promoted and which do not, when texts are released or scheduled and so on, but it is senior management within the cultural industries which usually decides these matters.

This combination of loose control of creative input, and tighter control of reproduction and circulation constitutes **the distinctive organisational form of cultural production during the complex professional era**. The form developed in the early twentieth century, persisted and became much more widespread. Clearly, it has enormous implications for the conditions of creative work – a key concern of this book. I have referred to this organisational form in the present tense throughout the discussion above. But the key issue for the argument of this book is: **To what extent have the dynamics of this distinctive organisational form changed since the late 1970s?** I explore this issue in Chapter 5.

### The cultural labour market and systems of reward

From the market professional era onwards, most creative workers were paid not through regular wages, which gradually became the norm in most industries in advanced industrial countries during the same period, but through royalties: that is, through a percentage share of either the revenues or the profits made by the work. Creative managers, meanwhile,

---

2 This stage is often referred to as distribution (Garnham's seminal discussion, 1990: 161–2). But I find this term confusing: it sounds as though it refers to wholesaling: the transfer of products to retail outlets. Circulation includes this wholesaling aspect; but it also more clearly includes the equally problematic and important issue of marketing than does the term 'distribution'.

have more usually been wage-earners in large organisations, or owner-managers of their own small companies. Technical personnel have tended to be wage-earners, or to have worked freelance for higher wages.

We can turn to Bernard Miège for a picture based on 1970s research, but which can serve as a picture of the cultural labour market in the complex professional era of cultural production. Miège (1989: 82–3) argued that creative workers bear the costs of conception on behalf of cultural-industry companies by being willing to forego the benefits of secure working conditions, and in nearly all cases earning relatively little when they do. Creative labour within the cultural industries is underpaid because of a permanent oversupply of artistic labour which takes the form of various reservoirs or pools.[3] The biggest pool is composed of non-professional cultural workers, who work occasionally and have to take other jobs to subsidise their artistic activities. Wages are also kept down by the ready availability and willingness of professional workers in other cultural industries to transfer across into another field (such as journalists who might want to publish books, or pop musicians who might want to compose film scores).

The result is job markets in which most creative workers are either underemployed, at least in terms of the creative work they actually want to do, or underpaid. This should not be seen as a natural phenomenon: it is a result of specific economic and cultural conditions. These conditions include the failure of creative workers to come together to defend their interests against such forms of low pay and exploitation – in part because symbol creators are permanently competing with each other for recognition and rewards (Miège, 1989: 87).[4] The main exceptions are difficult-to-enter guilds, such as actors' unions.

For those relatively few creative workers who do succeed in having their works released into the market, and for the cultural-industry companies who undertake the circulation of such works, copyright law is vital (see Box 2.4). Copyright law is the arena in which the rewards for creative cultural labour are determined; and battles over these rewards between creative worker and company are resolved in the form of contracts. Overseen by national copyright laws, these contracts determine which creative workers get what percentage of revenues or profits, how long for, and who has the right to say what happens to the cultural work produced under the term of the contract.

---

3 Elsewhere Miège, or his translator, uses the term 'tank'.

4 Caves (2000), writing from a mainstream economics perspective, discusses differential success for creative workers by referring to the A list/B list property of the creative industries. But B lists comprise very successful creative personnel: stars who are not superstars. Miège's pools suggest the existence of C, D and other lists right down to Z, involving levels of inequality which Caves fails to address.

> ### Box 2.4   Copyright and cultural work
>
> A vital and often neglected aspect of the cultural industries is copyright law. Since the nineteenth century, copyright has underpinned the ownership of cultural commodities, and therefore the cultural industries as a whole. Mainstream economists and policy-makers describe its function as providing an incentive for authors to create. If authors wrote books and they could simply be copied without paying the author, then there would be less incentive to produce books, so the argument goes. For political economy approaches (Garnham, 1990: 38–40 and Bettig, 1996), copyright law is better understood as an attempt to regulate one of the distinctive problems facing the cultural industries: that cultural commodities often tend to act like public goods, in that the act of consuming them does not diminish their value (see p. 19). Copyright law responds by limiting the right to copy, thus making cultural goods scarcer than they might otherwise be.
>
>   Copyright law developed in the seventeenth and eighteenth centuries in book publishing, and took its modern form in the nineteenth century. Anglo-American copyright law was founded on contradictory principles: authors were treated as the creators of cultural works, and their expression of ideas was protected from plagiarism under copyright; but copyrights were assigned to publishers for a fixed term of, say, 20 years. Other legal systems have provisions which are more protective of authors' rights, in terms of their right to say how the work might be further modified or reproduced, but the tendency in all modern copyright systems is for the cultural-industry companies to own rights.[5] In the twentieth century, this already contradictory and complex legal framework became vastly more complex, as new media forms developed, such as film and recorded music, requiring their own modifications to the copyright laws originally developed for publishing. Nearly all the new media forms involved a much more complex division of labour, bringing about further complexity about who is the 'author' of a cultural work. With the complex professional era of cultural production, cultural corporations, rather than publishing companies, became the main owners of rights.

The poor working conditions and rewards for creative cultural work have been obscured by the fact that, in the complex professional era, very generous rewards are available for symbol creators who achieve name recognition in the minds of audience members. This overreward of stars derives in part from the need to confront risk through 'branding' (see Introduction). By branding star symbol creators, the cultural industries drew on long histories of charisma, and in so doing transformed them. For centuries, some symbol creators have achieved greater recognition than others. But in the twentieth century, the cult of celebrity has grown (see Gamson, 1994 for a useful history) and through the mass media, star symbol creators now have an aura previously achieved only by royalty,

---

5 See Bettig (1996: Chapter 2) for an outline of the early history. After an initial period of, say, 20 years, the work entered into the public domain: that is, everyone could use it. Later modifications meant that copyright would revert to the author for a further fixed period (say, until 50 or 70 years after her death).

and by political and religious leaders. By the 1950s, there was already a marked division in most cultural industries between, on the one hand, star symbol creators and, on the other, those in the various pools, including lesser-known but moderately recognised workers. The star system was established.

The question we need to confront then, in thinking about the extent of change and continuity in the cultural industries, is: **To what extent have the cultural labour market and systems of reward for cultural workers changed since the 1970s?**

## Ownership and structure of cultural-industry companies

One of the most striking and significant features of the complex professional era was the increasing presence of large corporations in the business of cultural production. The biggest of these companies, such as RCA (Radio Corporation of America) in the USA, were huge conglomerates.[6] They dwarfed the publishing companies and newspaper empires that had formed the largest companies of the market professional era. In film, recording, radio and television, significant oligopolies had emerged before the middle of the century. The most famous oligopoly was the eight vertically-integrated Hollywood studios (see Box 2.5). Rather less famous was the oligopoly that dominated the recording industry: the British companies Decca and EMI, and Columbia and RCA in the USA, joined by Warner Bros and Dutch consumer electronics giant Philips in the post-Second World War period. Many of these companies were vertically integrated too, producing record players and developing new recording and playback technologies. In radio and television, the US networks, CBS and NBC, were dominant. There was significant cross-media ownership in the early years of the complex professional era: film studios such as MGM (Metro-Goldwyn-Mayer) had significant music-industry interests, RCA had its own record company and its NBC network.

Beneath this layer of vertically integrated giants, most large companies were involved mainly in one form of cultural production. An important change came in the 1960s, as conglomeration spread throughout the cultural industries. (A conglomerate is a corporation that consists of a group of companies, dealing in different products or services.) This was part of a more general trend in business as a whole. Neil Fligstein (1990: Chapter 8) provides evidence of the shared trend towards diversification in all industries from the 1940s onwards. Of the 100 biggest companies in the USA in 1939, 77 concentrated 70 per cent or more of their business in a

---

6 For example, including its non-media interests, RCA was the 39th biggest company in the USA in 1972 (Murdock and Golding, 1977: 27–8).

single industry. By 1979, only 23 corporations concentrated on one industry in this way. And whereas none of the top 99 companies in 1939 produced across different industries that bore no relation to each other, by 1979, more than a quarter followed this strategy (these figures are from Fligstein, 1990: 261). What is more, Fligstein shows that this shift in strategy was adopted across all industries, and was driven by the need of senior managers to be seen to be achieving growth.

Conglomeration first hit the cultural industries in the 1960s, as part of this trend towards diversification. In some cases, this took the form of industrial and financial corporations and business corporations buying up and investing in media interests. Box 2.5 summarises how conglomeration affected the film industry during the complex professional era. In the 1960s and 1970s, conglomeration mainly took the form of large general conglomerates, with their businesses based on interests as diverse as oil, funerals and financial services, buying up film production studios and 'libraries' of old films. In other industries, conglomeration was based on projected 'convergences' and 'synergies', although the terms were not invented until later. For example, in the 1960s, big American consumer electronics and manufacturing companies such as IBM (International Business Machines), RCA, Xerox, GE (General Electric) and GTE bought up book publishers, anticipating convergence between book publishing and computers (Tunstall and Machin, 1999: 107–8).

But ownership and structure in the complex professional period is not only about the rise of vertically-integrated conglomerates; and, to restate my earlier point, this is one of the reasons I prefer the term 'complex professional' to Williams' 'corporate professional'. Small companies multiplied. The widespread existence of small companies in the cultural industries reflects some of the distinctive features of cultural production discussed in the Introduction. The conception of cultural works could take place on a relatively small scale, even while the scale of reproduction and circulation of cultural goods grew. Making up stories and songs, for example, are activities that can be carried out pretty much anywhere. Feature films might be impossible to make for anyone without access to considerable capital, but in economic terms at least, anyone can write a script. Even inscription (e.g., putting a magazine design onto disk, or making the master copy of a recording) and reproduction (running off copies of magazines or CDs) can be relatively cheap.

As small companies proliferated, more and more importance was attached to them as sites of creative independence, and this reflected anxieties about the negative effects of big, bureaucratic organisations on cultural production. Commentary about popular culture was booming in the mid-century, as, for example, film and jazz and even rock criticism began to burgeon as important cultural forms in their own right. By the late 1960s, many young pop and rock critics equated the corporations with commercial control, and saw the independents as representative of a hucksterish entrepreneurialism (e.g., Cohn, 1989/1969) or as more in touch with trends developed in local settings (e.g., Gillett, 1971). We will return to the issue of whether independents really do offer some kind of 'alternative' to the conglomerates in Chapter 5 and Chapter 8.

---

### Box 2.5   The Hollywood oligopoly across the complex professional era

Eight companies dominated Hollywood during its 'classical' period (1925 to 1950). The major studios owned and controlled many parts of the value chain. They ran production facilities, made the films, had creative and technical personnel signed to contracts, owned distribution networks, and owned the cinemas where the films were shown. A Big Five both distributed films and owned their own cinemas; the Little Three had their own distribution arms but no theatres. A series of rulings by the US Supreme Court aimed at breaking the Big Five's oligopoly forced the studios to get rid of their cinemas from the late 1940s onwards, weakening their power. The studios increasingly subcontracted to independent film production companies from the 1950s onwards, in an attempt to lower costs, and to control risk and outmanoeuvre television by producing new and spectacular genres. The studios acted as national and international distributors, and retained great power. All have eventually become divisions of large conglomerates (see Chapter 5). As their names recur throughout this book, this box also provides a brief guide to the later history of these important cultural-industry corporations.

*The Big Five:*
- Paramount, bought by oil conglomerate Gulf & Western in 1967, now part of the Viacom media conglomerate.
- 20th Century Fox performed disastrously in the 1960s and 1970s, became part of a private corporation, and was sold (as Fox) to Rupert Murdoch's News Corporation in 1985.
- Warner Bros was taken over by a general conglomerate Kinney National Services (a business based on funeral homes) in 1969, merged with Time in 1990 to form the world's largest media group and is now merging with AOL to regain that position.
- Loew's/Metro-Goldwyn-Mayer – MGM was just one subsidiary of the most successful film corporation of the classic Hollywood era. It changed hands countless times from the 1960s to the 1990s, and (as MGM/UA since 1981) is hardly an industry player now.
- Radio-Keith-Orpheum (RKO) was broken up by Howard Hughes in 1954.

*The Little Three:*
- Universal was taken over by MCA in the early 1950s (along with Paramount's film library and Decca Records) and MCA-Universal prospered in the television age to become the biggest film studio. It was taken over by Japanese consumer electronics company Matsushita in 1986, by Seagram in 1995 and by Vivendi in 2000.

*(continued)*

- Columbia struggled in the 1950s and 1960s, was acquired by Coca-Cola in 1981, and by Sony in 1988. It continued to struggle under conglomerate control.
- United Artists was acquired by Transamerica Corporation, a 'multiservice' organisation involved in insurance and financial services, in 1967 and merged with MGM in 1981.

Disney was not part of the classic Hollywood oligopoly. It had no distribution wing, but had its pictures distributed by UA and later RKO. When RKO was broken up, it set up its own distribution wing, Buena Vista. On the back of its revitalisation as a creative and commercial force in the 1980s, it has grown to become one of the largest cultural-industry conglomerates in the world.

*Sources*: mainly Gomery (1986), supplemented by Guback (1985) and Dale (1997).

The above features of ownership and company structure in the complex professional period raise the following question for analysis in the book as a whole, especially in Chapter 5: **To what extent have changes in conglomeration and integration led to recognisably new and distinct forms of ownership and structure during the 1980s and 1990s?** This question is in fact closely linked to questions about the internationalisation of the cultural industries.

### Internationalisation

International movement of cultural texts and cultural workers goes back many centuries. The first global media corporations, however, date from the nineteenth century, in the form of the British and French imperial news agencies (Reuters and Havas) which 'in the 1870s established a world cartel in fast news by ocean cable' (Tunstall, 1994: 14). Tunstall also provides other examples of internationalisation, including:

- Cultural forms: the spread of the daily entertainment sheet from the USA, where it was introduced by moguls such as Hearst and Pulitzer, into Europe and across the world.
- Cultural technologies: such as the sound film, which spread across the world in the 1930s.
- Cultural industries: in particular, the 'speedy capture of the world movie market by the young Hollywood' from 1914 to the 1930s.

As Tunstall notes, these waves of internationalisation, in the twentieth century, mainly emanated from the USA.

So the decades preceding the complex professional era of cultural production had already seen considerable amounts of international traffic in cultural goods. This international activity grew in the post-Second World War period. Alongside developments in communication and transport, this led to much higher levels of transnational flows of texts, genres, technologies and capital. This can be seen, for example, in the phenomenal spread of Anglo-American rock music and pop music culture across much of the world in the 1960s and 1970s, including even the Stalinist states of Eastern Europe. The US television industry developed ahead of most other countries and the US system was dominant internationally in the early years of television. In particular, most countries drew heavily on US programming during the television boom years of the 1960s (very few countries had developed television systems before the late 1950s). Television exports from the USA reached their peak in the late 1960s and then 'in the early 1970s remained at around US$100 million a year – meaning a real decline against inflation' (Tunstall, 1994: 144).

How and why did the USA dominate international television flows, and indeed cultural trade in general, during the complex professional era? This question raises fundamental issues concerning the relative roles of capitalist economics, political power and symbolic form and content in determining developments in the cultural industries.

One important factor was **the role of the US state**. US government organisations played an important part in promoting US cultural industries abroad, as a means of securing export income but also in order to export a set of beliefs and values concerning how to organise production and consumption. In international forums such as UNESCO in the post-Second World War years, US representatives 'pressed relentlessly' for the notion of a free flow of information and entertainment across the world, which would allow multinational cultural corporations to operate abroad, and would limit national government regulation of their activities (Schiller, 1998: 19). US foreign aid in the post-war period was tied to stipulations that US cultural exports would be permitted. In addition, the US state contributed enormously to the development of communications infra-structures, such as satellites. US cultural exports boomed during the post-Second World War period (see Herman and McChesney, 1997: 18–21).

Another key factor was **the nature of the US domestic market for leisure**. This was, from an early stage, larger and wealthier than any other in the world, and this allowed US production companies, across all cultural industries, to cover their costs at home, and to treat overseas markets as sources of further profit. In the early years of television, US companies built up greater repertoires of programming, giving overseas importers or international partners a bigger range of products to choose from. In a period when many economies were rebuilding, in the aftermath of the Second World War, the US television market established itself much earlier. Television was able to draw on an already established global success in film and, to some extent, in popular music. Genres, stars and other creative personnel, and technicians too, could be moved across from these industries. What is more, the US TV industry could invest in the expensive process of putting its products onto film, at a time when many countries were still transmitting programmes live. Some writers (Hoskins et al., 1997: 44) also stress the positive effects of having to appeal to a diverse audience at home. This view of the USA as a 'melting pot' and the rest of the world as homogeneous is too simplistic.[7]

The complex professional era, then, saw the rise to dominance of the USA as a global cultural force. But, as Tunstall (1994: 62) notes, there were other international cultural flows too. These included long-standing flows of texts within particular regions, often dominated by a regional 'media imperialist', such as Egypt in the Arab world, and Sweden in Scandinavia. Britain reaped the benefits of empire, even after its empire went into decline. There were also cultural flows from Latin America and Africa into the USA and other advanced industrial countries, especially in music and dance.

**Has the US retained its international dominance? Have the spatial relations of international cultural flows changed sufficiently for us to speak of a new era in cultural production and circulation?** I address these questions in Chapter 6.

### Associated regimes of technology, consumption and policy

The four main dimensions of the complex professional era of cultural production, discussed above, were intertwined with particular regimes of cultural consumption, policy and technology. The most important changes in consumption habits derived from the increasing amount of leisure time and disposable income available to people in advanced industrial countries. Indeed, it appears that such changes may have been crucial in fuelling the growth of the cultural industries as a whole. Vogel (1998: 6) cites figures showing the huge decline, in the USA, in average weekly working hours between 1850 (70 hours a week) and 1940 (approximately 44 hours a week), the years of growth in which the cultural industries made their transition from the market professional era to the complex professional era. Working hours decreased much less markedly in the USA in later decades, and have steadily declined in Japan, France and Germany. In the UK, working hours declined up until 1981 and have remained fairly consistent since then.

This increase in time available for cultural consumption and the rise of the complex professional form of cultural production from the 1920s onwards were closely associated with – though not caused by – the rise of

---

7 Just as problematic is Hoskins et al.'s view that US success abroad is based on the benefits of competition between oligopolistic firms at home. Hoskins et al. do recognise more significant factors – such as vertical integration in very large and wealthy markets – but they complacently dismiss accounts that stress the active role of the US state in promoting the interests of those industries as 'conspiracy theory' (Hoskins et al., 1997: 45).

electronic media technologies. Before the cinema boom of the 1910s, most people's experience of texts was either via live entertainment or print (books, magazines, newspapers). The technology of cinema, which involved the consumption of narratives in what were effectively neighbourhood pleasure centres, was, from the mid-1920s, increasingly supplemented by more individualised and family-based consumption practices associated with radio, and from the 1950s with television. With the rise of the consumer electronics industries in advanced industrialised countries during the post-war era, this drive towards private media consumption was enormously intensified. For Miège (1979: 20), 'the most remarkable aspect' of the growth in cultural consumption over the period from the 1950s to the 1970s was 'the very rapid growth in the development of reproducible products for private purchase' including cultural hardware such as TV sets, video recorders, tape recorders, hi-fi sets, but also photo and movie equipment; and the software linked to this equipment (records, film stock). The effects of all this on cultural production were profound. The sheer amount of texts produced proliferated; cultural consumption became radically more complex as products vied with each other for consumer time and attention; and the different media became interlinked with each other, so that the products of each medium were advertised and marketed in other media.

The introduction and dissemination of new media technologies had huge impacts on consumption practices. Early- and mid-twentieth century commentators identified their own period as one of *mass culture*. Millions of people shared experiences of certain cultural products: Hollywood movies, radio and television shows, the records of Bing Crosby, Elvis Presley, the Beatles. Yet even in this period of unprecedented massification, the seeds were sown for later fragmentation. Radio and television, along with important changes in housing for many people (better heating, larger living spaces) led to the rise of family-based and individualised cultural consumption. This was greatly intensified in the 1950s and 1960s with the rise of hi-fi, transistors, tape players, personal cameras and so on.

Partly as a result of widespread anxieties amongst the dominant classes in industrial societies about mass culture, the complex professional form of cultural production was highly regulated and closely governed. Forms of cultural production which private corporations did not feel they could make profit from, such as 'serious' music, opera, ballet, plus forms of national 'heritage' such as museums and galleries, were subsidised by national governments in the interests of maintaining or widening access. Broadcasting – including the key medium of the late twentieth century, television – was in many countries largely owned and operated by the state.

I will defer a full characterisation of broadcasting and telecommunications policy to Chapter 4. Technological changes are discussed in Chapter

7. Sociocultural changes are referred to throughout. The main guiding question for my treatment of these issues is: **What have been the key technological, sociocultural and policy changes affecting changes in the cultural industries?**

◆  ◆  ◆

The outline above, of the main features of the complex professional era of cultural production, provides the basis for our *measurement* of change and continuity – our assessment of the degree to which cultural production really has undergone fundamental transformation – in the rest of the book. But how to *evaluate* these changes?

## Evaluating change and continuity in the cultural industries

In what follows, I outline the values I will bring to bear on questions of change and continuity in the cultural industries in the main body of the book. I am concerned with the relationships between the cultural industries and society, and with the cultural industries as a system for the management and marketing of symbolic creativity. I end each section with a summary of the questions generated by the discussion for the book as a whole, concerning the historical period from the late 1970s to the early 2000s. (These questions are summarised in Box 2.6.) My treatment will be transhistorical, for the most part leaving aside for now questions of whether and how the cultural industries have changed, in order to elucidate what evaluative questions we might eventually ask about change and continuity.

---

**Box 2.6   Summary of evaluative questions concerning change and continuity in the cultural industries, 1980 onwards**

The numbers in brackets indicate the chapter(s) that most substantially deal(s) with the particular question under consideration.

◆   What are the effects of the growth in size and power of cultural-industry corporations on cultural production and on wider society? (5)
◆   Have the rewards and working conditions of symbol creators – and indeed other workers in the cultural industries – improved? (5)
◆   To what extent has creative autonomy been expanded or diminished? What changes have there been in the extent to which symbol creators within the cultural industries get to determine how their work will be edited, promoted, circulated? (5 and 7)

*(continued)*

- To what extent does the increasingly global reach of the largest firms mean an exclusion of voices from cultural markets? What opportunities are there for cultural producers from outside the 'core' areas of cultural production to gain access to new global networks of cultural production and consumption? (6)
- To what degree has access to the means of cultural production and circulation been opened up? To what extent are the barriers between production and consumption breaking down? (7)
- To what extent are the texts produced by the cultural industries growing more or less diverse? (8)
- Has the overall quality of texts declined? (8)
- Do the cultural industries increasingly serve the interests of themselves and of the wealthy and powerful in society? (8)

## The role of large corporations in the cultural industries and in society

The increasing presence of large corporations in the cultural industries has already been discussed earlier in this chapter, and Chapter 5 will show that the size and scope of these corporations expanded enormously during the 1980s and 1990s. How might we evaluate this expansion? The role of cultural-industry corporations in society has been an important theme in political economy, especially in the Schiller–McChesney tradition. There are striking examples of the exercising of interests via cultural-industry ownership by media moguls – individuals with overall control of a company (see Chapter 5). But it can be argued convincingly that they are exceptions. Moguls are more prevalent in the cultural industries than in most other types of industry[8] but even in the cultural industries, most companies are governed by a number of different shareholders. It could therefore be argued that control is spread over many owners, and this prevents particular interests from being served. But this misses the point. It is not the interests of particular individuals that is at stake, it is the interests of the social class to which they tend to belong: wealthy and powerful owners of capital, with strong ties to other powerful and influential institutions and individuals.

This wider argument has been disputed. Many commentators on ownership and control in general (not just of the cultural industries) have argued that since the nineteenth century's 'managerial revolution', control has been delegated to managers, who represent a different social class, and who do not have such an interest in maintaining power relations (see Scott, 1995 for a survey of these debates). Companies thus become a

---

8 Some have attributed this to the need for cultural-industry corporations to be able to carry out often rapid changes of policy and strategy in a high-risk unpredictable business (see, for example, Wolf, 1999: 117–54).

mixture of fragmented class interests. Again, though, the idea that owners and senior executives represent different social classes is wide of the mark. Senior managers will often be drawn from backgrounds as wealthy and privileged as those of their owners. They might represent a different stratum of the dominant classes, but given that they too are wealthy and privileged, they may well share the interests and political inclinations of the owners responsible for their appointments.

We should be in no doubt about the continued exertion of control by owners and executives. In an important article, Graham Murdock drew on debates in the sociology of business enterprises to clarify a distinction between two types of control in organisations: 'allocative' and 'operational' (all quotations from Murdock, 1982: 122). Allocative control consists of the 'power to define the overall goals and scope' of the enterprise and to 'determine the general way it deploys its productive resources'. This includes decisions on whether and where to expand, the development of financial policy (including share issues) and the distribution of profits, but crucially it also includes 'the formulation of overall policy and strategy'. Operational control 'works at a lower level and is confined to decisions about the effective use of resources already allocated and the implementation of policies already decided upon at the allocative level'.

Does this mean, however, that wealthy and powerful owners and senior executives of cultural-industry companies are able to pursue their interests via the cultural industries? To answer this means considering what their interests are. We can speak of **three different types of potential interest**. First, there is an interest in maximising the profits, revenues, market share, share price, etc. of their own particular company (or companies – many directors serve on the boards of a number of companies). In this first respect, companies obviously pursue their own interests. Aiming for profit maximisation, all businesses will try to ensure that expenditure on wages and other costs is well below the level of revenues. Within this system, some companies will pay higher wages and provide better conditions than others. Some industries will have better working conditions than others. As we have seen, there are specific conditions surrounding the business of cultural production, whereby workers have been given greater creative autonomy than in other sectors. But exploitation is inevitable: the system of capitalist accumulation depends on it. As Miège pointed out, cultural industry companies subsidise costs through pools of reservoir labour, and through the use of casualised cultural work. Other strategies include moving work overseas into countries where wages are much lower (as is the case in most animation productions – see Lent, 1998).

The second type of interest that owners and executives are likely to pursue is that of companies like themselves. Obviously, such companies compete with each other, except when they are involved in cartel arrangements, usually forbidden by law. But even within a system of mutual competition, companies will affiliate to form trade bodies, lobbying groups and alliances. There is a deeply rooted tendency in twentieth-century capitalism for oligopolies of large companies to form in nearly all industries. These oligopolies of big corporations are particularly effective at forming lobbying groups, which campaign against what they see as obtrusive government legislation and regulation, much of it in fact intended to protect workers and consumers. Such corporate lobbying has been an important feature of cultural policy making (see Chapter 4). Oligopolies also come to embody a set of conventions for understanding how best to organise business. Non-profit enterprises and smaller commercial companies, including those aiming at lower profit margins and innovative working practices, will tend to be excluded or marginalised. They may even come to appear naïve or incompetent, because of the greater wealth and prominence of companies in the oligopoly.

That companies pursue the interests of owners and executives in these two ways seems to me to be undeniable. The controversies surrounding such a system of self-interested production are mainly ones regarding the wider system of capitalism as a whole: principally whether the advantages (such as dynamic growth, the production of greater amounts of total wealth) of economic systems based on such actions outweigh the disadvantages (systematic underpaying of most workers, oligopoly, massive inequality, social fragmentation).[9]

There is, however, a third type of potential interest that owners and executives might pursue. Other things being equal, all businesses tend to want conditions in which businesses as a whole can thrive: political and economic stability and lively demand. This will mean that businesses will, for example, make huge donations to political candidates they think are likely to achieve these general business-environment goals. They will oppose reform and the struggle for greater equality if they perceive that such developments might threaten their business interests. Here, the question of whether and how they pursue such interests in the general conditions for profit making is extremely controversial. The ability of cultural-industry corporations to give an account of such issues makes their role the subject of special debate. Do cultural-industry companies produce texts that systematically support the interests of businesses? Do they hold back progressive reform and try to prevent the forms of social conflict often necessary to bring it about? I will defer consideration of these questions until later in this chapter. For now, though, this discussion of interests will serve to inform a question I address directly in Chapter 5, when I survey the growth of cultural-industry corporations in the 1980s

---

9 There are also questions of how to imagine and/or bring about alternative systems, but such issues need never imply that criticism should not be mounted.

and 1990s: **What are the effects of the growth in size and power of cultural-industry corporations on cultural production and on wider society?**

### Conditions of creativity in cultural-industry organisations

Let us now look in more detail at the terms and conditions of cultural-industry workers. This has been a neglected issue, even in the political economy and sociology of culture. Many books exist on film, recording, broadcasting and publishing, and yet few make reference to the working conditions and financial recompense available to the people working in these industries. Such issues have been absolutely central to the sociology of work in general, so why have they been marginalised in the study of *cultural* work? It may be that the sociology of culture has been unconsciously influenced by analyses that view creative artistic work as fully (rather than relatively) autonomous: the very form of analysis that it has often sought to critique. Another likely explanation is that the sociology of work often examines the type of waged work that prevailed in western societies from the Industrial Revolution until the 1980s. Symbol creators and other cultural workers, by contrast, are often rewarded by copyright payments, and make their living by contracting themselves to a number of different organisations in the course of their career.[10] Finally, there is the fact that the most prominent symbol creators are extremely wealthy and famous, and some are arrogant and obstreperous. Even the least prominent symbol creators might seem fortunate in that they are doing creative work at all. Perhaps these factors cultivate a complacent sense that cultural workers have it easy.

The relative creative autonomy of symbol creators does not mean that they all have a wonderful life, idling about in recording studios and on film sets while everyone else toils and watches the clock. Most creative workers make very little money. Great sacrifices have to be made to achieve even limited autonomy. As we have seen, Miège (1989) has drawn attention to the status and conditions of cultural workers. He noted the reliance of cultural firms on the existence of 'vast reservoirs of under-employed artists' (Miège, 1989: 72). He also noted how bad creative workers were at defending their own interests. The situation of the majority of people attempting to make a living out of cultural production contrasts strongly, of course, with the small number of highly rewarded superstars. An important question for this book to consider is whether the

---

10 Given that much work is taking this more 'flexible' form (though that word masks the insecurities and anxieties surrounding such working conditions) perhaps the study of remuneration and status in the cultural industries can provide a template by which to look at changes in other sectors.

situation described by Miège has changed in any way during the 1980s and 1990s. **Have the rewards and working conditions of creative workers – and indeed other workers in the cultural industries – improved during this time?** This will be addressed in Chapter 5, and to some extent in Chapter 7 too.

If I am right in focusing attention on the role of the cultural industries as systems for the management of symbolic creativity (see Introduction) then a key issue here will be the relationship between symbol creators and cultural-industry organisations. This focus is not intended to devalue the lives of technical workers. It derives from the recognition of how crucial symbol creators are in determining final outcomes, and from the central place of symbol creators in fantasies and beliefs about what 'good work' might involve in modern capitalism.

We saw in the Introduction that thinking about symbolic creativity has a long history. The influence of the romantic movement and of modernism has been profound and helped to establish a widespread view in the west that symbolic creativity can only flourish as far away from commerce as possible. This view is embodied in prevailing myths about great artists. We often think of the greatest symbol creators as either being unrecognised by commercial success in their lifetime (Van Gogh) or as being driven to despair by the superficiality of the commercial world they come to inhabit (Kurt Cobain). This polarisation of creativity versus commerce can confuse and mystify our understanding of the media and popular culture. In everyday conversation, texts, genres, performers, writers, etc. are often judged on the basis of assumptions about whether or not symbol creators had commercial intentions. The assumption is often that those creators that reject commercial imperatives most entirely are the best. But this is an overly polarised view of the relationship between creativity and commerce. All creators have to find an audience, and in the modern world, no one can do this without the help of technological mediation, and the support of large organisations. Moreover, we can't assume that the input of creative managers (as we saw earlier, the professionals who mediate between the interests of cultural-industry companies and those of symbol creators) is negative in terms of textual outcomes. Take for example, the tendency of creative managers to push symbol creators in the direction of genre formatting, in order to facilitate marketing and publicity for a particular audience. This isn't necessarily a bad thing. Genre can be a productive constraint, allowing for creativity and imagination within a certain set of boundaries and for enhanced understanding between audiences and producers.

Yet it remains the case that the relationship between creativity and commerce is a matter of negotiation, conflict and even struggle. However rewarding they find their work, nearly all symbol creators seem at some point to experience the constraints imposed on them in the name of profit accumulation as stressful, and/or oppressive and/or disrespectful. Many are forced to do 'creative' work that they hardly experience as creative at all. Let me give two examples.

♦   Sam, a successful but impecunious children's author with aspirations to write serious fiction for grown-ups, had a script turned into a major television series, funded by a transnational media conglomerate. He was paid a great deal of money, but was required to make revisions to his script on an almost daily basis during filming, in line with the 'suggestions' of the producer. He was driven to the edge of collapse and vowed never to work in television again. The most stressful aspect of this collaborative work for Sam was being thrown together with 'humourless arseholes'. Sam felt that the bad experience was a result of his own naivety, in not realising the leverage he had as a writer. But the question remains: why was he allowed to go through such a miserable, stressful experience by those with whom he was 'collaborating'?

♦   Tanika wrote scripts for a British television soap. Storylines are decided by a committee of executives, creative managers and script-writers. She felt that she was merely 'filling in the gaps'. She saw this work as merely paying the bills, so that she could do the work she really valued, in theatre, where even though audiences were much smaller, working relationships with directors and producers were more collaborative and co-operative. These co-operative conditions were possible because her work there was sheltered from commercial imperatives – though it still had to find an audience (and it did).[11]

Such stories concern conflicts during the creative stage. Just as significant are conflicts and decisions, of which creative workers might not even ever be aware, concerning decisions about reproduction and marketing. The fate of the symbol creator's work is in the hands of various other workers. This can function well, of course; and marketing can ensure the wide-spread dissemination of creative work, to the satisfaction of all concerned. Alternatively, texts can sink without trace, as creative managers and marketers prioritise other projects.

Here we encounter a contradiction. However mystifying and confusing the polarised view of creativity versus commerce can be, it has some positive effects. For it allows people who want to work creatively to argue for more time, space and resources than they might otherwise get from their commercial paymasters. Whether this results in better work can only be judged in particular cases. But the existence of work that is autonomous

---

11 The names of those involved may have been changed to protect the guilty. The examples are from case studies in a related project on symbol creators.

of the demands of profit accumulation is, in my view, a good thing in itself. This is not to celebrate or romanticise symbol creators. It is simply to grant them due recognition.

So the other key questions regarding the status and conditions of cultural workers are: **To what extent has creative autonomy been expanded or diminished over the last 20 years? What changes have there been in the extent to which creative workers within the cultural industries get to determine how their work will be edited, promoted, circulated?**

### International inequality

The last 20 years have seen an intensification of the internationalisation of cultural-industry businesses and texts that we noted earlier in discussing the complex professional era. What have been the effects of such internationalisation? In the 1960s and 1970s, when the intensified international activity of cultural-industry businesses was relatively new, radical writers developed the concept of 'cultural imperialism' to refer to the way that the cultures of less developed countries had been affected by the arrival of cultural texts, forms and technologies associated with 'the west'. The term was also applied to the effects of the expansion of US-based cultural industries on other developed countries. The 'cultural imperialism thesis' held that, as the age of direct political and economic domination by colonial powers drew to an end, a new, more indirect form of international domination was beginning. This involved, in Herbert Schiller's words (1976: 9), the adoption in economically peripheral countries of 'the values and structures of the dominating center of the [modern world] system'. As Annabelle Sreberny (1997: 49) has pointed out, the concept of cultural imperialism is an 'evocative metaphor', rather than a 'precise construct'. But the term draws attention to a number of important issues, such as the imposition of 'western' cultural products on the 'non-west',[12] the potentially homogenising effects of western culture as it spreads across the world and the destruction of indigenous traditions by such cultural flows, and the transfer of belief systems from the west to the non-west.

As we shall see in Chapter 6, the cultural imperialism thesis fell from favour in the 1980s and 1990s, when globalisation theory pointed to important ambivalences and problems surrounding such issues. I outline the tensions between cultural imperialism and globalisation theory in that chapter, and make the point that, even if cultural imperialism analysis was sometimes simplistic, it drew attention to important questions surrounding international inequalities in cultural power. **To what extent does the increasingly global reach of the largest firms mean an exclusion of**

---

12 These terms are extremely problematic, for reasons to be discussed in Chapter 6. I'll desist from using scare quotation marks from now on.

voices from cultural markets? What opportunities are there for cultural producers from outside the 'core' areas of cultural production to gain access to new global networks of cultural production and consumption?

### New technologies, access and participation

A fifth set of questions concerns the effects of new technologies on cultural production. A series of new, digital media technologies have been introduced since the 1970s. These are surveyed in Chapter 7. Some of the questions I ask in that chapter concern the conditions of symbol creators, particularly those involving desktop publishing software and new musical technologies. Other questions, however, concern access, participation and specialisation. The internet and digital television are especially important here.

In the complex professional era, there is a marked inequality between producers and consumers (see Couldry, 2000a for important insights into the difference between 'media people' and 'non-media people'). This clearly has important implications in terms of the role of information in contemporary societies. Most of the information we get is from distant media sources, whom we can hardly question about the accuracy and objectivity of their reports.[13] But it is also significant for the way we understand creativity. For the central role of the media – especially that of television – in our leisure and entertainment means that we generally let other people be creative for us. It is hard not to see our own forms of creativity as inferior to the work of the 'real' creators, who are part of the cultural industries.

The conditions of production in some cultural industries allow for more access to their inside zones than do others. A broad, generalised comparison of the television and recording industries might serve as an example. It costs an enormous amount of money to make a television programme. There is a very strong professional discourse within television which places a high value on technical 'finish'. Training takes years and experience is hard to come by, even with the recent proliferation of channels across the world. It is very difficult to get to appear on television, whether in a paid capacity, or in order to present a viewpoint. It is even harder to appear on your own terms, without being considerably constrained by the very tight presentational conventions of television. Much the same is true of the recording industry. It is incredibly difficult to gain access to the budgets and resources necessary to have a hit record. However, there are important differences. It is still possible to make a record 'outside' the core recording industry, at relatively low cost, and to

---

13 Thompson (1995: Chapter 3) provides a useful discussion of the rise of such 'mediated interaction' and the 'monological' nature of media such as television.

find a small audience for it. Subcultures of consumption, maintained through niche media of magazines, radio stations, and increasingly websites, mean that there is a huge diversity of recordings being made every day, by all sorts of different people. And because music is often still associated with marginalised and transgressive living, a disproportionate number of musicians are working class or lower middle class, or black, or feel alienated from the mainstream of society. The recording industry isn't democratic: but there is more space within music-making for access than in television.

Periodically, technologies develop in new ways and are hailed by utopian commentators as representing the dawning of a new era of access to cultural production. This happened with community radio and video cameras in the 1970s, miniature computerised recording studio equipment in the 1980s. The 1990s has seen the most pronounced claims yet for new technologies: the internet and digital television have, in different ways, been seen as the means to transform present conditions of access. Chapter 7 will assess the degree to which these technologies really have transformed the social relations of production in the cultural industries.

The above discussion then prepares the ground for a crucial issue, in the ethical evaluation of change and continuity in the cultural industries from the late 1970s to the early 2000s: **To what degree has access to the means of cultural production and circulation been opened up? To what extent are the barriers between production and consumption breaking down?**

## Choice, diversity, multiplicity

I now turn to the most difficult and controversial aspects of evaluation: the textual outcomes of the cultural industries. There are three main ways in which the relationships between cultural industries and textual outcomes tend to be discussed: the issue of diversity and choice; questions of quality; and in terms of social justice, and in particular whether the interests of the wealthy and powerful are served (the question deferred from earlier). Only the last of these issues is likely to pay dividends in any *critical* analysis of the cultural industries, and I take up this point further in Chapter 8.

The issue of diversity has been particularly important in discussion of oligopoly, concentration and conglomeration. Mainstream economics has argued for many years that markets tend to oversupply products in 'the middle of the market' (Hotelling's Law – see Hotelling, 1929). Liberal-pluralist communication studies scholars and others have tried to show that concentration leads to homogenisation and standardisation, or at least reduced diversity, but with contradictory results (see Chapter 8). Even in the rare cases where decreasing diversity is clear, it is very difficult to show that concentration *caused* homogenisation. Indeed, it is possible to make the argument that concentration can, at least in particular cases at particular times, be beneficial for diversity. As Collins and Murroni (1996: 58) put it, 'risky new media markets require venture capital and market power in order to launch new products'. And, as they also point out, challenging, authoritative reporting needs lots of money to back it up.

In fact, there is evidence that the complex professional era has seen a marked increase in the range and diversity of cultural goods on offer: the high street record shops, newsagents and bookshops seem awash with products, and nearly everyone in the developed world can receive more radio and television stations than ever before. How can we possibly speak of a lack of diversity? One political economy writer (Mosco, 1995: 258) has responded to this criticism by making a distinction between *multiplicity* (the sheer number of voices) and *diversity* (whether these voices are actually saying anything different from each other).[14] This is an important point. There are hundreds of magazines available in the USA and Europe, catering for every kind of interest imaginable, from needlework to the mercenary soldier business, from gay porn to religious affairs. No doubt many of these magazines add pleasure and interest to their readers' lives. But is there real diversity when it comes to the expression of viewpoints about how we might understand public life? Similarly, are audiences exposed to a wide range of voices, or are we increasingly encouraged to stay tuned only to those channels of communication we have already decided we are interested in? These questions suggest the very real difficulties involved in providing any objective assessment of what constitutes diversity in the cultural industries. This is a great problem, because much writing that is critical of the present constitution of the cultural industries assumes the assent of readers regarding these questions. Nevertheless, the question remains on the agenda: **To what extent are the texts produced by the cultural industries growing more or less diverse?** I return to this issue in Chapter 8.

### Quality

It is common to hear claims that the quality of the texts produced by the cultural industries is in decline. Indeed, there is a huge tradition of cultural commentary devoted to this view (e.g., MacDonald, 1963; Bloom, 1987; see Ross, 1989 for a brilliant overview of this terrain). The most recent version of this approach has it that the faster, more frenetic way in which we read, watch and listen to texts has led to a decline in the quality of our cultural experiences, and in the quality of the actual texts themselves. According to such views, the cultural industries can 'get away with' investing less

---

14 A similar argument runs through Adorno and Horkheimer's analysis of 'the culture industry'.

energy, time and resources in high standards, because we are too dis-
tracted to appreciate quality anyway. Closely related to this is the view
that overall quality is declining because of an overfocus on making money.
As I will show in Chapter 8, such arguments are extremely difficult to
prove. This is not simply because judgements of quality are subjective. The
real problem is that many of those who argue for overall decline in a
particular industry offer very little substantial argument, in the form of
explicit reference to aesthetic criteria, to back up their case. Nevertheless,
the question remains an interesting one: **Has the overall quality of texts
declined?**

### Texts, social justice and the serving of interests

Here we return to the question raised earlier in the discussion of the
interests of cultural-industry corporations, specifically their owners and
executives. Let me take the breakdown of goals that cultural-industry
companies might pursue, provided in the section on the role of large
corporations in the cultural industries and in society. In each case I raise
the question of whether cultural-industry companies serve powerful interests, without anticipating too much the evidence to be discussed in
Chapter 8. The main aims here, however, are to clarify and justify the
evaluative criteria I will bring to bear on textual developments in the
cultural industries in that later chapter.

◆ *Companies promoting their own interests as companies through texts.* In one
obvious sense, cultural-industry companies clearly serve their own
interests via texts. Whatever the mixture of motivations amongst
individuals and across different roles, cultural-industry companies
release texts primarily in order to make money. But does this have
negative consequences? Not, I believe, in terms of quality of texts.
Companies sell commodities directly to the public and aim to make
more in revenues than they expend on costs. But many of the texts
that sell best will not have any textual qualities associated with
selling. Audiences value texts that are autonomous of commerce.
Some criticise certain texts and performers for pandering to an
audience, for being 'commercial' in the sense that they aim to please
too easily. I do not think it is possible or relevant to mount a criticism
of the cultural industries on this basis. I am not arguing that commercial motivation produces poor quality. This assertion is often made by
those who see creativity and commerce as polar opposites but it is
very problematic. There are plenty of underresourced, ill thought-out,
unimaginative texts, but their poor quality is not *necessarily* caused by
the fact they are sold for commercial gain, although budget-cutting
and penny-pinching may not help. Many texts that are commercially
produced are funny, beautiful, intriguing, clever and so on. This

is true even of advertising, the most commercially-oriented of all messages.[15] More problematic issues surround other ways of making money from texts, especially the selling of advertising to accompany texts. In my view, this potentially has negative social consequences. The fact that companies produce texts primarily for profit means there is a tendency for commercially-oriented texts to increase in number and presence in everyday life, as new media provide new advertising opportunities, and as the space allotted to advertising in existing media increases. Advertising helps to shape the view that the purchase of goods and services is the primary means of providing satisfaction, happiness and well-being. It helps to foster a society where individual consumerism is equated with the good life. People are encouraged to act less as citizens and more as consumers. Individuals spend huge amounts of effort and energy accumulating wealth and possessions but, for example, cannot raise the energy to speak in a meaningful way to friends and family. Clearly, there are many other factors contributing to the development of acquisitive societies. But advertising plays a large part. Recent years have seen the development of new forms of hidden advertising in the cultural industries, in the form of increasing product placement and the development of texts intended to produce synergies with other texts, such as the simultaneous release of films, novels, soundtracks and computer games.

♦ *Companies promoting the interests of cultural-industry companies as a whole (or those of fellow members of an oligopoly of major corporations) through texts.* The main way cultural-industry companies act as joint interest groups is through lobbying activities. There are textual ways in which this happens too. There is a strong tendency for texts made by the largest corporations to refer to products of other corporations. But this is not the result of conscious and deliberate attempts by large companies to reinforce each other's positions. The most important issue is whether the cultural industries issue texts that question the impacts of their own operations.

♦ *Companies promoting the interests of businesses in general and of the social class who own them.* The cultural industries have for many decades, through advertising and marketing, served the interest of businesses as a whole by creating a context in which consumption is stimulated, and satisfaction becomes associated with the buying of commodities, through advertising and marketing. It isn't nearly so clear that non-

---

15 It is often remarked that television advertisements are better than the programmes they interrupt. If this were true (and I don't think it is), it wouldn't be surprising. These advertisements often have larger budgets per minute.

advertising messages systematically support the business environment, however. Many texts celebrate selfish consumerism as a means to happiness, but many prioritise other values over acquisition. Promoting the interests of businesses above the interests of people as citizens and workers can lead to a deterioration in the quality of working life, the environment and personal relationships. The most difficult question of all is whether texts promote the interests of businesses and the dominant social class by encouraging political and economic stability, and by discouraging progressive social change. I assess the mixed evidence about this question in Chapter 8. But any increasing tendency for the cultural industries to support these powerful interests would clearly be negative.

The above discussion will hopefully have provided indication of the specific breakdown of the overall question to be applied in this case: **Do the cultural industries increasingly serve the interests of themselves and of the wealthy and powerful in society?**

◆ ◆ ◆

This chapter has laid the ground for the assessment of change and continuity in the following chapters by providing a means of measuring the extent of change in the cultural industries over the relevant period, followed by a framework for evaluating change. The task of the next chapter is to provide a model for explaining the major changes and continuities in the cultural industries.

## Further reading

Raymond Williams is usually named as one of the 'founding fathers' of cultural studies, based on early works such as *Culture and Society* (1958) and *The Long Revolution* (1961), but his later, sociological and theoretical work (for example, 1977 and 1981) is just as important. It is compatible with political economy and radical media sociology approaches to the extent that he can be seen as a parent of those approaches too. *Culture* (1981) is probably his most neglected major work. It provides the basis of the attempt here to construct a *historical* sociology of cultural production. Bill Ryan's *Making Capital from Culture* (1992) picks up Williams' Marxian, historical analysis of the 'corporate professional' form of capitalist cultural production, and brings an organisational studies perspective to bear on it. His book is specialised, exhaustive and difficult but I have found it invaluable. Much more readable is Jason Toynbee's *Making Popular Music*

(2000). It is rare to find such a theoretically sophisticated examination of a particular cultural industry. Its focus on symbol creators (that is, in the case of the music industry, musicians) has been a major influence on my thinking in this book and Toynbee's optimism about the human capacity for symbolic creativity has helped to balance my pessimism about the growth of large corporations. I have found the work of Jeremy Tunstall (1986, 1994) very useful in providing historical detail on the cultural industries, in spite of its empiricist lack of interest in theorising historical developments.

# 3 Explaining the Cultural Industries

## Three forms of reduction: technological, economic and cultural

Why have the cultural industries changed so much over the last 20 years? What are the forces driving these changes? We will need to avoid easy answers as we negotiate these questions. In complex societies, adequate explanations of social processes are rarely going to be simple. It would be wise therefore to avoid answers that *reduce* complicated, interwoven webs of causality to a single driving force. Of course everyone thinks that her/his account avoids such reduction. Yet the need to achieve coherence and directness often drags accounts into an overemphasis on one particular factor, at the expense of others.

The term most widely used in sociological and historical writing to refer to such an overemphasis on one factor is **technological determinism**, which obviously suggests that the factor being given too much weight at the expense of others is the causal role of technology. I prefer the term 'reduction' or (if pushed), 'reductionism' to determinism, because the problem is not that technology is given a determining role, but that this determining role is overemphasised, thus reducing complexity to simplicity. The term 'technological determinism' was introduced to social and cultural studies by Raymond Williams in his book *Television: Technology and Cultural Form* (1974), where he provided a critical account of such thinking as it applied to television, and indeed to technologies in general. But it is often forgotten that Williams was also criticising what he called 'sympto-matic technology' (Williams, 1974: 13), the view that technologies are merely by-products of wider social processes. What mattered for Williams was that technologies should never be seen in isolation, but should always be understood *in relation* to other processes and factors.

Obviously, technologies have effects. The introduction of the telephone has helped to transform the way that we communicate. The introduction of video recorders into the home has played an important role in changing the way many of us experience television. These are relatively uncon-troversial statements, involving no reduction. Reduction would come in if we were, for example, to answer the question 'What has caused the trans-formations in the way we experience television over the last 20 years?' with a broad response such as 'new technologies such as video, cable and satellite'. For this begs a number of questions. What caused these tech-nologies to be introduced in the way that they were? How did they take the particular form they did? In accounts that are afflicted by the techno-logical reductionism of their authors, the relationship of technologies to economic, political and cultural forces becomes obscured or even lost altogether.

It is also common to hear charges of **economic determinism**; and again, I think that reductionism is a more accurate term. This charge tends to be levelled particularly against political-economic accounts, for their sup-posed reduction of social and cultural events and processes to ultimately economic driving forces, such as the imperative of companies to make profit, or the interests of the social class who control the means of production. Indeed, some cultural studies analysts and many pluralist communications studies scholars (such as Neuman, 1991: 16) make the claim that Marxism is more or less inherently reductionist. But economic reductionism is by no means confined to Marxists. Orthodox, mainstream economics often makes strong claims for the explanatory power of its economic models. As with technological reductionism, the issue here is not whether economic forces have any causal effect. It is clear, for example, that the behaviour of companies in pursuit of profit does have important social effects. The question is whether an overemphasis on economic explanation means that the analyst fails to provide an adequate account of the relationship of such economic factors to other processes.

Neuman (1991: 17) has drawn attention to the much less often heard charge of **'cultural determinism'**, which he defines as the view that systems of values and beliefs have causal primacy.[1] Although it is not nearly so common to hear this phrase as it is to hear about technological and economic determinism, a belief in the causal primacy of culture is very

---

1 Neuman uses the concept of 'monism' – accounts of determination based on single factors.

widespread. A version of such cultural determinism underlies the commonly expressed but mistaken view that 'the media give people what they want': that is, the shape of the media is determined by its audiences' culturally-shaped desires and expectations. Few people are bold enough to go into print to attempt to justify such a view (an exception is Whale, 1977). But this view can be heard with alarming regularity in cultural-industry organisations and amongst public commentators and politicians. The main problem with it is that it ignores the huge role that the media themselves play in shaping the desires and expectations of audiences.

Once again, the objection to cultural reductionism is not that it attributes causal properties to cultural processes. Clearly, for example, changes in leisure time and practices have an enormous influence on what cultural-industry companies can do. The problem here as with any reduction is the begging of further questions about causality such as, 'how did these cultural practices come to take the form they did?' But there are added difficulties in discussing the causal effects of cultural processes, connected to the difficulties of definition surrounding the term 'culture', discussed in the Introduction. Culture has become such a widely-used word in contemporary societies, whether in academic writing or in journalism and popular publishing, that it has come to mean everything and nothing. Does it mean the prevalent attitudes, beliefs and values within a particular society? Or the ordinary, lived experiences of people? Or the general conditions of living within a particular place, organisation or institution? Everyone agrees that the term is difficult and contested, and yet it is commonly invoked as a means of explanation superior to an approach centred on 'technology' or 'economics', without any recognition of these difficulties. As should be clear from the Introduction, I prefer Williams' definition of culture as 'the *signifying system* through which . . . a social order is communicated, reproduced, experienced and explored' (Williams, 1981: 13). This at least helps to avoid the clumsiest invocations of culture, and draws our attention to the concept of the 'sociocultural', an inherently non-reductionist concept, involving interactions between such cultural dimensions and more broadly *social* systems and behaviours (for discussion of this difficult and neglected terrain, see Williams, 1981: Chapter 8).

## Contexts for change and continuity in the cultural industries: 1945–90

In what follows, I develop an account that attempts to combine analysis of economic, technological and cultural processes with other important dimensions, including politics, legal and regulatory frameworks, and the internal dynamics of cultural-industry organisations themselves. When I began thinking about issues of determination and change in the cultural industries, I thought that I would be able to summarise political economy work in order to provide a concise and coherent historical account, as a lead-in to my assessment of change and continuity. But political economy approaches have, to a remarkable degree, lacked an explanatory account of such changes. Even Nicholas Garnham and Graham Murdock, whose writings are scattered with insightful nuggets of explanation, have not provided any systematic, overall view of the relationship of economic and cultural change, via a historical examination of the cultural industries. This Chapter takes some steps towards an overview of change. To do so, it turns to a broader literature in social theory, politics and economics.

Having said that, social theory and social science have neglected the cultural industries. Some major contributions have attempted to deal with them, but nearly always in a very limited way. David Harvey's *The Condition of Postmodernity*, for example, attributes considerable importance to the cultural industries in terms of mastering and controlling sign systems in an era of new cultural volatility and unpredictability (see Harvey, 1989: 284–307). But Harvey gives no space to their distinctive organisational forms (apart from a brief reference on page 290) or to conflicts and contradictions within cultural production. Manuel Castells' chapter on media in *The Rise of the Network Society* (Castells, 1996) is the weakest in his entire trilogy on *The Information Age* (of which *The Rise of the Network Society* forms the first part). Castells resorts to futurology and simplistic descriptions of a previous era of media (Castells, 1996: 327–75 – see my comments in Chapters 7 and 8). A significant exception to such neglect of cultural production in social theory is Scott Lash and John Urry's book *Economies of Signs and Space* (1994). This devotes an entire chapter to the cultural industries, and has interesting things to say about the relationship between the cultural industries and wider economic and social changes.

But where to begin? In my view, the most promising starting point for understanding changes in the cultural industries is the Long Downturn which affected much of the world from the late 1960s onwards. A number of accounts (most notably for my purposes, Castells, 1989 and Harvey, 1989) have shown how corporations and governments responded to this economic crisis in a number of ways, in an attempt to fix the problem. In beginning my narrative from an economic event, am I guilty of economic reductionism? No, because I use the term 'starting point' advisedly here. This economic crisis was itself produced in part by social, cultural, organisational and technological factors. There is no single point of origin to the chain of cause and effect. The Long Downturn serves as a catalyst to accelerate and consolidate certain processes already under way. So while this is an account which begins from the political-economic, it recognises the fact that political-economic events were tangled with a large number of other factors.

## Political-economic change: The Long Downturn

It would be wrong to portray the era following the Second World War as an era of global peace and prosperity. Disease and poverty were wide-spread, and outside Europe, there was unprecedented military conflict. There is no doubt, though, that for the 'advanced' capitalist economies of Europe, North America and Australasia, the period from the 1950s to the early 1970s was one of steady economic growth, rising standards of living, and a relatively stable system of liberal democratic government. The Stalinist economies of Eastern Europe and the Soviet Union also achieved significant growth. There was even evidence that the increasing inequality in wealth and social opportunity which had marked feudal and capitalist societies was beginning to be reversed (see Hobsbawm, 1995: 257–86 for an overview of this period). Because of the relatively strong macroeconomic performance of advanced capitalist economies, some economists have referred to this period as 'the golden age of capitalism' (Marglin and Schor, 1992). In the late 1960s, mainstream economists were predicting an end to the cycles of boom and bust which, in the views of all commentators, be they from left or right, had characterised industrial capitalism for a 150 years.[2]

But in the early 1970s, after decades of these relatively favourable conditions, the advanced capitalist economies hit the beginning of a Long Downturn which continued into the 1990s, marked by particularly severe recessions in 1974–5, 1979–82 and 1991–5. In the G-7 countries between 1970 and 1990 profits fell significantly across all sectors, but especially in manufacturing. Other key economic indicators also showed a significant downturn, as can be seen in Table 3.1, which is drawn from Brenner (1998: 5).

There is some controversy over the causes of the Long Downturn. For David Harvey (1989), international financial movements began to under-mine the stability of financial system from the early 1960s onwards. For other scholars (e.g., Armstong et al., 1991), the primary cause was that the increasing power of working-class wage earners disturbed the balance of capital and labour that had been sustained during the golden age. As labour solidified its power, a 'wages explosion' squeezed profits, so leading to crisis. For Robert Brenner (1998), the main cause of the decline in profits associated with the Long Downturn was not the increased pressure brought about by labour, but the tendency by capitalists to compete with each other, without any regard for what happened to the

---

2 See, amongst other examples quoted by Brenner (1998: 1), the remark by Paul Samuelson, one of the most eminent mainstream economists of the twentieth century, that the National Bureau of Economic Research had 'worked itself out of one of its jobs, the business cycle'.

**Table 3.1** Comparing the post-war boom and the Long Downturn (average annual rates of change, except for net profit and unemployment rates, which are averages)

**Manufacturing**

| | Net Profit Rate | | Output | | Net Capital Stock | | Gross Capital Stock | | Labour Productivity | | Real Wage | |
|---|---|---|---|---|---|---|---|---|---|---|---|---|
| | 1950–70 | 70–93 | 50–73 | 73–93 | 50–73 | 73–93 | 50–73 | 73–93 | 50–73 | 73–93 | 50–73 | 73–93 |
| US | 24.35 | 14.5 | 4.3 | 1.9 | 3.8 | 2.25 | – | – | 3.0 | 2.4 | 2.6 | 0.5 |
| Ger | 23.1 | 10.9 | 5.1 | 0.9 | 5.7 | 0.9 | 6.4 | 1.7 | 4.8 | 1.7 | 5.7 | 2.4 |
| Jap | 40.4 | 20.4 | 14.1 | 5.0 | 14.5 | 5.0 | 14.7 | 5.0 | 10.2 | 5.1 | 6.1 | 2.7 |
| G-7 | 26.2 | 15.7 | 5.5 | 2.1 | – | – | 4.8 | 3.7 | 3.9 | 3.1 | – | – |

G-7 net profit rate extends to 1990; German net capital stock covers 1955–1993; Japanese net profit rate and net capital stock cover in manufacturing 1955–1991.

**Private Business**

| | Net Profit Rate | | Output | | Net Capital Stock | | Gross Capital Stock | | Labour Productivity | | Real Wage | | Unemployment Rate | |
|---|---|---|---|---|---|---|---|---|---|---|---|---|---|---|
| | 1950–70 | 70–93 | 50–73 | 73–93 | 50–73 | 73–93 | 50–73 | 73–93 | 50–73 | 73–93 | 50–73 | 73–93 | 50–73 | 73–93 |
| US | 12.9 | 9.9 | 4.2 | 2.6 | 3.8 | 3.0 | – | 3.0 | 2.7 | 1.1 | 2.7 | 0.2 | 4.2 | 6.7 |
| Ger | 23.2 | 13.8 | 4.5 | 2.2 | 6.0 | 2.6 | 5.1 | 3.0 | 4.6 | 2.2 | 5.7 | 1.9 | 2.3 | 5.7 |
| Jap | 21.6 | 17.2 | 9.1 | 4.1 | – | – | 9.35 | 7.1 | 5.6 | 3.1 | 6.3 | 2.7 | 1.6 | 2.1 |
| G-7 | 17.6 | 13.3 | 4.5 | 2.2 | – | – | 4.5 | 4.3 | 3.6 | 1.3 | – | – | 3.1 | 6.2 |

G-7 net profit rate extends to 1990; German net capital stock covers 1955–1993.

*Source:* Brenner, 1998.

system as a whole. As German and Japanese corporations increased their successful involvement in manufacturing, the world's key economy, the USA, experienced a crisis of over-capacity and production in manufacturing – which was, and remains, its key sector (see Brenner, 2000: 8) – and this triggered an international crisis, exacerbated by the OPEC oil price rise of 1973.

## Political and regulatory change: the rise of neoliberalism

Whatever the precise causes of the Long Downturn, there is widespread consensus that it had profound consequences. One set of consequences was political, and these provide important contexts for understanding changes in the regulation of the cultural industries (discussed in detail in the next chapter). The various advanced capitalist states responded to the crisis that hit capitalism in the 1970s by attacking the institutional strength of labour movements and by moving away from the arrangements for state intervention in economic life that had prevailed in the post-war period, whereby government spending was used to supplement consumer spending, whenever consumer spending was inadequate to sustain economic growth (see Harvey, 1989: Part II). Employers and governments ensured a long-term reduction in real wages, but this was not sufficient to restore profits. From 1979, after some years of attempting to reflate western economies, governments made permanent a set of anti-inflation strategies that had been tried in 1974–5. Emergency cutbacks in public spending and the stripping away of regulation by democratically-elected governments were promoted from emergency measures to permanent policy. The view that human needs are best served by an unregulated 'free market', a view that had been popular with various nineteenth-century liberal economists, but that had mostly been confined to cranks and nutcases for much of the late twentieth century, made a comeback: hence the term *neo*liberal economics.[3]

Such neoliberal free market thinking took particularly extreme forms in the UK and the USA, where far-right conservative governments were elected (by a small minority of the eligible-to-vote population) in 1979 and 1980 respectively. These governments were re-elected with massive majorities in 1983 and 1984 respectively, partly because an influential minority of people benefited from such policies, but also because the

---

3 In the USA, 'liberal' has come to mean politically centrist (as opposed to conservative or radical) but that is not the sense of the term involved in nineteenth-century liberal economics, or in the important term 'neoliberalism', where the sense is one of advocating individual freedom. However, the consequences of unregulated markets often deny important freedoms to many people.

labour movements in the USA and the UK, traditionally the basis of leftist politics in both countries, were in complete disarray, and chaos on the left helped make the rightist governments look competent, in spite of record levels of unemployment and inequality. This was an era in which the cultural industries had an especially important role in legitimising political and economic strategies, as press and television news portrayed trade unions as regressive.

From the late 1970s, most governments of whatever political persuasion attempted to weaken the bargaining power of labour in order to lower wage costs. Credit was restricted through the raising of interest rates, which forced unprofitable firms out of business, and weakened labour still further through the spread of unemployment (Brenner, 1998: 181). But as a result of the second election victories of Thatcher and Reagan in 1983–4, extreme neoliberal dogma spread into elected social-democratic, reformist governments, such as New Zealand from 1984 onwards (see Gray, 1998) and most governments of advanced capitalist countries in the late 1980s. When Stalinist communism collapsed in Eastern Europe, the Soviet Union and many of their client states in 1989–91, it was neoliberalism rather than social democracy that was adopted as a political model.

This is the vital *political* context for understanding changes in communications and telecommunications law and policy in the 1980s and 1990s: the revival of the idea that human needs are best served through the 'free' market. Such **marketisation** has been fundamental in bringing about a whole series of other changes in the cultural industries. I trace the paths of marketisation in a number of different contexts in Chapter 4, and analyse their effects in more detail.

## Changing business strategies

A second major consequence of the decline in productivity and profits associated with the Long Downturn was that capitalist businesses across the developed world began a period of intense innovation. There were three main aspects to this.

♦ A shift towards service industries: that is, away from the extractive (for example, mining and agriculture) sector and to some extent from the transformative (mainly manufacturing) sector towards the various industrial sectors which deal primarily with services: distributive, producer, social and personal services, to use the terms adapted by Castells (1996: 311) from Singelmann (1978).
♦ Internationalisation
♦ Organisational innovation

## Investment shifts towards service industries

There was a significant overall move on the part of businesses in advanced industrial countries away from agriculture, raw material extraction, construction and manufacturing towards service industries. This was a longer-term trend, as Harvey (1989: 157) shows, but it became irreversible in the wake of the Long Downturn. Companies in advanced industrial countries faced rising wages and increased competition, especially from the newly industrialised countries of the Asia-Pacific region (most notably South Korea, Taiwan, Hong Kong and Singapore) but also Latin America (principally Mexico and Brazil). However, this shift is often simplified or exaggerated. The figures in Table 3.2, based on Castells' data (1996: 282–93) provide some indication of the overall patterns. These figures are useful in providing a much more sophisticated picture of industrial change than the old primary–secondary–tertiary model of agriculture, manufacturing and services. Castells, drawing on industrial historian Joachim Singelmann, instead uses the broader terms 'extractive' and 'transformative' to describe the primary and secondary sectors; and breaks services up into four constituent sectors.

The decline of manufacturing tends also to be exaggerated. In Japan, for example, the transformative sector, including construction, utilities and manufacturing, showed only a very small decline in the proportion of employment during the post-1973 period. But there were substantial declines in the USA, France and the UK. Even more significant was the

**Table 3.2  The shift to services**

| Industry | US 1970 | US 1991 | Japan 1970 | Japan 1990 | France 1968 | France 1989 | UK 1970 | UK 1990 |
|---|---|---|---|---|---|---|---|---|
| Extractive | 4.6 | 3.5 | 19.8 | 7.2 | 15.6 | 6.4 | 3.6 | 3.3 |
| Transformative | 33.0 | 24.7 | 34.1 | 33.7 | 39.4 | 29.5 | 46.7 | 27.3 |
| Distributive services | 22.4 | 20.6 | 22.4 | 24.3 | 18.8 | 20.5 | 18.7 | 20.6 |
| Producer services | 8.2 | 14.0 | 4.8 | 9.6 | 5.0 | 10.0 | 5.0 | 12.0 |
| Social services | 22.0 | 25.5 | 10.3 | 14.3 | 15.1 | 19.5 | 17.7 | 27.2 |
| Personal services | 10.0 | 11.7 | 8.5 | 10.2 | 8.2 | 14.1 | 8.1 | 8.1 |

Figures refer to the percentage of total workforce.

**Sector definitions:**
Extractive: agriculture and mining
Transformative: construction, utilities and manufacturing
Distributive services: transport, communication and wholesale
Producer services: banking, insurance, real estate, engineering, accounting, legal services, miscellaneous
Social services: medical, hospital, education, welfare, religious services, non-profit organisations, postal service, government, miscellaneous
Personal services: domestic service, hotels, eating and drinking places, repairs, laundry, barbers and beauty shops, miscellaneous and unclassifiable services

*Source*: adapted from Castells, 1996: 282–93

decline in the extractive sector (agriculture and mining) in countries such as Japan and France with sizeable rural populations.

The 1980s and 1990s boom in the cultural industries needs to be seen in the context of this shift in investment strategies. Unfortunately, Singelmann and Castells' categories are not flexible enough to include figures specifically on the cultural industries; they appear to be hidden away as miscellaneous producer services – the area of greatest growth in nearly all advanced industrial countries. A European Commission staff working paper (European Commission, 1998) outlined the following figures, drawing on national governments' statistical data. Even taking into account the different methodologies adopted by different national governments, the figures are striking:

◆ Cultural employment in Spain went up 24 per cent between 1987 and 1994.
◆ Cultural employment in France went up 36.9 per cent between 1982 and 1990, ten times the increase in the total working population during the same period.
◆ Employment of 'producers and artists' in Germany grew by 23 per cent between 1980 and 1994.

What percentage of the workforce are employed in the cultural industries at the end of the period of growth? The UK government's 1998 *Creative Industries Mapping Document* (Department of Culture, Media and Sport, 1998) showed employment of about 1 million people in the creative industries, about 4 per cent of the total workforce. Even taking away non-leisure software to leave a definition closer to my definition of the cultural industries, this figure would still be about 3 per cent.

All this suggests that the growth of the cultural industries represents an important aspect of a general shift towards investment in service industries in advanced industrial countries. Let us examine the forces driving that shift in more detail. Nicholas Garnham argues (1990: 117) that demand for labour-saving domestic consumer electronic goods had helped fuel the 'golden age' of the 1950s and 1960s but western markets were fast becoming saturated by the beginning of the 1970s. Companies had the chance to use the vast amount of high-tech research generated by the US government in defence and space as a result of the Cold War.[4] By the early 1980s, as Europe and North America faced economic recession, and as newly industrialised countries in Asia continued to achieve high levels of

---

4 For example, although the internet cannot be explained entirely as a defence-driven phenomenon – the familiar story is that it developed as a means of maintaining computer systems in case of a nuclear strike – Brian Winston's account (1998: 321–36) makes it clear how the development of key research into switching protocols was primarily funded through defence spending.

economic growth, the perceived advantages for Euro-American corporations of moving into high-tech and cultural industries were even more
overwhelming, in spite of high research and development costs.

The cultural industries were profoundly affected by these changes. As
competition in the new consumer markets intensified, there was increasing
demand for advertising and marketing opportunities. This has been
crucial in fuelling a growth in media outlets which continued into the
1990s. Here are some relevant data:

♦   Table 3.3 shows how the proportion of gross domestic product (GDP)
    devoted to advertising in a wide range of countries increased sig-
    nificantly during the 1980s.
♦   Between 1984 and 1989, advertising expenditure in the European
    Union (EU) increased by more than 6 per cent every year, and
    increased by 10 per cent in 1988 alone (Howard, 1998).
♦   EU growth continued at a reduced rate in the early 1990s, but picked
    up again from 1993. Growth was 73 per cent in real terms between
    1980 and 1996, reaching €58 billion, or US$74 billion in the latter year
    (Howard, 1998: 117).
♦   The most striking growth figures were to be found in the developing
    markets of the Middle East and Latin America. Middle Eastern

**Table 3.3   Increases in advertising expenditure, 1980–90 (This
table shows the percentage of gross domestic product spent on
advertising)**

| Country | 1980 | 1990 |
|---|---|---|
| Austria | 0.47 | 0.63 |
| Belgium | 0.47 | 0.65 |
| Canada | 0.98 | 1.05 |
| Switzerland | 1.02 | 1.07 |
| Germany | 0.75 | 0.82 |
| Denmark | 0.76 | 0.84 |
| Finland | 0.71 | 0.94 |
| France | 0.48 | 0.78 |
| UK | 1.11 | 1.37 |
| Greece | 0.26 | 0.77 |
| Ireland | 0.65 | 0.82 |
| Italy | 0.37 | 0.62 |
| Japan | 0.95 | 1.12 |
| Norway | 0.77 | 0.74 |
| Netherlands | 0.87 | 0.87 |
| Portugal | 0.19 | 0.77 |
| Sweden | 0.64 | 0.80 |
| Turkey | 0.20 | 0.38 |
| USA | 1.32 | 1.51 |
| Europe | 0.70 | 0.91 |

*Source*: Sánchez-Tabernero et al., 1993: 125, drawing on Zenith Media Worldwide

advertising expenditure increased by over 1,000 per cent in real terms
between 1987 and 1996 (IJOA, 1998a: 515). In Latin America, growth
was 377 per cent in the same period (IJOA, 1998b).

◆   Growth in advertising expenditure in the USA in the 1980s and 1990s
    was slower, but the USA already had phenomenally high advertising
    expenditure in the early 1980s. In 1998, 42.9 per cent of all advertising
    investment was spent in North America, and the USA accounted for
    roughly 95 per cent of this figure (IJOA, 2000).

Such figures indicate the increasing economic rewards afforded by the
cultural industries during the period under examination. But the cultural
industries were more than just another investment opportunity: they
increasingly came to be seen as a *prestigious* form of profit making, as the
entertainment industries came to be perceived as a key economic sector, at
least in North America and the UK (see Wolf, 1999). Vast companies in
other sectors, such as General Electric in the USA or Sony in Japan made
significant investments in cultural production during the 1980s. Such
industrial conglomerates had intervened in the cultural industries before,
especially in the 1960s, but in the 1980s these companies were entering the
very core of the cultural industries: the television networks that dominated
the US cultural landscape (NBC and CBS, respectively). Meanwhile,
companies already involved in the cultural industries grew, and increasingly operated across different cultural industries. This meant that the
production of culture was increasingly the concern of ambitious and well-
resourced sectors of economic activity. The implications for the cultural
industries of these changes are discussed in Chapter 5.

### Internationalisation

A second major type of industrial and organisational restructuring in
response to falling profits in advanced industrial countries was what
Harvey (1989: 183) calls a 'spatial fix'. Owners and operators of capitalist
enterprises attempted to restore higher profits by investing abroad, in
order to spread fixed costs, and to make the most of cheaper labour
markets, as real wages rose in advanced industrial countries. Such internationalisation has a long history, as David Held et al.'s (1999: 242–55)
account shows admirably. There had been a massive expansion in foreign
direct investment (FDI) – a significant marker of business internationalisation – during the Gold Standard period, from 1870 to 1914, but this was
dominated by the UK, was highly concentrated in certain areas, and was
primarily based around the extractive industries. Cartels based around
raw materials such as oil began to form during the inter-war period.
Consumer goods were increasingly sold on an international basis, but
production tended to be organised nationally. In the post-war period,
particularly in the 1960s, there was huge expansion in the role of the

multinational corporation, especially on the part of US-based manufacturing corporations. Internationalisation of production began to be expressed in the emergence of global production and distribution networks, marking a qualitatively new phase of internationalisation.[5]

The last two decades have seen an acceleration of such internationalisation in response to the Long Downturn. Internationalisation was slowed by the severe recession of the early 1980s, but the next decade saw very large increases in the annual growth rates of foreign direct investment. The annual growth rate in FDI flow was 7.3 per cent in the period 1980–5, and 19.4 per cent between 1986 and 1994.[6] Meanwhile, the neoliberal economic policies of the 1980s and 1990s led to the removal of protection measures for national industries. The GATT Rounds, a series of negotiations between nations aimed at reduction and eventual elimination of tariffs and other barriers to 'free trade' culminated in the Marrakesh agreement of 1993 and the formation of the World Trade Organisation (WTO) in 1995. The removal of trade restrictions helped to fuel the internationalisation of business activity on the part of corporations of all kinds. A concurrent internationalisation of financial markets, beginning in the 1950s but culminating in the deregulation of international financial flows in the 1990s, helped further to delegitimate the role of national governments in managing economies, as such governments became apparently helpless when faced by speculators on currency markets. Vast regional trading markets were formed in Europe (the European Union), North America/Mexico (NAFTA) and the Asia-Pacific (APEC), forcing a rush to locate in these regions. There was a massive wave of mergers and acquisitions as transnational corporations bought up overseas companies to expand their production and distribution networks. By 1995, overseas affiliates accounted for 7.5 per cent of world GDP; in 1970, the figure had been 4.5 per cent (Held et al., 1999: 246).

The cultural industries internationalised their operations too, and there were sound economic reasons for their doing so, most notably the low marginal costs of some of their key products. But the general internationalisation of businesses as a whole affected the cultural industries in key ways, because international communications became crucial for business in general, and developments in the telecommunications industry came to have profound effects on the cultural industries. International communications became vital for multinational corporations of all kinds, as the different parts of these vast companies needed to communicate with each other, quickly and securely, through public and, increasingly, private

---

5 Held et al. (1999) use the popular but, in this context, confusing term of globalisation; but I prefer internationalisation, for reasons that I explain in Chapter 6.

6 These growth rates were considerably higher than the rates of growth of gross world product, indicating that growth in international activity was outstripping economic growth.

networks. Partly to provide for these needs, high-tech companies began a wave of technological innovation in communication technologies, in league with the huge European public telecommunication operators (PTOs) and the US private corporations. This culminated in the development of digital 'intelligent networks' in the 1970s and 1980s. Besides servicing the needs of multinational corporations, the development of these networks was in large part aimed at protecting the monopoly positions of public and private monopolies as new entrants came into the telecommunications market, as Mansell (1993) shows. Such innovations in telecommunications technologies have been vital in providing new distribution forms for the cultural industries, including of course the internet and the world wide web, but also digital television, and private information networks. Up until the 1970s, most telecommunications traffic was voice only; now images, text, graphics and music flow through the intelligent networks alongside phone conversations.

Internationalisation in another industry, consumer electronics, also had important knock-on effects on the cultural industries. Spreading fixed costs across many national markets funded expensive research and development for new hardware devices (see the section on technological change, below).

### Organisational innovation and restructuring

A third form of industrial and organisational change relevant for an account of the cultural industries was that new forms of organisational innovation were introduced, in order to achieve higher profits, to reduce labour costs and to win market share over competing firms. Writers from a number of perspectives have examined a general restructuring of businesses in the 1970s and 1980s, and many of them attribute this restructuring to a response to the Long Downturn. Various phrases have been used to label this restructuring, most notably flexible specialisation (Piore and Sabel, 1984), flexible accumulation (Harvey, 1989) and post-Fordism (Hall and Jacques, 1990). Castells (1996: 151–68) provides a valuable breakdown of some of the main elements of such restructuring.

♦ *The 'decline' of the large corporation and the rise of interfirm networking*: Castells argues, following commentators such as Bennett Harrison, whose 1994 book *Lean and Mean* (Harrison, 1994) argued for the continuing importance and vitality of the large corporation, that the large corporation is not nearly so much in a state of crisis as some 'post-Fordist' commentators suggested in the 1980s. Rather, says Castells, the traditional, vertically-integrated large corporation is in decline as a *model* for how to organise production, but it is still very much in existence. Corporations have changed their organisational structures, and increasingly subcontract to small and medium-sized firms. These smaller firms are potentially more dynamic and able to innovate; but they are increasingly involved in close relationships with the corporations that subcontract to them.

◆ *Corporate strategic alliances*: An important emergent pattern has been the formation of strategic alliances between corporations, not as in traditional cartel arrangements, but on the basis of specific projects. This is especially relevant, says Castells, in high-tech sectors, where research and development costs are enormously expensive. For Castells, the self-sufficient corporation is increasingly a thing of the past. What is more, small and medium-sized firms are often drawn into such alliances, in an extension of interfirm networking.

◆ *New methods of management, and corporate restructuring*: Many discussions of organisational innovation concern forms of production developed in Japanese car production (and therefore sometimes labelled Toyotism). Much of this involves using information sensibly to reduce inventories by delivering supplies just in time; and improving quality control. But most significant for the management of labour is the idea of involving workers in production, by reducing hierarchies, and creating autonomous working units. Castells also points to developments in the organisation of corporations, in particular the tendency to move away from traditional, hierarchical forms of organisational structure, towards the setting up of decentralised, sometimes semi-autonomous working units, sometimes even to the point of having these units compete with each other. The corporation becomes a network. The job of the corporate centre is to make sure the network communicates adequately. Castells says that such arrangements originally developed as cost-saving devices during the economic restructuring of the 1980s and that the horizontal corporation of the 1990s represents an extension of such arrangements. Closely related to such changes is the idea of flexibility: the idea was that, as markets become ever more volatile and unpredictable, firms need to be able to switch production rapidly to conform to changing tastes. These changes are particularly interesting in the present context because, as we saw in Chapter 2, the cultural industries have had this network form for much of the complex professional era.

◆ *Changing work patterns*: In a separate discussion, Castells (1996: 264–72) notes the new working conditions associated with new organisational forms. In particular, he notes the increasing disintegration of workforces, with substantial rises in temporary, part-time and self-employment. This may take the form of increased work options for the relatively privileged, but it also takes the form of casualisation and insecurity for the less well-off and less skilled and educated.

The discussion here of changes in businesses of all kinds paves the way for the discussion of industrial and organisational shifts in the cultural industries which I undertake in Chapter 5. An important theme there is the extent to which the cultural industries are becoming more or less distinct from other sectors. Are the cultural industries losing their distinctiveness as they become increasingly important in advanced industrial economies? Or are, as some writers (e.g., Lash and Urry, 1994) argue, other industries becoming more like the cultural industries as, for example, companies increasingly organise themselves into semi-autonomous divisions?

## Sociocultural and textual changes

Understanding changes in the cultural industries over the last two decades needs, then, to lay great emphasis on restructuring in response to the economic crisis of the 1970s. But an adequate account needs to go beyond restructuring too. We must avoid a model whereby economic change 'happens to' politics and production organisations, and this then brings about changes in the cultural industries, and then in cultural life more generally. There are three main ways in which we need to go beyond such an account.

First, an account of changes in the cultural industries since 1980 needs to acknowledge the complex interplay of, on the one hand, economic and political processes and, on the other, the social, cultural and institutional processes which are sometimes conceived as by-products of events at the macro level. The cultural industries could hardly evade the effects of the accelerating sociocultural transformations taking place in advanced industrial societies from the 1960s onwards: the dismantling of many forms of social authority in educational, religious and other institutions; changes in family life, in sexuality, in relationships between women, men and children, in the very meaning of what it is to be a person; an increasing emphasis on, and reflexivity about, issues of personal identity. In order to gain audiences in time-rich and/or newly prosperous constituencies, such as the baby boom teenager and student in the 1960s, or working women in the early 1980s, cultural firms had to appeal to changing values, at least in some market sectors. Not that cultural industry corporations were answering the pre-existing needs of consumers: they were simultaneously helping to shape these new needs. Obviously enough, citizens affected by these sociocultural changes, imbued with new ways of being and thinking, were allowed to enter the cultural industries and were able to transmit their values into the texts they created. One striking example is the development of new genres, forms and narrative modes in the New Hollywood cinema of the early 1970s. This was partly the result of organisational and institutional factors in that the old studio system had broken down and film studios perceived that the core audience for cinema was young baby boomers. But the shift was also sociocultural, as film-makers of a new generation brought new ideas and values into film production (see Tasker, 1996).

Second, an adequate analysis of the cultural industries needs to take account of continuity and of multiple and coexisting processes of change, occurring at different rates. An overemphasis on restructuring exaggerates short-term transformation at the expense of these different temporalities. The increasing centrality of the cultural industries in economic life, for example, was certainly not caused *exclusively* by post-crisis restructuring. Culture was already becoming increasingly central to modern social life throughout the twentieth century, as leisure time expanded, and as consumer culture began to pervade advanced industrial economies. When Stuart Hall refers to the increasing importance of culture as a long-term 'cultural revolution', taking place throughout the twentieth century, whereby 'the domain constituted by the activities, institutions and practices we call "cultural" has expanded out of all recognition' (1997: 209), he is surely right to think that this process predates the restructuring processes under discussion earlier.[7] We might be wise then to think of the transformations of the 1980s and 1990s as *accelerating* processes that were already in train.

Third, all histories need to recognise the possibilities of contingency and chance. An account of the cultural industries which sees transformations there as a seamless response to economic and political crisis may well fail to acknowledge such contingency. This is particularly important in an account of industries that are based on irrational (or at least arational) aesthetic experiences. This brings us back to the unpredictable ways in which people make use of aesthetic and informational products (see Introduction). This dimension of the cultural industries makes it especially likely that certain changes in the cultural industries might come about as a result of sudden, unexpected cultural phenomena, rather than as the outcomes of structural economic patterns.

It would be impossible to do justice to the immense sociocultural changes taking place across the world in the late twentieth century. But we can point to those aspects of most direct relevance to the cultural industries. First of all, working time. In the USA, the most important decreases in working time took place in the early twentieth century (as we saw in Chapter 2) and hours worked per year stayed roughly even during the 1970s and 1980s. But in most countries, according to OECD (Organization

---

7 In his important chapter, Hall uses what I believe is far too broad a definition of culture, which he seems at times to equate with 'discourse' or even 'meaning' (Hall, 1997: 225–6).

for Economic Co-operation and Development) figures, the trend in work-ing hours was markedly downward during the 1970s and 1980s (see Vogel, 1998: 8). Secondly, even in the USA, with its relatively stable working time versus leisure time split, the time spent on media consumption has increased enormously, from 50.7 hours to 65.5 hours per week (Vogel, 1998: 9). Leisure time is dominated to a quite remarkable degree by one activity: television. The amount of television watched by the average American increased considerably between 1970 and 1995, from 1,226 hours per person per year to 1,575 (Vogel, 1998: 9). Americans, on average, spend 30 hours a week watching television (Webster and Phalen, 1997: 108). This makes television by far the most heavily consumed medium. It represents over 46 per cent of the 65.5 hours per week spent consuming media, about the same proportion as in 1970 (Vogel, 1998: 9). Thirdly, expenditure on recreation has increased out of proportion to the increase in non-working time. In the USA, the figure has risen from $93.8 per person per year in 1970 to $395.5 per year in 1995, expressed in 1992 dollar terms, and therefore adjusted for inflation. This represents a doubling of the percent-age of total personal consumption spending made up by such recreation spending, from 4.3 per cent to 8.6 per cent. These are the factors that have most directly helped to bring about growth in the cultural industries during the period under discussion.

## Technological change: information technology and consumer electronics

Finally, we return to the factor of change most commonly invoked in journalism and popular publishing. Technological reductionism saturates everyday discourses about the cultural industries. This means that we need to be particularly cautious in addressing technology as a causal factor. For technologies are themselves the effects of choices, decisions, contingencies and coincidences in the realms of economics, politics and culture.

Technological innovation is nothing new. It is one of the main ways in which companies (and nations) try to outdo each other in competitive markets. But technologies are more than just economic opportunities; some become the repositories of hopes for a better life, or symbols for anxieties about the future. In the last 20 years, information and com-munication technologies have spawned huge amounts of commentary and debate. The key development that helped to fuel media obsession with 'the information society' was the development of computer-compatible and computer-mediated communication. The resulting waves of 'digitalisation' in various cultural industries, discussed in Chapter 7, represent the most important technological development of the period under discussion in this book.

The development of the computer is, then, a vital context for understanding change and continuity in the cultural industries (the following account draws mainly on Augarten, 1984). Intensive levels of research and development in microelectronics enabled the key transformations in information technology in the post-war period. The transistor, first produced in 1948, but developed in the 1950s, allowed for the cheap and efficient control and magnification of electrical current. Computer firms realised that such transistors could provide a much more efficient way of storing and moving information than previous devices (which had been mainly based on the vacuum tube). The crucial technical challenge was to get many transistors (or their equivalents) on the same circuit, in order to multiply this ability to control and magnify current, and therefore more efficiently and cheaply to move information. A key development therefore was the integrated circuit (IC) which was first produced in workable form in 1957, but which rapidly developed in the early 1960s. The IC allowed for the placing of dozens of transistors (devices which amplify electrical current) on the same surface without mutual interference. In the early 1970s, engineers at Intel developed the microprocessor: a whole set of integrated circuits (ICs) on one very small silicon chip. The entire functioning part of the computer could now be stored on a very small surface. But it was only in the mid-1970s that people realised that miniaturisation, in the form of the microprocessor, would allow for the development of *personal* computers. Even so-called minicomputers were, up until this point, envisaged as smaller versions of the vast, centralised mainframe computers that dominated the industry.

These remarkable technological developments were possible because of vast research expenditure. Why were such huge amounts of research resources diverted to advances in computing?

♦ First, because there were many perceived military uses for computing. The high-tech computer and communications sectors benefited from vast defence spending on computer-mediated communication. This was especially the case in the USA, where the Department of Defense was for many years 'centrally concerned in the development strategies of the entire US computer software business' (Tunstall, 1986: 41).

♦ Second, as we have already seen, transnational corporations were expanding rapidly during the post-war period, and they needed faster and more efficient communication technologies to bind their operations.

♦ Third, there was the later context of the downturn in western economies from the late 1960s onwards, and in particular the threat to

European and US manufacturing industries from newly industrialising countries in Asia. Many western governments and enterprises invested enormous amounts of money and resources in the development of high-tech sectors.

♦ Fourth, there were important social and cultural factors, in particular a widespread sense, mediated by journalists and other commentators, of an impending information revolution. This helped to feed the idea that the onward march of the computer was either beneficial or inevitable, or both. Importantly, there was a strong sense of the private and public benefits of a **do-it-yourself** (DIY) attitude as a means of countering the control of new information and communication technologies by corporations. Ironically, many of the computer enthusiasts inspired by this DIY ethos became entrepreneurs and ended up as part of large corporations themselves. The counter-cultural enthusiasm for hands-on computing was absorbed into capitalism, but its effects were not entirely neutralised, as we shall see in Chapter 7.

Thinking about the causes of technological innovation in this way takes us away from technological reductionism. Technologies should not be thought of as the best answers to pre-existing needs, which is the way we are often encouraged to think about them by media coverage. Their evolution is determined by many choices and decisions, and by unintended consequences of dynamics external to the companies developing them.

To repeat the point made towards the beginning of this chapter, in the discussion of technological reductionism, conceiving technologies in this way – recognising that they should hardly ever, if at all, be thought of as the main engine of transformation – is not to deny that they have important effects. Without a doubt, the impact of the computer on the cultural industries has been profound. Computers became increasingly central to many people's working and leisure lives during the 1980s. The cost of personal computers fell sharply in the early 1980s, when Apple launched as a public company and IBM entered the market (using Microsoft software). According to Forester (1987: 134), sales of personal computers went from none in 1975 to 7 million in 1983, 1.4 million of which were sold in the USA. In a decade, the number of personal computers installed worldwide grew from 200,000 to over 50 million in 1987.[8] The explosion in discussion of 'new media' dates from this period, when ownership of computers became sufficiently widespread for industry analysts, policy-makers etc. to envisage a future where digitalisation

---

8 The rise of the personal computer, mainly used for work, should not be confused with the rise of the home computer, which were fewer in number – 6 million in the USA by 1985 (Forester, 1987: 151) – and often underused.

would become the basis of home-based information and entertainment.[9] By the late 1980s, commentators were increasingly discussing the idea of convergence between three information/communication technologies and their industries: media, computers and telecommunications. I question this idea in Chapter 7, and challenge the view of digitalisation as progress.

There were other important technological developments besides those related to computers and information technology. Particularly significant were developments in consumer electronics, especially new technologies for the storage and retrieval of texts. The most notable were:

◆ Various tape formats, of which the audio cassette and its players (Philips) triumphed
◆ The video cassette recorder, where a battle was fought between Matsushita's VHS format and Sony's Betamax and Philips' V2000 formats
◆ The personal stereo/Walkman (Sony)
◆ The various compact-disc technologies (initially developed by Philips), especially music CDs, but also CD-ROMs, as personal computers developed, and later DVD as a means of replacing video cassettes

The effects of such technologies on the way that consumers experience cultural-industry products have of course been profound. The success of such technologies has drawn on the individualisation of social life noted by many commentators, but they have also made important contributions to extending such individualisation. Again, production contexts are important, in order to avoid seeing these technologies as 'solutions' to our need for more flexibility in cultural consumption. Consumer electronics transnationals were a significant part of manufacturing internationalisation from the 1950s onwards. Such new technologies were enormously expensive in terms of research and development, but these costs were spread by selling the devices across the world. The 'best' technology did not always win: Matsushita's VHS format triumphed over Sony's superior Betamax format because of Matsushita's more effective marketing, and because they agreed to license the technology, rather than manufacture it under their own name.

The replacement of old formats – such as vinyl records by CDs – and the appearance of new ones has helped to create new selling opportunities for the cultural industries. But the new technologies also represented

---

9 Debates about new media took distinctive forms in continental Europe, where there was also great emphasis on public 'videotex' systems. Most notable was the French Minitel network. See Castells, 1996: 343–5, who as part of his celebration of American entrepreneurialism and individualism, denigrates Minitel, in spite of his interesting and frank comments about his own involvement in the 'democratised sexual fantasy' of Minitel chat-lines in the 1980s.

threats: for example, they made the problem of controlling scarcity considerably more difficult. Seeing the money to be made from text production drew many consumer electronics companies into the cultural industries from the late 1980s on, with sometimes disastrous consequences (see Chapter 5).

◆ ◆ ◆

In this chapter, I have been discussing the major contexts for understanding patterns of change/continuity in the cultural industries in the last twenty or so years. The emphasis has been on factors external to the cultural industries: the end of the golden age and the beginning of the Long Downturn, the neoliberal political-economic response, general changes in the business environment, of which the cultural industries were a part; social and cultural transformations; and technological developments outside the cultural industries. I have been concentrating here on transformation but we should note that there was also important economic, political, organisational, sociocultural and technological continuity alongside these changes. Economies continued for the most part to be run by national governments, even if there were increasing interconnections between different parts of the world; liberal democracy remained the model for government in the advanced industrial countries; the legal frameworks governing businesses remained fundamentally intact in these countries; people continued to work hard, worry about their children, and to seek pleasure in watching and participating in cultural events; radio and television remained dominant as cultural technologies throughout most of the world.

Much of this chapter has been concerned with what explains change. But what explains such continuity? Even in a time of remarkable transformation, certain structures are hard to shift. Powerful groups feel threatened by change and fight for the retention of the status quo. There is the force of habit: it often seems easier to carry on doing things the same way. And then there are aspects of human life which are hard to change, and may even be rooted in long-standing characteristics of human beings across many different societies. The pleasures of having a story told to us can be found across many different societies, in many different contexts, even if the characteristic forms of such stories vary. There are powerful forces for continuity in the internal dynamics of the cultural industries too. A key argument of this book, outlined in the Introduction and expanded in Chapter 2, is that certain distinctive properties of the production and consumption of cultural goods, as opposed to other commodities, help explain why cultural production tends to be organised in particular, recurring ways. To recapitulate, the main dynamics were: the high levels of risk to be found in the cultural industries; high production costs and low reproduction costs; semi-public goods and the need to create scarcity; and various distinctive responses to these conditions, including offsetting misses against hits, concentration and integration, artificial scarcity, formatting and loose/tight control of production and circulation. For all the changes of the last 20 years, including the massive expansion of the cultural industries, and their increasing centrality in social and economic life, cultural businesses still have to manage these problems, which derive from the difficulties of managing creativity and information. Because the ways in which creativity and information are understood have very deep historical roots, problems and complexities surrounding the task of managing them persist, and are not going to be blown away by new technologies, new organisational strategies, or new market conditions. The growth and huge profitability of the cultural industries suggest that owners and managers have been largely successful in their strategies for controlling cultural production and consumption. But the management of creativity remains a fraught business. And the problems faced by cultural-industry corporations continue to push business strategies in certain directions rather than others.

The next five chapters build on the general outline of factors driving change and continuity, by attempting to distinguish fundamental changes from superficial changes; setting continuity against transformation; and separating out different types and rates of alteration.

## Further reading

Like grungy lumberjack shirts, ripped jeans and other trends of a decade ago, debates about postmodernity and postmodernism are now very much out of fashion. But David Harvey's book, *The Condition of Postmodernity* (1989) remains a scintillating read about the relationship between economic, political and cultural change, even if it sometimes overemphasises the causal effects of economic dynamics, and underplays cultural effects (see Morris, 1992 for a brilliant critique). Lash and Urry's *Economies of Signs and Space* (1994) has a similar breadth and similar degree of insight, although it drifts into social-theory jargonese at times. I am critical of some of the work of Manuel Castells elsewhere in this book, but his work is immensely exciting and stimulating (e.g., Castells, 1989; 1996). David Held et al.'s *Global Transformations* (1999) is an important contribution to debates about globalisation and a treasure-trove of information. I have found Robert Brenner's work in *New Left Review* (1998; 2000) enormously cogent and informative about economic change in the post-war era. An enjoyable and provocative book about technological change relevant to the cultural industries is Brian Winston's *Media Technology and Society* (1998), which even manages to be funny at times. Raymond Williams' opening chapter in *Television: Technology and Cultural Form* (1974) has no jokes whatsoever, but still has more to say about technology than most of the books published about the internet put together.

# PART TWO
# CHANGE AND CONTINUITY
# IN THE CULTURAL INDUSTRIES

# 4 Policy: Changes in Law and Regulation

In all areas of commercial life, governments intervene. The free market does not exist in modern, complex societies: it is merely an ideal to be aspired to by those who believe that the market, in its ideal state, is the best way to distribute resources and to answer human needs. Even those national economic systems based most on private enterprise, such as the USA, are built on a huge foundation of laws concerning competition, tax, contracts, the obligations of companies and so on. They also rely on government funding of infrastructures (for example, roads) and on regulation of companies, to ensure that market powers are not abused.

Governments intervene in *cultural* markets in three main ways:

- They **legislate**: that is, they create laws concerning the general issues mentioned above, such as competition and contracts, plus more specifically cultural issues such as copyright, obscenity, privacy, and so on. These are subject to constitutions and to the decisions of courts.
- They **regulate**: via these laws, governments create organisations which monitor a particular industrial sector, and which have powers to affect the behaviour of companies.
- They **subsidise**: directly through grants, in order to supplement the provision of texts provided by the private sector, in areas such as theatre, ballet, opera, fine art and so on; or indirectly, by allowing research and other knowledge created in the public sector (especially defence) into the private sector.

These three areas together are referred to as **policy**. It is impossible to understand the cultural industries, and changes in them over the last 20 years, without knowledge of media, communications and cultural policy. The changes in policy with the most far-reaching consequences for the cultural industries since 1980 have taken place in broadcasting and telecommunications, and these industries are my main focus in this chapter.

## Deregulation, re-regulation and cultural marketisation

First, though, an important issue of terminology. We saw in Chapter 3, how neoliberal political doctrine spread across the world in response to the Long Downturn. During the 1945–73 period, there had been some consensus amongst both left-wing and right-wing political parties about the need to protect workers and consumers from actions undertaken by private companies in pursuit of profit. In some countries, this involved the nationalisation of private companies. Neoliberalism, from the 1970s onwards, presented public ownership and close regulation as the causes of the economic downturn and undertook programmes of privatisation and of regulatory change. The neoliberal term for such programmes was **deregulation**.

The rhetoric of deregulation was particularly powerful in the cultural industries, because the notion of freedom from government intervention fed on anxieties about government interference in personal and political expression. The right to free expression of views is a fundamental of democratic liberal thought, and superficially government regulation might appear to undermine such rights. However, the term deregulation can potentially confuse the removal of censorship with measures that are actually intended to increase the access of citizens to a wider variety of personal and political expression. For example, one of the most important forms of state regulation has been to ensure that a small number of firms do not dominate a particular cultural industry, as this might mean less diversity of products, and a narrower range of political viewpoints.

Some advocates of the public interest have argued, in response to this use of the term deregulation, that **re-regulation** is a more appropriate name for changes in media and communications policy in the 1980s and 1990s (e.g., Murdock, 1990: 12–13). 'Re-regulation' points to the fact that legislation and regulation were not removed by these changes, and highlights the introduction of new legislation and regulation, much of which favoured, as we shall see, the interests of large, private corporations and their shareholders. What is more, as governments tried to negotiate competing interests during the deregulatory years of the 1980s and 1990s, in many cases they actually introduced new and more complex sets of regulations. The UK, as Peter J. Humphreys shows (1996: 191) introduced a number of new regulatory bodies, including the Broadcasting Complaints Commission (1982) and the Cable Authority (1984) during an era when it was supposedly beginning to deregulate. France's deregulatory legislation of the mid-1980s created a complex network of rules. For all its advantages, however, the term 're-regulation' also disguises an important issue, as Humphreys points out: much new legislation and regulation did in fact legitimate 'a lighter touch', the creation of a business environment in which commercial cultural-industry companies could operate in a relatively unhindered way. Often, however, the interests of such companies are not necessarily conducive to a fair and equitable system of cultural production, in the terms developed in Chapter 2.

The terms 'loose' and 'tight' and 'light touch', as opposed to 'tight' regulation may go some way towards avoiding the misleading implications of the terms 'deregulation' and 're-regulation', and I use them here, but these terms too have misleading positive connotations. The term I prefer to describe the policy changes of the period from 1980s onward is **marketisation** (see Chapter 3). This refers to the assumption underlying much new policy, that the production and exchange of cultural goods and services for profit is the best way to achieve efficiency and fairness in the production and consumption of texts. Markets can, in certain cases, be efficient and equitable allocators of resources. But the notion of the market operating in the policy changes of the 1980s and 1990s was one very much influenced by the conception of the market in neoclassical economics discussed in Chapter 1, and by the neoliberal political-economic ideas discussed in Chapter 3.

## Telecommunications and broadcasting: why was the state so involved?

Some of the cultural industries may seem to have relatively low levels of government legislation and regulation: the publishing, film and music industries in liberal democracies such as the USA, Australia, the UK and Germany, for example. But even these industries are governed by a mass of laws and regulations, concerning ownership, competition, copyright, libel, obscenity, restrictions and guarantees of press rights to provide information about state matters and so on. Broadcasting and telecommunications have been subject to other forms of legislation and regulation too. Until the 1980s, in liberal democracies as well as authoritarian states, most of the world's broadcasting organisations were owned and controlled directly by the state. The same was true of telecommunications. Though not a cultural industry in any meaningful sense of the term (see Introduction) telecommunications is an industry with vitally important implications for cultural markets. Even in the USA, with its long tradition of preferring private enterprise to public ownership, broadcasting and telecommunications were for many decades subject to tight regulation by government bodies.

Why were broadcasting and telecommunications more subject to public ownership and tight regulation than other cultural industries? We can divide the reasons into three, generalising broadly across very different political and cultural contexts.

### Telecommunications as a public utility

In most nations in the early twentieth century, telecommunications (telegraphs and telephones) were widely recognised as something that the state would want to make, in principle, available to their entire populations, in order to foster national identity and encourage economic development. In most liberal democratic states and in their colonies, the responsibility for organising telecommunications was passed to the authorities charged with dealing with the postal system. In some European countries, national post organisations expanded to become postal, telegraph and telephone authorities (PTTs): for example, the General Post Office in the UK, the Reichpost and, after the Second World War, the Bundespost in Germany, the Direction Générale des Telecommunications in France. In the USA, where businesses were especially fervent and successful in their resistance to democratic regulation of markets, the private company AT&T (American Telephone and Telegraph Company) was allowed to act as a private monopoly covering nearly all of the USA. US policy makers used their own distinctive language, whereby telecommunications was treated, like the roads and train-lines, as a common carrier, that is, a system or network which had to carry any messages, vehicles, and so on, paid for by customers, within certain legal boundaries. The justification for AT&T's monopoly was that the high costs of installing telephone infrastructure meant it was a 'natural monopoly', and that such a monopoly, closely regulated by government, was the best way of achieving standardisation, high quality and thus 'universal service' in providing a common carrier.[1] In return for being granted such a monopoly, until its partial break-up in the 1980s, AT&T accepted close regulation of its prices and a ban on its being involved in the production and distribution of programming.

## Broadcasting as a national resource and a limited one

Radio was developed as a form of one-to-one communication, envisaged as something like a telephone or telegram of the airwaves, rather than as the broadcasting (one-to-many) form it became. It was widely used by the military, and increasingly by amateurs for personal communication, in the 1910s, and was essentially unregulated. In the early 1920s, private companies in a number of countries began to experiment with broadcasting music and other entertainment. In the USA, a radio craze developed, but the airwaves remained unregulated for years, causing chaos and bad reception more or less everywhere. In Europe, however, the public ownership and regulation of national resources and utilities, such as gas, water, electricity and postal services, were considered desirable. The responsibility to provide public service was an increasingly important part of many national cultures, even if in many cases, such as that of the UK, this involved a 'paternalist definition of both service and responsibility' (Williams, 1974: 33). It seemed natural therefore that radio should be run, or at least overseen, by PTTs. This seemed particularly the case given *spectrum scarcity*: that is, the situation that frequencies used to transmit radio messages were very limited. Even in the USA, with its already strong tradition of resistance to regulation, it became widely accepted that the state had to be closely involved in the allocation of spectrum space, so that broadcasters did not overlap on the same frequencies, ruining the radio experience. As a result, a Federal Radio Commission was finally introduced in 1927. Eventually, in most countries, new bodies were formed to govern broadcasting. Many were initially under the auspices of PTTs, but eventually developed their own autonomy, including the British Broadcasting Corporation (BBC), and various similar organisations (some of them modelled after the BBC), such as the CBC (Canadian Broadcasting

---

1 'Universal' did not mean that everyone had equal access. It took decades for poorer sections of the population to reach high rates of installation, and then as a result of lowering costs rather than commitment on the part of government or company (Garnham, 1996: 3; Aufderheide, 1999: 16).

Corporation). When television, which of course relied on radio waves for transmission, was introduced, its regulation was passed on to these state organisations; or, in some countries, a dual system of public service and commercial television was established (as in Australia and Japan in the 1950s).

### The power of broadcasting

When radio became a broadcasting technology, rather than a technology for point-to-point communication, its potential social power quickly became apparent, both commercially (in terms of its power to advertise and promote goods) and politically (in terms of its power to affect people's voting habits and attitudes towards democratic goals and procedures). In nearly all countries, it was accepted that the state, again via democratic accountability, should be the agency to ensure that these powers were not abused. In some countries, such as post-1945 France, this meant very strong and direct state control of the main broadcasting organisation. In the UK, the BBC was (from 1926) a public corporation, governed by a Royal Charter which laid out its mandate, and by governmental appointees. Even in countries such as the USA, or in post-war Luxembourg, which favoured private enterprise, high levels of government regulation were widely accepted, compared with those in operation in other business sectors, largely because of radio's perceived power. When television became widely popular and available in the 1950s and 1960s, its obvious potential social power meant that it inherited legislative and regulatory frameworks from radio.

## The 1980s: the rationales are dismantled, marketisation follows

By the 1980s, the rationales behind such high degrees of government intervention in broadcasting and telecommunications were breaking down. We have already seen in Chapter 3 how the rise of neoliberalism in the 1980s helped to delegitimate public ownership and certain forms of regulation, in nearly all forms of economic activity. We also saw how commercial companies in Europe and North America, observing diminishing margins in manufacturing, were becoming increasingly aware of the potentially greater profits to be made in the cultural, communication and leisure industries. They put increasing pressure on national governments to remove restrictions on access to certain markets, in particular telecommunications and broadcasting, which had previously been very closely regulated.

All of the major rationales for broadcasting and telecommunications policy came under ferocious attack in the 1980s and 1990s, in particular from private corporations and from policy-makers and commentators who supported their interests. These interest groups argued instead for market-isation. They attacked each of the rationales listed above, in the following ways.

### Challenge to telecoms as utility rationale

Various writers (e.g., De Sola Pool, 1983) and agencies argued that the need to provide telecommunications as a national utility (or as a common carrier, to use the US concept) no longer applied, because telecommunications services were now already widespread amongst the populations of the advanced industrial countries. They argued that telecommunications needed to be opened up for national and international competition. This would, claimed the neoliberal proponents of marketisation, increase the efficiency of the sector by exposing it to the rigours of the market. This would in turn provide more advanced services that could help to drive the economies of these countries out of their Long Downturn. It should be noted that the large telecommunications companies and senior executives of PTTs (who stood to become enormously wealthy out of privatisation) were particularly keen to make such arguments. They nearly always claimed that they also needed protection from the rigours of the market, in the form of limitations to the entry of new rivals, so that they could compete with other large companies in the international market. Such contradictions in the discourses of marketisation have been a consistent feature of the policy landscape in the past 20 years.

### Challenge to broadcasting as scarce, national resource rationale

Instead of the limited part of the electromagnetic spectrum available for analogue broadcasting, new cable, satellite and digital technologies poten-tially offered almost limitless capacity for the transmission of information and entertainment. The proponents of marketisation claimed that new communication technologies meant that spectrum scarcity was coming to an end and that state intervention in broadcasting on the grounds of ensuring clear signal reception could no longer be justified. However, the strategic use of technological reductionism in such claims should be noted. Technology did not delegitimise existing policy in itself. Rather, these technologies should be seen as the result of investment decisions by private corporations. Cultural-industry corporations and their political allies were able to present such new technologies as inevitable motors of change, which required new forms of looser regulation, to allow companies to compete in national and global markets.

### Challenge to the power of broadcasting rationale

It became increasingly difficult for the advocates of public service and/or the public interest to argue that public ownership or tight regulation of television was justified by the medium's power of influence and persuasion. By the 1980s, corporations were involved in an enormous range of cultural enterprises. Why, they asked, were they excluded from entry into television, the most important (and lucrative) of all media forms? Television had become thoroughly absorbed into the fabric of everyday life. Although television was still authoritative, and was still the cause of great concern over its social and behavioural effects, arguments that viewers needed to be protected from the medium were increasingly difficult to sustain. But calls for the ending or relaxing of public ownership and regulation tied this sense of television's declining power to a different and much more problematic rhetoric: that existing systems of broadcasting provided insufficient choice for the viewer, and that the best way to increase choice was to provide more (commercial) channels (Peacock Report, 1986).

## Four waves of marketisation

As a result of the successful delegitimation of rationales for public ownership and regulation, the 1980s and 1990s saw an extremely important historical change in the policy landscape.

- Telecommunications authorities were privatised, and national telecommunications markets were opened up to competition, in particular from cable and mobile operators.
- Some public broadcasting institutions were privatised.
- Even where public broadcasting institutions remained in place, television systems were opened up to other terrestrial, commercial broadcasters, and increasingly to cable and satellite providers.
- Regulatory 'walls' between telecommunications, broadcasting and new media (such as cable and satellite) companies came down. Telecoms and cable companies were increasingly allowed to enter into television markets; cable television companies were allowed into telephony, etc.
- Marketisation created new contexts for the understanding of cultural policy in an era of technological innovation. When new communication technologies were introduced or disseminated more widely, they were often assumed to need minimal legislation and regulation beyond competition laws and rules.
- Restrictions on content were significantly relaxed: for example, on the amount of advertising allowed per hour, on how much educational

programming broadcasters were required to transmit and at what times.

♦ Laws and regulations governing media ownership were removed or relaxed.

♦ Also worthy of note, although it is beyond the scope of this chapter, are the reductions in subsidy to non-profit and public-sector cultural institutions, such as libraries, museums, theatre, film, etc. This made further space for private companies in cultural markets by opening up new market opportunities (for example, in providing private information databases) and in reducing competition (for example, by reducing the number of films made in most European countries, and therefore allowing Hollywood films even more access to European markets).

Specific examples of such changes in different countries are provided in the historical account which follows. These changes in cultural-industry policy played an absolutely crucial role in initiating and accelerating many of the changes which are the subject of this book. It cannot be emphasised enough that these changes were consciously and deliberately brought about in order to support the interests of large, commercial, cultural-industry companies. Any suggestion that they were made inevitable by, for example, technological change disguises the willed and intentional nature of these changes (though they had many unintended and unanticipated consequences).

There were four overlapping waves of policy change from 1980 onwards, all of which can be characterised as involving marketisation:

♦ The policy changes with the most profound consequences initially took place in the USA from 1980 onwards.

♦ Changes there had an important influence on changes in other advanced industrial states, in Western Europe, Canada, Australasia, and Japan from the mid-1980s, but of course with significant national and regional variations.

♦ Then, a number of countries with more authoritarian traditions of state control and ownership initiated policies of marketisation and 'liberalisation'.

♦ Finally, a further round of legislative and regulatory changes in the USA, Western Europe and elsewhere intensified a number of processes that earlier reforms had already set in place, including, most crucially, a potential convergence between various forms of communication (computers, telecommunications, media), and amongst companies involved in these businesses.

The next four sections outline these four waves.

## Changes in US communications policy, 1980–90

The state had a significant role in the development of radio in the USA, and in the setting up of RCA (later owners of the television network NBC, and the record company that released Elvis Presley's records). But in its 1934 Communications Act, the USA had radically departed from the norm in other liberal democratic countries, whereby governments would have a very pronounced role in media and telecommunications ownership and regulation.[2] The Act set up the Federal Communications Commission (FCC) to monitor 'public interest, convenience and/or necessity' (originally a phrase used in the 1927 Radio Act). A dual system was created of media and telecommunications regulation. In radio and, later, television broadcasters were given access to scarce spectrum in return for promising to serve this 'public interest, convenience and/or necessity'. There were restrictions on how many television stations these programme-making broadcasters could own nationally, but locally-owned stations up and down the USA affiliated themselves to what eventually (from 1955 to 1985) became a trio of major networks: NBC, CBS and ABC.[3] These companies formed a *de facto* vertically-integrated national oligopoly. Their revenues came mainly from advertising, rather than from a radio or television licence fee, which was the system favoured in Europe and elsewhere.

Meanwhile, in telecommunications, as we saw earlier, AT&T was granted monopoly control in the interests of efficiency. In return, they agreed not to have any involvement in content creation and circulation. The first big change in telecommunications regulation relevant to the main period covered by this book came in 1982, as a result of a Justice Department case against AT&T first brought in 1974 (which is typical of how slowly US regulation works). AT&T agreed out-of-court to be divested of their local business, and to be opened up for competition in long-distance markets (see Box 4.1). In 1984, as a result of this divestiture, seven 'Baby Bell' local phone companies were formed. Some of these have become key players in the 'converging' telecommunications, media and information technology markets of the late 1990s and early 2000s. In return for agreeing to this divestiture, AT&T were allowed access to information and computer markets they were previously forbidden from entering. Developments in the regulation of telecommunications took many years to have an effect.

---

2 Robert W. McChesney has shown how various commercial and right-wing interest groups played a crucial role in ensuring this outcome during debates over the best way to organise telecommunications, during the 1927–35 period (see McChesney, 1993; 1999: Chapter 5).

3 A fourth network, Dumont, lasted until 1955. News Corporation's Fox network began in 1985, and had established itself by 1991. Time-Warner and Viacom established new networks in the 1990s: WB and UPN respectively.

**Box 4.1 The peculiarities of US regulation**

One notable feature of US media and communications policy is that very little legislation has ever been passed by Congress: the Telecommunications Act of 1996 was the first major piece of legislation since the Communications Act of 1934. Many of the biggest decisions affecting communications have been 'made by Federal Judges adjudicating in merger and anti-monopoly cases' (Tunstall and Machin, 1999: 41). Such cases are often brought by the Federal Trade Commission or by the Justice Department, rather than by the Federal Communications Commission. Raphael (n.d.) adds a new twist to this view that the role of the FCC is sometimes overstated. He argues that the recent history of US regulation should be seen not as a move from stringent government oversight to a long process of deregulation, but as the gradual privatisation of regulation. Raphael shows that television journalism is now overseen less by the FCC, Congress and the Executive Branch of US government, than by tort law, public relations campaigns and market pressures.

Changes in broadcasting were more immediate in their impact. The most significant changes in policy took place in regulation, rather than in legislation (with the exception of the 1984 Cable Act). The key changes were brought about by a change of personnel at the FCC. Over the period in which television developed into a national mass medium, from 1945 to 1970, the FCC clashed with the broadcasters on a number of issues, most notably over 'the Fairness Doctrine', the rules by which the FCC tried to ensure that broadcasters would not abuse their power by acting as biased advocates. By the 1970s, the FCC had moved away from tight regulation of media content, but in general retained strong controls of structural issues, such as restrictions on concentration, cross-media ownership and convergence.

The far-right administration of President Ronald Reagan (1981–9) appointed a zealous neoliberal, Mark Fowler, as chair of the Commission. Fowler's FCC did away with numerous controls on concentration, leading to a surge in merger and takeover activity in broadcasting in the 1980s (Sterling and Kittross, 1990: 464, 532). It largely repealed the Fairness Doctrine in the late 1980s, and amongst other consequences for content, this helped to lead to the rise of right-wing talk show hosts on radio. Meanwhile, it took a harder line on issues of obscenity than ever before, leading to a series of conflicts with shock-jocks such as Howard Stern. Limits on the amount of advertising allowed per hour were relaxed. And in general the FCC encouraged an atmosphere in which the public interest, never defined, was equated with the economic prosperity of US commercial enterprises.

What were the forces behind the shift towards marketisation in the USA? The shift was the result of a struggle over how to regulate and organise cultural production. Jeremy Tunstall (1986) showed in a contemporary study how this struggle was to a very large degree waged within specific areas of Washington DC, by interest groups and their lobbyists. The pro-deregulation interests included, for example, the broadcasters, represented by their trade association, the National Association of Broadcasters; and the various cable companies, who succeeded in gaining ground in the early 1980s. Against them were ranged various groups seeking to represent the 'public interest', such as civil rights, consumer groups and church activists (see Aufderheide, 1999: 18–19 for details on such public interest groups). Some of the pro-marketisation forces had, in certain respects, competing interests and most were in favour of marketisation in their own interest, above all else (see Chapter 2). But they were united by a shared neoliberal commitment to the free market – that is, unregulated private business – to the notion of consumer sovereignty and choice (as opposed to citizens' rights), and to the goal of economic efficiency through competition. We have already seen the core arguments mobilised by these interest groups and their political allies on the radical right against traditional forms of communications policy: the need for competition to encourage efficiency, the supposed breakdown of spectrum scarcity as a rationale for regulation, and the privileging of consumer choice over citizens' rights. They drew on, and provided an important part of, the turn to neoliberalism.

Together, these changes made it clear that government policy was moving in a direction which would be highly favourable for corporations looking to expand their interests in the cultural industries. What is more, the success of American companies and conservative politicians in dismantling special regulatory apparatuses, especially in broadcasting, gave great encouragement to companies and policy-makers elsewhere with similar goals.

## Changes in broadcasting policy in other advanced industrial states, 1985–95

Historically, the liberal democracies of Western Europe, Australasia, Canada, Japan and other countries have followed a very different route from that taken by the USA in media and communications policy. In these countries, to different degrees, telecommunications have been run essentially as public utilities; and rather than a very loosely defined notion of public interest, as in the USA, the key concept in broadcasting policy has been **public service**. One of the most significant changes in the cultural industries in the 1980s and 1990s has been the dismantling of this public utility–public service mix. Particularly important was the challenge to non-commercial broadcasting. Television is the most important cultural industry of the late twentieth century, in terms both of the sheer amount of time people spend using it (see Chapter 3) and its cultural significance.

The marketisation of television in the advanced industrial states has already had enormous effects on the cultural industries not only in these states themselves, but in many other places too. The pulling apart of public service television has important implications for the social relations of cultural production and for the texts produced by the cultural industries.

### Defining characteristics of public service broadcasting systems

The key features of public service broadcasting (PSB) as outlined by its advocates (see Brants and Siune, 1992: 102; Blumler, 1992; and Tracey, 1998: 26–9) include:

- *Accountability to the public* (via their political representatives) beyond that provided by market forces.
- *Some element of public finance*, mainly carried out via an annual licence fee: in 1997 about £9 (US$12) per month in the UK, DM28.25 (US$14) in Germany. Revenue for public broadcasters can include commercial income from advertising, and from the sale and licensing of programmes and formats to other broadcasters. But, importantly, all profits must generally be fed back into programming or administration, whereas in a private system, a large chunk must be paid to shareholders. In the UK, the annual TV licence fee pays for public service radio and internet, as well as television.
- *Regulation of content*, including restrictions on advertising, violence and pornography (a feature of regulation of private broadcasting) but also rules concerning balance, impartiality and the serving of minority interests, the obligation to provide educational programming, and programming for all regions of a country.
- *Universal service* across all the territory of a nation and a 'comprehensive remit' (Blumler, 1992: 8) requiring public service broadcasters to encourage and satisfy the tastes of the full range of people in a society.
- Perhaps the most important feature of all in this context is that *audiences are addressed as citizens*, rather than as consumers. This is reflected in the provision of mixed and pluralistic schedules, whereas in a consumerist system, schedules would be determined primarily by the imperative to maximise ratings. In Blumler's terms, public broadcasters were charged with the responsibility of maintaining the cultural wealth and diversity of a nation. This concern with citizenship is also apparent in the way that, in Blumler's words, PSB 'assumed some responsibility for the health of the political process and for the quality of public discourse generated within it' (1992: 12). This meant, in general, a commitment to 'distance from vested interests', even if that was not always achieved, especially in times of war, conflict or crisis.

### Variations in public service systems

Of course, there were many variations in this generalised system of PSB. As Humphreys (1996: 177–8) observes, many of these differences can be explained by the very different political cultures in the countries involved. There is no space to provide a full classification of national differences here (details can be found in many comparative studies, including Humphreys, 1996; Hoffman-Reim, 1996; Euromedia Research Group, 1997; Raboy, 1997; Goldberg et al., 1998), but the most important variations include:

◆ *Funding of television system and of public service channels within it.* In most liberal democracies, television began as a public monopoly, funded only by a licence fee, consisting of just one channel. Further channels were added in the 1960s and 1970s. By 1980, most of these channels had begun to mix advertising with the licence fee. By 1990, as part of the changes to be discussed in this chapter, many countries had shifted to a mixed revenue (licence fee/advertising) public monopoly, but a roughly equal number had shifted to a dual system of public broadcasters alongside commercial channels (see Table 4.1). This represented a huge expansion of opportunities for cultural-industry corporations in the television market, with important consequences for the cultural industries as a whole.

◆ *State control of public service broadcasters.* In some liberal democracies, such as France (up to 1982) and Greece, there was direct state control of

**Table 4.1  Changes in television funding systems**

| System | 1980 | 1990 | 1997 |
|---|---|---|---|
| Public monopoly/ licence fee only | Belgium, Denmark, Norway, Sweden | | |
| Public monopoly/ mixed revenue | Austria, Finland, France, Germany, Greece, Iceland, Ireland, The Netherlands, Portugal, Switzerland, Spain | Austria, Denmark, Iceland, Ireland, The Netherlands, Portugal, Switzerland | Austria, Ireland, Switzerland |
| Private monopoly/ advertising only | Luxembourg | Luxembourg | Luxembourg |
| Dual system | Italy, UK | Belgium, Finland, France, Germany, Greece, Italy, Norway, Spain, Sweden, UK | Belgium, Denmark, Finland, France, Germany, Greece, Iceland, Italy, The Netherlands, Norway, Portugal, Spain, Sweden, UK |

*Source*: Siune and Hultén, 1998: 27

the broadcasting organisation. Much more commonly, public corporations, such as the UK's BBC, Australia's ABC, NHK in Japan, and the
CBC in Canada, were set up in order to be generally autonomous of the
state, though key appointments might be made by the government.
- ◆ *Relationship to political institutions.* In some countries, such as Austria,
  the governors of public broadcasters were appointed in proportion to
  the strength of the political parties in the country. In many countries,
  there were places on boards for non-political appointees from other
  sectors, such as trade unions, church groups and universities.
- ◆ *Programming styles.* It would be a mistake for readers from countries
  such as the USA, where public service broadcasting is positioned as
  a worthy supplement to an overwhelmingly commercial, weakly-
  regulated system, to think that public service broadcasters served up a
  programming diet consisting purely of highly serious, educational
  programming. The whole point of public service programming was
  that it should be mixed and diverse, though how this worked on a
  day-to-day level varied from country to country.

## The social and cultural role of PSB

To what extent did PSB systems promote social justice in the terms
presented in the model in Chapter 2? From the 1950s right into the 1980s,
public service broadcasting was subjected to considerable criticism from
the political left. It was criticised for its pseudo-objective notion of balance
and impartiality in current affairs coverage (Glasgow Media Group, 1976),
for management policies and labour relations that reproduced class power
(Garnham, 1990: 128–31), and for its failure to provide programming
which appealed to working-class or non-elite audiences (Ang, 1991). Yet
the achievements of PSB should not be underestimated. One laudable
result was near-universal service. Millions were spent ensuring that
remote regions were given access to national broadcasting systems, in a
way that would have been unthinkable in a commercial system. There was
also a constant commitment to providing the regions with access to the
national system. Many public service broadcasters achieved an impressive
mix of genres and programmes. In the UK, for example, the BBC specialised in high-quality drama and situation comedy in the 1960s and 1970s,
alongside its news coverage and authored documentary series.

## Public service broadcasting under attack: case studies of change

As with the shift towards marketisation in the USA, the pulling apart of
the PSB system in liberal democracies was based on a struggle over how

best to organise the cultural industries. Peter J. Humphreys (1996) has provided a very useful outline of the key actors in reformulating broadcasting policy in Western Europe in the 1980s and early 1990s (see Table 4.2).

The pro-market coalition worked through lobbying and public relations work with policy-makers and key opinion-formers in the media. Again, this echoed developments in the USA. But in Europe, the pro-market coalition's task was more substantial. In the US, deregulation mainly comprised the breaking-down of an unpopular private monopoly (AT&T), and important but obscure changes in concentration policy. In Europe, an often popular apparatus of public ownership and programming had to be dismantled.

In Western Europe, significant changes in broadcasting policy began in earnest in the mid-1980s, following an early and disastrous experiment in Italy in the late 1970s, and took nationally-differentiated forms. There is only space for a brief survey of a few countries here. What can be seen across the board in this survey is a huge growth in the commercial sector. In some countries, the public service system remains relatively strong, if under threat. There is also variation in the degree to which ownership laws work to prevent concentration and cross-media ownership.

**Table 4.2   Marketisation interest groups in Europe**

| The pro-market actors | Their interests |
| --- | --- |
| The electronics industry | To exploit markets for new TV sets; pay-TV decoders; satellite reception equipment, etc. |
| The cable and satellite television lobbies | Freedom to provide commercial services |
| PTTs | To develop and diffuse new media technologies; to maintain monopoly or dominant market position in telecoms provision |
| Newspaper publishers | To diversify media operations; to pre-empt further competition for advertising revenue[1] |
| Advertisers | To gain outlets and strengthen market position |
| Governments | To promote the economy; to attract media investors |
| Parties of the Right | Pursuit of neoliberal agenda; promotion of business interests |
| European Commission | To liberalise European markets |

| Public service supporters | Their interests |
| --- | --- |
| Public service broadcasters | Self-defence; continuance of public resources, etc. |
| Unions | Protection of employment and conditions of employment |
| Parties of the left | Promotion of public service ethos and communitarian values; promotion of labour interests |

[1] Not universally the case. In some countries the press remained a force resisting commercial broadcasting.

*Source:* Humphreys, 1996: 176

## The UK

Very much under the influence of US communications deregulation, the UK was very quick to privatise telecommunications, and to introduce 'light touch' cable regulation. The far-right conservative Thatcher government and the newspapers of her political ally, Rupert Murdoch, launched an attack on British broadcasting. Thatcher appointed a right-wing economist to run a public enquiry into broadcasting (Peacock Report, 1986). But the resulting legislation, the Broadcasting Act of 1990, was far less radical in its marketisation of British broadcasting than public service advocates feared. The BBC was not privatised; nor was Channel 4, set up by the previous Labour administration to serve minorities, and introduced early in the Thatcher years, in 1982. The BBC was not, as many had feared, forced to take advertising. This was for economic, not cultural, reasons: the commercial companies did not want the BBC taking their market. The deregulatory thrust was weakened by strong support on the traditional, paternalist wing of the Conservative Party for the mix of licence fee and commercial television which had existed in the UK since the 1950s. Moreover, strong controls were retained on concentration and cross-media ownership – eventually weakened in the 1996 Broadcasting Act. Nevertheless, the impact of Thatcherite legislation should not be underestimated, especially on ITV, the network of closely-regulated commercial franchises established in 1955, operating under a public service remit. In the 1990s, ITV moved quickly from 14 regional franchised stations, dominated by six companies, towards effective monopoly control by two companies, Granada Media Group and Carlton. Most advertising money went not on making national programmes, but to shareholders, and to the 12-yearly auction system for franchises set up by the Broadcasting Act of 1990 (Tunstall, 1997: 247). To fend off parliamentary hostility, the BBC was forced to introduce 'internal markets and a ruthless regime of cost-cutting dressed up in the rhetoric of Thatcherite management consultancy, allied to a play-safe news and current affairs policy' (Garnham, 1998: 216).

What is more, cable and satellite were introduced to the UK on terms that allowed Rupert Murdoch's British Sky Broadcasting (BSkyB) to gain a virtual monopoly over new television technologies in the UK. The Cable Act of 1984 attempted to introduce cable under a very 'light touch' regulatory regime, but cable failed abysmally because the Thatcher government of the 1980s gave none of the state support to the incipient cable sector provided by some other Northern European countries.[4] As a result

---

4 In 1995, only 6 per cent of British TV homes were connected to cable (Collins and Murroni, 1996: 92, citing UK government figures). According to Zenith Media figures, 95 per cent of Netherlands TV homes were connected in the same year. Only Turkey and Portugal had lower connection figures in Western Europe. From the mid-1990s, however, deregulation allowed cable companies to compete with British Telecom in the telephone market and cable penetration rates increased.

of the failure of cable, by the mid-1990s, News Corporation's BSkyB DTH satellite package was completely dominant in the UK pay-TV sector, helped by its purchase of key sports rights, providing a powerful base from which to launch its bid to dominate digital television.

### France

France had a long tradition of state intervention in the cultural industries, not only in broadcasting, but also in the form of ambitious communications and audio-visual strategies and programmes. This included enormous investments in very modern and efficient telecommunications infrastructure in the 1960s and 1970s, including the popular and widely used, state-run videotex system, Minitel. But in the 1980s and early 1990s, France was in some ways more radical in its marketisation of broadcasting than the UK, even though France was headed by a socialist president, François Mitterrand, from 1981 to 1995. Communications policy is very strongly influenced by presidents, but is officially a matter for governments, and for crucial periods in 1986–8 and 1993–5, Mitterrand cohabited with right-wing governments under Chirac and Balladur respectively. But in any case the leftist governments of 1981–6 and 1988–93 were also involved in commercialisation. One reason for this was that France's state broadcasting system was closely associated with the political right. Another was the general drift across Western Europe towards marketisation in all areas of public policy, even in France, with its long statist traditions. The state broadcasting system was modified into a public service system in 1982, with an independent regulator (fierce battles were fought over the name, make-up and status of this body throughout the 1980s and early 1990s). Commercial channels were launched in 1984[5] and 1986 to create a dual system, but then the right-wing Chirac government of 1986–8 went much further, and privatised a key public channel TF1, along with other publicly-owned communications companies, including the TV and advertising company Havas. An ambitious plan to cable France via public money was abandoned and cabling was turned over to the private sector. New commercial terrestrial and satellite channels appeared in the late 1980s and the socialist government of 1988–1993 did not reverse earlier privatisations. The result was that from 1990 onwards, France 'had one of the most marketised broadcasting systems in Europe' (Humphreys, 1996: 181) with its public service channels comparatively marginalised.

---

5 Canal Plus, privatised in 1986, and now a major player in the European subscription television market as part of the Vivendi conglomerate.

## Germany

By contrast, the third major European media market, West Germany, launched a new commercial sector, but its decentralised public service system remained intact, confirmed by a ruling of the Federal Constitutional Court in 1986. This ruling was partly a result of campaigning by the leftist Social Democratic Party (SPD). Nevertheless, the rapid growth of commercial channels had a huge impact on the German media landscape after unification in 1990. This growth was largely due to central state funding of a massive cabling programme in the 1980s. Relatively weak ownership laws mean that there are strong and significant links between publishing and broadcasting. Two 'families' dominate both publishing and television: Kirch and Bertelsmann. What is more, the growth in commercial channels has made German television extremely reliant on English-language imports from the UK, and especially from the USA (Tunstall and Machin, 1999: 198).

## Australia

Australia's television system was a dual one from its inception in the 1950s. It represented a distinctive mix of British public service and US commercialism, the latter in the form of regulated, advertiser-supported city-based stations and networks. Consequently, events in the period 1985–95 were concerned not so much with the introduction of commercial channels, as in much of Western Europe, as with changes in ownership laws, determining how much a particular company could control of the television market, and to what extent these interests could be combined with press ownership. In 1987, strict limits on how many stations a particular company could own (two), were considerably loosened, partly in order to generate improved television facilities in the less-populated areas, by allowing the wealthy stations of Southern Australia to expand. The new limit was 60 per cent of national audience, but this was in any case breached (by Network Seven). To pacify anti-concentration campaigners, new rules forbade cross-media ownership across print and broadcasting, traditionally a strong feature of the media landscape. As magnates such as Kerry Packer and Rupert Murdoch chose print, their stations were sold at huge prices to, as it turned out, corrupt and incompetent bosses (with the result that Packer bought back his Nine Network for a song in 1990). But the main deregulatory act came in 1992, with the Broadcasting Services Act, which weakened restrictions on broadcasters, abolished radio ownership laws almost entirely, and introduced pay-TV in such a way as to favour satellite, dominated by Packer and Murdoch. The 1980s and 1990s, then, can be seen as a period in which commercialisation was intensified, the public service broadcaster was weakened, and Australia added to its reputation as the (advanced industrial) country 'with perhaps the greatest degree of media concentration in the world' (Hoffman-Reim, 1996).

## The third wave of marketisation: transitional and mixed societies (1989 onwards)

Because most of the world's most powerful economies are to be found in Western Europe, North America and the Pacific Rim, changes there have had enormous effects in the rest of the world. As deregulation took hold in the USA, Europe and elsewhere in the late 1980s, other economies followed the lead of the more powerful nations, in moving away from public ownership and close regulation towards marketisation.

### Soviet Union, Eastern Europe, China

The neoliberal vision of the free market as the best route towards a prosperous global future spread across much of the world during the 1980s and 1990s. For many commentators, this view seemed to be affirmed most powerfully by events in Eastern Europe (1989) and the Soviet Union (1991), where Stalinist governments were replaced by a system of representative democracy and market economies. In the Soviet Union and Eastern Europe, a generally well-educated population of nearly 400 million people was opened up to international trade and investment in cultural goods and services. However, events in Eastern Europe and other 'transitional' societies have not justified optimistic projections of benign globalisation.

In all Eastern European countries, the press moved from subsidy and state control to advertising and subscription; and telecommunications and broadcasting were soon privatised. Regulatory authorities had to be created from scratch, and the regulatory vacuum created powerful local monopolies and relationships between government and businesses which often bordered on illegality, and in some cases was thoroughly corrupt (see, for example, Goldberg et al., 1998 on Hungary). As Colin Sparks (2000) remarks, however, the resulting interpenetration of media ownership and political influence can actually be seen as the global norm, rather than as an aberration from idealised models of public or commercial broadcasting. (We have already seen evidence of the great influence that cultural-industry corporations can have on national governments and policy-makers in Europe and the USA.) As Eric Kit-wai Ma (2000) shows, state and market are now thoroughly intertwined in China. In Kit-wai Ma's words, 'lively and commercially vibrant media are actually essential to the continued governance of the state' (2000: 28). Under China's market-led reforms, leisure is encouraged in order to stimulate consumption, and the burgeoning Chinese cultural industries are essential to this.

## Latin America

Latin America, meanwhile, underwent transitions of a related, but different kind in the 1980s and 1990s. US Cold War propaganda often contrasted the Soviet bloc with the 'free world', but in the mid-1970s, more people were living under military, authoritarian regimes in Latin America, the USA's 'back yard', than in the whole of the Soviet Union and Eastern Europe together. Most television systems were thoroughly commercial, after the US model, but they were subject to authoritarian, rather than public service, monitoring; and private owners were often in close alliance with military rulers (see Chapter 6 on the Brazilian company, Globo). Under the influence of critiques of 'cultural imperialism', many democratic and authoritarian Latin American governments sought to protect their nascent television industries from US imports and direct investment in the 1960s and 1970s. But by the time of the neoliberal 1980s and 1990s, as television internationalisation intensified, experiments with state-funded alternatives were largely discredited through their association with the military authoritarian regimes of the 1960s and 1970s (Waisbord, 1998). The result has been a lack of substantial resistance to cultural marketisation in the region, even on the left. The introduction of satellite television is transforming the broadcasting environment in Latin America, but very much on terms favourable to partnerships between dominant Latin America companies and transnational cultural-industry corporations.

## India

Marketisation has proceeded apace in Asia in the 1990s but the continent is too vast and diverse to survey here. A discussion of transformations in India will at least give an indication of the huge importance of changes in Asia for the international cultural industries. India is not only the largest democracy in the world, it also has the world's largest middle class, estimated to be between 200 million and 250 million in number (Thussu, 1999: 125), a potentially huge and lucrative market for multinational cultural-industries conglomerates. The liberalisation (marketisation) of Indian broadcasting from 1991 onwards is extremely significant, then, for these conglomerates and for Indian audiences. Up till that date, Indian television was essentially a single-channel state system, often criticised for its close relationships to the dominant Congress Party, and for its worthy dullness, but with important and sometimes effective commitments to public service ideals, including national spread and the provision of education (Thomas, 1998). The same was true of other South Asian systems, including Pakistan, Bangladesh and Sri Lanka. However, commercials were allowed on the Indian state channel, Doordarshan, from 1976 onwards. In a country dominated by cinema, the massive potential of television as a cultural industry only began to be realised with the transmission of two serials based on Hindi religious epics, *Ramayana* and *Mahabaratha* (1987–90). By 1991, transnational satellite transmissions, including CNN and the Hong Kong-based STAR TV (before its takeover by Murdoch's News Corporation in 1993) were being received in India in large numbers (Sinha, 1997). At the same time, the Indian government initiated a wholesale marketisation of the economy, including the media. The result was a huge explosion in television channels throughout the 1990s, especially of pay-TV. By 1998, nearly 70 cable and satellite stations were operating in India (Thussu, 1999: 127). Many, including STAR, initially transmitted 'western' programming, but were increasingly oriented towards local content by the late 1990s. There were debates within India about whether this explosion represented a new diversity or the strangling at birth of an incipient public sphere. There is no space to assess those debates fully here, but India indicates how global marketisation has helped to trigger significant internationalisation. This can be seen not only in the investment by multinational conglomerates such as News Corporation in India; but also in the increasing presence of Asian broadcasters, such as India's Zee TV, in Europe and the USA. The significance of such complex and new flows of culture, which to a significant degree are a result of marketisation, will be addressed in Chapter 6.

## A fourth wave: towards convergence and internationalisation (1992 onwards)

The most important consequences of telecommunications marketisation were in the longer term, and they happened in conjunction with longer-term effects of changes in broadcasting, and of crucial changes in the computer and IT industries. A key issue here is the prospective convergence of the cultural industries with telecommunications and information technology. Crucial policy decisions were made in the late 1990s, which effectively treat this notion of convergence as inevitable. These can be seen as part of a fourth wave of marketisation.

From the early 1980s onwards, policy-makers and analysts had raised the future prospect of convergence between telecommunications, computers and media (one influential example was De Sola Pool, 1983). Information and entertainment would, it was envisaged, increasingly be consumed via some kind of hybrid of the computer and the television set, and would be transmitted via cable, satellite and telephone lines as well as, or instead of, via the airwaves. Such convergence is still a long way from happening, even in the most prosperous countries. But the very idea of convergence has fuelled many of the more recent changes in the cultural industries that I deal with in this book. It is now sufficiently advanced that extremely important mergers and alliances have been formed across the different sectors, including most notably AT&T's purchase of TCI (1999) and the merger between AOL and Time-Warner (2000–1). Many new technologies have been introduced because companies perceive that profits will be made out of such convergence. The most important of these are various forms of digitalisation (see Chapter 7), and the provision of broadband telecommunications channels. Because powerful companies that provide jobs and prestige envisage such profits, national policy-makers have introduced policies clearing the way for further rounds of convergence-led activity.

The most important piece of legislation at the national level in this respect has been the 1996 US Telecommunications Act (see Aufderheide, 1999 for indispensable context and overview). The Act solidified perceptions of emergent convergence, and paved the way for it, in three main ways. First, it freed the local Bell telephone companies created by the AT&T divestiture to enter long-distance markets, in return for allowing competition in their own regions. This allowed these enormous companies access to huge markets in new communications technologies. In the wake of the Act, these Baby Bell companies became major players, as a series of massive telecoms mergers 'seemed to presage a reduction from about 10 or 12 big telecoms companies to about four major survivors. The seven regional Baby Bells were melting down to only two or three big regional telecoms players' (Tunstall and Machin, 1999: 56). Second, it provided legislation enormously favourable to the cultural-industry corporations that dominate US broadcasting. Free spectrum was allocated to the main broadcasters for digital television, with only minor and difficult-to-enforce legislation preventing them from using this spectrum for non-media services. New rules made it easier to renew broadcasting licences, and the period for holding them was extended, giving broadcasting companies new control of a vital node in the new, converged cultural industries. These changes made them key partners in future convergence mergers and alliances. Third, the Act favoured existing cable companies by relaxing the regulation of charges, and it allowed phone companies to enter the cable market to provide content. The 1984 Cable Act had removed cable price regulation, and had reduced the powers of local government to demand public interest facilities from cable operators. By 1992, cable had to be re-regulated, as its prices had soared, and the cable industry had become deeply unpopular with the public and with policy-makers. The 1996 Act took away these regulations once again, with effect from 1999, leading to big increases in rates in that year.[6]

The Act was immediately followed by massive consolidation and frenetic trading. It helped pave the way for a wave of megamerger in the late 1990s (see Chapter 5) by drastically reducing barriers to consolidation, cross-ownership and vertical integration. It represents the culmination of the trend towards marketisation in US policy, enshrined in legislation, rather than embodied in regulation.

Another vital component of the fourth wave of marketisation in cultural-industries policy is the increasing importance of international policy bodies. These institutions have increasingly tended towards pro-convergence policies in the name of marketisation. The most important of these are outlined in Box 4.2.

---

### Box 4.2   Main international policy agencies

EU – the European Union, comprising 15 countries as of 2001.

NAFTA – the North American Free Trade Association, comprising the USA, Canada and Mexico.

MERCOSUR – Southern Cone Common Market, comprising Argentina, Brazil, Uruguay and Paraguay, established in 1991.

ASEAN – the Association of South East Asian Nations, and its organisation for developing free trade in the area, APEC (Asia Pacific Economic Cooperation)

GATT – the General Agreement on Tariffs and Trade, originally signed in 1947 and developed and expanded over a series of rounds, most recently the Uruguay Round (1986–93) culminating in the Marrakesh Agreement of 1993. This last round set up the much more powerful and formalised WTO.

WTO – World Trade Organisation, which consists of over 100 members and which can make binding judgements on cases where trade rules are subject to dispute (Held et al., 1999: 165). China is applying to join.

GATS (General Agreement on Trade in Services) and TRIPS (agreement on Trade-Related Aspects of Intellectual Property Rights) are the most important elements within GATT/WTO related to the cultural industries. The latter integrates intellectual property into a world trade regime governed by free-trade principles (Galperin, 1999).

---

These bodies have fuelled business internationalisation of all kinds by encouraging trade between countries, but they have also, in some cases, provided regulation to protect industries through setting quotas on how much content can be exported, to limit concentration and so on. All of

---

6 On this and numerous other important points of detail in this chapter, I owe thanks to Chad Raphael.

them work in the direction of enabling free trade between member countries. Because such marketisation tends to favour the wealthier and more powerful companies and nations, some of these organisations have been opposed by activist groups, most famously in the form of the actions at Seattle in November and December 1999 against the WTO. The cultural industries have been exempted from some of these free-trade agreements, in order to protect cultural diversity by insulating national cultural industries from the effects of US cultural exports. The most notable such instances were the exemption of Canadian cultural-industries protection measures in NAFTA and the provision in GATS for cultural industries (argued for by the EU under French pressure). However, the general drift of policy in these bodies has been heavily towards marketisation.

This can be illustrated by the case of the EU, which of all the international bodies named, is the organisation most informed by social-democratic notions of public interest. Advocates of the public interest have put constant pressure on proponents of deregulation, and have achieved occasional victories, but there has been a relentless drift towards marketisation. EU policy bodies have moved away from sector-by-sector legislation regarding the social impacts of the media, and towards regulation whereby telecommunications, computers and media are governed by general competition legislation, and regulators ensure compliance (Østergaard, 1998).

The *Television Without Frontiers* initiative of the 1980s (Commission of the European Communities, 1984) aimed to develop European audio-visual industries which could form a power-bloc to match those of the USA in the global market, while respecting national diversity. It may be that this was an impossible goal to achieve, given the national diversity within Europe (Collins, 1998; Galperin, 1999). After years of discussion, a directive based on the policy (Council of the European Communities, 1989) finally came into effect in 1991. It has been widely condemned as an ineffective and confused failure. It set quotas for the proliferating television channels of Europe, in terms of how much they could import from outside the EU, but rendered the policy useless by including the qualifying phrase 'if practicable'. Its fudged attempts to combine economic growth and cultural diversity contrast with the supposed 'success' of EU telecommunications policy. Here, because the implications for content were not fully understood, there was consensus over policy, and the consensus was pro-deregulation. Ten years of EU telecommunications marketisation culminated in the agreement of all EU member states to open up their telecommunications markets to privatisation and free competition from 1 January 1998. Meanwhile, public service advocates continue to do battle with the marketisers over 'information society' policy, and these often take the forms of battles between different sections of the EU's vast bureaucracy.[7] This was particularly apparent in debates over the EU's evolving information society policy. The Bangemann Report of 1994 (Commission of the European Communities, 1994) advocated an extreme pro-market approach, but a High Level Group of Experts (including Manuel Castells) appointed by the Commission focused on issues of access and exclusion to this information society in their response. Nevertheless, the Green Paper on Convergence issued by the Commission of the EU in September 1997 (European Commission, 1997) was heavily pro-market, and while public interest advocates succeeded in having it revised more in the direction of public interest, that remains the thrust of EU information society policy. Underpinning EU policy is the assumption that convergence on corporate terms is inevitable and therefore that the EU's role should be to allow European corporations to compete on equal terms with other companies in the global economy. So convergence functions as a self-fulfilling prophecy. Policy change is both brought about by perceived convergence, and at the same time is likely to accelerate it. The drive to marketise telecommunications across Europe in the 1990s has been very much propelled by such convergence talk, although advocates of public interest and public service broadcasting continue to fight hard to resist such notions (see Downey, 1998; Murdock and Golding, 1999).

The EU illustrates the pressures towards marketisation in even the most social-democratic of trade organisations. It suggests that the pressures towards globalisation and convergence are proving extremely difficult for policy makers to resist. Such trade associations seem to be pushing the cultural-industry landscape even further in the direction of the domination of large conglomerates operating on a global scale. And convergence seems increasingly to be accepted as a technologically-driven fact. Whether such convergence of telecommunications, computers and media is inevitable and/or desirable will be discussed in Chapter 7.

◆ ◆ ◆

The push towards marketisation has not gone unresisted. Activist groups and national governments have put many obstacles in its way at different times. Public service broadcasting has been surprisingly resilient in the face of barrages from its commercial rivals. Nevertheless, the four waves suggest that, across very diverse national and regional contexts, neoliberalism and the neoclassical conception of the market have made huge advances in the cultural sphere. Much of the world seems to have looked increasingly towards the USA as a model for how to regulate culture.

---

7 Such as the battles between Directorate General (DG) X for Communication, Culture and Audiovisual Media, and DG XIII on Telecommunications.

Policy changes have had massive consequences for the cultural industries as a whole. Policies are responses to, and products of, sociocultural, economic and technological conditions. But they are fundamental in triggering and/or inhibiting transformations in the cultural industries. This is particularly the case in broadcasting and telecommunications policy, where there have been strong traditions of public ownership and regulation, but where such traditions were abandoned or severely limited during the neoliberal turn of the 1980s and 1990s. The changes described above have played a vital role, in conjunction with the changes and continuities described in the next four chapters, in determining the new landscape of the cultural industries at the beginning of the twenty-first century.

## Further reading

Two sources have been invaluable for me in understanding the history of US policy, law and regulation: Aufderheide (1999) and Sterling and Kittross's textbook history of US broadcasting (1990). Useful statements of the principles of public service broadcasting include those in Tracey (1998); Blumler (1992); and Brants and Siune (1992). Of the many useful comparative accounts of national media policy published in the 1990s the most valuable (and readable) is Humphreys (1996). The work of Jeremy Tunstall provides many useful insights into cultural and media policy. Especially good are Tunstall (1986) and Tunstall and Palmer (1990), though these are now outdated; Tunstall and Machin (1999) update this earlier work. An encouraging development in media studies is the publication of collections that deal with policy and media histories in countries outside Europe and North America. I have found Smith with Paterson (1998) and Curran and Park (2000) very useful. Cultural policy in the era of international policy organisations is an important area for future work. Galperin (1999) is a groundbreaking article on this topic. Collins (1998) is a detailed study of some aspects of EU policy. Finally, Garnham (1998) provides a characteristically crisp and astute overview of policy issues.

# 5 Ownership, Organisation and Cultural Work

The changes in government policy discussed in the previous chapter created a new business environment for cultural-industry corporations, for cultural workers, and for consumers from the late 1980s onwards. In short, marketisation helped to create a situation in which the cultural industries became an increasingly important sector for business investment. As we saw in Chapter 3, in response to the Long Downturn of the 1970s and 1980s, private corporations in the advanced industrial world began to intensify the longer-term shift in investment away from extractive and transformative sectors, and towards service industries, including the cultural industries. But at the same time, businesses of all kinds were going through a long phase of organisational innovation and restructuring. How did these changes affect the cultural industries?

The first part of the chapter provides evidence of the considerable growth in size and scope of large cultural-industry corporations. It examines trends in the strategies of these corporations, including conglomeration and vertical integration. I relate the discussion here to the first of the questions raised in the evaluative framework outlined in Chapter 2. What have been the effects of the growth in size and power of the largest cultural-industry corporations on cultural production and on society?

Changes in ownership and corporate strategy tell us only a certain amount about the environments in which creative work takes place, about the way in which cultural industry owners and executives attempt the difficult business of managing and marketing creativity. As Chapter 2 showed, even in the complex professional era, as large corporations began to dominate cultural production, much cultural work was nevertheless based on a certain amount of operational autonomy for creative workers and managers. So in the second part of the chapter, I turn to questions of organisation and control. To what extent were the organisational features associated with the complex professional era of cultural production, outlined in Chapter 2, radically altered? Here I address the second set of evaluative questions raised in that chapter: have the rewards and working conditions of symbol creators – and indeed other workers in the cultural industries – improved during this time? To what extent has creative autonomy been expanded or diminished over the last 20 years? What changes have there been in the extent to which creative workers within the cultural industries get to determine how their work will be edited, promoted, circulated?

## Ownership and corporate structure: the big get bigger

One of the most important transitions from the market professional era of cultural production to the complex professional era involved the increasing presence of large corporations in cultural markets. This trend has intensified in the 1980s and 1990s. There has been a massive growth in the size and scope of cultural-industry corporations. A small number of transnational corporations have enormous power. I will begin by outlining the growth and current scope of these corporations before dealing in more detail with two vital aspects of corporate strategy – conglomeration and integration – and how these strategies have changed over the last 20 years.

The growth in size and the conglomeration of cultural-industry companies were part of a long-term trend in mergers and acquisitions in all industries that quickened during the 1980s in response to the Long Downturn. There were 4,900 mergers in the USA between 1968 and 1973, and this number increased in the 1970s and 1980s. There were over 3,300 corporate acquisitions in 1986 alone (Greco, 1995: 229–30). This was the period of marketisation in US broadcasting policy and two of the three great US broadcasting networks (CBS and NBC) changed hands in huge deals in 1985–6.

Following the Wall Street Crash of October 1987, the US House of Representatives eliminated certain tax breaks that encouraged acquisitions; as a result, mergers of all kinds substantially decreased in the USA in the following years (Greco, 1995: 230) though this move did not put an end to spectacular international mergers. Consumer electronics company Sony purchased CBS Records in 1988 (US$2 billion) and Columbia Pictures Entertainment (US$3.4 billion) in 1989. Time-Life and Warner Communications merged in 1989, in the form of a 'friendly' US$14.9 billion buy-out by Time-Life. Then, after the brief hiatus of the late 1980s, the 1990s saw a huge explosion of mergers in industry as a whole. For example, 1997 saw the highest ever figures for US mergers and acquisitions up to that point: US$912 billion worth of deals (*Business Week*, 30 March 1998: 47). This was echoed in the cultural industries. According to Greco (1996: 5), there were 557 reported media business acquisitions between 1990 and 1995, only just short of the entire total of such deals between 1960 and 1989. Particularly significant have been two waves of mega-acquisitions, in 1994–5 and in 1999–2000. See Table 5.1 for details of other major cultural-industry mergers and acquisitions in the 1990s.

**Table 5.1   Some major cultural-industry mergers and acquisitions**

| Date | Acquiring firm | Acquired firm (new name in brackets) | Price US$ billions[1] | Strategic motivation |
|------|---------------|--------------------------------------|----------------------|----------------------|
| 1994 | Viacom | Paramount Comms | 8.0 | Conglomeration across publishing, film, broadcasting, cable, theme parks |
| 1994 | Viacom | Blockbuster | 8.5 | Distribution control |
| 1995 | Disney | Capital Cities/ABC | 19 | Vertical integration and control of content creation |
| 1995 | Time Warner | Turner Broadcasting | 7.4 | Vertical integration and conglomeration/ synergy |
| 1995 | Seagram | MCA (Universal) | 5.7 | General conglomerate moves into diversified media |
| 1995 | Westinghouse | CBS | 5.4 | General conglomerate moves into broadcasting |
| 1998 | AT&T* | TCI (including Liberty Media)* | 48** | Telecoms-media convergence |
| 1998 | Seagram | PolyGram | 10.6 | Recording market share plus European film interests |
| 1999 | Carlton* | United* | 8.0** | Merger of major European media groups |
| 1999 | Viacom | CBS | 22 | Media conglomerate consolidates broadcasting power |
| 2000 | Vivendi | Seagram/Universal | 35 | Very diversified European leisure conglomerate diversifies further |
| 2000 | AOL* | Time-Warner* (AOL Time-Warner) | 128** | Internet service provider merges with media conglomerate |

[1] Prices and values are based on reports at the time that the merger or acquisition was announced, except for AOL Time-Warner, which was evaluated at US$350 billion in January 2000, when the merger was first reported, but at US$128 billion, when the merger was finally approved by the US regulatory body, the Federal Communications Commission. The fall in value reflected the fall in share values over the year, as internet and new media hype subsided.
* indicates a merger
** indicates evaluation of new merged company rather than price

There is another important context for the growth of cultural-industry corporations in the late 1990s. The US economy began to boom from 1995 onwards; finally, the Long Downturn seemed to be in reverse. There was rapid growth of gross domestic product, labour productivity and investment. Even real wages went up. This boom led to what Robert Brenner (2000: 5) has called 'the greatest financial bubble in American history', as equity prices lost touch with reality, and household, corporate and financial debt all reached record levels, leading to an explosion of consumption. As a result of the boom, and of mergers and acquisitions in the cultural industries, a situation had arisen by the late 1990s whereby a small group of corporations were clear leaders in terms of the revenues they gained from global cultural-industry markets. The names and organisational structures of these companies change regularly, as further mergers, acquisitions and sell-offs take place, or are put on hold by regulators; but Table 5.2 lists the six biggest cultural-industry businesses, as they stood in mid-2001, based on company reports for the year 2000. These six corporations have a significant presence in both North America and Europe, the world's two largest continental cultural-industry markets. But only News Corporation can be considered a truly global corporation, in that it has significant market share across numerous cultural industries in three continents (North America, Europe and Asia/Australasia).

Below these six vast cultural-industry corporations, each with annual revenues of over US$10 billion, sits a 'second tier' (Herman and McChesney, 1997: 53) of regional giants, consisting in 1999 and 2000 of 42 companies with revenues in excess of one billion dollars per year from media and cultural operations. Apart from three Latin American companies and one Australian concern, all are based in either North America, Europe or Japan. Some of these companies have ambitions to join the elite club of cultural-industry mega-corporations, such as Comcast (US, primarily cable) and German group Kirch. Collectively, the Big 48 have an enormous impact on the cultural-industry landscape, in terms of policy lobbying, and in terms of the standards they set for what constitutes standard practice in the cultural industries. Concentrating only on the largest six

**Table 5.2  The Big 6 cultural industry corporations**

| Company | Revenue in US$ billions |
|---|---|
| AOL Time Warner | 36.2 |
| Walt Disney | 25.4 |
| Viacom | 23.4 |
| Vivendi Universal | 21.2 (24.3 billion euros) |
| Bertelsmann | 19.1 |
| News Corp. | 13.8 |

*Source*: *Variety's* Global 50, August 27–September 2, 2001, based on annual reports for 2000.

corporations can distract attention from the huge importance of these 48 corporations. It is the Big 48 we should focus on to get a real sense of the expanded role of large corporations within the cultural industries.

Even below these two tiers of global giants, there are many other companies, exerting a sizeable influence on particular markets. A report by Zenith consultants (cited by Sánchez-Tabernero et al., 1993: 100) usefully classifies the biggest cultural-industry companies into the following categories:

- Companies dominant in one cultural industry in one country
- Companies influencing one cultural industry across several countries
- Companies having interests across more than one cultural industry in one country
- Companies with interests in more than one cultural industry internationally

Nearly all the cultural-industry corporations in the Big 48 are in one or more of the first three categories. With conglomeration and internationalisation, more and more companies are entering, or moving into, the final category.

## How central are the cultural industries in global business?

The figures involved in mergers and acquisitions, and the now massive size of revenues accruing to the biggest cultural-industry companies, reflect the increasing centrality of the cultural industries in global business. However, we should not make the leap made by some commentators (e.g., Lash and Urry, 1994: Chapter 5) and suggest that the cultural industries form a 'new core' to global business. Cultural-industry corporations are becoming much bigger, but they still have a long way to go to match the largest corporations in the world.

In terms of market valuation, the AOL-Warner deal of 2000 was the biggest merger of any kind of all time. Surely this is evidence that converged media and computer companies represent a new core? In fact, such figures need to be interpreted carefully. The size of the AOL-Warner deal is closer to the hugely-inflated telecommunications mergers of the late 1990s which took place in the wake of the pro-convergence 1996 Telecommunications Act. And even in the new climate of the 1990s, following years of spectacular internal growth and mergers, corporations primarily based on cultural-industry business were still dwarfed in terms of the most relevant indicators by other kinds of corporation. Table 5.3 shows the biggest corporations with significant cultural-industry interests, along with their

**Table 5.3** **The largest corporations with cultural-industry interests**

| Ranking | Company | Revenue in US$ billions |
|---|---|---|
| 1 | Exxon Mobil<br>(No media interests – included for sake of comparison.) | 210.4 |
| 8 | General Electric<br>This extremely diverse conglomerate owns the US TV network NBC, but this is only one of 21 divisions. | 129.9 |
| 30 | Sony<br>Has five main divisions: consumer electronics, games, music (Sony Music Entertainment), films (Columbia Tristar), and insurance. Consumer electronics accounts for most of its sales. | 66.1 |
| 91 | Vivendi<br>Based in France, centres its business on 'environmental services', such as water, energy, waste management, transport, construction and property. Prior to its purchase of Universal Music Group from Seagram (1999 revenues: US$11.784 billion, 418th in Global 500), its ownership of Canal Plus made it one of the most important players in the European media market. The acquisition gives it the biggest music company in the world plus Universal's film interests, but its other interests still considerably outweigh its media concerns. | 38.6 |
| (103) | *AOL Time Warner*<br>The biggest cultural-industry corporation in the world, when this is defined as a corporation where most of the revenues come from cultural-industry concerns. The merger was completed in early 2001. Because the merger was underway throughout 2000, the company is not listed in the 2001 Global 500, but its combined revenues would put it at 103rd on the list. | |
| 174 | *Walt Disney* | 25.4 |
| 201 | Microsoft<br>Included for the sake of comparison here. It is building up many alliances with cultural-industry companies. While it is one of the most highly-valued companies in the world, and has very high profit returns on its revenues, it is important to realise that its revenues are still dwarfed by older corporations. | 23.0 |
| 245 | *Viacom* | 20.0 |
| 299 | *Bertelsmann* | 16.6 |
| 371 | *News Corporation*<br>Note that this ranking underestimates the influence of News Corporation mogul, Rupert Murdoch. Another company of which he has main control, *BSkyB*, is a major player in European digital and satellite television, but reports its figures separately (ranking 24th on the Variety 50, with US$3.2 billion of revenue for 2000). | 14.1 |

*Notes*: italics indicate that most of the company's revenues come from cultural-industry interests. The disparity in revenue figures between Tables 5.2 and 5.3 comes from rounding off, and the different methodologies employed by *Fortune* and *Variety*.

*Source*: the *Fortune* Global 500 list for 2001, based on annual reports 2000/2001.

rank in the *Fortune* magazine list of the biggest 500 companies in the world by revenue in the year 2000. As is clear from the table, even the very biggest cultural-industry corporations – that is, corporations that gain most of their revenues from cultural-industry operations – are dwarfed by the biggest corporations in the world. These corporations are automobile giants (GM, number three in the 2001 Global 500; Ford, number four and Daimler-Chrysler five, Toyota at ten), oil companies such as Exxon Mobil (number one) and Royal Dutch/Shell (six) and BP (seven), retail giants (Wal-Mart, at two) and general conglomerates (Mitsui, at eleven).

These figures should put into perspective the growth of the largest cultural-industry corporations.[1] It may be that in the wake of convergence hype, cultural-industry companies will merge into vast telecommunications conglomerates – as was the case with AT&T's media holdings, for example – or even internet service providers (such as AOL). But these trends have not yet been established firmly enough to warrant the description 'convergence'. What is more, even where such mergers and acquisitions take place, cultural-industry corporations will operate as separate divisions, just as they already do now, within vast consumer-electronic corporations (Sony) and general conglomerates (Vivendi).

Nevertheless, we should not forget the essential fact: the increasing presence of vast companies in the cultural industries. As indicated in Chapter 2, this has important implications. These corporations are able to mobilise massive lobbying powers and can put tremendous pressure on governments not to put into place legislation and regulation which goes against their interests as profit-making companies. This often works against the public interest. The growth of large corporations also affects prevailing conceptions of how to carry out the management of creativity. The biggest firms often tend to be the most prestigious, and set the standard by which other businesses carry out their work, with important implications for conditions of cultural work.

## Changing strategies (I): conglomeration

An important feature of the complex professional era from the 1960s onwards was conglomeration (see Chapter 2). This has continued into the 1980s and 1990s but corporate strategy with regard to conglomeration has changed in important ways. The recent fashion has generally been to build a portfolio of *related* industries, whereas in the 1960s and 1970s, as we saw

---

1 Historical comparison of the relative size of the largest cultural-industry corporations is difficult. Companies based on 'services' were only included in the *Fortune* 500 and Global 500 from 1995 onwards.

in Chapter 2, the trend was for non-cultural-industry conglomerates to buy into the cultural industries.

One of the ways in which the Long Downturn of the 1970s and 1980s forced a rethinking of the way businesses operated was that there was an increasing emphasis on the notion of 'synergy'. This was originally a medical term: it referred to the way that two elements (such as two drugs, or two muscles) might work together to produce a result greater than the sum of the two parts. The idea behind the metaphor was that the different parts of a corporation should relate to each other in such a manner as to provide cross-promotion and cross-selling opportunities, so that sales would exceed what was possible from two separate divisions. As the popularity of such ideas spread from business schools and management gurus and into corporations, conglomerates began to specialise again, but not on one activity, as in the pre-diversification era of the early twentieth century, but on a set of related ones.[2]

The form of conglomeration that received the most publicity in the late 1980s was the purchase of media producers by consumer electronics companies: so-called hardware/software synergy.[3] Sony's purchases of CBS Records and Columbia Pictures Entertainment in 1988 and 1989 respectively were widely assumed to represent the future shape of cultural-industry corporations. The idea was that Sony would be able to use prestigious American rock music and cinema to help persuade consumers to buy new consumer technologies, such as the mini-disc. Other significant purchases in the late 1980s were based on very different strategies, such as general conglomerate General Electric's purchase of NBC. However, it was the acquisitions by Japanese corporations, such as the Japanese conglomerate Matsushita's acquisition of MCA Records in 1990, which received most attention: they fed recession-fuelled fears on the part of US businesses about a loss of global economic domination.

But by the mid-1990s, such hardware/software synergies were widely viewed as a failure. Some commentators have explained this apparent failure by referring to the different production cultures needed to produce consumer electronics on the one hand, and music/films/TV programmes on the other. Some of these accounts are convincing (Negus, 1997) but

---

2 Very diverse general conglomerates continue to be a feature of the South East Asian business landscape right up to the time of writing. The struggles of, for example, Korean general conglomerates such as Daewoo may or may not affirm European and North American commitment to synergy-based diversification. Some North American general conglomerates such as General Electric thrived in the late 1990s.

3 Such hardware/software synergies were not unprecedented by any means: the Dutch consumer electronics group Philips had its own record division (PolyGram) for decades until it sold it to Seagram in 1995. And the US networks were founded on such synergies: NBC was part of the communications conglomerate RCA, which made radio equipment.

some press versions of this view bordered on racism: the implication was that the Japanese were incapable of producing entertainment; they could only produce efficient machines. When hardware/software mergers were deemed to be a failure, the electronics companies began to sell off their media properties, and to form alliances and joint ventures with media producers on particular projects.

There is no fundamental reason why mergers, as opposed to alliances and joint ventures, between electronics companies and media producers will not return to fashion. But the 1990s were dominated by three more tenacious forms of synergy-based cultural-industry conglomerate. (The following typology is adapted from a study by consultants Booz, Allen & Hamilton, summarised by Sánchez-Tabernero et al., 1993: 94.) The first was **the media conglomerate**, based almost entirely around a set of core media interests (for example, News Corporation). The media are also important for the second category, **the leisure conglomerate**, but take their place alongside other leisure interests, such as hotels and theme parks (for example, Disney). From the mid-1990s onwards, however, a third type of cultural-industry conglomerate was becoming increasingly significant as a potential model: **the information/communication corporation** (perhaps best symbolised by AT&T's 1998 takeover of cable group TCI, including the Liberty Media Group). Media, telecommunications and computer corporations have been merging and acquiring each other, in anticipation of further convergence between these markets (see Chapter 7).

The marketisation of broadcasting has been absolutely crucial in the formation of all three types of conglomerate. For marketisation meant that many new cultural-industry sectors, including radio, plus terrestrial, cable, satellite and digital television, became available as targets of purchase and investment for conglomerates wishing to extend their portfolios, as governments removed restrictions on market concentration and cross-media ownership and as the cultural industries therefore came to be perceived as major new growth areas for business.

Conglomeration clearly entails an increase in the scope and power of individual cultural-industry corporations, in that the same corporation can have stakes in many different forms of communication. Fewer companies therefore come to dominate the cultural industries as a whole. This has an effect on the lobbying power of the corporations, and on their general influence on the way in which cultural production is carried out. Internal dissent amongst the major conglomerates is less likely, as they decrease in number. It undoubtedly allows the corporations to cross-promote their products (whether texts or other commodities). This in turn reinforces the power of the oligopolies dominating the cultural industries. Some also assert that conglomeration leads to diminished diversity and quality – but there are real problems surrounding the evidence for this (see Chapter 8).

## Changing strategies (II): vertical integration

The imperative towards vertical integration is strong in the cultural industries, because of the vital importance of circulation. This in turn derives
from the need to control relationships with fickle audiences, and the need
to create artificial scarcity for public goods (see Introduction). That is why
so many of the key industries have been dominated by an oligopoly of
vertically-integrated companies. However, as with conglomeration, vertical
integration strategies are subject to change; and there are signs of partial
disintegration in some industries, and new forms of integration.

Whereas in the late 1980s commentators thought that Sony would
be the archetypal cultural-industry corporation, in the 1990s the future
seemed to be represented by Disney. For the success of Disney in the 1990s
was based on an understanding of the importance of intellectual property:
that the cultural industries increasingly operate around the ownership of
rights to films, TV programmes, songs, brands. By circulating these
symbols across many different media, characters, icons and narratives
become increasingly present in public consciousness. New characters and
icons can be launched through intensive cross-promotion. Crucial to this
strategy though has been vertical integration. Disney not only owns a
remarkable back catalogue of films and recordings, its theme parks, hotels,
and so on, it also has its own television network and cable channel (it has
had its own international distribution company, Buena Vista, for decades).
With its purchase of Capital Cities/ABC in 1995, Disney became one of the
largest cultural-industry companies in the world. But it was not just the
size of the corporation that made this a significant event, it was also the
perception that Disney had understood the nature of the new cultural
industries: that combining ownership of content and distribution was the
way forward. In its list of the biggest media companies (by turnover) in
1998–9, *Screen Digest* (July 1999: 176) noted that 'the top companies are all
highly diversified – vertically and horizontally integrated'.

We must be cautious about portraying developments in the cultural
industries as a steady advance of vertical integration. By 2001, analysts
were speculating that Disney's fortunes were in reverse, after the poor
performance of the blockbuster film *Pearl Harbor*. There has been plenty of
movement in the last 20 years *away* from vertical integration. One of the
major organisational forms of the early complex professional era, public
service television, represented a striking example of vertical integration in
the public interest, justified on the grounds that it ensured a coherent
schedule of entertainment and information for national citizens. Many of
the public service monopolies had programme-makers of all kinds, technical and creative, on permanent contracts, made programmes, controlled
broadcasting distribution and some even made the television sets. In the
1990s, however, there was a boom in independent television production

across much of the world, driven mainly by two processes: public service corporations dealt with budget cuts by subcontracting production; and policy-makers wanted to encourage growth in the independent sector by measures such as setting quotas of how much production had to be outsourced. This led many commentators to talk of a new era of post-Fordist television, involving flexible working arrangements and networks of interdependent firms, rather than monolithic organisations (Lash and Urry, 1994: Chapter 5; see Robins and Cornford, 1992 for a more sceptical account). Whether this resulted in greater creative autonomy for programme makers is another matter. We shall return to the issue of whether independent production has allowed greater autonomy for symbol creators later in this chapter.

The trend in the US audiovisual industries has been towards vertical integration. It is ironic that while classical public service television permitted vertical integration, the US system, associated with a more market-oriented approach to cultural production, aimed at discouraging it. With marketisation, the disintegration amongst European broadcasters has been reversed in the USA. One of the main ways in which US policy-makers sought to control the mighty power of the networks was to restrict vertical integration by limiting how many local stations the networks could own. And from the early 1960s on, the broadcasters bought nearly all of their TV and radio programmes in packages from independent production companies, such as MTM (which made *The Mary Tyler Moore Show* and *Hill Street Blues*) and Lorimar (*Dallas*, *Knots Landing*) (see Sterling and Kittross, 1990: 559–63). Some Hollywood studios acted as 'independent' producers in this system, most notably Warner Bros. In the late 1990s, all this changed. The networks were increasingly part of the same media and leisure conglomerates as the major Hollywood studios, and consequently turned to these sibling companies for most of their productions. Those networks not owned by studio-owning conglomerates followed suit, as the studios gained in prestige. According to a report cited by McChesney (1999: 21), the six Hollywood major studios produced 37 out of 46 new prime-time shows scheduled for the Fall/Autumn of 1998. Such integration was apparent further downstream too. Not only were companies such as Columbia (that is, Sony) buying up cinemas, but the studios were now owned by the same companies that owned the other major outlets for films: broadcast and cable television, plus video hire networks. Disney owned ABC, plus numerous cable networks; News Corporation owned Fox and had launched a new television network of the same name in the mid-1980s; Viacom owned Paramount Studios and the fledgling network UPN and in 1999 bought CBS, one of the big three networks; Time-Warner dominated cable networks, and through its purchase of Ted Turner's company TNT in 1997, owned the key cable channels. Even here, in the case of the USA, such transformations cannot be portrayed as an entirely new era of vertical integration. The integration of Hollywood studios with television networks represented a return to the strategies Hollywood used during the classic studio era, from the 1920s to the 1950s (see Box 2.5). The recording industry also shows high levels of vertical integration. For decades, the major companies have owned pressing and distribution, as well as contracting musicians to them. However, the majors have rarely attempted to own retail outlets, in part because of the complexity and multiplicity of the market for music. What is more, the relationship with independent production is more complex in the music industry than in any other industry (see the section on small companies, below).

Vertical integration is best seen not as a constant process, whereby companies get more and more vertically integrated over time, but as something historically variable across different industries. Changes in government policy, the arrival of new technologies and new business fashions can all bring about shifts towards or away from vertical integration.

## Market concentration and its limitations

The issue of market concentration has been central to work on the cultural industries in liberal-pluralist communication studies and in political economy approaches to culture. Chapter 2 noted high levels of market concentration in the cultural industries but pointed out that, in some cases, the arrival of corporations in new markets actually reduced the level of market concentration. Good, historically comparative statistics on market concentration are hard to find. Instead, we have to rely on snapshots of particular times, and these need to be treated with caution.

What have been the effects of conglomeration on corporate domination of cultural markets? Ben Bagdikian (2000) provides something of an indication of the effects of such conglomeration in terms of general cultural market concentration. For the first edition of his book *The Media Monopoly*, Bagdikian compiled an apparently unpublished list of the dominant media firms in the US market in 1983 in the following industries: newspapers, magazines, television, book publishing, motion pictures. For each industry, he worked down the lists of dominant companies, counting how many companies it took to account for more than 50 per cent of market share (measured in different ways for different media). He then added the figures together and calculated a total of 50 dominant corporations across the media as a whole.

Bagdikian has repeated the exercise for every subsequent edition of his book, and in the most recent edition (Bagdikian, 2000: xx–xxi) summarises the results.

1983 – 50
1987 – 29
1990 – 23
1997 – 10
2000 –  6

This is a crude method of measuring overall cultural-industry concentration and conglomeration, but it draws attention to the increasing size and scope of the biggest corporations, and their increasing tendency to work across all the different cultural industries.

Writing about the USA, McChesney (1999: 17–18) provides a number of examples of concentration in recent years, with some historical comparison:

♦ In 1997, the six largest film studios dominated over 90 per cent of US box office revenues and produced 132 out of the 148 films to receive wide distribution.

♦ The five largest music groups account for over 87 per cent of the US market.

♦ In cable, which was once a market without significant oligopoly control, according to McChesney, six cable companies had effective monopoly control over local markets across 80 per cent of the USA by 1998.

♦ Four radio chains controlled one-third of the radio industry's annual revenues of US$13.6 billion (though in fact some would say that this does not suggest a particularly high concentration ratio compared with most industries of comparable size).

♦ In 1985, the 12 largest theatre (that is, cinema exhibition) companies in the USA controlled 25 per cent of the screens; by 1998, that figure was 61 per cent.

♦ Between 1992 and 1998, the share of books sold by independent booksellers fell from 42 per cent to 20 per cent, as Barnes and Noble entered the market.

The accumulation of evidence suggests an irresistible tide sweeping the cultural industries towards ever-greater levels of market concentration. But much depends on the historical framework we decide to examine. Radio became more concentrated in the light of the 1996 US Telecommunications Act, but it was still much less concentrated than in the days of network control; in 1945, 95 per cent of all radio stations were affiliated with one or more of the four national networks (Sterling and Kittross, 1990: 260). And concentration levels in cinema exhibition are still relatively low compared with other industries, and certainly compared with the days when the major studios owned them, that is, prior to 1948, when government antitrust action resulted in the studios selling off their cinema interests.

As for new industries such as cable, there is bound to be a process of oligopolisation as such industries mature and as smaller firms are snaffled up by those aiming to increase market share. That's capitalism. This is not to be complacent about existing levels of market concentration. But such statistics do not prove, in themselves, the existence of long-term processes of *increased* concentration in US markets. Market concentration levels are high across all industries – but even in the wider economy, there is evidence that market concentration does not always go up in advanced industrial economies as a whole.[4]

What about European figures? In their study of media concentration in Europe, Meier and Trappel (1998: 51) provide some figures on concentration based on European Union sources (see Table 5.4). They suggest very high levels of concentration in book publishing, newspapers and television. But again these are non-historical and, given that in many countries television was entirely dominated by one or two channels until the 1980s, there may even be significant reductions of concentration, at least in the terms used here.

**Table 5.4  Media concentration in Western Europe**

| Country | Circulation share of top five publishing companies | Circulation share of top five newspaper titles | Audience market share of top two TV channels |
|---|---|---|---|
| Austria | 45 | 69 | 68 |
| Belgium (fr) | 77 | 55 | 47 |
| Belgium (fl) | – | – | 58 |
| Denmark | 50 | 49 | 78 |
| Finland | 42 | 39 | 71 |
| France | – | – | 60 |
| Germany | – | 23 | 31 |
| Ireland | – | – | 60 |
| Italy | – | – | 47 |
| Luxembourg | 100 | – | – |
| The Netherlands | 95 | – | 39 |
| Norway | 53 | 38 | 80 |
| Portugal | 55 | 91 | 88 |
| Spain | – | – | 51 |
| Sweden | 49 | 33 | 55 |
| Switzerland (d) | – | – | 45 |
| Switzerland (fr) | – | – | 49 |
| UK | 95 | – | 68 |

*Source*: Meier and Trappel, 1998: 51, based on EC statistical sources

4 Ghemawat and Ghadar (2000) arguing against global megamergers as a business strategy, present evidence to show declining global concentration levels in automobiles, oil and other key industries, including even high-tech industries. Systematic comparisons of market concentration in the cultural industries with levels elsewhere are extremely rare. Murdock and Golding (1977) is a rare and obviously outdated exception.

**Table 5.5**  **Changes in newspaper market concentration**

| Country | 1975 (%) | 1990 (%) |
| --- | --- | --- |
| Austria | 55 | 68 |
| Belgium (fl) | 26 | 59 |
| Belgium (fr) | 52[1] | 68 |
| Switzerland | 20 | 21 |
| Germany | 35[2] | 29 |
| Denmark | 38 | 48 |
| Spain | 24 | 29 |
| Finland | 26 | 39 |
| France | 15 | 35 |
| UK | 53 | 58 |
| Greece | 61 | 36 |
| Ireland | n/a | 75 |
| Italy | n/a | 32 |
| Netherlands | 36 | 35 |
| Norway | 48 | 45 |
| Portugal | 60[1] | 30 |
| Sweden | 30 | 31 |
| Turkey | 46 | 34 |

The figures refer to the share of circulation held by the two largest newspaper groups.
[1] estimate
[2] 1976 figures

*Source*: Sánchez-Tabernero et al., 1993: 102, reporting European Institute for the Media figures.

Sánchez-Tabernero et al. (1993: 102) compiled statistics comparing the market share of the two largest daily newspaper groups in 1975 and 1990 across 17 European countries (see Table 5.5). Even here, however, the trends were mixed across the 15 countries where figures were available. Five recorded significant increases; four small increases; three large decreases and three small decreases. This certainly does not point to a Europe-wide trend towards signficant market concentration in this cultural industry though, as Sánchez-Tabernero et al. point out, their figures do not capture regional trends within countries. In some countries, such as the Netherlands, fewer and fewer cities had more than one newspaper.[5]

My concern here is primarily with the difficulties of proving that levels of market concentration have substantially increased in the cultural industries since the late 1970s. But economists find it difficult to agree on any reliable measure of market concentration even in the same period (see Iosifides, 1997), leaving aside the difficulties of historical comparison. One issue amongst many others, for example, is whether different divisions of the same corporation, which at least in principle compete with each other,

---

5 Sánchez-Tabernero et al.'s market share statistics for radio and television are also ambiguous. They show that private companies were becoming involved in these markets but do not provide evidence of significant market concentration.

should be counted as competitors.[6] Even more difficult to prove via reliable statistics is that increased levels of market concentration lead to reduced levels of diversity of output. I return to this issue in Chapter 8.

None of this is to deny the importance of the presence of large corporations in cultural markets. Indeed, as Chapter 2 suggested, it is on this particular point that analysis should focus, rather than on the red herring of market concentration. The case for increased corporate control cannot be made via analysis of market concentration figures in quite such a clear-cut way as some writers would have us believe, through a rhetorical piling-up of statistics. Processes of conglomeration and integration, and the increasing size and scope of the largest cultural-industry corporations, are more important. These require separate treatment.

## The continuing presence of small companies

We saw in Chapter 2 that independent producers proliferated – and became important to debates about cultural production – even as large corporations became dominant in the cultural industries in the middle of the twentieth century. As cultural corporations have become bigger and more dominant, small companies have continued to boom in number. According to one analyst, 80 per cent of the Hollywood film industry is made up of companies with four employees or fewer (Jack Kyser, cited by Magder and Burston, 2002). Even during the period when the book industry was involved in successive waves of mergers and acquisitions, the number of book companies active in the USA increased from 993 in 1960 to 2,298 in 1987, according to Department of Commerce figures (Greco, 1996: 234).

The continued importance of small companies can partly be explained by the factors analysed in Chapter 2: the conception stage of texts remains small-scale and relatively inexpensive, and still takes place in relatively autonomous conditions. But there are other factors, more specific to the 1980–2000 period, accounting for the still-prevalent role of small companies.

◆ The onset of new media technologies brought about by the combined factors of government marketisation policy and intensified business interest in leisure and culture: This has created new types of cultural industry, and before industries 'mature', there is often more room for

---

6 Christianen (1995: 89–91) argues that concentration in the music industry should take account of different record company divisions as separate entities, so that all the different labels under each conglomerate's control would be counted separately, because they are in internal competition with each other. This would make concentration figures much lower, and would help account for the greater diversity of product that followed from some periods of apparent market concentration (see Chapter 8).

manoeuvre for independents. Key examples of such independent-friendly new cultural industries over the last 20 years are computer games, multimedia production (for example, educational CD-ROMs) and website design. But the introduction of new technologies is also a product of, and in turn a cause of, a proliferation of new sub-sectors within longer-established industries. For example, as live performance by successful rock acts has become more and more important, from the 1970s onwards, a host of new companies have sprung up providing technical and other forms of support, including amplification specialists, but also lighting and set designers, and so on.

◆ The rise of a discourse of entrepreneurialism in the economy as a whole (Keat and Abercrombie, 1991): There has been increasing emphasis since the 1970s on the value of 'going it alone', separately from large bureaucratic organisations. This has not only made people willing to set up their own businesses, but it has made large businesses more willing to interact with them.

◆ As culture has become recognised as a valid form of profit making, banks have become much more prepared to lend venture capital to small and medium-sized cultural businesses.

◆ As we have seen, industries such as television, dominated by vertically-integrated companies, have seen some disintegration. This has not only brought about an independent production sector, it has also created many ancillary and technical support companies, from film and television catering specialists to companies that rent out editing suites and personnel.

◆ There has been an increasing emphasis in cultural-industry companies on marketing. So there are also scores of design studios, independent advertising agencies and so on aimed at servicing companies that are increasingly willing to pay more to market their goods and services. What is more, actors, performers and other symbol creators can subsidise their other work, which they may feel is their 'real' work, by operating in these sectors. This has always happened, but now more than ever.

Accounts that focus on conglomeration, integration and the increasing size of the cultural-industry corporations (such as many accounts from the Schiller–McChesney tradition) often understate the importance of small companies. Such companies may account for small levels of market share, but they are important in terms of the numbers of people they employ, and in terms of their potential to foster – or at least act as a conduit for – innovation. This, along with other factors, has meant a strong ethical and aesthetic premium has been placed on institutional independence.

This is particularly apparent in the film industry (I discuss film indies in Chapter 8) and in the recording industry. Crucial in many music genres has been a discourse of independence amongst musicians, fans and journalists. This has allowed independent record companies, in some exceptional cases, to serve as the centre of commercial networks which form something of an alternative to prevailing systems of cultural production and consumption. For Jason Toynbee, the particular importance attached to independent production in popular music derives from a long-standing history of 'institutional autonomy' (Toynbee, 2000: 19–25) in popular music-making, which cuts against the efforts of large companies to make profits out of music. This derives from the dispersed, decentralised nature of music-making. Institutional autonomy means that not only do companies cede control of production to musicians (as in all cultural industries); there is also a tendency towards 'spatially dispersed production in small units' (rock groups, swing bands) and 'a strong continuity between production and consumption' in musical subcultures (Toynbee, 2000: 1). Audiences and performers come together in 'proto-markets', which are only partially commodified, and where there is a great deal of resentment towards the industry and 'selling out'. The possibility of institutional autonomy and the high value attached to it in musical subcultures means that spaces have been created where alternative arrangements for the management and marketing of creativity can be tried out. I discuss an important example of such an 'alternative' dynamic later in this chapter.

## Interdependence, interfirm networks and alliances

Small companies, then, not only continue to exist; they are multiplying. However, there is a vital caveat, already referred to in passing in the above discussion of independent record companies. A key change in the cultural industries in the years since the 1970s has been that small and large companies are increasingly interdependent: they are involved in complex networks of licensing, financing and distribution.

One of the most important ways in which corporations have changed their organisational structures, in nearly all major areas of business, is that they increasingly subcontract to small and medium-sized firms (see Chapter 3 on organisational innovation in the wake of the Long Downturn). These smaller firms are potentially more dynamic and able to innovate; but they are increasingly involved in close relationships with the corporations that subcontract to them. This is true too of the cultural industries.

Such webs of interdependence are not entirely new in the cultural industries. In the film industry, as the Hollywood corporations lost their control over production in the 1950s, new independent production companies entered the market to cater for specialist products, but the Hollywood studios acted as distributors and financiers of independently-produced films (see Aksoy and Robins, 1992). Even in an era in the recording industry when 'majors' and 'independents' were seen by fans, musicians and critics as polar opposites, in truth they were often linked in licensing, financing and distribution deals. Such arrangements, whereby small and large companies form interdependent webs, became increasingly prevalent in the 1980s and extended into new areas of the cultural industries, most significantly in European broadcasting, where traditionally production had been handled 'in house' by large state and public service broadcasters (Robins and Cornford, 1992).

There are rewards for both corporations and small companies in such systems of interfirm networking. For the corporations, acting as distributors and financiers of independent producers is an extension of what they already do, in acting as distributors and financiers of their own semi-autonomous divisions. A large multi-divisional corporation might get a lower cut of revenues from a text produced by an independent company than from the sales of a text created within one of their own divisions, but the arrangement means that they can get independent companies to bear some of the risks associated with the difficult business of managing symbolic creativity. What is more, symbol creators might well *feel* as though they are more autonomous of commercial pressures, especially in cultural industries where there is a mistrust of corporate bureaucracies.

This makes interdependence sound very rosy. However, in the eyes of many, increasing levels of interdependence in the cultural industries mean the end of an era when independents could provide an alternative to the majors: another sign of corporate takeover. And many forms of interfirm networking involve links between very large companies in different industries, and increasingly in different sectors. These involve strategic alliances between corporations, not as in traditional cartel arrangements, but on the basis of specific projects. Such 'alliance capitalism' has been a feature of a very wide range of businesses over the last 20 years. It is especially relevant, says Castells (1996: 162–4), in high-tech sectors, where research and development costs are enormously expensive. For Castells, the self-sufficient corporation is increasingly a thing of the past.

While cultural-industry companies compete with each other, at the same time, they operate complex webs of joint ventures and ownership. Auletta (1997: 225) lists a number of reasons for such alliances with potential rivals:

- To avoid competition
- To save money and share risks
- To buy a seat on a rival's board
- To create a safety net, as technological innovation makes for increasing uncertainty
- To make links with foreign companies to avoid 'arousing the ire of local governments'

The interconnections amongst the six biggest cultural-industry corporations and the 'second tier' of the Big 48 are almost impossible to encapsulate neatly. One of the best attempts to capture the complexity of links between different corporations was printed by *The New Yorker* in 1997 (see Figure 5.1). It shows the 'web of collaboration' between six of the most powerful cultural-industry corporations in the world at the time, plus Microsoft, and lists some of the many joint ventures between them. In the rapidly-changing world of the cultural industries, this diagram is already a

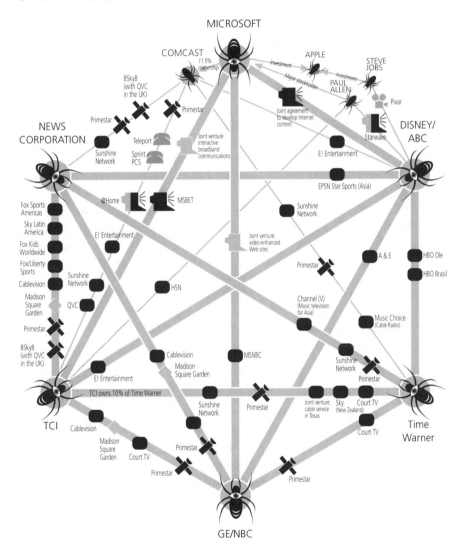

**Figure 5.1   A web of collaboration. This diagram, reproduced from a 1997 edition of *The New Yorker*, illustrates the many complex connections existing at the time between a number of companies in the cultural-industry and IT business (Auletta, 1997: 227)**

historical document; but it gives a good sense of how closely intermeshed the major companies are, in terms of joint ventures and ownership. Auletta (1997) describes such links as an American version of keiretsu – the 'ancient Japanese custom of co-opting the competition' through creating structures of collaboration with rivals; a system of 'co-opetition' (Murdock, 2000: 48, quoting *The Financial Times*) rather than competition. As Auletta (1997: 226) suggests, such alliances have implications for texts. As more and more companies become tied to one another, will their journalists cover controversial stories about other companies in the web? Without question, it helps to reinforce the economic power of the biggest corporations. Such alliances have been further encouraged by speculation about future convergence of the telecommunications, computers and cultural industries (see Chapter 7).[7]

## Governance, control and creativity

So far, I have been mainly discussing the structure and strategies of cultural-industry companies. We have seen that these companies have become larger and more powerful, and that there is more to an analysis of structure and strategy than a story of ever-increasing power. Strategies change with fashion; and small companies remain important. None of this, however, has addressed certain questions that I signalled as crucial in Chapter 2 of this book: How has the distinctive organisational form of the cultural industries changed in the 1980s and 1990s? How have the terms and conditions of cultural work changed during this period? There is a vast field to cover here, but Howard Davis and Richard Scase (2000: 104–27) provide a way into understanding changes in the management of symbolic creativity. They argue that there has been a shift in organisational form in the cultural industries. Using a Weberian approach that focuses on bureaucracy and charisma, they posit four ideal types of cultural-industry organisation, based on how companies control and coordinate work (Davis and Scase, 2000: 99):

♦ *Commercial bureaucracies*, where control and coordination are highly explicit and formalised, emphasising hierarchical reporting mechanisms and the close measuring and monitoring of employees for performance; there is a very strong emphasis on making profit built into the functioning of the organisation.
♦ *Traditional/charismatic organisations*, in which a high level of coordination is achieved through shared values but where 'mechanisms of

---

7 See Herman and McChesney (1997: 56–8) and Murdock (2000: 47–51) for further discussion of such alliances.

formal control are relatively less developed'; these tend to be small businesses. There is less emphasis in working life on profit. Charismatic leaders – often owner-managers – tend to provide direction.

♦ *Cultural bureaucracies*, usually operating under a public service remit, where there is a high degree of formalised control and hierarchically structured authority relations, but coordination is achieved through relatively autonomous departments; there are strong clashes over commercial pressures. Davis and Scase seem to have the BBC in mind here.

♦ *Network organisations*, which tend to be micro-companies and are essentially too small to have formalised control or coordination; they operate in networks with other companies.

Davis and Scase believe that a major shift in cultural-industry organisations during the 1990s has been the decline of the traditional/charismatic organisation and the cultural bureaucracy and the corresponding rise of the commercial bureaucracy and network organisations (p. 102). Traditional/charismatic firms, such as the small publishing houses that were the centre of the book industry until the 1950s, have been bought up by corporations, and put within commercial bureaucracies. Cultural bureaucracies such as the BBC are under threat from commercial pressures. Network organisations have proliferated as more and more work is outsourced from cultural and commercial bureaucracies. For Davis and Scase, changes within commercial bureaucracies have been just as important as the increasing presence of such companies in the cultural industries. They claim that as large conglomerates entered into the cultural industries in the 1960s and 1970s, they attempted to bureaucratise creative work in a number of ways: by rationalising and specialising work tasks, curtailing the autonomy of employees by stipulating duties and by establishing strict line management. But, according to Davis and Scase, such practices soon fell out of favour, and were replaced by new, organisational innovations. In order to move beyond mere compliance on the part of employees and in order to foster the kinds of commitment found in smaller companies, commercial bureaucracies began to break the larger organisation into smaller autonomous operating units. Instead of strict, hierarchical line management, workers were given autonomy for operational decision making. In Davis and Scase's account, this resulted in 'highly decentralised organisational structures operating units functioning as subsidiary companies' (139). Under this new system, control was exercised through tight financial budgets, the setting of deadlines and through measuring outputs (140–1). These changes took place 'in the 1990s, and sometimes earlier' (130). Management–worker relations become more like those between purchasers and providers and because work could therefore either be done in-house, or out-of-house, this led to the growth of network firms outside the company (and presumably 'downsizing' within the commercial bureaucracy).

This is an interesting attempt to understand change, but it is a flawed one. Davis and Scase overemphasise organisational change, especially in commercial bureaucracies.[8] In particular, they misrepresent the 1950–80 period, drawing on assumptions derived from other industries. Substantial operational autonomy for creative personnel has been a feature of large cultural-industry companies throughout the complex professional era, not only in the 1990s (Ryan, 1992; Toynbee, 2000). Davis and Scase recognise that creative personnel are given relative autonomy, and it may be that they are referring primarily to the operational autonomy of creative managers. But even here, their historical assumptions are not supported by the evidence. In the large publishing companies established in the post-war era, for example, commissioning editors were given considerable autonomy (Coser et al., 1982), as indeed were A&R personnel in record companies. The film industry made the kind of move from 'bureaucracy' to 'networks' that Davis and Scase describe, from the early 1940s onwards, and producers (the key creative managers in the industry) increasingly came to operate as independent companies during the 1950s and 1960s. It is true that some companies did try to control production more closely during the period 1950–80 – the period Davis and Scase are discussing as the era of the 'old' commercial bureaucratic model. One example would be formatted popular fiction, such as Mills & Boon's romance novels. But such formatted production with tight control over budgets and outcomes long preceded the 1950–80 period and often took place in smaller companies which Davis and Scase might categorise as 'traditional/charismatic' rather than in the commercial bureaucracies. There *have* been organisational innovations during what I am calling the complex professional era, but Davis and Scase are wrong to assume that the 1990s was the crucial period for change. Many shifts long precede the 1990s: for example, an important move towards divisional structures in the major record companies took place in the 1970s and was based on generic divisions that were already in place when record companies were smaller (see Christianen, 1995: 89–91; Negus, 1999: 47–50).[9]

In my view, Ryan's work on cultural-industry organisations provides a better basis for assessing change and continuity than does Davis and

---

8 It would have been helpful if Davis and Scase had given concrete examples of pre-1990s commercial bureaucracies of the 'old' kind.

9 There are strong echoes in Davis and Scase's model of the faulty historical assumptions in work on 'post-Fordism' and 'flexible specialisation' in the cultural industries. See Christopherson and Storper (1986; 1989) and Lash and Urry (1994: Chapter 5) for the most sophisticated versions of cultural-industry post-Fordism; and Aksoy and Robins (1992) and Hesmondhalgh (1996) for critiques of their positions.

Scase's model. Chapter 2, building on Ryan (1992), outlined the division of cultural labour and organisational form characteristic of the complex professional era. As we saw there, four main cultural-work functions had emerged by the middle of the twentieth century: primary creative personnel/symbol creators, technical craft workers, creative managers and owners and executives. The organisational form common across nearly all cultural-industry companies was one in which creative personnel were loosely controlled, by creative managers acting on behalf of the interests of owners and executives, but circulation and reproduction were much more tightly coordinated. In smaller companies, owner-managers acted like creative managers in dealing with creative personnel, but like executives in negotiating relationships with outside distribution, reproduction, marketing and publicity organisations.

To what extent is the distinctive division of labour and organisational form, involving loose control of creativity by creative managers but tight control of circulation by executives, a stable one? I want to argue that, although there are superficial signs of a loosening of control in some cultural industries, the strongest trend is towards a much more careful coordination of cultural work, rather than in the direction suggested by Davis and Scase, towards looser control in networks.

## The increasing importance of marketing

The most important change in organisational control in the cultural industries is that the variety of activities known as marketing has become professionalised and more important to the coordination of activities in the cultural industries. This represents a further tightening of control over circulation strategies.

One important example of the increasing importance of marketing is the increasing intensity of efforts to use market research as a means of controlling risk. Justin Wyatt, for example, argues that although market research was used occasionally in the classic Hollywood era, it was only in the late 1970s that the studios seriously engaged in such methods (Wyatt, 1994: 155). Wyatt attributes the shift in part to the purchase by general conglomerates of film companies in the 1960s. Films were now part of a culture that was used to market research in packaged goods. As releases fell and as costs rose, executives wanted more accountability (Wyatt, 1994: 156). Keith Negus has described a shift in record-company strategy away from 'inspired guesswork, hunches and intuition' and towards the widespread use of various research methods, including electronic monitoring of sales, large-scale interview panels provided on subscription by a separate company, and various broadcast data systems (Negus, 1999: 53). Again, the shift seems to have taken place in the 1970s, and although Negus does not attribute the shift to this, it was during this period that the recording industry was increasingly integrated into larger, general conglomerates. As for television, here is one television executive discussing the importance of research:

> Research is the key instrument in the selling of air time because if I'm selling a minute or half a minute of air time in *Coronation Street*, *Coronation Street* will have a number of categories, demographic categories of viewers watching. It will have young ABC1 men or whatever. No, unless you know precisely which demographic groups in which proportions are watching these programmes very scientifically you can't sell that audience at the optimum value to the advertiser. So for example an advertiser can buy adults in *Coronation Street* for eight pounds a thousand but if he wants to buy ABC1 adults it might be forty-eight pounds a thousand. And if he wants to buy 16–24 year old adults it might be seventy-eight pounds a thousand and that's a hell of a different yield. So it's a bit like an aeroplane or a hotel. You're maximising the yields of your rooms or your airtime seconds by optimising who buys what audiences . . .[10]

This way of talking about research would have been impossible 30 years ago in Europe. Only in the last 30 years has market research become such a priority that software packages of sufficient sophistication have been developed to undertake such exact calculations. But it is not technology that has driven the change. Such technology came into being largely because of the desire on the part of executives to control more carefully the value chain in broadcasting, partly because of the erosion of public service imperatives, but also because of an enormous increase in competition in the television market.

The other major relevant aspects of marketing besides research – design, packaging, advertising, and publicity management – have been present in the cultural industries for many decades, but have also increased their importance and visibility. Budgets for advertising in films produced by the major Hollywood studios soared in the 1980s and 1990s. Even though the average cost of producing the negative/first copy of a major-produced film more than doubled between 1980 and 1995 to US$39 million, during the same period advertising budgets greatly increased their proportion of total costs, to nearly 45 per cent (based on Dale, 1997: 31). Advertising has long been important in the film industry, but there has been a move towards 'blitzkrieg marketing' (Dale, 1997: 32) whereby blockbusters open simultaneously across a particular country, rather than being 'rolled out' in different regions. Publicity marketing has also become much more important in industries where it has traditionally played a minor role. This is true of television in particular, where there is now a greatly increased emphasis on trailers, on print and billboard advertising

---

10 From an interview with the Chief Executive of a British media group, February 2001, for a related project on the conditions of creative work.

to support premium programmes, and on back-up articles in newspapers and magazines. Unless a programme has such backup, even if it is shown in a relatively prime-time slot, it has little chance of success.

All the above illustrates the increasing importance of marketing in the cultural industries. But an even more significant issue is the role of marketing in the conception stage of cultural production. This is important, because it potentially undermines the traditional division between loose control of creative work, and tight control of reproduction and circulation, which as we have seen constitutes the distinctive organisational form of cultural production in the complex professional era. Marketing departments have been consulted for decades on the likely success of cultural products that require significant investment – whether in the form of production costs, or on the basis of large payments to the creators. What is new is the increasing prestige of marketing departments, and their increasing clout in settings where decisions are negotiated concerning the selection of prospective acts or products, and how they might be modified to achieve 'success'. This may in turn derive from a partial erosion of the principle that creative work ought to be autonomous of commerce. It may be that people working in cultural-industry organisations are finding it harder to argue against short-term commercial imperatives in the name of prestige, or providing creative innovation.

Wyatt argues that the increased role of marketers in making decisions over what movies – and which types – get made led to the rise of the 'high concept' movie in 1980s Hollywood. The high concept movie is, in essence, one whose central idea can be conveyed in a single sentence, both in the initial pitch of the film to financiers, etc; and also to audiences in the marketing of the product. The film *The Player* (1992) dramatised high concept beautifully in the form of numerous such pitches. At the core of high concept, then, is the reduction of narrative to a simple, underlying idea. Wyatt considers that the rise of high concept was a major factor in bringing about a decline in the quality of Hollywood cinema during the 1980s and 1990s following the years of Hollywood's embrace of cultural prestige in the 1970s (see Biskind, 1998). It is not impossible for qualities of complexity, richness and ambivalence to survive the domination of high concept – and Wyatt pays insufficient attention to this possibility. But in my opinion high concept makes such qualities more difficult to achieve, other things being equal. Although there are many countervailing tendencies against formula and repetition in cultural production, and although marketers are quite happy to promote original products as distinctive and unique, there is a strong tendency in marketing to embrace the familiar. As Bill Ryan puts it (1992: 220): 'Marketers need predictable commodities to work their magic on'. Or in the words of one veteran market researcher, Hy Hollinger, quoted by Wyatt (1994: 59), 'Anything that is innovative is hard for market research to clue in on'. A particularly notorious use of market research in what is effectively still the creative stage of cultural production is the screening of movies to test audiences, with a view to amending the film in response to audience questionnaires. The most quoted example is *Fatal Attraction* (1987) – Glenn Close's character originally committed suicide to an aria from *Madam Butterfly* but after poor test responses, the ending to the film was changed, and her character was killed. Most major Hollywood films are now tested, and nearly all tests are carried out by the National Research Group based in Los Angeles (Lerner, 1999). Many successful films test poorly, but go on to achieve success. They include innovative movies such as *The Blair Witch Project* and *Reservoir Dogs* (Lerner, 1999). The National Research Group recruit an audience whose demographic characteristics supposedly match those of the film's target audience. They fill in response cards and some may take part in a focus group discussion. Some directors, especially those of comedies, embrace the process; many resist, and find that executives can use tests as ammunition. The tests are a means of attempting to find objectivity in order to deal with the perennial unpredictability of the film business. But directors opposed to the process think that it favours restrictive control of creativity. As one director puts it, 'If the test is bad, the studio panics. If it goes well, they say, "It doesn't mean anything" ' (Andrew Bergman, quoted by Willens, 2000: 11).

## Control of creativity: still loose, but tighter

The increasing presence and status of marketing, then, represents a shift in the organisational structure of cultural production. But not all changes in the cultural industries can be uniformly understood as an increase in commercially-oriented aspects of cultural-industry work at the expense of creative autonomy. Sean Nixon (1997) writes about the 'creative revolution' in British advertising in the late 1970s and 1980s, a development which was 'established in opposition to what was represented as the boring and unimaginative advertising produced by the large multinational agencies' (Nixon, 1997: 195). The old advertising practices were more reliant on the written or spoken word, and attempted to convey the 'unique selling point' of the product. The new, more creative advertisements worked at the levels of desire and identity, rather than via the 'hard sell'. Nixon attributes the shift towards 'creative' advertising, involving much greater levels of autonomy for creative staff, primarily to new forms of market research in advertising agencies, which meant that advertisers were much more concerned to target specific market segments than entire social classes or 'the mass audience'. So here a greater use of market research seemingly led to greater levels of operational autonomy for creative personnel, in the most commercially-oriented of all cultural industries. However, it may be that Nixon is dealing with a very particular case here. Creative personnel in advertising are highly unusual in the context of the cultural industries as a whole. The main goal of their work is to sell goods and services – or to increase the value of the companies they promote. Advertising creatives were probably more tightly controlled in terms of being judged on financial outcomes than most creative personnel in other cultural industries. So a relative loosening of control for the most highly-paid and prestigious creatives is not necessarily typical of trends in the cultural industries as a whole.

As a contrasting example, we might take an area of creativity that was previously well protected from commercial imperatives in the conception and execution stages: live theatre. This is an industry which may once have been classifiable as peripheral, in the terms established in the Introduction, but which is moving nearer to the core cultural industries, as it becomes a multimillion dollar industry, with much investment from some of the largest transnational cultural-industry corporations. Jonathan Burston (1999) argues that, as the profit-making potential of live entertainment has become more apparent, and as the sector has therefore become increasingly integrated into entertainment conglomerates, assembly-line production methods have become increasingly apparent in theatre. Burston examines the megamusicals which have dominated live theatre economics over the last 20 years: shows such as *Cats*, *The Phantom of the Opera*, *Miss Saigon* and *Disney's Beauty and the Beast*, large-scale musical works with very big casts and a strong emphasis on special effects. The huge amounts of money invested in, and made from, these shows, has meant that production companies very carefully control what can be done with their intellectual property after the original production of the show. Shows are 'franchised' by their owners, and can only be put on if very specific conditions are met. The consequence for those involved in such productions is, in Burston's view, increasing alienation. One of his interviewees, a director, described his deep dislike of 'having to be the person who stands there and says, "[male principal], you're six inches too far to the left" . . . and who trains endless [male principals and female principals] to go through the mechanics again' (Burston, 1999: 75). This raises important questions concerning the working conditions of creative personnel that I shall return to below.

Davis and Scase's case for the loosening of control through the growth of network organisations in the cultural industries in part rests on the idea that, within commercial bureaucracies, creative managers are gaining more autonomy. The key creative managers in British television, a system that encouraged creative autonomy in the name of public service, were producers. Examining the extent to which their working conditions changed during the 1980s and 1990s provides a good test case of the fate of creative autonomy. How did their creative autonomy fare in the profound transformations that swept through British broadcasting in those years? British television producers have always had some managerial role, and because of the public service nature of the British system, they were less driven by commercial imperatives than was the case with other creative managers such as editors in publishing companies, or A&R personnel in record companies. This was true even in the commercial sector of British television, which was strongly governed by public service obligations from its inception in the 1950s. Television producers effectively functioned in many cases as leaders of creative teams which, in many situations, they could build themselves (see Tunstall, 1993: 24–6). They were answerable to a number of higher decisions from senior management, especially regarding scheduling, overall budget and number of programmes and broad editorial directions, but their autonomy within these overall guidelines was considered the guarantee of quality within the British system.

Jeremy Tunstall (1993) provided a rare, detailed study of British television producers across both commercial and cultural bureaucracies, to use Davis and Scase's terms. The roles of producers had changed by the early 1990s, according to Tunstall. This was partly because of changes in the BBC and the ITV companies, but also because more and more production took place in independent companies. Tunstall says that producers became 'more autonomous' (Tunstall, 1993: 202) but this increased autonomy from senior managers came at a cost. Many producers were increasingly insecure in their jobs, or had lost them altogether. But even those producers who kept their jobs were being asked to do more and more things. Increasingly, producers were expected to raise their own funds. They had to spend more time talking about, and working on, budgets and money than ever before. They had to commission out to other producers as well as making programmes themselves. They had to make more decisions about resources, including which freelance crews to use. Tunstall sums up their changed roles as less secure, more responsible and more autonomous (1993: 203). Here we see the contradictory nature of the creative autonomy characteristic of the cultural industries. In this case, increasing independence from senior managers means slavery to administrative concerns. There seems often to be a trade-in between finding creative space and the huge 'emotional investment' (Tunstall, 1993: 202) necessary to undertake such creative work.

## Journalistic autonomy and media moguls

Questions regarding autonomy from commercial and ideological pressure have been particularly debated in studies of journalism. Journalists put great emphasis on their autonomy from owners and from other powerful influences in society. A series of important sociological studies in the 1970s suggested that journalists worked relatively autonomously of the demands of newspaper owners and senior executives (Tunstall, 1971; Tuchman, 1978; Gans, 1979). But others, particularly those writing from political economy approaches, have argued in response that such studies over-stated the independence of journalists. James Curran (1990), for example, preferred the term 'licensed autonomy' to 'relative autonomy' and remarked that 'journalists are allowed to be independent only as long as their independence is exercised in a form that conforms to the require-ments of their employing organisations' (1990: 120). Curran argued that the British press had shifted in the 1970s and 1980s to a more partisan stance than for many decades, under the influence of a new generation of interventionist owners. Curran provided evidence of how, under this new regime, British press journalists were pushed by their senior executives to write stories presenting the left-wing Greater London Council of the 1980s in a negative light; broadcasting organisations portrayed the Council much more favourably, for a mixture of organisational and cultural reasons.

Curran's point is supported by the evidence which emerges from time to time of conglomerates using news organs to promote their business interests. Bagdikian (2000: xxv–xxvii) recounts incidents that suggest increasing damage to 'the Wall of Separation between Church and State' – the Church in this metaphor being editorial independence and the State being the business interests of the newspaper. He tells the story of how in the late 1990s a new CEO of Time-Mirror Company, one Mark Willes, reorganised the company's flagship paper, *The Los Angeles Times*, so that news stories would be allocated by a staff which included someone from the business department of the newspaper. News staff were, it seems, increasingly involved in special corporate advertisements.

The notion of journalistic autonomy is further qualified by the increas-ing efforts on the part of other organisations and institutions to position themselves as key sources. There has been a huge explosion in the public relations industry over the last four decades, across a number of fields. In the UK in 1963, there were an estimated 3,000 public relations professionals; in 1995, the top 150 consultancies alone employed a total of 4,854 staff (Miller, 1998: 67). While journalists in general retain an attitude of pro-fessional scepticism towards efforts to attract their interest and sympathy, in practice this involves forming hierarchies of sources, from most trusted down to unknown and therefore untrustworthy. Naturally, the most powerful organisations often have the most credibility. Recent studies have shown that the access to journalists does not depend entirely on resources; sometimes weaker and oppositional sources are given great prestige (Schlesinger and Tumber, 1994). Nevertheless the pressures on journalists exerted by the more powerful and wealthy organisations can be tremendous. Journalists, then, even if they act in relative autonomy from the requirements of owners and executives on a daily basis, are not independent of other pressures to pursue particular interests; and their everyday autonomy is shaped and formed by the overall interests of the organisation they work for.[11]

It is worth looking at Curran's point about interventionist owners in more detail. In the market professional era (late nineteenth century and early twentieth century) strong individuals dominated the family firms that ran the newspapers and publishing companies at the heart of the cultural industries. In other industries, family firms with dominant figures have given way to complex systems of control, under boards of directors, where most directors represent other companies, and where there are many interlocking directorships. This has happened in the cultural industries too, but the figure of the media mogul, who owns a dominant interest and has an overpowering control over his own company, has been remarkably persistent in the complex professional era. Even as cultural-industry corporations grow in size and complexity, a large number remain under the control of such individuals.

Many media moguls are prepared to push their own political views extremely hard through their cultural-industry interests. Perhaps the most spectacular example of the pursuit of political ambition through media ownership in advanced industrial countries in recent years is the case of Silvio Berlusconi, who by promoting his political party 'Forza Italia' across his various television, publishing and sports interests, managed to make himself prime minister of Italy in 1994 (see Mazzoleni, 1995) and again in 2001.[12] But the most internationally prominent of all media moguls is Rupert Murdoch. Curran (1990) showed how *The Sunday Times*, once it had been taken over by Rupert Murdoch's News International, moved from a centre-right, even liberal newspaper to a Thatcherite one (1990: 132–3). Murdoch revived the strategies of direct control associated with press barons of the early twentieth century, such as Northcliffe, Beaverbrook and Hearst (the man on whom Orson Welles based *Citizen Kane*). Murdoch would apparently rewrite leaders that were insufficiently supportive of the hard-right Prime Minister Margaret Thatcher, and removed left-leaning or moderate conservative editors. He exerted pressure on his liberal editor at *The Times* by refusing to fix an editorial budget, and thereby gaining the chance to approve any editorial decision that needed significant spending. The centre-right editor at *The Sunday Times* was forced out to make way for the Thatcher-supporting Andrew Neil. Overt and abrasive pressure was applied to journalists to reorient the editorial direction of the paper. More

---

11 An interesting, important and neglected issue is the degree to which the notion of professional autonomy in other, non-journalistic fields differs from autonomy in journalism.

12 Mancini and Hallin (2001) argue that Berlusconi's 2001 success was not achieved by using his television stations for propaganda, but rather through using his television empire as a resource for negotiation and bargaining with other political, economic and social individuals and institutions.

than 100 journalists left the paper between 1981 and 1986 (the staff was 170 strong in 1981). *The Sunday Times* has pursued a far-right editorial policy ever since.

But surely, given that Murdoch owns a vast global media empire, operational autonomy is left to editors? Not necessarily. In a more recent chapter, Curran (1998: 87) quotes Andrew Neil, now a senior executive elsewhere, on his experience at *The Sunday Times*:

> Rupert has an uncanny knack of being there even when he is not. When I did not hear from him and I knew his attention was elsewhere, he was still uppermost in my mind . . . Rupert expects his papers to stand broadly for what he believes: a combination of right-wing republicanism from America with undiluted Thatcherism from Britain.

Moguls receive tremendous amounts of attention, partly because the media thrive on reporting the actions of charismatic individuals. Such interventions are extremely important but they are, in the context of the cultural industries, relatively rare. They illustrate that autonomy is never irrevocable. But focusing to an excessive degree on media moguls can distract attention from systemic features of the cultural industries. It can obscure the central importance – and ambivalence – of the operational autonomy granted to journalists and other creative personnel in cultural-industry companies. Direct intervention by owners and senior executives of the kind analysed by Curran must not be ignored, but neither should the very indirect coercion exercised in professional cultures. The notion of journalistic autonomy still holds strong as a means of gaining legitimacy and credibility for cultural-industry organisations. Gitlin (1997: 8) suggests that since 1990, NBC has routinely covered scandals involving its parent company General Electric; and that ABC News's Peter Jennings has 'gone out of his way to cover criticisms of Disney'.[13] In Gitlin's view, the greater danger is self-censorship: that journalists decide not to pursue certain interests that might clash with a corporate culture; and that news media will be used to promote entertainment aspects of the conglomerate's business. (I return to these issues in Chapter 8.)

## Terms and conditions of cultural work

How have the terms and conditions of cultural work changed during the 1980s and 1990s? We can examine this question by looking at the working

---

13 McChesney (1999: 52) offers more recent evidence of corporate interference: he claims that ABC dropped a report on the conditions of workers at Disney World in 1998. But the *New York Times* report he cites (Carter, 1998) suggests that the item was not about workers' conditions, but about inadequate checks on employees' criminal records, and was mainly based on conservative sources.

conditions, career paths etc. of three of the four main types of job in the cultural industries. Before doing this, we should note the increasing importance of new categories of cultural work, including most notably *agents*, who act as mediators between cultural-industry organisations and the pool of creative workers. Caves (2000) suggests that such agents were once shunned by companies but are now welcomed as a means of reducing recruitment costs in book publishing, in film and television, and the various performing arts. He explains why by quoting figures by Coser et al. (1982: 130–2) that only three or four out of 10,000 books submitted for publication are accepted. Agents do some of the publishing company's filtering work for them. Artist managers perform a similar function in the recording industry; and an important change in recent years has been the increasingly entrepreneurial role played by managers, or management teams, in recruiting and training bands, often using finance capital they have raised themselves. In this respect, the recording industry is becoming a little bit more like the film industry, with managers acting as independent producers who attempt to 'develop' a particular project.

Having noted this change, another preliminary remark is in order: to note the *continuity* involved in the division of labour characteristic of the cultural industries. The four types of cultural work discussed in Chapter 2 remain broadly intact.

### Technical personnel

The number of people performing relatively humdrum, but essential, work in the cultural industries has vastly increased, partly because there is so much more product available than ever before, but also because much of it involves factory-style reproduction and wholesaling. While some unionised technical workers are paid relatively well (for example, camera operators in the film and television industries), in general technical workers are now exploited on an unprecedented scale. In the advanced industrial countries, there has been large-scale de-unionisation. Internationalisation means that many humdrum tasks can be shifted abroad to countries where labour laws are even weaker than in the USA or the UK. This has been the case in animation, as John A. Lent (1998) shows. Although the working practices he examines are not so exploitative as offshore production in the clothing/fashion industries (see Ross, 1998), US companies such as Hanna-Barbera have achieved huge economies by opening major offshore studios in Australia (1974) and Taiwan (1978). Most animation is now carried out for US and European companies in Asia. Disney contracted for many years to a set of Japanese subsidiaries, and by the 1990s Disney Japan was subcontracting most of its work to South Korea or China.

## Creative management

Ryan (1992: Section 4.3.2) argues that creative management has become much more professionalised in recent years, in that its roles and duties are established and are even, in some cases, formally taught on courses. The creative management function has become completely established in all 'mature' cultural industries, and has increasingly come to be carried out in teams. This has spawned internal divisions of labour and hierarchies. For example, the A&R department in a record company will include a senior manager who might have responsibility for dealing with more established artists, or for pushing through the signing of an expensive act, while younger, new members of the team will take on more of the work of making contacts and sampling new acts, whether in the form of recordings or live shows. Some creative managers achieve a kind of stardom within their own area, and because such managers are now increasingly mobile, can command higher financial rewards than ever before. After the conglomerates entered book publishing in the 1960s, and introduced strict accounting and bureaucratic managerial practices, it became common for successful commissioning editors (the main form of creative management in that industry) to leave the conglomerates in order to set up their own smaller company – which is often taken over by a conglomerate years later. In the last 30 years, there has been a trend towards the same thing in the recording industry, as A&R personnel leave to set up their own independent company. Once again, we see the 'networked' nature of much cultural work: creative managers move back and forth between independent production and corporate cultures.

## Symbol creators

The pool or reservoir of underemployed creative labour discussed by Miège (see Chapter 2, in this book) is getting bigger, because of a number of interrelated factors. The cultural industries might *appear* to be more open in access to their prospective workers, because of the proliferation of cultural forms and technologies. Yet people are prepared to spend longer in the pool. This is partly a result of the fact that people are increasingly aware of the intensely competitive nature of entry to the cultural industries. Also, casualisation in advanced industrial economies means that more and more people are prepared to accept long periods of time without secure employment, and to mix jobs. More than anything else, though, the willingness of so many hundreds of thousands of people to take their place in the reservoir of cultural labour is the consequence of a commitment to doing creative work which they can be proud of. Discourses of creativity, in other words, continue to play an important economic function.

Creative workers work tremendously long hours under difficult conditions. They trade in financial reward and security for creative autonomy.

But a model of power as coercion is insufficient to explain this. There is rarely an authority figure present to tell symbol creators to work so hard for so little reward. In fact all cultural workers, creative workers, and to some extent creative managers and technical personnel, sometimes accept poorer working conditions (for example, long, difficult hours) for the benefits of being involved in creative projects. And some cultural-industry work is hardly creative at all, such as outsourced animation work done according to order (Lent, 1998).

Rewards for creative work continue to be very uneven, with very high rewards for the few superstar creative workers and much less for other workers, including creative managers and technical personnel. Montgomery and Robinson (1993; cited by Caves, 2000: 79) provide some figures on this, and though they are drawn mainly from the world of artists and professional classical musicians, they indicate some of the dynamics likely to be found in other cultural industries. A 1989 survey of 2,000 visual artists found that median earnings from art were only about US$3,000. The same study showed that the costs of pursuing such a career were about US$9,625, so median net income was minus US$6,000! Median total earnings, including other work, for the various artists in this group came to between US$10,000 and US$20,000. Family and other jobs provide the support to get creative workers through.

What about symbol creators who do manage to achieve access to the cultural industries? Their rewards are dependent on the contract they sign, as we saw in Chapter 2. But creative workers are dependent on more than just the contract for their rewards; they are also dependent on the work done by the cultural-industry company. Deals in the recording industry will serve as an example. Publishing and recording deals for musicians have generally taken the following form during the complex professional era. Musicians agree to render their services exclusively to a company for a specified period and in certain specified territories. In return, the company will normally make commitments to promote the work of the artists. The musicians are paid an advance and then, when this advance has been recouped via sales, they are paid a royalty. The long history of dubious contracts and career-breaking rip-offs cannot be told here.[14] But there are two main areas of controversy surrounding the 'standard' advance-royalty/exclusivity contract between musicians and company. The first area concerns the financial rewards available for artists. The advance is essentially a loan against money that the musicians' recordings will make in the future. Repayment is 'cross-collateralised' against costs such as recording and touring: that is, the musicians pay for these promotional

---

14 Some important developments in contractual law in the cultural industries are surveyed by Greenfield and Osborn (1994); and, in a journalistic account, by Garfield (1986).

expenses out of their loan. In many cases, the advance is never recouped and musicians can be in debt to their record company for many years. Many young bands enter into this system unaware of the difficulties of recouping the substantial advances that they initially welcome.

There have been important changes since the 1970s. Musicians are much more aware of the dangers of rip-offs, and of the need to take legal advice when signing contracts. Royalty rates have risen considerably since the 1970s, when 7 to 9 per cent was common (Caves, 2000: 62) The level of royalty rate is set in the initial contract as a certain percentage of retail sales. Big stars gain much higher royalty rates (16 to 20 per cent, according to Caves, 2000: 62) whereas middle range acts get 14 to 16 per cent, and new acts get something like 11 to 13 per cent. Generally, the level of the royalty rises, as the musicians make more records – the justification for this is that the company has to invest more resources initially, in order to establish the musicians' careers. In most contracts, however, costs are still recoupable against royalties – in other words, musicians pay for their recording and for many promotional expenses out of their earnings. Yet the company retains the lion's share of the money and retains control of copyrights – increasingly, the source of much of the wealth in the cultural industries.

The second area of controversy relates to the creative autonomy of musicians and the level of commitment shown by a company to a symbol creator's output. A particularly important issue in the music business in recent years has been the restraints on symbol creators brought about by the long-term nature of the recording and/or publishing contract. Although established star names are able to negotiate relatively high royalty rates, many contracts remain very long term in nature – and this is actually a disadvantage for the artist. Normally, the company has a right to exercise an option or a series of options to retain the musician's services. Nearly all contracts are asymmetrical, however, in that the musician must fulfil certain criteria if s/he wants to be retained by the company, but s/he cannot choose to leave. These criteria will usually include sales – which are dependent on the efforts of the record company. A danger for musicians in being held to a long-term contract is that the sympathetic staff who signed them may leave the label, to be replaced by creative managers with little interest in the band. Another is that any change of direction by a musician may receive an unsympathetic reception from the record company.[15] These dangers remain current in the recording industry. In this particular respect,

---

15 This was a central issue in Panayioutou versus Sony Music Entertainment (UK) Limited – the George Michael case. Michael tried unsuccessfully to argue in this important dispute with his record company that his long-term contract with Sony was a 'restraint of trade' under European law. Other aspects of the 'standard contract' have recently been challenged in a lawsuit brought by Courtney Love against Universal Music Group (see *Financial Times: Music and Copyright*, March 2001).

little has changed since the 1970s except that record company staff are even more prone to moving between companies.

An important intervention in the recording industry attempted to change these arrangements and here we return to Toynbee's argument, referred to earlier, that the recording industry is marked by unusually high levels of 'institutional autonomy' (Toynbee, 2000: 19–25). At various independent record companies associated with punk in the late 1970s and 1980s, new ways of dealing with artists were developed which challenged the standard arrangements in the music industry. Deals with musicians were often on a 50-50 basis, rather than the single-figure percentage royalty rates usual at the time. Long-term contracts were rejected in favour of deals based on personal trust. The aim of such deals was to be as 'musician-centred' as possible. Contracts were avoided on the grounds that the standard contracts were loaded in favour of companies and that if the personal trust between musicians and companies broke down, there was no point in pursuing the relationship anyway. These companies generally favoured record by record deals, which gave artists the freedom to move on to other companies, should they wish to do so. The 50–50 deals meant that payment rates for musicians were enormously higher than the single-figure percentage royalty rates common even for established bands on major labels. If a band could achieve high sales on such a deal, they would make a great deal of money. Recognising the vital strategic importance of circulation, British punk independents formed distribution and retailing networks. What is more, many extremely talented musicians came to work with the punk independents because they wanted to work with people whom they felt had a closer understanding of their music than the creative managers in the transnational corporation divisions. Their records achieved considerable success and brought very different voices into the mainstream of British cultural life.[16]

The post-punk intervention illustrates the potential that many musicians and audiences have attached to independence, not only in terms of musical innovation but in terms of the politics surrounding the conditions of symbolic creativity. It also serves as an example of attempts to transform the apparatus of *commercial* cultural production. All too often, the literature on attempts to construct alternatives is confined to very small, marginal interventions, operating so far outside most people's experience of popular culture, that they are known only to small groups of activists and intellectuals. Here, however, activism took place actually in the field of commercial entertainment production itself. In the end, the post-punk rebellion was unsuccessful. The key companies went bankrupt; many

---

16 See Hesmondhalgh (1997; 1999) for a more detailed examination of the post-punk independents.

musicians became disenchanted with the limited promotional budgets available in small record companies; and gradually more and more independents forged distribution and/or financing deals with transnationals (Hesmondhalgh, 1999). But new genres continue to develop in proto-markets, and independent record companies still act as vital conduits for the more widespread dissemination of the music produced within them (see Hesmondhalgh, 1998 on electronic dance music).

◆ ◆ ◆

This chapter has provided evidence of considerable change in the ownership and organisation of the cultural industries, and in the nature of cultural work. Bigger-than-ever corporations tower over this new terrain. Their growth has been encouraged by the policy changes outlined in the previous chapter, along with various waves of mergers and acquisitions, and a growing perception amongst business investors that the cultural industries represented a good opportunity for high returns. This growth has helped to make the cultural industries more central in advanced industrial economies than they have been in the past – though they are still not in the league of Big Oil, the car industry, and the banks. The growth of the corporations has significant implications because such corporations can mobilise huge resources to campaign on behalf of their interests, and can put together the kinds of promotional budgets that allow their texts to gain more attention than any others. Within companies of all kinds, owners and executives are altering their strategies for managing creativity, resulting in what may be a diminution of creative and journalistic autonomy in the face of commercial imperatives. New types of relationship between companies have emerged. There are increasing numbers of strategic alliances between cultural-industry companies and large corporations in other industries. Small companies increasingly form complex licensing, financing and distribution deals with the major corporations.

But there is considerable continuity too. Small companies continue to play an important part in the cultural industries. The dynamics identified in the Introduction continue to drive company strategy, even if the exact form vertical integration and conglomeration take vary according to general business fashion. And loose control of symbolic creativity remains at the heart of the way companies manage creative work.

## Further reading

The best way of keeping in touch with developments in the ever-changing cultural industries is by reading business publications, such as *The Financial*

*Times*, the entertainment trade paper, *Variety*, or if you can tolerate the ultraconservative political perspectives they take, *The Wall Street Journal* and *The Economist*. *Variety* publishes its list of the top 50 global media companies every August. But knowing the details of who owns what this year, this month, this week is perhaps less important than understanding significant overall trends and what they say about issues of power in the cultural industries: hence my focus on trends and issues in this chapter. The most comprehensive treatment of the issues of concentration and integration is an obscure and hard-to-find book: Sánchez-Tabernero et al.'s 1993 study. Shorter treatments, also from a liberal-pluralist communication studies perspective, can be found in chapters by Werner Meier and Josef Trappel in McQuail and Siune (1998). On cultural work, Negus's studies of the recording industry (1992; 1999) suggest how fruitful organisational sociology can be for understanding the entertainment-based cultural industries, though his focus is primarily on creative managers, and symbol creators are sidelined. Work in empirical sociology of culture, especially that of Howard S. Becker (e.g., 1982) and Richard A. Peterson (e.g., 1997) needs to be paid far more attention by cultural studies and political economy approaches than it has in recent years. Bourdieu's work on cultural production (e.g., 1993) is surprisingly neglected. Jeremy Tunstall's work (e.g., 1971; 1993) has provided important information about the attitudes and working lives of media professionals of various kinds. The richest treatments of issues of creative autonomy have been from within studies of journalism, such as work by Schlesinger (1978), Tuchman (1978), Gans (1979) and Curran (1990). Caves' book (2000) on creative industries deals with many areas of creativity that I have not had the space to treat here. But, to reiterate from the discussion in Chapter 1, it is the cultural-industries approach that has had most to say about symbol creators and conditions of creativity, especially Miège (1989).

# 6 Internationalisation, Globalisation and Cultural Imperialism

We have already seen (Chapter 2) that there were significant instances of internationalisation of technologies, texts and genres in the late nineteenth and early twentieth centuries, and that one of the features of the complex professional era of cultural production was the intensification of such internationalisation. An important feature of the cultural industries throughout the twentieth century has been the domination of much international cultural trade by the USA and, to a lesser extent, Europe. One of the key developments in the cultural industries over the last 20 years has been the further and accelerated intensification of international cultural flows, including – as we shall see – much greater internationalisation on the part of cultural-industry businesses. This took place partly in response to the need on the part of businesses of all kinds to generate higher levels of profit during the Long Downturn. Also important was the increasing ease of doing business across national borders as communications and transport improved. As leisure time and disposable income increased in some parts of the world, such as Asia and Latin America, European and North American cultural-industry corporations took the opportunity to expand. Meanwhile, Asian and Latin American companies made attempts to internationalise into European and North American cultural markets. The successive waves of marketisation discussed in Chapter 4 were extremely important in paving the way for such internationalisation, by removing many policy barriers to cultural trade.

## Neither cultural imperialism nor globalisation

How can we analyse and evaluate these developments? Chapter 2 outlined the most important way of analysing the internationalisation of the cultural industries amongst radical scholars in the early complex professional era: the cultural imperialism thesis. We saw there some of the key themes of the thesis:

◆ The imposition of western cultural products on the non-west[1]
◆ The potentially homogenising effects of western culture as it spread across the world
◆ The destruction of indigenous traditions by such cultural flows, and the transfer of belief systems from the west to the non-west

The term cultural imperialism was at its most popular during the 1970s and early 1980s, when concern about such developments found expression in a series of UNESCO reports, seminars and declarations (most notably MacBride Report – UNESCO, 1980). From the early 1980s onwards, however, a paradigm shift occurred in the way radical writers understood international mass communications (see, e.g., Fejes, 1981). Many writers began to react against the cultural imperialism thesis. Some began to prefer the term globalisation to cultural imperialism. Globalisation was a term developed by writers (Robertson, 1990; Giddens, 1990) in a very different tradition from the international policy forums and activist circles where the cultural imperialism thesis became widespread. Globalisation was intended to capture the increasing interconnectedness of different parts of the world. Partly because it referred to a wide variety of economic, political and cultural practices, it spread quickly to become the most widely-discussed social science concept of the 1990s, going beyond academia to reach many other circles. Most notably, in the late 1990s, the term came to be used to denote a certain aspect of economic globalisation: the removal of barriers to trade across national borders. For many radical writers and activists, such 'free trade' in fact favours the wealthiest countries in the global system of nation states. (Hence the protests against globalisation in this sense in various cities around the world over the last few years, most famously in Seattle in 1999.) As a result of the dissemination of the term globalisation across many different contexts, confusion surrounds the idea (see Box 6.1 on one confusing use of the term).

---

1 Terms such as 'western' and 'non-western' are very problematic. Western societies are not only extremely different from each other; they are internally heterogeneous too. The same is true of non-western societies. Nevertheless, the adjectives have real political resonance in certain parts of the world, as a means of resisting some of the worst aspects of modernisation and commodification.

**Box 6.1    Herman and McChesney: globalisation as cultural imperialism**

The most thorough recent treatment of internationalisation of the cultural industries, Herman and McChesney's *The Global Media* (1997) uses the term globalisation in a way which strongly echoes the concept of cultural imperialism, and which goes against the notion of a complex and ambivalent interconnectedness to be found in social theory's use of the term. This is partly because Herman and McChesney are deriving the term from its uses in activist circles, to refer to economic globalisation. What is striking, however, is their almost complete failure to address conceptual debates regarding cultural imperialism. They initially indicate some recognition of the contradictory effects of global interconnectedness. They point briefly to some positive effects of cultural-industry internationalisation, associated with the dissemination of commercial popular culture, such as 'a greater connectedness and linkage between peoples' and the export of certain positive values, such as scepticism of authority, and the questioning of repressive traditions (1997: 8). But Herman and McChesney are clear that, for them, the primary effects of internationalisation (or globalisation, as they would have it) of cultural products are systematically and almost uniformly *negative*: the implantation, extension and intensification of 'the commercial model of communication' (1997: 9). Indeed, the rest of their book is devoted to a cataloguing of the activities of media companies in spreading this model, and in creating an entertainment-based culture which in their view is incompatible with real democracy. They are therefore best understood, in terms of my argument here, as using the term globalisation to mean cultural imperialism.

Some work on globalisation deals with empirical issues. There are fierce debates about the extent to which globalisation, in the sense of significantly new global interconnectedness, has actually taken place over the last decades, and about whether it is a long-term or a more recent development. David Held and his co-authors argue that 'contemporary [that is, post-1980] patterns of globalization have . . . surpassed those of earlier epochs' and that the 'contemporary era represents a historically unique confluence or clustering of patterns of globalization in the domains of politics, law and governance, military affairs, cultural linkages and human migrations, in all dimensions of economic activity and in shared global environmental threats' (Held et al., 1999: 425). Held et al. usefully describe the increasing and quickening interconnectedness of the world, examining how this affects various economic, political and cultural phenomena in very different ways. But such empirical work on globalisation tends to be concerned only very marginally with *cultural* aspects of global interconnectedness.[2]

Much more common in work on cultural aspects of globalisation is a theoretical invocation of globalisation which reacts against the cultural

---

2 For example, Held et al.'s treatment of cultural globalisation is confined almost entirely to issues of cultural trade, without reference to debates about cultural identity.

imperialism thesis and related Marxian approaches and which attempts to develop a more sophisticated way of understanding the complexity and contradictions of global cultural flows. Conceptual advances associated with globalisation theory have helped to bring about the rapid fall from favour of the cultural imperialism thesis.

Firstly, some writers have argued that it is no longer possible to portray the global cultural system as one in which the countries of the west (or, in a slightly more sophisticated version, the 'core', to include powerful 'eastern' countries such as Japan) impose their cultures on the non-west. The rise of newly industrialised countries, according to such writers, makes such a perspective outdated, if it was ever valid (see Tomlinson, 1997: 140–2).

Secondly, whereas some cultural imperialism writers assumed that the spread of western cultural goods and technologies involved homogenisation or cultural synchronisation (Hamelink, 1983), critics of the concept have pointed out the very strong processes of cultural differentiation taking place throughout the world. As Hall (1997: 211) puts it, 'there are many countervailing tendencies which prevent the world from becoming a culturally uniform and homogenous space'. Indeed, it is possible to argue that diversity may well have increased as new syncretic cultural texts and genres circulate within societies exposed to western cultural influence. Whereas a previous generation of writers was deeply concerned that western cultural exports might inhibit or destroy indigenous cultural traditions, cultural-studies approaches tend to see cultures as 'hybrids' of older forms (Chambers, 1994; Canclini, 1995), and the idea of a pure, uncontaminated tradition as problematic, and even dangerous, because it might serve to support racism and reactionary versions of nationalism (see Chapter 1). Culture can no longer be equated with place in any simple way, argue these critics. Globalisation involves 'deterritorialisation' (Canclini, 1995) – (nearly?) all places are full of influences from elsewhere. Again, this suggests heterogeneity rather than a universal sameness – and a much richer theorisation of internationalisation than that to be found in the cultural imperialism thesis.

Thirdly, whereas the cultural imperialism thesis tended to assume the negative impact of western cultural exports, many writers have stressed the creative and active uses made by audiences of internationally-distributed cultural goods: most famously the study by Liebes and Katz (1993) of the reception in different countries of the US TV series *Dallas*, a classic of 'active audience' theory in liberal-pluralist communication studies.

Globalisation theory has been effective in exposing some of the conceptual limitations of cultural imperialism, then. But globalisation theorists (and other critics of cultural imperialism) have their limitations too. For a start, there is an almost spectacular lack of empirical evidence in the work of commentators such as John Tomlinson, Stuart Hall and others associated with globalisation theory; whereas cultural imperialism writers such as Herman and McChesney (1997) are all empirical evidence and no adequate theory. Active audience theory usefully problematises the assumptions in some cultural imperialism writing that non-western populations accept the values of western cultural products. But it fails to confront broader 'non-media' questions. What, for example, are the relationships, if any, between flows of texts and the continuing international and intranational inequalities of wealth and opportunities? Active audience theory certainly does not provide the answers to this; it merely tends to suggest that such relationships are more complex than were thought by a previous generation.

Similarly, Tomlinson puts great stress on the ambivalence of cultural globalisation, which he describes as 'double-edged: as it dissolves the securities of locality, it offers new understandings of experience in wider – ultimately global – terms' (1997: 30). He also portrays globalisation as an essentially *undirected* process:

> The idea of imperialism contains, at least, the notion of a purposeful project: the *intended* spread of a social system from one centre of power across the globe. The idea of 'globalisation' suggests interconnection and interdependency of all global areas which happens in a far less purposeful way. (Tomlinson, 1991: 175)

Tomlinson's stress on ambivalence and undirectedness is intended to counter the functionalism and lack of recognition of complexity in cultural imperialism writing. But this emphasis leaves certain questions – often raised by Tomlinson in the course of his thorough treatments – unanswered. How do we assess global economic and cultural inequality? Which actors are involved in the creation and maintenance of such lasting economic and cultural inequalities?

In this book, I am attempting to deal with these questions more adequately, by putting the interests of the companies that dominate the international production and circulation of culture at the centre of the narrative, but in a way that recognises the complexity and ambivalence of their motives and outcomes. With the treatment of questions of assessment and explanation outlined in Chapters 2 and 3 behind me, my aim in this chapter is to ground the abstractions of globalisation theory by asking 'middle level' questions about internationalisation. To recapitulate from Chapter 2, these are: **To what extent does the increasingly global reach of the largest firms mean an exclusion of voices from cultural markets? What opportunities are there for cultural producers from outside the 'core' areas of cultural production to gain access to new global networks of cultural production and consumption?** I will investigate these questions across three cultural industries: television, film and recorded music.

It should now be clear that my use of the term internationalisation is intended to avoid the problems surrounding the term 'globalisation'. To clarify further, however, there are three main aspects of cultural internationalisation that I am concerned with here.

♦ *Internationalisation of cultural businesses*: More and more cultural-industry companies invest in more than one country. This might mean producing in many countries; more usually, it will mean distributing texts made in one place across many others. Some claim that the transnational corporation has no identity and that even though the head office of the corporation might be based in one country, the company itself has no nationality. But much of the money made from the operations of the transnational corporation will (at least in electronic form) be 'returned' to the base country.

♦ *Internationalisation of cultural texts*: Cultural texts originated in one country are increasingly seen, heard, and so on in other countries. Because of this increasing flow of cultural texts, audiences and symbol creators can, in many places, draw on texts from many other different places. Texts, genres and even technologies (such as musical instruments) will be often reinterpreted and adapted by symbol creators in other contexts.

♦ *The local is increasingly affected by the global*: Partly as a result of this increasing movement of cultural texts, but also because of other, wider factors, cultural identities are increasingly complex. It probably never was wise to think of culture as being linked to territory in a simple, one-to-one way, but more and more the culture of a particular place is comprised of inputs from many other places. Many texts are now based not on the interests, concerns and culture of particular nations, but on those of a variety of nations, or of sections of people who share a transnational culture.

Clearly, my main concern here, given the topic of the book, is the first of these aspects of internationalisation. But this can never be fully separated in analysis from the other two.

## Television and geocultural markets

As we saw in Chapter 2, the USA dominated international flows of television programming in the 1960s. Television became closely linked to concerns about American popular culture more generally. For some (Schiller, 1969) television was the latest and most significant development in US cultural domination. This view was based on programme exports, but also on direct investment by US companies in overseas broadcasters, especially in Latin America (see Wells, 1972). Other commentators were concerned about the *quality* of US television products, culminating in 1980s debates about whether the dominance of US programmes and formats would lead to 'wall-to-wall *Dallas*'.

Ironically, in the period when the cultural imperialism thesis was at its peak, the domination of US television was in decline. Already, well before the time Jeremy Tunstall first published his groundbreaking analysis of media and cultural imperialism (Tunstall, 1994) in 1977, most prime-time programming, including the most popular programmes, was local in origin. Prime-time television, Tunstall points out, tended to be produced either within the home nation, or by a larger nation with similar linguistic and cultural traditions. US programming was primarily used to fill less popular times more cheaply. Direct investment by US television companies in Latin America was short-lived, and US firms had withdrawn from such ventures by the mid-1970s – in many cases as a result of protectionist measures introduced by national governments, such as Brazil. These measures should not be thought of as an enlightened resistance to US cultural imperialism, however: they were often introduced by military, authoritarian governments.

The 1970s and early 1980s saw further declines in television imports. According to Varis and Nordenstreng (1985), in the television stations of The Third World, the proportion of foreign programmes broadcast declined on average by over 15 per cent between 1973 and 1983. In the six largest Latin American countries, imports fell by 29 per cent between 1972 and 1986 (Berwanger, 1998: 192).

Tunstall's work suggests that it is too simplistic to see the international cultural industries as dominated by the USA (or the USA plus the UK). One recent attempt to move beyond this 'concentric perspective', which sees ' "the West" at the centre dominating the peripheral "third world" with an outward flow of cultural products' has been made by the Australian writers, John Sinclair, Elizabeth Jacka and Stuart Cunningham (1996: 5). Sinclair et al. introduced the useful concept of 'geolinguistic regions' (1996: 11–14) to capture the increasing complexity of international television flows. Geolinguistic regions are groups of countries defined by common cultural, linguistic and historical connections. They might be actual geographical areas, where countries with these kinds of connections are actually next to each other. But in many cases, these relationships rely on cultural rather than physical proximity, in that they are forged out of long histories of transnational contact, including especially the legacy of colonial empires. It is possible, for example, to see the USA, Canada, the UK, Ireland, Australia and New Zealand as forming one such geolinguistic region, based on the use of English as a first language, and primarily white, Christian cultural traditions. Another potential region comprises Spain, Spanish-speaking Latin America, plus Spanish-speaking parts of the former Spanish empire and the massive Spanish-speaking population of the USA. Some might include Portugal, Brazil and the former Portuguese colonies in Africa and Asia in the same 'region' within a broader set of countries influenced by Hispanic languages and cultures.

I prefer the modification **geocultural markets**. Geocultural is better than geolinguistic because language is only one of a number of potential cultural connections between places and peoples. The countries of Eastern Europe and the European nations of the former USSR, for example, form a particular geocultural region, with shared histories of Soviet oppression and longer Christian traditions, but there is no shared language. 'Markets' is a better term than 'regions' because such cultural connections can work across enormous distances that transcend geographical proximity. It is important to note that a particular country can belong to more than one geocultural market, because nearly all countries contain different groups of people, with varying cultural identifications. More significantly still, and this is an insight of cultural-studies approaches, the same people can have multiple cultural identifications. A woman of Indian origin living in the UK might feel part of an Anglophone geocultural market, familiar with a wide range of programming from the UK, the USA and Australia. Yet she may well also feel affiliated to a different geocultural market, comprising India itself, plus substantial Indian migrant communities in the Arabian Gulf and elsewhere. Her affiliations may shift according to her different experiences in life, who she is with, and even her personal mood.

These different geocultural markets have other centres of production besides Hollywood. Sinclair et al. draw attention to some of these: 'Mexico and Brazil for Latin America, Hong Kong and Taiwan for the Chinese-speaking populations of Asia, Egypt for the Arab world, and India for the Indian populations of Africa and Asia' (1996: 8). They note that these regional television production centres were built upon previously existing centres of film production and I will discuss some of these later in this chapter.

But the new complexity of global television culture is more than a matter of recognising that trade takes place *within* these geocultural markets. Sinclair et al. are clear that these regions are not bounded, discrete spaces: in the new era of television culture, 'global, regional, national and even local circuits of programme exchange, overlap and interact in a multifaceted way' (1996: 5). To make this more concrete, and to delineate further this complex, polycentric picture of global television, I will deal with two important but ambivalent examples of recent developments.

♦   The circulation of non-US programming in Europe, the USA itself and other geocultural markets – the most commented upon case of this is the export of Latin American *telenovelas* (a type of drama serial): To what extent does this represent the rest of the world exporting its culture back to the west? Can this be understood as a breakdown of the cultural imperialism model, and a move towards a more equitable model of transnational cultural flows?

◆ The breakdown of the system whereby programmes were transmitted nationally, and whereby schedules comprised a mixture of domestically-produced programming, plus foreign (often mainly US) imports; and the associated rise of systems of satellite transmission, where channels are received across national borders: To what extent can this be seen as a move away from a system of national broadcasting, towards a truly international audiovisual system? And, crucially, to what extent can such shifts be understood as progress towards systems of greater choice and diversity?

## Reversing cultural flows? The case of Latin American television

Latin American television is often invoked in order to question the simplistic notion that non-Euro-American television is dominated by Hollywood television and US conglomerates. It has also been used to suggest a model for how non-core television-producing countries might gain more presence in the international television market.[3] There has been a developed television industry across most of Latin America, particularly in Mexico and Brazil, since the late 1960s. A significant development in the 1980s and 1990s has been that both these countries, and other Latin American countries such as Venezuela, have become exporters of considerable amounts of programming to other countries, not just within the Hispanic geocultural market, but also beyond to many other countries, such as the USA and the UK: countries that are usually considered to be at the geographical core of the cultural industries.

The international presence of the Mexican and Brazilian television industries is founded on the domestic strength of two mighty corporations. In Mexico, Televisa takes about 80 per cent of the domestic television market share, and this is higher in peak times. In Brazil, Globo has a market share of about 76 per cent, in a huge market of 160 million people where television dominates advertising spending (Sinclair, 1996: 35). Televisa can also draw on a formidable overseas market in Spanish-speaking Latin America, Hispanic USA and Spain. Globo can rely less on linguistic ties overseas, but it founded its export success on initial success in Portugal in the late 1970s.

---

3 See, for example, Mattelart and Mattelart (1990: 2), citing Italian policy research of the 1980s.

Telenovelas have been central to debates about Latin American television. The term telenovela is sometimes translated to mean 'Latin soap', but the term 'soap', complex enough in Anglophone contexts, is misleading – even though early telenovelas were sponsored by British and US detergent companies. Whereas British prime-time soaps and US day-time soaps run in principle forever, and have no overall narrative resolution, telenovelas move towards closure over a large number of episodes. US prime-time soaps take the form of a series of about 20 programmes, transmitted in 'seasons' over a number of years. Telenovelas do not run in series, but form one continuous serial of about 100 episodes. Unlike US and UK prime-time soaps, they are shown five to six times a week. As many as 15 telenovelas might be shown by different channels on the same day, often in blocks, in the afternoon and evening. They share with British and US soaps a concern with family relationships, and they invite strong emotional responses. There is often much more emphasis on polarised moral forces than in the British soaps[4] but there is a strong 'quality aesthetic' apparent in some telenovelas, especially those from Brazil (Sinclair, 1996: 50). Some of the most important telenovelas have been literary adaptations. Whereas soaps have traditionally been thought of as debased, trivial entertainment in the Anglophone world, telenovelas are often more prestigious in Latin America. But as in the UK and the USA, the fact that the programmes are enjoyed by women and by less educated audiences (Vink, 1988: 221–2) is often implicitly, and sometimes explicitly, interpreted as a sign of their supposed lack of worth.[5] Nevertheless, telenovelas are the central television genre in Latin America, in a way that has no parallel in Australia, Canada, Britain or the USA. Although introduced to television in the early 1960s, they draw on a much longer history of melodramatic serials in Latin America, in popular fiction, film and radio (Mattelart and Mattelart, 1990). Telenovelas then must be understood as culturally specific.

It follows from this that the success of Latin American television outside Latin America represents, at least to some degree, a significant new international presence for Latin American culture. One of the reasons for the international spread of the telenovela was economic. Mattelart and Mattelart show, for example, that the cost to Italian television of importing a telenovela was between US$3,000 and US$6,000 per 40 minute episode, whereas US dramas cost between US$6,000 and US$48,000 per half hour. As the desire for more content boomed with television marketisation in the

---

4 This emphasis is sometimes called 'melodramatic'. Jostein Gripsrud (1995: 242–8) has shown, in his brilliant study of the US prime-time soap *Dynasty* how complex this notion of melodrama is, and how the term is sometimes misapplied in the study of soap opera.

5 As in the UK, figures suggest that audiences are in fact comprised of an even balance of women and men (Vink, 1988: 247).

1980s, Globo's exports increased healthily. Various novelas became television events in the countries to which they were exported: Globo's *La Escrava Isaura* in China, Czechoslovakia and Cuba, *Gabriela* in Angola, *The Rich Also Cry* in Russia (Paterson, 1998: 62). How can the widespread success of telenovelas be explained? Clearly, economic factors such as cost are insufficient: there must be cultural factors at work too. Mattelart and Mattelart (1990: 144) speculate that such non-western programmes are increasingly popular in the west as a kind of exoticism, as apparent 'responses to the tired logos of Western modernity' (1990: 152).[6] They also claim that melodrama in the late twentieth century increasingly revealed its 'potential for universality' and argue that melodrama serves as a kind of supergenre, which can be all things to all people, at least some of the time, incorporating suspense, comedy, grief, action, and so on (and this argument is echoed by Liebes and Katz, 1993 in discussing the success of *Dallas*).

However, it is important not to exaggerate the significance of telenovelas. Telenovelas form only 8 per cent of television hours produced by Televisa (Sinclair, 1996: 49). A significant and often overlooked fact is that the news was a more popular form of programming in Brazil than telenovelas during the period when the latter were being widely discussed in academic and policy circles (see Vink, 1988: 11). Whereas 50 per cent of US television sales come from overseas, in the mid-1990s Globo was gaining only 3 per cent of its revenues from abroad, even including Latin America. The figure for Televisa was 10 per cent, much of it from the sale of telenovelas and other genres to the US market, with its large and increasing Spanish-speaking population (Sinclair, 1996: 49, 52). Attention to telenovelas might help to correct the picture of a homogeneous world market dominated by the USA, and it suggests the possibility *in the future* of more cultural exports from periphery to centre, or to other peripheries. But economically speaking, telenovela exports are relatively insignificant, and culturally they still form a small part of the television landscape, even in countries such as Russia, where they have been very popular. In most countries, domestic programmes continue to attract higher ratings than do US imports (Hoskins et al., 1997: 29). Most non-domestic programming is US-produced: the USA accounts for at least 75 per cent of all television programme exports (Hoskins et al., 1997: 29). It may be premature to speak of a new era of transnational television on the basis of the sporadic success of a few telenovelas.

---

6 There are echoes of Mattelart and Mattelart's dubious invocation of universality in the argument of Liebes and Katz (1993) that *Dallas* had qualities of primordiality and seriality which made it almost universal in appeal.

In any case, we should be cautious about celebrating the existence of such Latin American corporations, as a means of countering cultural imperialism. As Mattelart and Mattelart (1990) show, companies such as Globo and Televisa monopolise their domestic markets in a way that the CEOs of US conglomerates can only dream of. Both companies rely on significant horizontal integration: Globo was built up by the Marinho family from its ownership of a leading daily newspaper; Televisa has significant press and radio interests. Globo has, at various points, owned record and video manufacturing and distribution, an electronics firm, an advertising company, and major art galleries. Mattelart and Mattelart (1990: 42) cite *Variety* estimates from 1987 that an average telenovela helps sell an average of 200,000 records in Brazil and up to 1 million records internationally. Both are strongly vertically integrated too. Each company produces 78 per cent to 80 per cent of the programmes it airs. Virtually all Brazilian actors with name recognition are under contract to Globo.

Portrayed in the west as examples of Latin American commercial vigour, Televisa and Globo were both founded on close links with repressive, authoritarian states. Cultural imperialism theorists were particularly concerned about 1960s US investment in the Latin American industries. The US broadcasting network ABC was involved in a joint venture with Televisa. Time-Life (later merged with Warner) worked with Globo to launch a joint channel. But the deal was ended by the military government in 1968 – a military government with which Globo had very good relations throughout the 1960s and 1970s. The military government paid for the satellite infrastructure that united the huge territories of Brazil into one television market; it was this unification of the television market that allowed Globo its dominance. In Mexico, private companies benefited too from government expenditure on developing television infrastructure. Here the relationship with the state was especially contradictory. Televisa was formed out of two commercial channels, in opposition to the Mexican government's newly-established Channel 13. Yet Televisa had close relationships with the party that ruled Mexico (PRI) from the 1910s to the year 2000. In both Mexico and Brazil, there was extremely weak government regulation, allowing significant cross-media ownership and massive commercialisation – Brazilian broadcasters were allowed in the 1980s and 1990s to transmit 15 minutes of advertising per hour.

So while the close study of Latin American television helps us to appreciate the complexities of the changing international television landscape, and while its products may be of great cultural interest, it would be wrong to see Latin American television as offering a significant counter to the forms of cultural inequality towards which the cultural imperialism thesis, however simplistically, tried to direct attention. There is little real democratisation of international communication here. There is little evidence of significant transfer of cultural and economic resources from South to North, alongside long-standing flows from North to South. The corporations that dominate Latin American television provide no significant organisational alternatives to dominant models of television available elsewhere. This suggests that while globalisation theory might be better than the cultural imperialism thesis at registering the complexity of international cultural flows, issues concerning the interrelation of economic, political and cultural power remain pressing.

## Transnational transmission and reception: neoimperialism or a new diversity?

The second major aspect of television internationalisation I want to examine here is the increasing transmission of entire channels across and beyond national borders. The 1980s and 1990s have seen increasingly complex cross-cultural flows in television which cannot be reduced to the notion of cultural imperialism. The global spread of the video cassette recorder during the 1980s meant that diasporic populations could import films and television programmes from their countries of origin. Cable and satellite technologies, available in many countries from the early 1980s onwards, have made this practice of cross-border programme consumption even more widespread. Naficy (1993: 62), for example, writes about an independent station, Channel 18 (KSCI TV) which, at the time of his research, provided 'round-the-clock programming in some 16 languages produced by various diasporas in the United States or imported from their home countries', including Arabic, Armenian, Cambodian, Mandarin, French, Tagalog/English, German, Hungarian, Hindi/English, Periona, Italian, Japanese, Hebrew, Korean, Russian and Vietnamese. Across many of the advanced industrial countries, such 'diasporic television' has boomed in recent years. It must not be assumed that such stations are necessarily addressing and fulfilling the cultural needs of the communities they address; and there are many places outside the major metropolitan cities where such services are unavailable. Few people would watch these programmes who were not from the specific diasporic population being addressed. Nevertheless, the availability of such 'peripheral' programming at the 'core' defies the simplifications of the cultural imperialism thesis.[7] A number of studies have cast important light on these new forms of cross-border reception, and some have argued that there are potentially progressive cultural consequences. Marie Gillespie, for example, argues that 'the juxtaposition of culturally diverse television programmes and films in

---

7 One of the most interesting aspects of Naficy's account is that he shows how Iranians, because they were an exile culture, rather than a transnational one, were forced to produce their own programming, rather than import it from their homeland.

Punjabi homes stimulates crosscultural, contrastive analyses of media texts' within those homes (Gillespie, 1995: 76). This, she says, heightens awareness of cultural difference and intensifies the negotiation of cultural identities, and leads to aspirations for cultural change.

But the implications for international television of the development of cable and satellite go beyond such diasporic channels. It also means that, in certain regions, there is much greater transnational transmission. This is the case in Europe: British viewers of satellite television can watch German video channels, badly-dubbed Polish pornography, and many other delights. There is a long way to go before television contributes to the ideal of a pan-European identity, however: there are too many different languages and cultures to be so easily reconciled. Developments in Arabic television are interesting in this respect. The first major developments in the transformation of Arabic television from a national system to a transnational one took place in the early 1990s.[8] Egypt, though not the first Arabic country to introduce television, had dominated programme production and trade from the early 1960s onwards, partly because of its highly-developed film industry, with its high numbers of trained technical and creative personnel. Egypt introduced its own satellite channel, Space-Net, in 1991; and had a huge impact, providing alternative coverage of the Gulf War during that year. SpaceNet was closely followed by MBC, a privately-owned Saudi station, and by the Kuwaiti Space Channel. Soon after, national terrestrial channels were made available on satellite, and many of the wealthier countries of the Arab world vied to put their own national satellite stations into operation, as a means of gaining national prestige. The channels were also aimed at reaching the 5 million people of Arabic origin living in Europe, and the 2 million living in the USA. Again, it is important not to portray such developments as an indication of a brave new world of diverse and imaginative television: Arab-sourced television remains under very strict state controls and the new, private stations such as MBC and Orbit are often run by the wealthy elite, including the Saudi royal family or businessmen close to them (Boyd, 1998). (Cultural imperialism accounts tended to neglect such *intra*-national power dynamics.)

Of course, the arrival of cable and satellite also meant that western, in particular US-based, channels such as MTV, developed initially to cater for the US domestic market, were increasingly available for consumption overseas, via satellite-cable and direct broadcast satellite. For some, this was an extension of cultural imperialism, and a challenge to cultural pro-

---

8 In fact, Arab countries had teamed up to fund their own satellite in 1976 (Amin, 1996: 106–8). Although this would have made satellite programming possible, the satellite remained massively underused for 15 years.

tectionism, in that audiences could choose these channels over domestic channels. But as Kevin Robins (1997) shows, channels such as MTV and CNN soon found that they had to adapt their programming to local audiences. New hybrids were produced, often US-owned, or jointly-owned with local businesses or states, and transmitting a mixture of locally-sourced news or popular culture.

Such strategies of local adaptation do not mean that the expansion of the mega-corporations into global television networks is without consequence. Rupert Murdoch's News Corporation purchased the struggling Asian satellite service, STAR TV, in 1993 and within a few years it had made significant inroads into television markets in a number of countries, including China (PRC), India and Taiwan. It reaches 300 million people with a variety of country-specific packages. All the mega-corporations are keen to gain access to the huge markets of Asia, but Murdoch has been particularly assiduous in courting the Chinese state, suspending the BBC's World Service from STAR in 1994, and making sure that his publishing company, HarperCollins, did not publish the memoirs of former Hong Kong governor Chris Patten, one of the PRC's main international political bogeymen. STAR TV is a distribution network for entertainment. Rather than a vehicle for the thoughts of Chairman Rupert, it transmits programmes which offer a similar mix to that familiar in the west. Individualist and consumerist values are emphasised, but so also are other values which do not straightforwardly support capitalist accumulation, including stories emphasising the virtues of family and community loyalty (see the discussion of Ong, 1999 later in the chapter). Would this system take a substantially different form were it owned by Asian business-people, rather than by Rupert Murdoch and his other chief shareholders? The likely answer is no – though News Corporation might have more resources to offer a convincing and seductive version of such a mix. Once again, we return to the issues discussed in the previous chapters. The negative effects of cultural-industry corporations such as STAR TV are on the general field of cultural production. It offers corporations yet more power to influence government strategy. It makes alternative forms of cultural production and of programming more difficult to imagine and achieve in more places around the world. And it continues to direct huge amounts of money into already wealthy hands.

## The international film industry: Hollywood power

The film industry offers a parallel but different perspective on these issues. Here, the domination of the USA over international production and distribution has been much greater than in television (the reasons for this are discussed in Chapter 2). Cinema was the first cultural industry where the cultural products of a particular nation gained significant domination in international markets. From the 1920s onwards, Hollywood, that is, the major studios located in that suburb of Los Angeles but mainly run from New York City, became the economic and cultural centre of film in the western hemisphere. Herman and McChesney (1997: 14) quote statistics from film historian Ian Jarvie that in 1925 American films accounted for over 90 per cent of film revenues in the UK, Canada, Australia, New Zealand and Argentina, and over 70 per cent in France, Brazil and Scandinavia. In the 1930s, foreign revenues provided Hollywood studios with about 45 per cent of their total international gross revenues (Segrave, 1997: 115). According to Thomas Guback (1969: 3), the incomes from overseas territories were perceived by the Hollywood studios as a relatively unimportant part of revenues. The Hollywood studios did little to suit foreign tastes, and they had no elaborate overseas organisations. It was Hollywood's vertically-integrated structure that gave the Hollywood studios enormous control over the US domestic market – the biggest film market in the world. This in turn gave them the opportunity to dominate the international market, by being able to cover even high production costs at home. When the US courts ordered them to end their vertically-integrated control of the US market, the studios not only began to use independent producers to reduce costs, they also turned to internationalisation. They made more concerted efforts to maintain their domination in an increasingly prosperous Europe. According to Guback (1969), this involved a range of strategies, including more focused marketing efforts, but also the inclusion of European locations.

To what extent has Hollywood dominated the international market in more recent years?[9] Garnham (1990: 176) estimated that the US majors and mini-majors accounted for over 70 per cent of non-socialist world gross film rentals from the cinema in 1979. Across the EU, the Hollywood share of box-office receipts rose from 60.2 per cent in 1984 to 71.7 per cent in 1991 (Held et al., 1999: 356). Figures vary significantly from country to country. In the UK, US films took 93 per cent of the 1991 market, but in France the figure was 58 per cent, the lowest in any major European economy (Wasko, 1994: 222). But even in France, indigenous productions' share of box office had plummeted to 26 per cent by 1998 (*Variety*, 25 January 1999). This further wave of internationalisation on the part of Hollywood can be linked to the spiralling production and marketing costs discussed in

---

9 Reliable data are difficult to come by, amongst other reasons because of the reluctance of the US trade association, the Motion Picture Association of America, to release full figures (see Garnham, 1990: 171, 174; Wasko, 1994: 293). However, as national governments have become more concerned about the cultural industries, figures have become more widely available, particularly for Europe.

Table 6.1  Most prolific feature film producing nations

| Country | Average number of feature films produced per year, 1989–98 | Average investment per production in US$ million in 1998 |
|---|---|---|
| India | 787 | 0.08 |
| USA | 591 | 14.00 |
| Japan | 255 | 3.57 |
| Hong Kong | 169 | 0.58 |
| Philippines | 160 | figure not provided |
| France | 148 | 5.26 |
| China (PRC) | 127 | 0.42 |
| Russian Fed | 124 | figure not provided |
| Italy | 105 | 3.93 |
| Thailand | 73 | 0.15 |
| South Korea | 73 | 0.72 |
| UK | 67 | 8.25 |

*Source*: *Screen Digest*, June 1999: 130

Chapter 5 (this, for example, is the view taken by the various executives quoted by Wasko, 1994: 223). Even as the EU and national governments have established programmes to support film production, Europe has slipped further and further behind Hollywood. European films are particularly bad at making money outside their own territories because of a lack of marketing and distribution clout. German and Spanish films make less than 0.5 per cent of total box office receipts in any major European country other than their own (*Screen Digest*, June 2000: 189).

But in the film industry as in the television industry, the domination of the USA has sometimes served to obscure the widespread production of films elsewhere. There have been significant film industries in many non-western countries since at least the 1920s. It is important to realise that the vast majority of the films made around the world are not American. As can be seen from Table 6.1, eight other countries besides the USA have produced more than 100 films per year on average over the period 1989–98. In spite of the very high proportion of the global box office taken by Hollywood, there are many other areas of the world in which films are produced besides Hollywood. Many of these cinemas have significant national markets; and some have significant international ones.

## Other industries, other texts: India and Hong Kong

The Indian film industry is often cited as an example of a challenge to cultural imperialism, and the international dominance of Hollywood. There are echoes here of claims surrounding telenovelas. Since independence, India has always produced more films than the USA, though the gap has closed since the 1970s, as US film production has greatly increased. India still produces more films per year than any other country in the world, averaging 787 productions per year in the period 1989 to 1998, compared with the US average of 591 productions during the same period (see Table 6.1). The term 'Bollywood' is often used to describe the Indian film industry as a whole, and the 'B' in Bollywood comes from Bombay (now Mumbai), where the best-known, Hindi-language, 'all-India' films are made, many of which are distributed internationally. However, only about 20 per cent of Indian films are made in Bombay (Pendakur, 1990). Most films produced in India are not exported, but are made for local markets. This is partly because of generous support for film production on the part of regional, state governments.

India's exports of film are important economically and culturally. In 1988, the main markets were the Arabian Gulf, the USSR and Indonesia, but significant importers also included the UK, Morocco and Latin American countries (Pendakur, 1990). Via video and new television technologies, the demand for Hindi-language films amongst the millions of Indian subjects living abroad has boomed. Indian film exports were worth about US$10 million in 1989, but this had climbed to more than US$100 million by 1999. This is a significant source of foreign income for a developing country, and the Indian film industry is now valued at US$5.5 billion globally (Trikha, 2000). Hollywood, meanwhile, has had surprisingly little impact on the Indian domestic film market. Up until the 1990s, this was for reasons of national protectionism: India did not allow foreign films to be dubbed into Hindi. But even when this ban was lifted during cultural marketisation in the early 1990s, Hollywood films were only sporadically successful. This was partly because Indian films are markedly different in their aesthetic from Hollywood films. Their plots and narrative forms owe much to long traditions of theatre and religious epic (Thomas, 1985). They are generally about three hours in length, rather than the 90–100 minutes average length characteristic of Hollywood films. The classic Hollywood narrative works according to realist conventions, even where it deals with fantasy. The emphasis in Indian films is on emotion and spectacle rather than tight narrative (Thomas, 1985). A certain kind of verisimilitude is expected, concerning ideal family behaviour, but particularly in the song sequences which are a fundamental feature of Indian cinema, continuities of time and place (nearly always respected in the Hollywood musical) can be subordinated to mood and spectacle. Whether the distinctive textual features of Indian cinema can maintain a cultural barrier around the Indian film industry remains to be seen.

Another significant film production centre is Hong Kong, often associated with either the kung fu films popular throughout much of the world in the 1970s,[10] and violent action films. But as Stephen Teo (2000: 166) points out, Hong Kong had been a significant film centre throughout the 1950s and much of the 1960s. Film production peaked at 311 per year in 1956–7, when musical melodramas and swordplay-based historical epics were dominant (Lent, 1990). In the late 1960s, Cantonese cinema fell from fashion, and Mandarin-language production became dominant, serving the Mandarin Chinese diaspora throughout East Asia. In the 1970s, however, there was a huge growth of audiences as Hong Kong's economy boomed. Venture capitalists moved into the industry, recognising the potential for profit. Cantonese cinema became central to the colony's cultural industries. Local Cantonese-language television provided a new source of Cantonese-speaking stars, as did the Hong Kong-based Canto-pop music industry. Local television also provided a new wave of 'technically proficient, socially conscious, and aesthetically polycultural' directors (Stokes and Hoover, 1999: 24).

Aihwa Ong (1999: 161–7) has written of how the massive expansion in middle-class consumers throughout Asia has vastly increased the market for Chinese mass media. Ong stresses the fact that this Chinese-diasporic public, spread over the USA, South China, Hong Kong, Taiwan, Malaysia, Singapore and elsewhere in Southeast Asia, is connected not only by news media but just as importantly, by TV, films, magazines and videotapes. New forms of transnational Chinese identity are, she claims, being forged by media products, including popular kung fu novels, and satellite television, but in particular the kung fu and gangster movies which form the main products of the Hong Kong industry. For these films, Ong argues, 'are a medium for exploring reified Chinese values . . . in conditions of displacement and upheaval under capitalism' (162). They are 'all about brotherhoods, hierarchized allegiances, and kinship loyalty', and the films demonstrate the vulnerability and importance of these values in a way which Ong believes resonates with audiences.

Nevertheless, Ong is careful to draw attention to the lingering influence of US cultural-industry corporations and cultural forms, including most notably STAR TV, which was beaming programmes to 38 countries at the time of Ong's study (Ong, 1999: 167). India and Hong Kong may be examples of significant regional production powerhouses, with their own distinctive modes of address, but European and especially North American corporations and cultural products remain enormously powerful. This is apparent in the fact that although Hollywood films and some US television programmes nearly always have some presence in overseas markets,

---

10 The Kung Fu genre was not of specifically Hong Kong origin, although films made there were the most successful internationally. Japan, South Korea, Thailand, Indonesia, Taiwan and the Philippines all produced kung fu films (Lent, 1990: 5).

there is very little presence for Indian and Hong Kong films in the US itself, and practically none outside the Indian and Chinese-language diaspora. US distributors rarely market and promote foreign films beyond the art-house circuit. Foreign films take less than 3 per cent of the US market ('Culture Wars', *The Economist*, 12 September 1998). This means that the Hollywood studios dominate the USA's vast domestic market. This supposed aversion to foreign films is not something natural to audiences; it is a product of particular sociocultural and economic circumstances, including deeply-held cultural beliefs about the superiority of US popular culture over other forms (see Chapter 8). Naturally, Hollywood has an interest in cultivating such beliefs.

From an already dominant position, the US film industry has increased its international hegemony in the 1990s. Its share of global receipts increased from 38 per cent in 1995 to 41 per cent in 1999 (*Screen Digest*, September 1999: 122), in spite of the growth of indigenous film industries in Europe, Latin America and Asia. In most countries, local films (that is, involving some domestic financial or production input) experienced a decline in market share during the 1990s, in part because of an increasingly globalised film market, where films from more countries circulate to other countries; but also because of 'an even greater dominance of US product'. Only in 1997 did Hollywood overtake the market share of local films in Hong Kong. In 1998, Hong Kong movies took more than 45 per cent of Hong Kong domestic box office – one of the highest local shares in the world – but this represented a decline of more than 30 per cent since 1990 (*Screen Digest*, July 1999: 173). In India, early predictions of an Hollywood invasion proved to be wrong; but it would be surprising if Hollywood did not increase its cultural presence there in the coming years.

But what does all this mean for cultural creativity and *experience*? Portraying the Indian and Hong Kong industries as resistant alternatives to Hollywood hegemony is tricky. It is worth remembering that, in spite of the quick dismissals of some political economy writers, there is no simple equation between Hollywood and cultural homogeneity. Hollywood distributes a range of genres and texts, partly because of the vast and diverse audience it serves in its domestic market. Hollywood budgets may represent an appalling squandering of resources, and they may reflect disturbing inequalities of income. But the tiny budgets of Hong Kong films mean that quality is sometimes elusive. There is significant textual repetition within the products of other film industries, including those of India and Hong Kong. Stokes and Hoover (1999) write, for example, about the very short production time and lack of adequate postproduction that characterises Hong Kong cinema. There are often poor working conditions for actors, and poor technical finish to films. Apparently, organised crime is closely involved in the industry.

Nevertheless, such local cinemas cannot be so easily dismissed on aesthetic grounds. Although Stokes and Hoover are generally writing in praise of Hong Kong cinema, it may be that they are bringing 'western' aesthetic criteria to bear on the film industry they analyse. One leading film scholar, David Bordwell, has recently used Hong Kong cinema to argue that mass-produced films can achieve great aesthetic merit. His book amounts to something of a celebration of Hong Kong cinema:

> Hong Kong films can be sentimental, joyous, rip-roaring, silly, bloody and bizarre. Their audacity, their slickness and their unabashed appeal to emotion have won them audiences throughout the world . . . These outrageous entertainments harbor remarkable inventiveness and careful craftsmanship. They are Hong Kong's most important contribution to global culture. The best of them are not only crowd-pleasing but also richly and delightfully artful. (Bordwell, 2000: 2)

If Bordwell is right, this suggests that the survival and development of non-US film industries can contribute in important ways to international aesthetic diversity and quality.

## Cultural imperialism and popular music

Debates about the cultural and aesthetic consequences of internationalisation and globalisation can be pursued further by examining the international recording industry. Popular music is a particularly testing arena for the cultural imperialism thesis, and some of the most effective critiques of the cultural imperialism thesis have come from popular music studies (e.g., Laing, 1986; Goodwin and Gore, 1990; Garofalo, 1993). The cultural imperialism thesis was felt to be inadequate to understanding international musical flows in the late twentieth century for a number of reasons.

### Authenticity versus hybridity

Some ethnomusicologists (e.g., Lomax, 1978/1968) echoed the cultural imperialism thesis in warning of a 'cultural grey-out' as western popular music affected indigenous cultures. More recent writers have tended to stress the value of mixing, syncretism and 'hybridity' in popular music. A number of studies have shown how various local popular musics are the result of complex reinterpretations of imported styles and technologies (Hatch, 1989 on Indonesia; and Waterman, 1990 on Nigeria). Often, the imported music is itself the product of other groups marginalised within the world economy, such as the Hawaiian guitar-playing which influenced the Nigerian palmwine musicians in Waterman's account. Indeed, much of the popular music which traverses the globe is the result of the creativity of the African diaspora and very often of African Americans. Transnational corporations may control the circulation of this music, but it would be wrong to identify it culturally as simply the product of a dominant western culture.

### Western cultural products can be interpreted in different ways

The internationalisation of rock and roll in the 1960s is often given as an example of how some 'western' popular music has encouraged people to question dominant forms of power in the societies in which they live. Laing (1986: 338), for example, stresses how rock and roll was 'an instance of the use of foreign music by a generation as a means to distance themselves from a parental "national" culture', and Wicke (1990) has written about the positive dimensions of this use in post-war Stalinist Eastern Europe. Against this, proponents of the cultural imperialism thesis stress that much of the most prestigious popular music of the world is sung in English. While local musicians might eventually synthesise distinctive versions of imported music such as rap (see Mitchell, 2001), these local variants are often denigrated by local audiences, as well as by consumers in the more lucrative Anglophone markets. Arguably, too, the emphasis on English in many genres excludes non-English-speaking audiences from full identification and engagement with the global popular music on offer. Critics of the cultural imperialism thesis have claimed, however, that lyrics are relatively unimportant in many key pop genres (e.g., Frith, 1991). More significantly, perhaps, Chinese and Spanish-language shares of global sales are gradually increasing (*Financial Times: Music and Copyright*, 22 November 1995). As with film and television, it is possible to speak of geocultural markets with their own centres of production. British and American acts achieve more globally widespread success than acts from any other country. They particularly dominate Anglophone countries and, to some extent, Europe. Japan has continued to import styles and records from the UK, the USA, Brazil and elsewhere. Taiwan dominates production for the Mandarin markets of South East Asia. But what is striking about music, compared with film and television, is how many centres there are, overlapping and competing with Anglo-American domination. Thus Zairean musicians and companies dominate much Central and West African popular music.[11] Brazilian music has been influential and widely-sold throughout much of Latin America, but Cuba, Puerto Rico, Argentina and Columbia have also exerted strong influences throughout the continent at different times, and in different ways. This multicentric aspect of popular music production and circulation may derive from its significantly lower costs of production, compared with film and television.

---

11 I am grateful to Malka Shabtay for enlightening me on this point.

## Spread of ownership

In the 1970s, the dominant transnational companies were mainly from the USA, apart from Philips/PolyGram. In the 1980s, Japanese companies such as Sony and Matsushita entered the fray, along with German publishing giant Bertelsmann.[12] In studies of the music industry, some claimed that the spread of ownership of the dominant corporations meant that it is no longer possible to talk of an imperial centre imposing its popular music on the 'periphery' (e.g., Frith, 1991: 267; Garofalo, 1993: 22, 27). On the other hand, this may simply entail a reconfiguration of the notion of the centre, rather than its eclipse. Again, cultural imperialism theory was at fault in placing too much emphasis on the geographical location of the major corporations, rather than on the practices associated with these corporations. But there are still nodal points in the musical world, from where it is much easier to gain access to international distribution than from other places: Los Angeles, New York, London, Paris and Hong Kong are amongst them. Musicians shift cities and even continents in order to gain access to the gigging circuits, recording studios and informal knowledge networks which will allow them to achieve success.

Popular music, then, provides some evidence against the cultural imperialism thesis. But even if we should not talk in such functionalist terms of the conscious imposition of one culture on another, the logic of the global market means that access to audiences and committed publicity and promotion still seems to be extremely unequal for musicians and this inequality is geographical, and nationally differentiated. There are also of course significant inequalities in what is available to different sets of audiences. This may mean that it is possible to hold on to a modified version of the cultural imperialism thesis. The continuing currency of issues which the term 'globalisation' does not always seem adequate to address can be indicated by reference to recent debates surrounding two controversial categories: 'Euro-pop' and 'world music'.

With rare exceptions, continental European popular musicians have often been held in contempt by British and American audiences. 'Euro-pop' was a scathing term for the pidgin English and perceived lack of authentic musicianship amongst a generation of 1970s and 1980s European acts. Laing (1992: 139) concluded a survey of national and transnational trends in European popular music by speculating that the next U2 might come from Wroclaw or Bratislava. But there have been few signs of the emergence of such acts. In the history of European acts on the global scene, only Abba have even come close to being at the centre of pop myth, and

---

12 At time of writing, five corporations own the companies that take over 70 per cent of global recorded music revenues: AOL Time-Warner (US); Vivendi-Universal (France); Bertelsmann (Germany); EMI (UK) and Sony (Japan).

even their significance since the 1970s has been primarily based on a kitsch aesthetic. Indeed, the mid-1990s saw the re-establishment of London as the European centre for the most fashionable pop sounds, whether in dance music or in indie/alternative pop/rock. The power centres are not shifting as quickly as some critics of cultural imperialism have predicted.

The term 'world music' (in the USA 'world beat' is sometimes preferred) was adopted by a number of recording and music-press entrepreneurs to allow non-western popular musics to be promoted more adequately in the UK. Without doubt, some non-western musicians have achieved international success and recognition. The most notable examples include Nusrat Fateh Ali Khan (Pakistan) and Youssou N'Dour (Senegal). But the impact of such musicians has been limited. They are enjoyed by a rather older, middle-class audience. They hardly register as popular, either in terms of total sales, or in terms of their centrality in global popular culture. In addition, such musicians are often the subject of discourses which see their music as valuable only to the extent that it conforms to certain western notions of authenticity and tradition (see Feld, 1994 for a superb examination of such discourses). Thus the notion of world music tends to serve as an all-embracing category for that which is not perceived as western pop, and this in turn functions to exclude non-western musicians from global pop markets by defining them as exotic.[13] In this respect, as Goodwin and Gore (1990) point out, the existence of world music as a genre can be seen as the product of the effects of cultural imperialism, rather than a significant counter to them.

◆  ◆  ◆

The situation of continental European and non-western musicians in the international recording industry suggests, then, that even if the cultural imperialism model has conceptual flaws, as indicated throughout this chapter, it draws attention to problems that continue to exist in the world of popular music: in particular, systematic global inequalities in cultural prestige and economic profit. Much the same can be said of the television and film industries. Producers from outside the 'core' countries still have only limited access to global networks of cultural production and consumption. The US cultural industries are still remarkably dominant. In this respect, there has been significant continuity.

Nevertheless, we should not underestimate the very real changes in the extent and complexity of international cultural flows. The internationalisation of the cultural industries over the last 20 years has, as suggested in

---

13 The term is also used sometimes to refer to the work of western musicians who draw on non-western sources, most notably Paul Simon's 1986 *Graceland* album.

Chapter 3, been driven by the need, on the part of 'western' companies of all kinds, to find new markets for labour and for their products. They internationalised largely in order to counteract the effects of the Long Downturn. However, the big US/European/Japanese corporations do not entirely dominate global production. There are other important flows too. We can see a growing complexity in the social relations of cultural production on an international scale, as new industries emerge, old industries grow, and new technologies are introduced on terms that allow for new relations between distant places. Globalisation theory attempts to capture this, but fails to capture the agency of large, profit-making corporations in affecting, but not completely determining, the new cultural world order. It downplays the economic and cultural dimensions of international inequality. Neither cultural imperialism nor globalisation theory is adequate to assess spatial and geographical changes in the cultural industries across the world. Grounding analysis by examining particular industries and texts may provide a way out of the impasse between the two sets of theory.

## Further reading

Tunstall's *The Media Are American* (1994, originally published in 1977) remains the most informative source about the history of cultural-industry internationalisation. The work of Herbert Schiller frequently addresses internationalisation (1969; 1976; 1989), but is often richer in polemic than in analysis. Herman and McChesney's *The Global Media* (1997) is the most important recent contribution by US political economy to consideration of internationalisation. For more information on specific industries, see Gronow (1998) and Burnett (1995) on the international recording industry; Guback (1969) and Segrave (1997) on film; Mattelart (1991) on advertising; Sinclair et al. (1996), Barker (1997), and Smith with Paterson (1998) on television. *Screen Digest* is the best source of information about contemporary developments in internationalisation in the audiovisual industries (including the internet). *Variety* is also very useful.

# 7   New Media, Digitalisation and Convergence

The new media could never be a minor part of any book about change and continuity in the cultural industries. No other area of debate about cultural production has seen such remarkable claims for transformation – but this makes it all the more paramount to assess such claims carefully and soberly. After all, many parties have an interest in overstating the impact of new communication technologies. For journalists and academics, sensational reports of a transformed future draw attention from readers, editors and funding bodies. For companies, the introduction and dissemination of new technologies provide new market opportunities. For politicians and policy-makers, predicting and supporting transformation can appear progressive.

The very term new media illustrates how much confusion hype about technological transformation can cause. The phrase is, more often than not, used to refer to technologies which are really quite old, such as the use of coaxial cable and satellite broadcasting in television. Both of these 'new' technologies have been around since the 1960s. And new media technologies such as e-mail are primarily based on person-to-person or person-to-group communication, and can therefore hardly be thought of in any meaningful way as media (in the sense in which the term is usually employed, to mean *mass* media) at all. Nevertheless, cable, satellite and e-mail are often included in discussions of new media alongside new mass cultural forms such as CD-ROMs.

## Defining new media

At the core of the issue, when all the variety of conflicting definitions are put to one side, is *digitalisation*. The 'old' electronic media that grew up alongside print media in the period from 1850 to 1950 – photography, phonography (that is, sound recording), cinema, radio, television – relied mainly on analogue systems, rather than digital ones. In analogue broadcasting, for example, the main components of communication and cultural expression – words, images, music and other sounds and so on – were translated into a continuous body of information, radio waves, which would in some way reproduce the form or appearance of the original performance, image or whatever. The radio waves (remember that, like radio, television was broadcast by radio waves) would then be decoded by radio or television receivers. In other words, the radio waves were *analogous* to the original act of communication – they resembled or corresponded to it. In photography, cinema and video, an analogy of the image to be captured would be imprinted in negative form on film, and would then be 'decoded' in the developing process. In phonography, the sound waves produced by musical instruments or the voice were converted into a signal, which was coded into the grooves of a record or on to magnetic tape, to be decoded at some later point by a record player or tape player.

The vital innovation associated with the development of digital electronic storage and transmission is that the major components of cultural expression – words, images, music, etc. – are converted into binary code (elaborate sequences of zeros and ones) which can be read and stored by computers. This is an extremely important change because it makes communication more transportable and manipulable than before. Perhaps most importantly of all, it also makes different media potentially interconnectable.

While digitalisation represents a remarkable technical achievement, and makes certain processes easier and more convenient, it is important not to read the development of digital technologies as unambivalent progress towards a more efficient communications world. It takes an enormous amount of resources and energy to make computers and microprocessors, and to learn software programmes. They save time and money only because incredible and often unnoticed amounts of money are spent elsewhere: for example, on research and development, and in building up the banks of computers in schools, colleges and workplaces where computer use is still concentrated.

But in any case, I am not primarily concerned here with such issues of *efficiency*. There are more pressing questions in the present context, derived from the main aims of this book. My overall concern is with whether digitalisation represents a fundamental shift in the cultural industries. I am especially interested in implications for the social relations of cultural production, including effects on the division of labour in particular cultural industries, and this involves returning to some issues already explored in Chapter 5, but with a new twist: has digitalisation allowed 'ordinary' consumers more easily to become producers? Digital music technologies, desktop publishing software and of course the internet are all relevant topics here. But I am also concerned with textual issues, to be addressed more fully in Chapter 8, though germane here too: has digitalisation allowed for more or less creativity, diversity and innovation? (See the sections on video and computer games, and again on musical technologies.) Has it led to greater choice for consumers (an important theme in discussions of digital television)? Underlying all these various issues is a focus on the effects of digitalisation on questions of *power* in the cultural industries.

Since the 1960s and 1970s wave of interest in the information society (see Webster, 1995), there have been plenty of optimistic treatments of digitalisation, proclaiming new information and communication technologies as the gateway to more democratic and decentralised cultural forms. Such optimism has proliferated in the 1990s (Negroponte, 1995). The pessimistic, dystopian voices were there from the start too (Schiller, 1981) but have become quieter – or less often heard – in recent years. Steering a more sensible, middle way involves careful delineation of the different social uses of various digital technologies. I begin, then, by separating out various applications of digitalisation, in a number of very different cultural industries and forms, via a historical overview.

## Overview of digitalisation in the cultural industries

Digitalisation had begun to have effects on the way businesses were run from the 1960s onwards, but this happened principally through the effects of mainframe or minicomputers. People in advanced industrial countries had increasing contact with airline reservation systems, electronic databases and so on during this period. These were systems in which remote terminals would be linked by phone line to a central mainframe computer. The effects of such systems on the cultural industries were first felt in news gathering, as news agencies such as Reuters began to provide electronic financial data and news services to news organisations (see Tunstall and Machin, 1999: 80).

But it was only in the late 1970s and early 1980s that digitalisation began to have a more substantial impact on the cultural industries as a whole. In many cases, the most immediate impact of digitalisation was on technologies of cultural *production*. With the development of the personal computer in the 1980s (see Chapter 3) digitalisation of production has spread through all of the major cultural industries, with important effects on the working practices of photographers, film animators, radio producers, television editors and so on.

In the music industries, for example, musical instruments and, in some cases, recording studios were increasingly moving over to digital methods in the early 1980s, because it meant less interference in the signals, more accurate reproduction, and more manipulability. As prices fell, such technologies were then offered to the consumer market, and marketed on the basis of their convenience and clarity. This has had extremely important effects on musical production, as we shall see in the section on digital music technologies. Referring to controversies and debates, I assess whether these new technologies made music-making less creative, less collaborative, and whether they have substantially affected the copyright system at the heart of the music industry.

Another industry where digitalisation and miniaturisation were to have profound effects on production was magazine publishing, as desktop publishing software (that is, software that could be used to produce and design documents, magazines and other publications on a personal computer) and other digital technologies became cheaper and more widely available from the early 1980s on. I briefly outline the implications for the magazine publishing industry in the section on desktop publishing and the magazine publishing industry.

Digital music technologies, desktop publishing and other forms of digital cultural technology had substantial impacts on *existing* cultural industries. But the availability of relatively cheap and compact microprocessors from the late 1970s began to spawn *new* cultural industries. The earliest new form of any substance was the video game. This was initially a part of the arcade and pub entertainment business in most countries, but as the ownership of personal computers spread in the 1980s, the computer game increasingly became a domestic cultural artefact – and a very sophisticated, profitable and controversial one. In the section on video and computer games, I look at the features of video and computer games as a cultural industry: are they substantially different from 'pre-digital' industries? Are they as aesthetically and socially regressive as some critics claim?

Apart from computer games, domestic personal computers (as opposed to those introduced into cultural-industry workplaces) have up until recently had a relatively limited impact on cultural markets. Enormous hype has surrounded the introduction of personal-computer (PC) related CD technologies such as the CD-ROM since the 1980s; along with games, educational software has been the main factor in encouraging sales of personal computers for individuals and families (Winston, 1998: 237). But the penetration of various new CD technologies – other than of course the music CD – has been minimal, in spite of years of hype about the benefits of CD-R, DVD, etc. From the PC boom of the mid-1980s through to the internet boom of the late 1990s, domestic PCs were mainly used as very, very expensive typewriters or games consoles.[1]

This began to change in the late 1990s. With increasing ownership of personal computers, and the spread of the internet and the world wide web beyond a tiny group of users in the mid-1990s, new cultural forms such as the website and the chat room have become available to a wider public. In a separate section I outline the early history of the internet, and show how it was interpreted and employed as a new, democratic form of communication. To what extent has the internet fulfilled its early promise? As a cultural industry, does it allow for greater access and decentralisation than the cultural industries already discussed throughout this book? What have been the effects of commercialisation and professionalisation on the net?

I then discuss one of the most fashionable terms in coverage of the cultural industries in recent years: convergence of media, computers and telecommunications. It is important to realise that this is a term used, in most cases, to describe possible future events, rather than past developments. This serves as a prelude to discussion of new television technologies, including cable and satellite, but especially digital television – the leading contender for the role as the major platform for converged information/entertainment services. What will be the effects of digital television on cultural consumption, and on cultural production?

In summary, then, this chapter will assess the impact of digitalisation on the cultural industries by unpacking the idea of digitalisation, and by analysing separate technological devices and systems.

## Digital music technologies

Digital technologies began to have a substantial impact on music-making in the early 1980s. The three key new (and interrelated) production technologies were:

---

1  CD technology has been slow to spread in other areas of cultural consumption too: the analogue video still, at time of writing, holds sway over the DVD except amongst the wealthiest North Americans and Europeans.

◆ *Samplers*: These are computers that can store sounds and then manip-
ulate them. Samplers can take tiny sections of music, such as four bars
of bass line from an old record, and then replay it when the sampler is
triggered. This can include noises of all kinds as well as music.

◆ *Sequencers*: These are simply digital programmes or devices that
record musical data and can play them back. Sequencers take many
forms: 'as a basic component within drum machines and many
synthesizer keyboards, as stand-alone hardware devices, and in computer software form with elaborate, graphical representations of the
[musical] data' (Théberge, 1997: 222). Sequences of music are triggered
by hitting certain keys or strings. Sequencers offer great flexibility and
control in terms of tempo, sound texture, rhythm, etc.

◆ *MIDI (Musical Instrument Digital Interface)*: This is not a device but a
standardised set of machine protocols and computer languages, agreed
by musical instrument manufacturers as digital machines began to
develop, replacing analogue synthesisers in the early 1980s. In effect,
the MIDI protocols allowed samplers, sequencers and various digital
instruments to talk to each other. The introduction of MIDI hastened
the commercial development of a great many devices, as buyers
became confident that different components would be mutually compatible. It is common to hear changes in music-making over the last 20
years described as the 'MIDI revolution'.

Debates about the consequences of digitalisation in musical production
concern a number of key issues.

### Aesthetics, creativity and originality

It seems almost laughable now that in the 1970s and 1980s synthesisers –
the generation of new musical instruments immediately preceding digital
sequencers and samplers – were thought of by many rock writers and fans
as 'cold' and 'inhuman', whereas the electric guitar was thought of as
expressive and authentic (see Frith, 1986 for an important deconstruction
of such thinking). Such attitudes were of course the result of certain
dominant ways in which these instruments were played and how the
resulting genres were interpreted. Samplers and sequencers – especially
the drum machine – inherited these discourses. This way of thinking has
fallen from favour (though it is still widespread) and now the interesting
possibilities opened up by digital instruments are better understood. Alan
Durant (1990) provided an extremely useful summary of some of these
possibilities at a time when such instruments were relatively new. First,
samplers opened up new textural or sound–colour possibilities. They could
borrow conventional musical sounds from elsewhere or 'conventionally
non-musical sounds, such as birdsongs, roadworks or water-dripping'
(184). Some of these sounds were (and are) provided by instrument

manufacturers, but more adventurous musicians could create their own sound library by recording sounds from other disks and from the world around them. For Durant, this meant that music-making was no longer limited by 'technical facility' or even by general human capability; sequencers could produce drum patterns faster and more relentless than the strongest drummer, for example. Second, sequencers and samplers created new composition and editing possibilities, by offering solutions to problems of inaccurate, incomplete, or technically impossible perform-ance, and 'by allowing for intensive scrutiny, manipulation and repair of anything entered into the machine' (Durant, 1990: 185). Third, samplers allowed for new forms of collage as musicians could draw on other songs, records and so on, with new possibilities for innovation, as has been the case in hip hop, and in various forms of electronic dance music.

Durant was careful to point to some of the 'unresolved issues' sur-rounding these new possibilities, and I'll come back to these shortly. But it would be foolish to deny the very real flexibility afforded by these new digital technologies. Of course, these machines are often used in an uncreative way. The ability to repeat the same uninteresting rhythm over and over again can lead to repetition. But sequencers allow for random variation to avoid this problem; and live drummers can play boringly and badly too. Many pop tracks use the rhythm track off an old record, rearrange it and add a new vocal hook. Such a process is often criticised as being unimaginative, but such a reworking is not so different from what musicians do anyway, even when they are composing and performing an 'original' piece. In Jason Toynbee's formulation (drawing on terms devel-oped by Bourdieu, 1993) they work within a space of possibilities, consti-tuted by the relationship between their own dispositions and the field of music production, and by the field of works – the 'historical fund of practices, textual forms and codes' available to them (Toynbee, 2000: 40). Sampling, then, represents a different means of plucking elements from the field of works and recombining them, still constrained by the limita-tions of the space of possibilities. So for all the anxieties about digital instruments, new creative opportunities were offered, within a system of musical activity that was essentially continuous with what had gone before.

### Working practices of musicians

A second set of issues concerns how music is made. In the most important study of changing music technology to date, Paul Théberge (1997) is pessimistic about the impacts of digitalisation on the working practices of musicians; and indeed about its effects on music as a collective, social activity. MIDI technologies generally have a design based 'metaphorically' on the dominant mode of popular music recording from the 1960s onwards: the analogue multitrack studio. Up until this time, musicians would go into a studio, perform live and have the performance recorded by two or three microphones. But from the late 1950s onwards, it became possible to use parallel tapes to combine different musical tracks. This was *multitracking*.

Sequencers use multitracking as a 'metaphor' in arranging information, by dividing the different elements into tracks, as on an analogue recording console. For Théberge this is more than a mere marketing decision. In multitracking (in most cases) musicians laid down tracks individually and at different times, and a sound mixing/engineering team combined the tracks at some later point. In an earlier article, Théberge (1989) portrayed such temporal and spatial separation of musicians as an example of rationalisation, in the Weberian sense, putting economic performance ahead of human interaction. He drops the term in his book, but a sense of this normative framework lies just beneath many passages. He sees the various MIDI technologies as encouraging a mode of music-making which is 'fragmented and disjointed' (1997: 228). Théberge is unclear about what the negative consequences of such separation might be, but he seems to feel that it reduces the possibility for music to act as a means of human sociality. This emerges in his discussion of *the home studio* – the setting-up of digital recording equipment in the house, so that high-quality recording can be carried out at low cost, and maximum convenience to the musician. Théberge describes the typical components: 'several synthesizers, signal processors, a mixer, a digital recorder and a computer' (234). Whereas some – including of course the musical instrument industry's own marketers – have hailed the home studio as a potential democratisation of the recording industry, because it frees musicians from the need to create tracks in expensive professional recording studios, Théberge sees home studios as another sign of individualisation and rationalisation. The rise of 'the hyphenated musician' – the 'singer-songwriter-producer-engineer-musician-sound designer' (221–2) strips away the collective nature of musical collaboration, he feels. He describes the isolation of home studios: 'Studios tend to be located in bedrooms, dens, or basement rec rooms, far from the main traffic of everyday life' (234). In Théberge's view, the headphones commonly used while working on digital instruments reinforce the cutting-off of the (mainly male) musician from the rest of a family, or from friends.

Théberge's view is provocative but it seems overly pessimistic. Some musical activity has always taken place in relative isolation, especially practice. Music isn't necessarily always a matter of sociality. And making (or listening to) music in privacy needn't necessarily be a matter of individualisation and isolation. The positive side of 'private' music consumption and production is expressed well by the ethnomusicologist Steven Feld, talking about his use of music in his 1950s US suburban home: 'I remember when I discovered headphones – the ultimate way to tune out my parents and the world was with headphones, what an incredible invention! They got me through high school' (Keil and Feld, 1994: 9).

### Systems of payment and reward

New musical technologies have important implications for the ownership of sounds, and for how financial rewards for the sales of musical works are distributed via copyright. Anglo-American law protects what it calls 'original' works but original in this context does not mean innovative or challenging, it simply means 'origin in an author'. The idea of origin in an author as the basis of what should be protected in copyright law is a remnant of the forms of cultural production prevalent when copyright law was first being formulated, in the eighteenth century. But in the twentieth century, as we saw in Chapter 2, copyright is increasingly based on complex divisions of labour, often involving a number of people who could claim to be authors. Twentieth-century copyright law has tended to deal with this problem by assigning copyrights to the companies that organise production: film studios, record companies, television channels, etc. In so doing, however, it relies on a definition of a work as *a fixed entity*: a particular film, book, recording and so on. Some cultural forms fit uncomfortably with such an idea – in particular, cultures which place greater emphasis on oral tradition, on the passing-on of stories, tunes and representations within a particular cultural formation. This is true of so-called primitive, pre-industrial cultures; but it is also true of some forms of industrial culture associated with peoples who have been denied access to widespread literacy, or who have come to associate dominant forms of culture with oppression. A number of writers, for example, have discussed the important presence of such practices in African American and diasporic Caribbean cultures (Gates, 1988; Gilroy, 1993).

For some commentators, digital sampling encourages cultural practices that challenge the notion of cultural work as being primarily about fixed, finished artefacts. Sampling allows musicians to borrow from whatever sound sources come to hand, whether on previous audio or film recordings, or in the world around them. Many recent musical forms have involved the extensive use of such collage via the sampler. The most significant example is rap/hip hop, which in the eyes and ears of many, owes its tendency to sample, borrow and rejuxtapose sounds to the tradition in African American culture of borrowing and recombining snippets of older stories, songs and so on (a process known in vernacular African American English as 'signifyin' – see Gates, 1988). This has led some writers to suggest that rap and, by extension, sampling in general, have a tendency to undermine the notion of cultural property as it is embodied in copyright law. For example, Thomas Porcello argues that 'rap musicians have come to use the sampler in an oppositional manner which contests capitalist notions of public and private property by employing previously tabooed modes of citation' (1991: 82).

There may be a tendency in particular uses of the sampler towards a certain, implicit questioning of such notions of ownership, but arguments such as that made by Porcello tend to downplay the actual role of the courts in determining how such ambiguities are legally resolved. Thomas Schumacher (1995), for example, shows that the US courts have consistently ruled in favour of copyright owners (that is, publishing companies that own the song, or record companies that own the specific recording of it which has been sampled) whenever such copyright owners have brought legal action against musicians making records that use samples. So the particular use of sampling may have raised questions about copyright, but the existing legal apparatus, however contradictory in its origins, has tended to answer those questions in a fairly unambiguous way. What is more, the sampler can also be used, even by well-meaning musicians, in ways that are very much compatible with the inequities of existing copyright law. In previously published work (Hesmondhalgh, 2000) I analysed the practices of certain musicians with a multiculturalist aesthetic/ethic based at a West London record company, who sampled non-western music in what they saw as a sympathetic and supportive way. Some musicians and the small independent record companies distributing their work achieved considerable sales from club hits based around such samples. While some musicians and record-company workers made strenuous efforts to credit and reward the sampled non-western musicians, others claimed that they were powerless in the face of copyright laws and practices, and that as the money would in any case only go to the companies holding the copyrights, rather than the musicians, the best thing to do was to evade copyright payments and accreditation. Yet this seemed to me to be, in some cases, a self-serving evasion. Sampling makes unethical borrowing practices more likely in some contexts.

This is not to say, however, that uses of the sampler have no positive potential. Some uses could indeed, as Porcello, Schumacher and others suggest, contribute to a rethinking of copyright law which does not rely on a notion of cultural work based on individual authors publishing complete and finished texts, but which acknowledges the fact that creativity is social (Toynbee, 2001): not only in the sense that it is often complex and collaborative; but also in the sense, referred to earlier, that the creation of all texts owes a great deal to other texts already in circulation. However, such a contribution to reassessing copyright law would rely on activism and argument in the relevant public policy arenas. The technology itself will not do the work of reform.

These debates are relevant for recent controversies about the digital distribution of music. In 1999–2000, speculation was rife in newspapers and magazines that new musical technology, associated with 'peer to peer' software would undermine existing regimes of ownership by allowing swapping of digital music files. Such technology would, claimed many, undermine one of the most important means of profit accumulation in the recording industry: the sale of musical commodities to consumers. The Napster site was the focus of enormous amounts of press coverage but after a US federal ruling against Napster, and various agreements between Napster and the major record companies, copyrighted material was withdrawn from the site, and visits there rapidly dwindled. A second generation of peer to peer software allows for swapping without actually having to revisit a particular site, once the initial software is downloaded. Controversy continues to rage over whether free downloads serve as publicity for acts and records and indeed for popular music itself (as opposed to other forms of cultural activity) or whether they diminish sales substantially. The purchased CD remains a desirable consumer object, and CD sales seem not to have been reduced by the file-swapping craze. Just as the cassette compilation often stimulated the purchase of records and pre-recorded CDs, downloading/CD burning may well encourage participation in musical subcultures, ultimately leading to greater sales for the music-industry companies. But there is no doubt that the major companies are finding the prospective effects of such internet-based software worrying and challenging, and they have responded by forming alliances amongst themselves to set up digital distribution services. The next few years will be interesting times, as the music industry grapples with technological innovation, and the do-it-yourself inclinations of young music fans.

## Desktop publishing and the magazine publishing industry

Newspapers all over the world saw a rapid transition from analogue to digital systems of production in the 1980s. Change in magazine publishing was slower but nevertheless swept through the industry in the late 1980s and early 1990s in the form of desktop publishing (DTP) software packages. Here, as in all the technological examples discussed in this chapter, we must be careful to avoid technological reductionism (Chapter 3): DTP was not something which 'happened to' magazine publishing; it was introduced for specific reasons. Driver and Gillespie (1992; 1993) show how falling revenues and profits in the UK magazine publishing industry from the late 1970s (the Long Downturn again) forced a number of innovations. The circulation for mass market magazines was shrinking. Internationalisation meant that publishers faced new competition from foreign companies entering the UK market. Magazines faced increasing competition from other industries for their share of the national advertising cake. The large companies that dominated the industry responded in a number of ways. They looked to niche markets to supplement their core mass market titles; they placed a stronger emphasis on marketing; companies such as EMAP established divisional structures whereby semi-autonomous companies specialised in specific markets; and they introduced the DTP packages developed by computer software companies in order to reduce costs. DTP was one of a number of innovations intended to deal with difficult market conditions.

Driver and Gillespie examine the effects of DTP on the traditional division of labour in the magazine industry. Figure 7.1 shows the effects on the production process in magazine publishing. In the old, pre-digital system, publishers would be in constant interaction with the pre-press companies: typesetters, who would key in the copy written by journalists, and repro houses which would deal with illustrations before the typesetters made up the final pages. Each stage involved great skill and expertise, and the pre-press and printing stages were highly unionised. In the UK, conflicts between print unions and newspaper publishing companies (including a particularly vicious conflict in 1986 after Rupert Murdoch's News International moved its newspapers from the traditional home of newspaper printing and publishing in Fleet Street, Central London to a specially built,

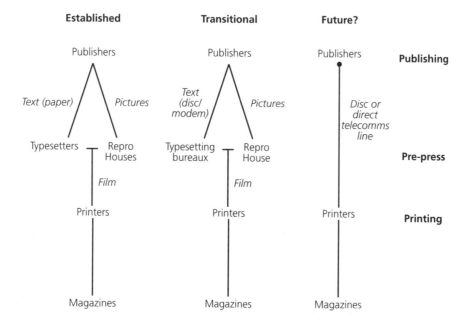

**Figure 7.1  Changing divisions of labour in magazine publishing (Driver and Gillespie, 1992)**

fortified site in Wapping, East London) ended in defeat for the unions. This should not be interpreted as the inevitable triumph of progressive technology over Luddite workers. The printers and typesetters were skilled people defending their jobs and their profession in a climate of tremendous state hostility towards trade unionism. Their defeat paved the way for the introduction of DTP in most large British publishing companies.

DTP brought efficiencies for publishers. It meant that magazines could 'stay open' (accept copy) later, and this in turn meant that advertising copy deadlines could be shifted closer to the printing day; last minute advertisements attract higher rates (Driver and Gillespie, 1992: 155). But its impact has been mixed in other respects (see Daly et al., 1997: 162–81). For many years, even the most developed packages resulted in lower quality than traditional methods. The tighter deadlines resulted in greater pressure for all staff. The traditional division of labour dissolved and editors, artists and others strayed into each other's patches, creating turf wars. New generations of DTP technology meant constant retraining. These disadvantages accounted for the relatively slow, mixed introduction of DTP (Driver and Gillespie, 1992) and hybrid analogue/digital systems persisted into the late 1990s. DTP may have allowed for small-scale magazines to achieve higher quality at lower cost than in previous generations and for larger companies to ride out an economic downturn. But its main, short and medium term impact in the magazine industry was to lower standards, create workplace tensions and to remove a level of skilled technical work.

## Video and computer games

We can begin to see, then, that talk of the effects of digitalisation as a whole on the cultural industries is almost meaningless. What matters is the specific effects of particular digital technologies in each cultural industry. Computer games, or video games, represent an interesting case, because they formed a *new* cultural industry based on digital technology. The console games software market was worth US$3.6 billion in the USA alone in 1999; PC games, which include education and reference as well as actual games, were worth another US$2.2 billion (*Screen Digest*, October 1999). How distinctive is this new cultural industry, based on digital technology?

The games industry does have some distinctive features. The console games industry, unlike all other cultural industries, is dominated by Japanese corporations, namely Nintendo, Sega and Sony. It is far more oriented around hardware/software synergies than any other cultural industry in recent times. The small companies commissioned to produce innovative texts are very much reliant on developments in the hardware sector; and this sector is even more prone to the introduction of new gadgets than is consumer electronics equipment in the music and film industries. The hardware companies are reliant on the software for their profits – the hardware consoles are sold at relatively small profit margins, whereas games have a very high mark-up (Caves, 2000: 215). Games players tend to be loyal to a particular console (Poole, 2000) and hence to its associated software; or, rather, most people find it too expensive to own two consoles. Every few years, a new generation of console hardware is introduced, backed up by increasingly massive marketing campaigns in an attempt to shift devotees of another company's hardware over. Box 7.1 summarises three generations of hardware.

---

### Box 7.1   Generations of computer game consoles

| Company | 1980s/early 1990s | mid 1990s | Late 1990s/2000–01 |
|---|---|---|---|
| Nintendo | NES, SNES and Game Boy | Nintendo 64 | Dolphin |
| Sega | Mega Drive | Saturn | Dreamcast |
| Sony | | Play Station | Play Station 2 |

Each generation has involved better graphics, resolution and so on and better player control of the action. Sega and Nintendo dominated the early phase of the industry, as it developed out of arcade entertainment games. Nintendo's most famous early games were *Mario Bros.* (1983) and *Super Mario Bros.* (1985). Poole (2000: 18) compares Nintendo to the Beatles – 'wholesome fun for all the family' and Sega to the Rolling Stones – 'the snarling, street-smart gang'. Sony entered the market in the mid-1990s and the success of Play Station was helped by *Tomb Raider* (1996), designed by the UK games company Eidos. Sony gained a market lead in many countries, as Saturn flopped and Nintendo 64 lacked sufficient software. Sega's Dreamcast represented a surprise re-entry into the console market in 2000, closely followed by the launch of Sony's Play Station 2.

---

For all its newness, the industry follows the 'editorial model' of commodity production identified by Miège (1987) as characteristic of the production of books, records and films. In this model of cultural production, texts are 'reproduced on formats conferring a private good character', a publisher/producer organises production, many small or medium-sized companies cluster around oligopolistic firms and creative personnel are remunerated by copyright payments. Miège contrasts this with a number of other 'logics' of production, mainly 'flow' production of broadcasting, where instead of individual commodities for sale, the emphasis is on the provision of an uninterrupted flow of entertainment (an idea Miège borrows from Flichy, 1980); and the production of written information: that is, principally the press, including magazine publishing. The computer games industry, then, represents a certain amount of continuity in terms of its organisation. Firms such as Nintendo and Sega are the oligopolistic companies at the centre of the industry. They have designed games in-house, but increasingly games are commissioned by the large corporations from specialist companies. There is a premium on inside knowledge of what fan subcultures are looking for, and large corporations gain access to this knowledge by entering into transactions with small companies made up of enthusiasts: in this respect, there are important parallels with sections of the popular music industry (see Chapter 5).

Like many new cultural industries, the games industry has been the object of much public anxiety about the effects of its products. For many years, games were dismissed or worried over as simple, violent fare for the young. In the late 1990s, the games industry was in a boom period. Although competition for market share between the three formats was fierce, the corporations and their software associates were competing for an ever expanding cake, as games devotees continued to buy games in their twenties and thirties, while the next generation of boys and girls joined the audience (Poole, 2000). Some recent statistics also suggest that the gap between male and female users is diminishing fast (see Poole, 2000: 157). *Screen Digest* (October 1999) attributes the success of the games industry to 'a far greater depth of quality product than the filmed entertainment market'. Now writers are noting the increasing sophistication and quality of games. Poole (2000: 35–58) usefully analyses the considerable variety of genre available in the games market, including shoot-em-ups, racing games, the platform game, fighting games, strategy games, sports games, role play games and puzzle games. Jenkins (2000) notes the possibility that a new generation of games will legitimate video games as a new popular art form, just as the films of the late 1910s and 1920s legitimated the then infant form of cinema.

## Digital networks, the internet and the world wide web

### The development of the internet

Patrice Flichy (1999) interprets the internet as the product of an encounter between two cultures with a certain amount in common: university computing cultures and the counterculture.[2] The internet developed in a series of laboratories, mainly university ones. Their work on the internet was mainly financed by ARPA, the US Department of Defense Research Agency. The main aim was to enable university teams to share mainframe computers and to enable distant connections, file transfers and messaging. Unlike commercial research, the research was essentially collaborative, aimed at providing a shared resource. In Flichy's view, 'the characteristics

---

2 My colleague Tim Jordan has convinced me that Flichy is wrong to label countercultural IT interventions as specifically 'Californian'. Many important developments took place elsewhere, especially in Europe and in other parts of the USA – see Jordan (1998).

of the Internet are related, to a large extent, to the fact that this technology was designed for and by the academic community' (36). The fundamental principles of the internet were 'free circulation of information, belief in the productiveness of confrontation and interaction, autonomy, and individual responsibility' (36). In parallel to the development of the internet, 'a sprawling computer counterculture emerged in the United States' (Castells, 1996: 353), including hackers, consisting most notably of Bulletin Board Systems. This parallel use of the internet was based on similar values to the academic use of the internet.

By the late 1980s and early 1990s, both state-funded and counter-cultural, alternative internet cultures had developed considerably. The internet inherited an association of information technology with indi-vidual freedom and autonomy, and decentralisation. The idea of doing it yourself, of the potential of information technology to be appropriated by 'ordinary people' had a long history in the USA: radio hobbyists had an important effect on spreading radio as a technology in the early twentieth century. As with radio, hobbyists were crucial in disseminating informa-tion technology, as popular electronics magazines promoted self-assembly computer kits to make the first minicomputers (Winston, 1998: 233). Important PC businesses such as Apple were created by hobbyists with close links to the counterculture (Flichy, 1999: 37). The role of small and medium-sized companies in developing innovations in information tech-nology was significant (Castells, 1996; Forester, 1985: 50–80). The emphasis on Silicon Valley in many accounts, including that of Castells, may play down the role of very large corporations, but it appeals to a long-standing tradition of US entrepreneurialism. This love of small business, combined in many cases with the countercultural ethic of a hands-on, do-it-yourself (DIY) attitude to technology, meant that IT became associated with innova-tion and with a resistance to 'mainstream' values, even as major corpora-tions such as IBM, always heavily invested in business and military markets, entered the personal computer business in the early 1980s and as small companies founded by countercultural enthusiasts, such as Apple, grew into major corporations.

So digital networks – especially the internet and the world wide web – inherited the countercultural understanding of personal computing as democratic. What is more, because the academic and countercultural computing cultures were made up of intellectuals, these cultures were able to produce accounts of themselves which were extremely influential in disseminating a utopian notion of the internet as a new, liberatory medium of communication (Rheingold, 1992; Negroponte, 1995; and *Wired* maga-zine). Digital networks have, to a limited extent, altered existing social relations of production and consumption. They have produced huge amounts of small-scale cultural activity. They have enabled new ways for people to communicate with each other. They have provided mechanisms to enhance political activism. The internet is full of material that is arcane, bizarre, witty, profane, as well as the inept, the mundane and the banal. These many minor forms of subversion, insubordination and scepticism don't cancel out the enormous concentrations of power in the cultural industries. But they do, I think, represent a *disturbance*. The problem is that this disturbance of existing relations of cultural production and consumption has happened mainly within a very specific section of the world's population. What is more, this disturbance has been largely contained by developments described below.

Some of the most optimistic projections for the progressive use of the internet as a whole were based on the era when it was used by academics and (mainly professional) countercultural enthusiasts. Since 1991, however, when the US National Science Foundation changed its acceptable use policy to allow commercial traffic across its NSFNET (then the main component of the internet) the internet has expanded and altered. Use of the internet for commercial means has enormously expanded. The development of the world wide web (developed in similar academic computing cultures to the internet, and based on similar principles of shared knowledge) enabled far greater use of images and graphics, and this increased the interest of businesses of all kinds in the internet.

The relevant question, then, is how the internet *as it has developed* is likely to affect cultural production and consumption. It is the internet as it stands at the beginning of the twenty-first century which is the relevant object of analysis, not the internet of the early 1990s, featured in so much of the internet literature. Of course, as the internet has developed, it has become commonplace to hear optimistic claims about its effects questioned. Some accounts make it sound as though the exciting potential of the internet has been utterly exhausted, save for the efforts of a few political activists. I think such pessimism is premature, but certainly there are some worrying features of current usage of digital networks which need to be set against the optimistic claims of internet proponents.

### Access and decentralisation

According to Manuel Castells, the internet produces communication that is 'largely spontaneous, unorganized, and diversified in purpose and membership' (Castells, 1996: 355). This involves consumers becoming producers, as on the world wide web, where 'everybody with access can produce her/his/its [sic] "home page" '. Even as the net changes, 'what remains from the countercultural origins of the network is the informality and self-directedness of communication, the idea that many contribute to many, and yet each one has her own voice and expects an individualized answer'. The micro-networks formed on the web 'are characterized by their pervasiveness, their multifaceted decentralization and their flexibility'. Castells acknowledges inequalities in access and the appeal of the internet to a cosmopolitan elite and its potential for 'reinforcement of the culturally dominant social networks' (363). Others, however, tend not to acknowledge that the liberatory aspects of the medium will be restricted for many years to come to relatively few people and, crucially, to particular social groups (Gates et al., 1996). They fail to acknowledge how such inequalities undermine claims about the communicative freedom offered by the internet. There is massive inequality in access to the internet, not only between advanced industrial countries and 'developing' countries, but also within some of the 'developed' countries themselves. Raphael (2001) provides a devastating series of statistics on this – see Box 7.2.

---

### Box 7.2   Access to the internet

Raphael (2001) presents the following statistics, amongst others:

◆ By the end of 2000, the internet was still only used (by a very generous definition of use, as at any time in the previous three months) by about 7 per cent of the world's population.
◆ The developed world dominated content, with 64 per cent of internet host computers located in the USA and Canada, and another 24 per cent in Europe.
◆ There were more hosts in New York than in all of Africa.
◆ 78 per cent of internet web pages were in English, which is spoken by only 15 per cent of the world.
◆ The average Sierra Leonean would have to pay 118 per cent of her or his earnings to pay for a month of internet access.
◆ But low internet penetration is not confined to poorer, developing countries. Even in Southern Europe, only 8 per cent of homes had internet access in 1999, according to Eurobarometer figures cited by Murdock (2000: 53).

But, even aside from this international inequality, there are also huge inequalities in access to the means of cultural production even within relatively wealthy countries.

◆ Drawing on US National Telecommunications and Information Administration data, Raphael shows that the internet-connection figures for black and Latino households in 1999–2000 were in each case about 18 per cent less than the figure for 'all homes', and that this gap had widened, not diminished, over the previous two years.
◆ Even in 1999, after years of hype about the on-line revolution, only 45 per cent of US households had PCs and only 60 per cent of these (that is, 27 per cent of all households) were on-line (McChesney, 1999: 148).
◆ In 1997, the UK Office of National Statistics showed that of the 20 per cent of households with the lowest income only 8 per cent owned home computers, whereas 79 per cent owned telephones. But of the households in the highest 20 per cent of income, 57 per cent had a PC.
◆ These figures had changed little by 1999. According to Anderson et al. (1999) nearly 60 per cent of households in the highest (professional and managerial) social classes in the UK own computers, but this declines dramatically in skilled and semi-skilled households to 25 per cent and 12 per cent respectively.

The response to such statistics from internet optimists is that such figures will change: once again, futurology replaces actual analysis (and in response we must resort to some futurology too). As the technology spreads, and markets grow, the assertion goes, costs will come down, encouraging even the lowest income-earners to gain access to the technology. This ignores fundamental questions about continuing and increasing inequality in on-line worlds. Those on lower incomes might gain access to on-line technology in the coming years, but the access they will gain will probably be to technology that will increasingly seem outmoded and outdated as a new generation of networked devices arrives. Nearly all predictions about digital information and entertainment envisage a future where sounds and images will be piped down *broadband* digital networks (Gilder, 1993; Cairncross, 1997). This will require massive bandwidth in the form of faster line connections, computers, modems and so on. These will become the premier technologies. The poorer sections of advanced industrial countries will gain access to machines that are capable of e-mail and of downloading basic text-and-image websites. These may well enhance the lives of some people, but it should be remembered who benefits most from the use of e-mail: those who have lots of distant friends and relatives, and those who need to communicate with dispersed networks of people for work purposes. Such people are still generally those in the wealthier, cosmopolitan echelons of society.

### Subcultures, professionalisation and commercialisation

This still leaves the possibility that, for the relatively privileged few who have access to the internet, there have been important democratising effects, including the ability to form the kinds of micro-networks mentioned above. Jordan (1998: 59–87) provides unusually concrete discussion of on-line life. He discusses the fluidity of individual identity on some applications of the internet, especially in the world of MUDS and related technologies.[3] Jordan is clear that 'hierarchies based on identity', such as gender, race and class, do not 'disappear from cyberspace but will be reinvented on the basis of new forms of online identity'. Nevertheless such identity-hierarchies are dislocated and disturbed, through the ability of individuals to play with the very idea of identity, but also through 'many-to-many communication and its ability to include more people in decision making than was previously practicable' (81). We should also note the emphasis amongst many user communities on the 'free circulation of

---

3 MUDS are 'programmes set up on a computer that accept connections from many users at once' (Jordan, 1998: 60), involving either adventures and quests, or non-goal directed social interaction. It should be noted that Jordan is less optimistic about other aspects of the internet.

information' (Flichy, 1999: 36) and 'the rejection of . . . undeclared commercial interests' (Castells, 1996: 354).

But how have such interesting and positive aspects of digital networks, amongst the relatively privileged social groups with access to the internet, fared during the late 1990s and early 2000s? Since 1994, when 'business "discovered" the Net' (Sassen, 1998: 177), the way in which the internet has developed has caused serious damage to its potential as a challenge to the forms of cultural communication prevalent in other cultural industries. First of all, the web has become *professionalised*, in that there is now a large sector of people who are paid to write for, and to design, websites, putting back up the barriers between producers and consumers on the internet, which were removed in early uses of digital networks. Secondly, the internet and world wide web have become *commercialised*. Advertising encroaches on nearly all aspects of web communication, in the form of banner headings and pop-up advertisements from the automatic start-up pages on web browsers, to the search engines and portals, to the websites you might visit. Signing on to any service, buying any product, risks a flood of unwanted e-mail messages over the next few weeks and months. Much web content is permeated by advertising to the extent that it is sometimes difficult to tell where advertisements end and the content begins. This is particularly true of the news services offered by the main portals[4] (McChesney, 1999: 175).

Between 1997 and 1999, the main portal sites doubled their advertising revenues year on year (*Screen Digest*, November 1999); and by 1999, advertising revenues accounted for more than 25 per cent of revenue – a figure that looks set to increase. Forms of communication that come to rely on advertising, rather than subscription, as their main source of income tend to become beholden to their advertisers, as a number of political economy writers have pointed out (see, for example, Curran, 1986 on the history of advertising in newspapers). But advertising on other companies' websites is just part of web commercialism. As Dan Schiller (1999: 132) points out, corporate websites must also be seen as a category of web advertising; and billions of dollars have been spent on them over the last few years.

A final aspect of web commercialisation is that networking technology has been appropriated in such a way that practically all uses we make of the web are recorded for market research purposes. Surveillance of web users as consumers rather than as citizens has been built into the very structure of web technology via cookies (files which are left on your computer when you visit a site) and logging software. Marketing and advertising agencies might claim that all this is doing us a favour: it allows

---

4 Portals are the sites which operate as gateways to the web, as default start pages or as book-marked websites which operate as 'home pages'.

us to be targeted more efficiently, and saves us the effort of having to sift through irrelevant advertisements. We can all, then, look forward to the day when we only see advertisements and marketing information for products we intend to buy: a niche marketing paradise. Well, maybe.

Castells seems to think that the liberatory nature of the medium will survive its commercialisation because of inherent properties of the technology. Castells is clear that commercialisation is changing the medium, but he believes that 'while its most heroic tones and its countercultural ideology fade away . . . the technological features and social codes that developed from the original free use of the network have framed its utilization' (Castells, 1996: 354). In such passages, Castells edges close to technological reductionism. Technologies do have lasting features, based on the social codes and discourses surrounding their development; but these features can be reshaped by powerful users and interpreters. Flichy provides a valuable corrective to Castells' assumptions. Asking whether the democratic features of the internet are a product of the technical characteristics of the medium, Flichy replies: 'It seems not, for other models of data processing networks do exist. IBM and other manufacturers have developed centralized networks for businesses, where the role of each actor is clearly defined: some input data, others consult it' (Flichy, 1999: 39). Sassen (1998; 2000) draws attention to the 'enormous growth of private digital networks' (2000: 19). She claims that 'the leading Internet software design focus in the last few years has been on firewalled [that is, protected from access by outsiders] intranets for firms and firewalled tunnels for firm-to-firm transactions. Both of these represent, in some sense, private appropriations of a "public" space' (Sassen, 2000: 20). The social uses of the technology, in other words, outweigh what might appear to be fixed features of the 'technical architecture'.

### Internet industries and control over circulation

The idea that the internet evades control through its decentralised nature is a key feature of optimistic writing about the medium. As Castells (1996: 352) puts it, 'the architecture of this network technology is such that it is very difficult to censor or control it'. Another factor which is helping to curtail the disturbance to existing inequalities in symbolic power caused by the internet is one which will be familiar from earlier chapters: control over which products get to audiences. Just like any other cultural industry, the world wide web can be thought of as having separate elements of creation, reproduction and circulation (including marketing and promotion). There are plenty of symbol creators and enormous amounts of information and entertainment in cyberspace. But which sites get visited and which don't? This depends on the equivalent of circulation in the online world.

Supposedly, we can go anywhere we choose on the web by clicking on whichever icons and sections of text we choose. For some right-wing proponents of the internet (Gilder, 1993), this supposed interactivity was what distinguished on-line experience from off-line cultural industries; the individual consumer could rule. In fact, this is not so different from wandering round a big bookshop: we can go anywhere we like and choose anything we want to buy, as long as we have the money or credit. The problem is that where we go will, to a significant degree, be determined by our existing knowledge and inclinations. How do we know where to go? Early users – the amateur enthusiasts – got over this problem by spending enormous amounts of time on the internet. Most users have limited time and since the commercialisation of the internet, from the early 1990s on, a number of new cultural forms have appeared, which aim to guide users through the world wide web. Particularly important in guiding us are search engines and portals. These are linked to the crucial commercial internet service providers (ISPs) which for many people provide the connection to an internet-linked computer. A number of companies have emerged as the leading players in the ISP sector, most notably AOL in the USA and across much of the advanced industrial world. In most such countries, the leading telecommunications and cable companies have established themselves in ISP markets. The ISPs have evolved increasingly influential codes of conduct and portray themselves as making the chaos of the internet safe and structured, and catered to the individual's needs (Patelis, 1999: 97–8). This has further eroded the DIY ethos at large on the internet. ISPs select search engines and they prioritise certain portals, including in some cases their own search engines or portals.

Raphael (2001) describes how the formation of portal sites serves as a strategy for reducing risk for cultural-industry corporations. Portal sites allow cultural-industry companies such as Disney, computer software companies such as Microsoft and hardware companies such as Compaq to limit the damage to their business caused by people surfing instead of watching videos, using non-internet software and so on. Portal sites do this by ensuring such companies a presence on the web and by cross-promoting and selling their other products. Portals bring together a number of sites and services, such as e-mail, news and chat rooms, enticing audiences to stay longer, which means that portal owners can charge advertisers more. They also bring together different ways of making money from audiences: selling audiences to advertisers (the main way in which web divisions of cultural-industry corporations make money) but also subscriptions to services, and direct sales.

As anyone who uses the internet will know, search engines are a particularly important means of affecting which sites get visited and which don't. Introna and Nissenbaum (2000) provide a valuable explanation of the problems of search engines. There are two main categories of engine: directory-based and those that use spiders (software robots which crawl out over the web, retrieving information). In the case of directory-based search engines, such as Yahoo, web-page creators submit their sites to the search engines. There is a huge queue for inclusion, only a quarter of sites are accepted and the explicit grounds for inclusion are not made available (Introna and Nissenbaum, 2000: 171–2). Webmasters and designers can submit their websites to spider search engines but this has mixed results. Mostly, website creators have to depend on being visited by a spider. Only 16 per cent of sites are included on individual search engines, and only 42 per cent collectively on all the major engines (Introna and Nissenbaum, 2000: 170, citing a report by S. Lawrence and C.L. Giles in *Nature*, 1999).[5] Spiders use various criteria to determine which sites get visited. The backlink method is so called because it uses a count of backlinks: that is, how many links to the web page appear over the entire web. But this means that less-known autonomous sites are much less likely to be visited and hence indexed by the search engine. The PageRank method is even worse because it weighs very highly links from pages which themselves have lots of backlinks. The third method uses location – not just geographical, but also in terms of domain name (such as .com rather than .edu). All of this concerns the issue of indexing, of which items even *appear* on a search engine database. To be *highly ranked* in the search engine's list of sites is even more difficult for small, poorly resourced sites. Engines rank according to various criteria, such as links to the site, frequency of keywords at the beginning of a document and other means. Designers and companies are desperate to get high on search engine rankings because it seems that few people look beyond the top 10 or 20 rankings on a search engine's results. Some websites attempt to 'cheat' by, for example, adding in extra keywords early in the site in invisible text. Increasingly, search engines allow web owners to pay for high rankings, and for automatic display of advertisements when particular items are entered. Yet, as Introna and Nissenbaum note, few web users are aware of these issues and many treat search engines as near-objective catalogues of information, much like a library catalogue. Search engines are reluctant to reveal their ranking criteria, and one of the reasons they give is that such openness would encourage 'cheating' of the kind described above. But at least it would help to make people more realistic about the limitations of the notion of the web as infinitely open and decentred.

◆  ◆  ◆

The internet is an extremely important and interesting development in cultural production and consumption. Its radical potential has been

---

5 Meta-engines such as Ask Jeeves rely on the major engines.

largely, but by no means entirely, contained by its partial incorporation into a large, profit-oriented set of cultural industries. Such cycles of radical potential and appropriation are a feature of most technologies invested with utopian hopes. Similar hopes surrounded, for example, the development of lightweight video cameras (see Garnham, 1990: 64–9). But because such technologies exist within cultural and political-economic contexts marked by inequality, concentration of power and the pursuit of profit, they often come to be dominated by less utopian interests. They can have positive aspects, nevertheless.

## Convergence: the promise of further wonders

Euphoria about the economic and communicative possibilities of the internet in the late 1990s helped to fuel a great deal of speculation about the issue of *convergence*. We saw in Chapter 4 how the long-extant idea of telecoms-computers-media convergence operated as a self-fulfilling prophecy in US and European cultural-industry policy in the late 1990s. Because they believed something called convergence was inevitable, policy-makers worked hard to enable it, for fear that corporations in their domain would lose out in global competition for profits. These efforts intensified in the late 1990s, all the more so in the wake of the US Telecommunications Act of 1996. But what are the implications of the term convergence for the cultural industries? To what extent is such convergence already under way, and to what extent is it likely to develop in the future? Dealing with these problems will help to clear the way for consideration of digital television, and for analysis of the future of the internet.

Graham Murdock (2000: 36–9) has helpfully disentangled some of the different meanings that have clustered around the term convergence.

First, there is *convergence of cultural forms* – often referred to in the distant days of the early 1990s, before convergence became the new buzz word, as 'multimedia'. Murdock comments that we 'are just at the very beginning of what many observers predict will be a far-reaching recomposition of cultural forms' (2000: 36). He points to CD-ROMs and websites as a possible picture of textual convergence, where the major components of cultural expression (music, sounds, words, images, graphics) are brought together in one place. This, combined with the user's ability to navigate her own way through material on offer, is one of the aspects of the supposed digital future that has most excited and intrigued observers. For example, much of Castells' analysis of the media (1996: 327–75) is devoted to the idea of a 'grand fusion' of multimedia: see Chapter 8 for a critical discussion of his approach.

Second, there is *convergence of corporate ownership*. I think it will be increasingly common in the next few years for advocates of political economy approaches to argue that this is the 'real' convergence, that this is where the boundaries between media, telecommunications and computing have really come down. Peter Golding, for example, argues that 'convergence should be read as an organisational and economic phenomenon, recognisable most obviously at the level of corporate strategy and structure' (2000: 179). This is indeed important: the introduction of digital television and the dissemination of the internet as a communication technology have meant that new players have entered the broadcasting market from consumer electronics (for example, the Hughes Corporation, which owns the main US digital satellite company, DirecTV), computing and telecommunications. However, there was very little actual convergence across these industries, in terms of permanent mergers, until the AOL–Warner merger of 2000–2001. Most moves towards convergence have been tentative, involving the purchase of minority stakes, alliances and joint ventures of the kind discussed in Chapter 5.

Third, there is the possibility of *convergence of communication systems* (or, as I would prefer it, media technologies). The 1980s and 1990s have seen a proliferation of such technologies. In 1980, most households in advanced industrial countries had a limited repertoire of media technologies receiving a limited number of channels: newspapers, magazines and books, a radio or two, a television (no VCR), some form of audio playback. The increasing penetration of VCRs, cable and satellite throughout much of the 1980s and early 1990s meant more television channels for most people. The personal computer brought computer games and CD-ROMs. The digitalisation of telecommunications meant that personal computers could be networked more easily, and eventually helped lead to the introduction of digital television. But in the late 1990s, suggestion that this range of media technologies might converge was aired more and more, because digitalisation makes it theoretically possible for all information and entertainment to be converted into compatible strings of 0s and 1s; and in the 1990s, digitalisation was proceeding apace. By the end of that decade, it was possible to distribute digitally the basic components of cultural communication (words, images, sounds and so on) in a number of ways, including analogue terrestrial television, analogue cable and satellite and even mobile phones. But there were only two serious contenders to be the basis of any significant convergence of media technologies: the internet and digital television.

As internet hype prevailed in the late 1990s, many assumed that convergence would take place in the form of the internet-linked personal computer. But gradually the sober truth began to be discussed more and more: that for the home computer to become the basis of converged information and entertainment the widespread availability of an *integrated broadband system* would be required. At the moment, it takes half an hour to download a four-minute album track on even quite advanced, expensive machines, and music takes up very little bandwidth compared with video. For entire films or television programmes to be practicably downloadable would require enormous leaps in infrastructure (that is, telephone lines and switching devices), modems and the affordability of vast amounts of computer memory. In North America, cable internet took the lead in broadband access, but even after massive promotional efforts by the two leading operators, AT&T/TCI's Excite@Home and Warner's RoadRunner, only 2 per cent of US homes had cable internet by July 1999 (*Screen Digest*, August 1999) and at the end of 1998, only 25 per cent even had broadband cable available. Cabling the rest of the advanced industrial world will require continuing economic optimism in the wealthiest countries and enormous investment on the part of governments (in the usual forms of corporate welfare, such as tax-breaks, etc), companies and consumers.[6] And we should recall that the numbers of people having any access at all to the internet are still small. In the words of *The Wall Street Journal*, the web is still imprisoned inside the PC (McChesney, 1999).

Meanwhile, television is already embedded in the lives and homes of consumers. The idea that the internet would quickly replace television, prophesised by internet gurus such as Negroponte (1995) and Gilder (1993) has been comprehensively demolished by audience research. Coffey and Stipp (1997), for example, showed that television viewing has hardly declined at all during the era of the personal computer, even amongst regular personal computer users. It requires relatively little adjustment in cultural habits for television users to begin to search for information, shop and so on on their television; indeed many people already use their televisions for this purpose via relatively primitive teletext systems. Digital television is therefore far more likely to emerge in the next 10 years as the major converged media platform/distribution form – and it is hardly worth speculating beyond then. So the most meaningful way to discuss convergence, in my view, is to consider digital television.

## Digital television

Most advanced industrial countries will gradually change over to digital transmission for all broadcasting services in the next few years, meaning that television owners will have to replace their sets – a boon for the consumer electronics firms that dominate set manufacture. For most consumers, this will mean getting the main five to eight channels in digital form, rather than analogue. Digital offers better pictures, but only an

---

6 For this reason, the type of internet-based multimedia system on which Castells bases his discussion of media in the network society, is almost certainly at least 10 years away from realisation, for all but a privileged few.

expert would be able to tell the difference. The main novelty of digital television is its potential to offer a supposed abundance of programming choice. Through compressing digital signals, digital television, whether delivered by cable, satellite or terrestrial relay-aerial systems (see Box 7.3) is capable of delivering literally hundreds of channels. This, it is often claimed, means more than just an extension of what was offered by the system of terrestrial broadcasting plus cable and/or satellite, developed from the early 1970s in North America and from the 1980s in most of Europe. Essentially, outside the USA, this consisted of one to three analogue channels plus a few cable or satellite niche channels (music, sport, news, films). There will be certainly more of such channels but digital television also involves very different types of programming, often described by the digital television industry as 'interactive', in that the viewer is supposedly given the tools to find her or his own way through the programming. Digital television represents the television industry's response to the challenge of new media and the type of interactivity offered on digital television has been very much influenced by the type of interactivity available in CD-ROMs and websites. So, for example, viewers can choose from which camera angle to view a football match; or they can select answers to questions in a quiz show they are watching. Amongst the most important of these services is 'near video on demand': the same film is programmed to start showing at, say, 15-minute intervals; the viewer orders the 8.45 or 9 pm start. But they also include: information services, more akin to a newspaper page or a website than to television as we have known it; channels which relay radio stations, along with some display about what is being played; and web access via the television. It should be clear, then, why digital television is a hot prospect when it comes to convergence.

## Box 7.3   Digital television

Digital television takes three main forms:

- Digital cable: where the digital signal is delivered via cable lines.
- Digital satellite: where the digital signal is delivered straight to homes and businesses via a satellite dish.
- Digital terrestrial: involves using the analogue aerial and television set to deliver pictures. It therefore has the advantage of cheap installation. And yet it looks set to fail, and has only been introduced seriously in two or three countries.

Cable and satellite companies are competing across Europe and the USA to take the lead in dominating digital. Cable is winning out in the USA; satellite is leading the way in Europe.

Digital television will not be the only such distribution form. Wealthier consumers are likely to use both digital television and the internet, with mobile telephony providing an important third platform, to rival and supplement portable computers. The domination of a single digital super-medium, of the kind predicted by Castells (1996), appears to be a long way away and, in my view, will probably never happen. Indeed, it may be that television represented the height of convergence, in the sense of a dominant medium incorporating many different forms of cultural com-munication. Instead, we have seen a *proliferation* of media technologies and communication forms since the 1970s. Digital television and the PC are extending this proliferation as plug-ins and accessories abound. Recent examples are MP3 players, various forms of DVD, and the TiVO box, a computer device that allows the user to store television programmes with much more flexibility than the VCR or DVD. Some of these technologies will be withdrawn by the corporate alliances that developed them. But some will stick. The term 'convergence' is as much a misnomer for media technologies as it is when applied to cultural forms and industrial strategies: we are likely to see continued proliferation of media technologies rather than convergence.

Nevertheless, the emergence of digital television as a transformed version of television as it existed from the 1950s to the 1990s is very significant. How to assess digital television in the early days of its emergence? To what extent does it genuinely offer an expansion of choice and interactivity for consumers? What have been its effects on the cultural industries so far, and what will be its likely future effects?

## Effects on consumption

As we have seen, the corporations leading the way in its dissemination portray digital television as offering choice and interactivity to its viewers. But such choice comes at a cost. For digital television, even more than cable and satellite, has become associated with *pay*-television. The advertis-ing market for television has been saturated (Kleinsteuber, 1998): expansion can only be funded by charges for programming. 'Old' television, espe-cially public service broadcasting, was cheap, even if some of its costs were hidden in the form of huge advertising expenses which were passed on to the consumers of the goods being marketed. When cable and satellite subscription services were introduced in most of Northern Europe in the late 1980s and early 1990s, the transnational cultural-industry corporations owning these services used their vast resources of capital to outbid rivals, including public service broadcasters, for the rights to premium program-ming, especially major sports leagues and events, and films. This has meant enhanced, more detailed coverage of sport, but it has also meant that, in the UK, football matches between leading domestic teams are rarely shown live on free-to-air television. Fans must pay a subscription of about GB£35 (US$50) a month for a package which includes live Premiership football, or find a pub showing the match.[7] But digital television takes this a stage further. The set-top box which, in most digital systems, acts as a decoding device for the encrypted digital signals, has a sophisticated ability to charge for pay-per-view programming. So digital television subscribers are increasingly encouraged to follow the US practice of paying for individual items, such as recent Hollywood movies, porn items and boxing matches. This allows the companies to profit from sudden, impulsive and sometimes drunken purchasing decisions in a way that was unimaginable 30 years ago. The costs of subscription and pay-per-view means that television may become increasingly vulnerable to the inequalities of access apparent in other media, such as the internet. Whether or not this is the case will largely depend on the effects of digitalisation on the industry as a whole.

Although digital television offers an apparent abundance of choice, it seems that viewers tend not to be able to make real use of that choice. Research shows that 'when people have forty-eight channels to choose from, they basically use eleven; with seventy-five choices, they use twelve on average; when the number jumps to two hundred channels, people still only use thirteen' (McChesney, 1999: 148, citing research reported in *Adweek*, June 1998). After all, for all the pleasures of television, there are other things to do with your life – even if it's just to surf the internet. And what about the supposed interactivity of digital television, which is supposed to transform TV viewers from passive zombies to active internet-style explorers? Beyond the occasional experiment with choosing from camera angles, it is difficult to see any real inroads in this respect. The core of programming remains recognisable as television. As broadcast-industry journalist Rod Allen puts it, 'the dominant purpose for which consumers use screen-based material will continue to be to enjoy narrative material. At its most fundamental, what this means is that people will look for *good stories well told*' (1998: 63). Allen extrapolates from this that the internet will not radically challenge the dominance of television; and he also predicts that the extra, interactive services offered by digital television will form a second level of programming, which will be reliant on mainstream television's ability to maintain loyalty through the creative organisation and promotion of narrative material.

---

7 I invite anyone tempted to argue that pay-TV has revived communal sports viewing to join me on a Sunday afternoon or Monday evening to watch such soccer delights as Southampton versus Blackburn Rovers in English pubs, deserted except for the pub manager, his dog, and a few stray drinkers uninterested in the match.

## Effects on the cultural industries

What have been, and are likely to be, the main effects of digital television on the cultural industries, in terms of production and circulation? First, the introduction of digital television has involved, to a degree unprecedented in any other medium, the kinds of strategic alliances discussed in Chapter 5. Complex networks of companies have worked together, because a number of difficult and expensive technologies need to be combined to produce a workable system. The most important of these are the conditional access systems, which involve encrypting the transmitted programmes, and then developing decoding software in set-top black boxes. But it also involves systems for installing boxes and (if necessary) satellite dishes, and systems for sending out decoding cards, subscription bills and advance information about programming. Add in the cost of subsidising installation in order to gain a critical mass of subscribers capable of attracting advertisers, and the huge resources necessary for research, development, expertise and infrastructure make it clear why alliances of enormous telecoms, cable, computer and cultural-industry corporations dominate the communications business today.

Second, huge amounts of content are needed to fill the hundreds of new channels. This favours a number of groups:

- Those who hold the rights to existing catalogues of audiovisual material. This confirms the increasing importance of ownership of intellectual property rights, apparent over many years (see Bettig, 1996 for details of how the cultural-industry corporations consolidated their hold over film rights in the 1980s).
- Hollywood film companies, US networks and those at the centre of the all-powerful US content creation business, who will see their exports boom. The various foundations of US domination, outlined in Chapter 6, look stronger than ever.
- New independent producers, the largest of which have become significant industry players and lobbyists. Some of these make vast amounts of money from the international sale of programming ideas and formats.
- The 'creative talent' at the top of the celebrity scale, including sports people; and the talent agencies and managers who represent these people. This widens still further the enormous inequalities noted by Miège between the underused pool of creative talent, and a vastly overpaid few. In the 1990s, these stars increasingly operated as businesses in their own right, with significant independent production companies based around them.

Third, though, circulation remains central in spite of the increasing importance of content and the increasing rewards for it. Those who run the distribution systems for digital television have a large say in which channels are adopted. Although regulators have attempted to ensure that producers and 'publishers' (that is, the television channels that make the programmes or commission them from other producers) are not discriminated against, there is no doubt that distributors use their competitive advantage to favour their own programming. This is particularly so in the design of electronic programme guides. In some ways, the situation here is akin to internet search engines. There are so many channels on digital television that traditional print guides are increasingly redundant; viewers instead tend to look for quick information on-screen about what is showing. But by placing their own programmes at the top of lists of particular 'bouquets' of channels, companies such as BSkyB, who own the dominant digital TV system in the UK can ensure that their shows are likely to be chosen ahead of those of rivals. For example, if you go to 'films' on the electronic programme guide for Sky Digital, you have to scroll down about 12 channels operated by BSkyB, consisting mainly of imports of US films, and on to the next page of listings, before you come to a rival film channel, FilmFour (a company set up by the UK's non-profit, publicly owned Channel 4).

Fourth, key companies which had established themselves in analogue cable and satellite pay-TV in the late 1980s and early 1990s have gained very dominant market positions in digital television distribution. The most startling example is in Germany, the biggest market in Europe, where Kirch's DF1 digital satellite service is dominant. In France, Canal Plus remains completely dominant. In the UK, BSkyB has one rival in the digital field: ITV Digital (formerly On-Digital) a terrestrial system owned by the two biggest British commercial channels, Carlton Communications and Granada Media Group, which looks set to fail because of its far fewer channels.

All this means that the commercialisation of television has made an important stride forward. Public service broadcasters are more beleaguered than ever, fighting to maintain their legitimacy, as they are attacked by newspapers often owned by companies with a strong interest in the television market. Conditional access systems mean that the charging mechanisms exist which may make the whole principle of television as a public resource redundant in the future. Those sections of the public with relatively high levels of disposable income seem to have accepted that it is worth paying a lot more for something not that much better – if at all – than what existed before. And for all the rhetoric about choice and interactivity, much of it derived from internet-speak, digital television very much remains the centralised, top-down medium that developed in the era of analogue broadcasting.

It is worth comparing the internet and digital television as new media. The decentralising potential of the internet may have largely been captured by cultural-industry and computing corporations, but this capture is not total: alternative organisations such as Linux and Apache exist, and the internet is still a medium where control is relatively dispersed. As we have seen, this is because of a mix of factors, including its technological architecture and the countercultural values of its early users. Digital television may mean that individual channels and programmes have less public impact and power than in the analogue era. But new accumulations of power have appeared around circulation – which was always important but is now more so – and in certain types of content creation. The marginalisation of the notion of public service may mean the end of some dubious paternalist monopolies, but it also means that the best things associated with this ideal – that everyone in a society had the right to access to high-quality programming of all kinds – are being eroded. As I write this, in early 2001, the internet and digital television represent the culmination of the story so far of transformation in the cultural industries.

◆　◆　◆

The introduction of digital technologies into the cultural industries was ultimately the product of post-war developments in the computer and consumer electronics industries. No development of the 1980s and 1990s has been accompanied by such wild claims as has digitalisation (see Feldman, 1998 for an example of a Panglossian treatment of digital media). This chapter has shown that the term 'digitalisation' makes little sense unless it is discussed in the context of *specific* applications, *particular* digital technologies. Have these various technologies opened up access to cultural production and circulation, and greater choice for consumers? Have the barriers between production and consumption been eroded? Has digitalisation produced greater creativity and innovation? The answers, of course, vary across the very different applications. Digital music technologies have been the subject of unjustified fears regarding their implications for music-making; on the other hand, they have been seen as more subversive and transformative than they actually were. It is their insertion into existing regimes and traditions of copyright law, not to mention global political-economic inequality, that has produced the most negative effects in sampling. Desktop publishing has wiped out craft trades, but has allowed small-scale publishing to thrive. Computer games are treated as dangerous, but have produced exciting innovations. The internet has been hailed as the most democratic communications technology in history, but its exciting and progressive uses are in danger of being submerged by commercialism. In all these technologies, we see the dangers of generalising about uses and effects.

These technologies have all had significant effects on cultural production and consumption, but not even the internet and digital television have yet had such an impact that we can speak of a new era in cultural production. New industries such as digital television, internet service provision and computer games all carry very strong inheritances from relatively stable ways of organising cultural production. The characteristics of the complex professional era are still intact in the era of digitalisation: even down to the continuing domination of television.

## Further reading

Garnham's chapter on technology in *Emancipation, the Media and Modernity* (Garnham, 2000) is a very useful overview of issues concerning technological change in general. On digital music, the work by Durant (1990) and Théberge (1997) discussed above is extremely useful. Poole (2000) provides an entertaining but informative treatment of video and computer games. Driver and Gillespie's work (1992; 1993) on desktop publishing was by far the best I found on this neglected topic. The internet literature is already vast. I found Tim Jordan's *Cyberpower* (1998) lively and balanced. The most detailed history of the internet is *Where Wizards Stay Up Late* (Hafner and Lyon, 1996). Steemers (1998) is a useful collection on digital television, but many more books and articles on this topic will surely follow.

# 8 Texts: Diversity, Quality and the Serving of Interests

I now want to address the point at which the cultural industries arguably have their most profound effects on social and cultural life: texts. In what significant ways did texts and their audiences change during the 1980s and 1990s? And in what ways has textual change/continuity then had reciprocal effects on the institutions, organisation and economics of the cultural industries? I'll divide my discussion roughly according to the issues raised when I dealt with textual issues in the evaluative framework offered in Chapter 2: choice, diversity and multiplicity; questions of social justice in relation to texts; and the issue of aesthetic 'quality'. One of the main themes of this chapter is the difficulty of providing definitive answers to questions concerning such textual issues.

## Choice, diversity and multiplicity

One outstanding feature of the texts produced by the cultural industries in the complex professional era has been their proliferation. Greco (1996: 234) reports figures showing that the number of new book titles published in the USA grew from 15,012 in 1960 to 53,446 in 1989 – and this does not even include the huge numbers of back titles available. The theatrical release of motion pictures went up from 233 in 1980 to 509 in 1998. In 1990, there were 104 cable and satellite channels across Europe. By 1994, this figure had almost doubled to 198. But by 1998, this larger figure had more than tripled to 659 channels, including digital terrestrial (*Screen Digest*, May 1999). Wolf (1999: 89) claims that nearly 900 magazines were launched in the USA in 1998 alone. In 1992, 10,716 albums were released on to the UK market; in 1999, the figure was 17,865 (*BPI Handbook*, 2000: 28). There is proliferation in news too: in advanced industrial countries, more news is available to us than ever before, in the shape of specialist rolling news radio and television channels, on the world wide web, and in newspapers and magazines.[1]

Add to this increased output across the different cultural industries, the increasing number of media technologies that most of us make use of in our everyday lives, and it is clear that we are being exposed to an unprecedented potential amount of entertainment and information. But, to recall the discussion from Chapter 2, does this proliferation under conditions of increasing conglomeration, integration and corporate growth represent 'real' diversity, or just 'meaningless' multiplicity (Mosco, 1995: 258)? In Chapter 7, I argued that the case of multichannelling in television suggests that even as the number of channels increases enormously, there is not necessarily any real increase in diversity, as the various new channels tend to provide only slightly modified versions of what was already provided on the core channels that existed before. Most significantly of all, the availability somewhere in the market of many channels, or albums, or magazines, or films, does not equate with knowledge or awareness on the part of audiences about a wider range of forms. Here again we return to the centrality of circulation in the cultural industries. The bookshops, video shops and record shops in any reasonably-sized city are bursting with more produce than most of us could consume in a decade of leisure (maybe even in a lifetime). How to select from amongst them? As consumers, we rely on information provided in the form of promotion and publicity, often filtered for us by friends. So those who assume that proliferation equals diversity have to be careful. Or take the example of film consumption. Most of us mainly consume films made either in the USA or in the country in which we live. Films from other countries are available in video shops but most of us 'choose' not to watch them. This might be because of laziness: 'Why would I want to watch a film with sub-titles?' (though in many countries, many non-US films are dubbed). It could be the result of an arrogant parochialism on the part of some people, who might feel that they couldn't possibly be interested in anything foreign (unless it was from the USA). It could even be because

---

1 Newspapers are slowly losing circulation in most countries, but only slowly, and they remain formidable shapers of opinion.

US films are great, and everyone else's films aren't very good. But this seems unlikely: even with their greater resources, why would people based in the USA be more creative than people anywhere else? The most likely explanation is that audiences are given little idea of what pleasures these non-US foreign films might bring: they haven't been promoted. So narrowness of consumption remains a problem, even in an era of proliferation, because of problems concerning the information audiences receive about which products are available.

Proliferation does not necessarily equate with diversity, then, but is there any way of providing harder statistical evidence concerning trends in diversity? In surveys of the cultural industries as a whole, even those commentators who are concerned about concentration, conglomeration and integration have found it difficult to provide hard evidence of diminished diversity. Sánchez-Tabernero et al. (1993: 151–160) for example, in their chapter on consequences of media concentration, are reduced to offering observations on potential links, which they recognise are unproven. Neuman, who has a remarkable grasp of empirical work in the pluralist communication studies tradition, can cite only one 1970s survey of dubious relevance (Neuman, 1991: 141–2).

Some of the most developed debates regarding trends in textual diversity have been in popular music studies, and the failure of scholars in that field to find adequate measurements is instructive. Also revealing are the difficulties of attempting to pin down the causes of any perceived trends in diversity.

## Popular music, concentration and diversity

A seminal but flawed article by Peterson and Berger (1990/1975) attempted to quantify musical diversity and innovation and to examine the relationship between changing industry structure and musical texts. Focusing on the period 1948 to 1973, they claimed to find evidence for two hypotheses: that there was a weak but inverse relationship between concentration and diversity/innovation (that is, the more concentrated the ownership of firms, the less diversity there was); and that this inverse relationship formed a series of cycles, whereby long periods of gradually increasing concentration and homogeneity were followed by brief bursts of competition and creativity.

Peterson and Berger's study had serious methodological limitations. They used top 10 hit singles as the basis of their samples, even though by the late 1960s and early 1970s albums were a more significant format, and even though the hit charts were an inaccurate measures of sales. They measured diversity by reference to lyrics, rather than to musical form. But aside from these problems concerning how to define diversity, their study also illustrates that there are simply too many other, unquantifiable variables around to 'prove' any kind of link between concentration and diversity. For example, their figures for 1964 to 1969 show increasing concentration and increasing diversity – seemingly against their hypo- thesis of a weak but inverse relationship between concentration and diversity. They explain this problem by reference to sociocultural and organisational factors, such as new lyrical diversity brought about by the US civil rights movement and the Vietnam war, and increasing creative autonomy brought about by increased competition for talent amongst the oligopolistic firms. Similarly, increasing diversity in a period of reconcen- tration in 1970–3 is brought about, in their view, by the conglomerates forming separate divisions which compete with each other. These sug- gestions are fruitful: so fruitful in fact, that it is hard not to see such sociocultural and organisational factors as more important than ownership concentration.

Burnett (1992) applied Peterson and Berger's analysis to the 1980s and found historically high levels of concentration and historically high levels of diversity – a troubling conclusion for critics of oligopoly. Lopes (1992) reinforced these conclusions. Burnett (1995: 107–10) felt that the main factors behind such an apparently surprising conclusion were organisa- tional. His explanation was that the maturing recording industry had found a way to deal with the problem of innovation in risky musical markets, by co-opting independent record companies and working with them in interdependent networks (see Chapter 5).

Christianen (1995) in the most sophisticated attempt I have yet found to examine statistically the relationships between concentration, diversity and innovation in any cultural industry, went much further than these previous studies by gaining access to a database of all albums released in the Netherlands between 1975 and 1992. He analysed diversity according to the amount of music available within 27 different popular music genres and found that during a period of generally decreasing concentration, diversity and innovation generally increased, in that there was more of each and every genre in the Dutch market. This supported Peterson and Berger's argument, but he found that total demand was more significant than concentration in determining diversity and innovation. Yet even Christianen's thorough analysis raises questions about definitions of diversity. His attempt to use genre as a means of thinking through diversity is admirable but it flounders. For his genre classification is based on an old industry model unusable in the 1980s and 1990s, where a huge undifferentiated super-genre called pop coexists with dozens of regional folk musics and a few fringe genres (military music and the like). Genres mutate, hybridise, disappear and appear so rapidly that no genre classifi- cation would work over any historical period greater than three or four years.[2] The quest within liberal-pluralist communication studies and sociology of culture for the Holy Grail of an objective, measurable conception of diversity constantly runs into insuperable problems.

## Convergence as homogenisation?

The obverse danger in cultural commentary is that blithe assumptions will be made about homogenisation, without any adequate content or textual analysis. In *The Rise of the Network Society* (1996), Manuel Castells talks of how 'in the second half of the 1990s a new electronic communication system started to be formed out of the merger of globalized, customized mass media and computer-mediated communication' (364). The past tense is odd and revealing, given that the book's publication date suggests it was completed by March 1996 at the very latest. Castells acknowledges that 'the newness of multimedia' makes it difficult to assess their cultural implications (369), but once he has paid lip service to such caution, he proceeds to develop a theory of cultural change around the emergence of the grand multimedia fusion (369–75), even though by his own account, it started happening only after his book was completed! Some of the changes he discusses such as audience differentiation and stratification have been debated for decades, and are discussed below. But the key changes he discusses are textual. First, there is the integration (or convergence) of messages in 'a common cognitive pattern' (371): news, education, and entertainment are blurred together. To illustrate this, he draws on changes in television programming, where different genres of programming borrow from one another. How this reference to the television past is supposed to illustrate the multimedia future is not clear. Second, multimedia 'capture within their domain most cultural expressions, in all their diversity' (372). The distinctions between audiovisual and printed media, popular and learned culture, entertainment and information, are eroded. The result is (Castells, of course, actually means 'will be') a 'culture of real virtuality . . . in which reality itself is entirely captured, fully immersed in a virtual image setting, in the world of make believe' (373). In other words: if you're not in the system, you effectively don't exist. This culture of real virtuality is important in Castells' overall account of social change, because it produces profound transformations in the experience of space (376–428) and time (429–68). Yet the only evidence he provides for such a transition is this reference to genre-blurring in television. This surely illustrates the perils of futurology in social and cultural theory (though the tenuousness of Castells' analysis of the media seems to have gone unnoticed

---

2 Toynbee (2000: 135–8) provides an invaluable discussion of how music can be prone, in certain periods, to generic hyper-innovation, as musicians and audiences obsessively pursue musical pleasures when certain music details become aesthetically salient.

by reviewers of his book). The homogenisation-through-convergence that Castells describes/predicts seems unlikely; in predicting it, Castells shows the influence of the worst kinds of mass culture criticism. The complex professional era has seen a pattern whereby new technologies tend to supplement existing ones, rather than replacing or merging them, leading to an accretion of separate devices, though of course with television dominant. In fact, what Castells seems to be describing is television as it has actually existed during the complex professional era. As I pointed out in Chapter 7, television is about as close to a convergence of cultural forms as we are likely to get in any short-term projected future.

Curtin (1999) provides a more adequate understanding of textual change in television, via a case study of representations of femininity. Curtin outlines a transition from the 'high network era' in which television was a mass medium, offering widely shared political and cultural experiences, premised upon 'an interlocking system of mass production, mass marketing, mass consumption, and national regulation' (59). In the neo-network era of cable and satellite television, from the 1980s onwards, the cultural industries have pursued new strategies of transnationalisation (familiar from earlier chapters in this book) but also of fragmentation and an increasing focus on niche-marketing. As a result, cultural-industry executives now seek to expose texts through 'multiple circuits of information and expression. They . . . seek less to homogenize popular culture than to organize and exploit diverse forms of creativity toward profitable ends' (60). The dual strategy of transnationalisation and fragmentation involves, according to Curtin, dual textual strategies, one focused on mass cultural forms aimed at national or global markets, and demanding low involvement; and the other targeted at niche audiences, and aimed at producing/circulating texts with 'edge', that produce very intense responses in their audiences. As an example of the type of text that results from the first strategy, Curtin discusses the huge global success of the song 'Macarena' by Los del Rio, which began as a hit in Spain on a small label, but which was distributed globally, in remixed form, by Bertelsmann's BMG record company. The video for this single, shown right across the world, provides complex representations: Macarena is portrayed as powerful, in charge of her life, but ultimately the video contains her feminine desire through the appreciative gaze of the two, middle-aged male singers who approve her, and it turns Macarena's active pursuit of pleasure into a mirror image of masculine fantasy (62). Curtin discusses two texts as examples of the second strategy: First, *Absolutely Fabulous*, a BBC production that was a big hit on the cable/satellite niche station, The Comedy Channel, a show in which feminine desire is represented as 'voracious and uncontrollable' (62). Unlike 'Macarena' (song and video) it makes little apparent effort to broaden its appeal. (Curtin is quite clear that the challenging nature of the programme is permitted by the nature of its audience: middle-class women in advanced industrial countries). Second, Alisha Chinai's 1995 indo-pop music video, 'Made in India', which Curtin feels inverts dominant representations of desire 'by transforming the male body into the sight of spectacle', thus raising suppressed questions, such as 'What does an Indian woman want, need and deserve?' (64). Whether or not you agree with Curtin's specific interpretations, his analysis is a suggestive and, I would argue, successful effort to make links between changing cultural-industry strategies and changing texts. And he provides a compelling argument against the assumption of homogenisation.

Perhaps issues of homogenisation and diversity are easier to address in cultural industries dealing in information, rather than in entertainment. One example, discussed amongst others by Humphreys (1996: 77), is the British national daily press, which has enormous levels of readership and political influence, and has undergone a marked homogenisation in terms of its political views, as its ownership has concentrated since the war. In 1945, there were four Conservative national daily newspapers, two Liberal ones and two Labour ones. But by the 1987 General Election, seven out of 11 national daily papers supported the Conservatives, two were Labour, and two did not commit. What is more, the two Labour papers represented only 20 per cent of the total readership, even though Labour receives between 30 and 42 per cent of votes in general elections. In 1992, '70 per cent of the national daily readers and 62 per cent of Sunday readers were advised to vote Conservative'. Yet even here there are problems in making the argument that there has been overall political homogenisation. It is not clear that support for the two main political parties provides an adequate measure of political diversity. Newspapers include stories elsewhere, other than in their leader columns, and some of these can be antagonistic to the party-political position taken by the newspaper at the time of a general election. *The Financial Times* (the UK equivalent of *The Wall Street Journal*) supported Labour in 1992, but its entire ethos is pro-business.[3] *The Daily Mail* takes right-wing stances on most issues, and yet its television and entertainment pages feature sympathetic coverage of, for example, soap storylines with progressive implications (this may derive from the greater editorial autonomy allowed to writers in these departments). Nor do the figures quoted prove that concentration *caused* homogenisation. There were other factors, such as the decline in circulation of *The Daily Mirror*, the main pro-Labour mass-circulation newspaper.

The proliferation of texts in the last 20 years, then, does not automatically mean diversity; nor can we assume that increasing size and scope of

---

3 A number of traditionally Conservative newspapers, such as *The Sun*, supported Labour (or, rather, the Labour Party's leader, Tony Blair – and this reflects the increasing 'presidentialisation' of British politics) in 1997 and 2001. Most justified this support on the basis that the Labour Party would more competently deliver economic growth than the Conservative Party.

cultural-industry corporations have led to homogenisation or standardisation. The jury remains out. The task must be to find more rigorous ways of discussing diversity, without falling into empiricist traps.

## Social justice and changes in texts

Chapter 5 showed that there has been a huge increase in the size and scope of cultural-industry corporations. These corporations are owned and operated by people with a significant interest in maintaining existing power relations within societies. Have the last 20 years seen any changes in the nature of the texts produced by the cultural industries, in terms of the interests they support and their potential role in promoting or inhibiting the pursuit of social justice (see Chapter 2)?

### Commercialisation/commodification

In one respect, I think, a clear answer is available. The cultural industries have brought about an unprecedented commercialisation of our everyday lives over the last 20 years. In doing so, cultural-industry companies have expanded their role, already emergent in the early years of the complex professional era, as the promoters of their own interests as companies (always their primary interest) and of the interests of businesses in general. Advertising is of course intended to sell goods and services, and in so doing, it often sells the idea of happiness through consumption. Advertising is a cultural industry in itself, but nearly all the other cultural industries act as important vehicles for advertising too. In fact, most advertising comes to us inserted in other media, except for billboard advertising (which in a sense is inserted into our living environments but is not carried by another medium). An important change in texts is that there is now more advertising around than ever before. All the major US networks, for example, have increased the average time per hour they devote to product advertising: ABC from 9 minutes per hour in 1991 to 11:26 in 1996; CBS from 9:10 to 10:29; Fox from 11:03 to 11:40; and NBC from 9:57 to 10:33 (Andersen, 2000). The growth of advertising is also strongly implied by the growth in advertising revenues (see the figures collated in Chapter 3).

Just as significant as the increasing space devoted to advertising is a huge increase in the amount of promotional material carried by the cultural industries in texts that we do not consider to be advertising. Andersen (2000: 3) claims that placing brands in films really took off after the time when in *ET* (directed by Steven Spielberg, 1982) the title alien ate a certain brand of candy/toffee and sales increased by 300 per cent. Andersen provides many examples of more recent product placement and cites evidence showing that audience recall of products is two and a half times greater when products are submerged in TV programmes than when they are advertised separately. Specialist product placement agencies match products to shows, such as *Dawson's Creek* to J-Crew clothes. Andersen hints at the ethical questions surrounding a situation where clothes are being promoted not in a section marked as an advertisement, but hidden away in what purports to be 'just a story'. One such agency believes the greater effectiveness of product placement is because 'products shown in motion pictures or in television are perceived by the audience to be chosen by the star thus receiving an implied endorsement' (Andersen, 2000: 2). Product placement often masquerades as 'hip cynicism' (4). Andersen gives an example from *The Wedding Singer* (1998), starring Adam Sandler:

> Sandler, playing the wedding singer, is lying in bed depressed after his fiancee has left him. A friend comes to visit, lies down on the bed [fully-clothed] and says, 'Hey, these sheets are soft. Do you use Downy?' Sandler replies, 'No, all-tempa-cheer. You can wash your clothes at any temperature and the colours don't run together'. (Andersen, 2000: 4)

So obvious, it's funny. Maybe; but the humour here is not at the *expense* of product placement, as in *Repo Man* (directed by Alex Cox, 1985). It is laughter at the sheer cheek of the film-makers for getting away with such blatant placement. Perhaps this is less offensive than the submerged quality of much product placement, but it is a close call.

Another important change in texts over the last 20 years is that texts often promote other texts produced by the same cultural-industry company. We can consider this on two levels. First, a particular channel or product will promote itself. In 1999, US TV network ABC aired 7,000 promos for its own programmes, nearly twice what it had aired 10 years before (McAllister, 2000: 111). But as a result of conglomeration and strategies of corporate synergy (see Chapter 5), companies increasingly plan and design texts in order to encourage subsidiary, spin-off texts, often of low quality. At the most prestigious, high-budget end of the market, there is the example of *Batman* (Meehan, 1991). The rights to the character were bought by Warner Communications when they bought DC Comics. Besides reviving the comic, Warner (Time-Warner from 1990) produced three films, plus soundtracks, novelisations and huge amounts of merchandising. The films and comics had their merits, but the spin-offs were blatant and imposing in their promotional quality.

I have already examined some of the implications for news of conglomeration. I mentioned in Chapter 5 that news organisations that are part of conglomerates do not necessarily fail to report negative stories about their owners: indeed, such reporting can be a badge of their objectivity, concealing other silences and absences. Nevertheless, there is evidence that conglomerates use their news organisations to promote their entertainment products. Gitlin (1997: 9) gives examples from *Time* magazine, the world's most widely read news magazine. *Time* put author Scott Turow, a Warner Books author, on its cover, at about the time that Warner Bros released the film of his book *Presumed Innocent*. It featured a cover story on tornadoes in the week that the Warner film *Twister* started showing in cinemas.

The most important feature of the commercialisation of texts is that it reinforces a continuing shift in the conception of political subjects under neoliberalism: we are less and less encouraged to think of ourselves as citizens; more and more we are treated as consumers. It would be quite wrong to say, however, that *the entire function* of the cultural industries is to support the interests of businesses, or of some abstract system called capitalism. This issue can be investigated by examining changes and continuities in entertainment texts over the last 20 years.

**The cultural politics of entertainment**

Is there any tendency, during the various changes (and continuities) of the last 20 years, for entertainment texts to have become more compliant, more likely to favour dominant interests in society? The answer is an ambivalent one. Many of these texts reflect the massive inequalities to be found in contemporary societies. They are riddled with sexism, racism and homophobia. They often show a cynical lack of interest in questions of public democracy or private suffering. Yet alongside these undoubtedly worrying tendencies, the media and popular culture are full of emotions and sentiments that do not simply coincide with the interests of business. Rupert Murdoch has consistently supported the most socially and politically conservative causes as an individual and through his newspapers; but his Fox Television network commissions and broadcasts *The Simpsons* – which, at least in the early years of its run, provided a powerful and politically-charged commentary on the traumas and limitations of American family life. But this is only one example from tens of thousands that can be construed as *not* supporting a system in which corporations can do business.

Here are examples of 'structures of feeling' to be found not just on the margins of the cultural industries, but often right in their very centre, at peak time, in prime time, and with huge audiences.

♦   Popular culture is full of cynicism, anger, sarcasm, the celebration of lazy hedonism. Irony and pastiche are to be found everywhere – even in advertising, which was an irony-free zone until the rise of 'creative advertising' in the 1980s. In this sense, media texts have become generally more reflexive about their own operations. If a cliché develops, there is often – though by no means always – a team of comedy writers waiting somewhere to develop a sketch about it for a programme.

◆ Alongside the many texts that fawn on power and wealth, in the shape of glamorous portrayals of the rich and influential, there is also evidence of radical scepticism about the claims of the powerful, and a questioning of authority. The powerful and the prestigious are regularly satirised. The British Royal Family are treated in some sections of the media with reverence and respect; elsewhere, they are the objects of ridicule and scandal-mongering.

◆ There is plenty of evidence of anger and rage in the media and popular culture. This is often undirected, or is directed against those with no real power in society (e.g., hip hop lyrics directed implicitly towards an imaginary peer-group enemy). But cultural forms such as hip hop and thrash metal draw attention to the widespread existence of social suffering, against the sentimental and optimistic implicit claims of other kinds of popular culture.

◆ A utopian belief in the hope of a better world, and a better society, has been present in popular culture throughout the twentieth century (see Dyer, 1981), but it continues to be expressed in many musical cultures (such as rave in the UK in the late 1980s and 1990s) and in much popular film.

These modes of thought and feeling are hardly ever directly subversive of oppressive economic and political power. They do not cancel out inequality. But they reflect, and reinforce, the fact that the naturalisation of existing power relations is never complete.

Associated with these changes has been a reconfiguration and partial questioning of cultural authority (an issue raised by debates about postmodernism, but rarely addressed with adequate sociological imagination). There are new relationships between 'high' and 'low' culture. These relationships have not been fully democratised; the rich continue to have extremely different cultural habits and tastes from the poor. As Peterson and Kern (1996) have shown, the educated have become more omnivorous in their tastes: they indulge in low culture, while maintaining an interest in high culture. This is easily mistaken for a postmodern blurring of high and low, but the less educated continue to be excluded from, and/or are uninterested in, high culture.

We need, then, to keep in mind the notion of *contradiction* in examining the role of transnational corporations in the cultural industries. As I pointed out in the Introduction to this book, such contradictions derive in part from the fact that cultural-industry companies are happy enough to disseminate cynical or even angrily political works, as long as it produces a profit (or prestige that can be turned indirectly into profit). However, they are perhaps less happy to allow for the provision of information which provides an analysis of overall power relations; and this takes us to the issue of changes and continuities in news journalism.

**The new news**

Journalism can play an important role in providing citizens with the informational resources to ensure that social justice is being pursued by their representatives and by the professionals. We have seen in Chapter 5 that there is more commercial pressure on news organisations than ever before, and I noted evidence above that this has had some impact on some aspects of news reporting. But has journalism's capacity to promote social justice been diminished in the period under discussion? Has there been a decline in standards?

Robert W. McChesney's response is unequivocally yes. For him, recent trends in journalism represent a collapse of the standards of professional journalism, which were founded on the goals of objectivity and public service. McChesney is careful to point out the limitations of professional journalism as it developed in the USA in the twentieth century: journalists were never as objective as they claimed and were always prone to falling in line with commercial and government forces. He highlights long-standing silences and absences in news media coverage, concerning the incredible size of US military budgets, and the activities of the CIA. Nevertheless, he portrays the period after the Second World War as a kind of golden age when 'the caliber of professional journalism prospered and developed a certain amount of autonomy from the dictates of owners and advertisers, and from the corporate sector as a whole' (McChesney, 1999: 51). As evidence, he points to staff cuts and an increasing tendency towards soft news, such as celebrity lifestyle pieces, court cases, plane crashes, crime stories and shootouts, which are uncontroversial and cheap to cover. He cites figures which show that international news has been cut back from 45 per cent of the network TV news total in the early 1970s to 13.5 per cent in 1995. Meanwhile the annual number of crime stories on network TV news programmes tripled between 1990–2 and 1993–6 (McChesney, 1999: 54).

Daniel C. Hallin (2000) addresses these issues. He points to a number of changes marking a new era in American journalism: the fragmentation of the news media, with more and more outlets claiming to be journalism; a blurring of the line between news and entertainment; and a growing uncertainty on the part of journalists about their role: should they be objective informers, or should they take partisan stances, showing empathy with the people they deal with (Hallin, 2000: 221)? Hallin outlines a number of reasons for these shifts. Some are commercial, such as increased competition from local news, the rise of news magazine programmes, and the greater concern of the conglomerates with 'the bottom line'. Others are political and cultural, including a decline in the high prestige of public affairs in the decades after the Second World War, the increasing presence of women and ethnic minorities in newsrooms (which made the former model of professional objectivity harder to sustain, as female, Latino and African American news workers detected bias in such supposed objectivity) and the increasing challenge to the separation of private and public realms from feminism and from media texts themselves. (Hallin thus allows for feedback from texts back into the cultural industries.)

Hallin refuses to portray changes in journalism over the last 20 years as either out-and-out decline or steady improvement. He finds that new formats of representing political debate do have a certain inclusiveness, which was not present in the golden age. Against those who mourn the rise of 'infotainment', he points out that news and entertainment have never been absolutely separate, and that good journalists have always been good storytellers. Tabloid television does at times, Hallin claims, give a voice to individuals who would not have gained access to the old journalism. Some of the stories mourned as 'soft' by professional journalists, such as when the character and actress Ellen came out as a lesbian on the sitcom of the same name, can, says Hallin, be seen as equally important in public life as the inside-the-beltway Washington stories that passed for hard news in the golden age of professional journalism. Nor is Hallin sure that the move towards interpretative reporting, whereby journalists bring their own subjective responses to bear on a story, necessarily represents a fall in standards.

Nevertheless, Hallin is absolutely clear about the negative aspects of developments in journalism. There is a tremendous amount of sensational coverage of ultimately trivial matters. Tabloidised news, on television and in newspapers, depends 'heavily on the exploitation and amplification of fear' (231). The ethos of professional neutrality helped to resist the imperatives of owners, but was increasingly eroded in the 1980s and 1990s. While there has not yet been a return to the era of newspapers acting as vehicles for the views of their owners, Hallin worries that the 'new Fox news division . . . reflects the politics of owner Rupert Murdoch in a way we have not seen at a major news organization since the death of *Time* founder Henry Luce' (233).

In Europe, the decline of news journalism's potential to promote social justice has also been the subject of much debate. Here, the split between broadcast news and the press is very strong. The decline of public service broadcasting has brought about debates very similar to those in the USA, regarding the decline of journalism. But the press has always been much more partisan, and this has been true of both tabloid and broadsheet newspapers. In the UK, the tabloid press was already heavily reliant on sensationalism and scandal even before the new era of conglomeration; but these tendencies seem to have been reaffirmed. Every so often, a tabloid newspaper surprises its readers with a piece of excellent journalism. One example was when in November 2000, *The Daily Mirror* led its front page with an exposé of George W. Bush's record of prisoner executions. Four pages of photographs and descriptions made clear the horrendous nature of the crimes involved, but also how many of these executions were of men from ethnic minorities. This drew attention amongst British working-class readers to the practices of the man who would become the next president of the most powerful country in the world, and helped raise awareness of some of the complex social issues behind violent crime. But in general there has been continuity in British journalism: the ethical standards of British tabloid newspapers were abysmal in the 1960s and 1970s, and they have remained abysmal.

### Social fragmentation and market segmentation

Another important and much discussed change over the last 20 years has been that more and more texts are produced for particular segments of the audience, rather than for a 'mass', undifferentiated audience. This was partly a result of more products entering cultural markets, as leisure time and disposable income increased in advanced industrial countries. It was probably also a result of social fragmentation, as people diverged more and more in the way that they spent their leisure time. What have been the main causes of this social fragmentation? For Neuman (1991: 116–7) the key factors are increasing levels of education (the strongest demographic predictor of breadth of cultural pursuits); a 'rebirth of pride in social differentation', plus the increasing numbers of unmarried (Neuman probably means 'childless') young adults, with energy and income to spare. We can assume that social fragmentation was itself accelerated by the increasing number of cultural options available for people as a result of developments in the cultural industries.

Segmentation was also a result of changes in the way that executives and creative managers conceived of their relationship with audiences. Feuer (1984: 3–4), for example, describes the shift in US network television at the beginning of the 1970s away from 'total audiences' and towards 'demographics'. It was discovered that young, urban adults (especially women) aged 18–49 were the main consumers of the types of goods advertised on television. The result was that, in the early 1970s, the networks competed to offer programmes aimed at this demographic group, alongside the 'mass' programming that had formed the staple of prime-time programming since television became widespread in the late 1950s. Driver and Gillespie (1993: 186) describe how, as the circulation of mass-market magazines in the UK market declined from the 1960s to the 1980s, magazine publishers sought refuge in targeted readerships and niche markets. This has helped to drive the proliferation of magazines, as advertisers use specialist publications to target consumers more specifically.

Some commentators have been concerned that audience segmentation means the end of television's role in producing a 'public sphere', in which issues of common concern for a society can be highlighted (see Stevenson, 1999 for a sophisticated discussion of a number of related issues) – and here we see the relevance of the issue of segmentation for questions of social justice. This is particularly a concern for European writers (Keane, 1991), impressed by public service broadcasting's ability to introduce people to new subjects and ways of thinking. However, we should not rush to hasty prognostications about segmentation without more examination of the evidence.

Are we really seeing a transition, brought about by the changes in the cultural industries in the 1980s and 1990s from an era of mass audiences to an era of segmentation and specialisation, as many commentators claim (e.g., Castells, 1996: 340–1)? Audiences have always been very much segmented, particularly along gender lines, in that movies, magazines, radio serials, etc. were often explicitly aimed at women. And mass markets continue to be central to the cultural industries. Magazines are perhaps the most niche-oriented of all the cultural industries, and there were over 18,000 consumer and business titles being published in the USA alone in 1997, according to the Magazine Publishers of America (MPA). Yet, according to *Advertising Age*, the advertising and circulation revenue brought in by the 10 largest consumer magazines represented over 26 per cent of the US$25.8 billion achieved by the top 300 titles (Standard & Poor's *Publishing Industry Survey*, 13 May 1999: 10). *TV Guide* alone earned US$1.1 billion. As we have seen, the film industry still revolves around the production of mass market blockbusters – and the recording industry is still centred on the big hit that cancels out the misses, and the global superstar who provides a 'brand' across a series of releases. Surveying an impressive range of audience research, James G. Webster and Patricia F. Phalen (1997: 114) conclude that 'mass appeal network television still dominates media consumption in the United States. That is not likely to change anytime soon'.

Segmentation is best thought of as a gradual process, linked to social fragmentation; and it is best to avoid predictions about its future course. It certainly cannot be dismissed as a bad thing, in and of itself. It is hard to object to the provision of television channels catering to specific minority audiences. Nevertheless, we can point to some unfortunate ways in which segmented viewing practices reflect and reinforce more negative aspects of social fragmentation, in ways consistent with the concerns of writers working in the Habermasian tradition of 'public sphere' thinking. One is the long-standing and perhaps increasing tendency for black and white audiences in the USA to consume different media products. Gandy (2000) cites some statistics on this: only *Monday Night Football* occurs in the top 10 most-watched television programmes of both black and white audiences. This suggests that the super-commercialised world of US sport at least provides some kind of common culture for white and black people; but more strikingly, the figures also suggest that, in general, a vast gulf is apparent between the tastes of these different ethnic groups. Of course we can value difference, and recognise the fact that different peoples might have different tastes. But with disparities this pronounced, it is hard to imagine any kind of national public sphere which would bring together black and white US citizens over issues of common public concern. Another worrying aspect of segmentation is that programming that requires effort, skill and creativity (all of which cost money) might increasingly come to be provided for wealthier, more educated audiences, while working-class audiences are left with cheaper, less prestigious programming. In the old television system, the urban upper middle class might have been more inclined to watch *Hill Street Blues* – the most acclaimed US drama series of the early 1980s – than the working class, but the programme was still available for the working class to watch – and sure enough as the series developed, it gained a mass audience (see Feuer et al., 1984). The early 2000s equivalent to *Hill Street Blues* is probably *The Sopranos*; but this programme is shown only on a specialist premium cable channel. This channel is in principle available to working-class viewers, if they can afford it. But it is generally advertised only in publications targeted at the upper middle class. The same might become true of news: the wealthy and educated, who feel they have a stake in national policy, get hard news; while the working class get tabloid television. Debates about the erosion of national public spheres have helped draw attention to such potentially negative aspects of segmentation.

## Declining quality?

### Short attention spans, shock and cultural authority

Does the proliferation of texts produced by the cultural industries in fact represent an abundance of rubbish? One important issue here is the increasing volatility and ephemerality of culture referred to by David Harvey (1989), and explained by him as a product of time–space compression, in turn brought about by the need of capitalist businesses to accumulate profit. Speeding-up is manifested in audience behaviour. Audience research suggests that cultural consumers increasingly want their products in bite-sized and portable chunks, as people monitor their daily time much more carefully, and form it into grids (see Wolf, 1999: 38–40). There is an increasing tendency to skip between texts, not only in channel-surfing or skipping between tracks in a CD selector, but in moving between the various media on offer. There are pleasures in such skipping, but does this have negative effects on the quality of cultural texts, as many cultural commentators have argued? The proliferation of texts means that cultural-industry corporations are faced with the task of finding new ways to capture and retain attention, with potentially negative consequences for the human experience of narrative and argument. Ratings-hungry producers increasingly resort to shock tactics in order to keep the attention of audiences. This means much greater sexual explicitness, which might help to challenge prudery and puritanism, and in some cases encourage people to experiment with different forms of sexual behaviour and identity. In many cases, however, it means an explosion of unsubversive titillation and unimaginative, unerotic pornography. The impulse to shock has also led to much greater levels of violence on television, as study after study has shown (though whether this makes people more violent has never been proven conclusively).

But audience fickleness has other, more ambivalent consequences. Industrial cultural production is not nearly as special as it once was. Television has lost the massive cultural authority it had in the 1960s and 1970s, as low-budget variations have proliferated. If press representations of audience views of television are anything to go by, controversies in the UK about 'docusoaps' and talk shows are a sign of increasing disenchantment and scepticism about television.[4] Such scepticism can coexist with trust of the media and even gullibility, but I think that widespread public scepticism about the aura of television and indeed other media is on the whole a positive development, insofar as it exists.

Of course, proliferation does not represent democratisation. It has negative consequences in terms of further concentration and conglomeration, for example, in that corporations are better at dealing with the media glut than are smaller companies. In order to generate a feeling of specialness amidst the mass of product, conglomerates spend more and more money on promotion. The concept of the media event, developed by Dayan and Katz (1992) to describe important moments arranged outside the television institution but covered by television, needs to be supplemented more and more by the television-generated event, even if these events are rarely yet as significant as major sports events, coronations, royal weddings and funerals. The last episode of *Seinfeld* and the release of *Star Wars: The Phantom Menace* in 1999 were just two successful examples of where massive promotional efforts by cultural-industry companies helped to create a special level of publicity for a text. As the rhythms of consuming television change and people become less accustomed to watching scheduled programmes on a weekly basis, broadcasters are turning to 'event television' such as *Big Brother* and *Survivor* to generate ratings.

---

4 An unpublished paper by Nick Couldry (n.d.) is the most stimulating consideration of these issues I have yet found; Couldry is quite rightly sceptical about how sceptical and cynical audiences might be. Of course, more audience research is needed on these matters.

There are countercurrents though in the way that audience attitudes to texts feed back into cultural-industry structure. It is not just texts and audience behaviour that speed up; so do cycles of fashionability. One long-standing trend in the cultural industries has been the way in which certain genres, styles and textual forms are imbued with a sense of being innovative in particular ways, often because they have been formed in a context which seems to evade such widespread commercialisation. These texts are then introduced to other audiences, which may be perceived as 'mainstream' by the original audience. A burgeoning set of specialist journalists gain money and credibility from being able to spot such forms of underground activity, and to bring them to the attention of some wider audience, whether in the form of comics, fanzines, music genres, or movements of film-makers. Yet the sense of the underground as a sacred political sphere, away from profane commerciality, remains undiminished, and is perhaps even enhanced by the institutionalisation of such cycles. Such undergrounds are rarely a real 'resistance' to the large corporations that dominate the cultural industries, but they often represent a partial questioning of them.[5] They help to maintain an independent sector in many cultural industries, at least until the conglomerates become aware of a new scene.

### Comparing quality: book publishing

Proliferation and speeding-up have ambivalent results then. But let me now turn more directly to the issue of whether the overall quality of cultural texts has declined. Many people assert that this is the case; providing substantial evidence is a different matter altogether. A rare, brave example of someone who is prepared to take this issue on is a chapter by a leading US political economy writer Mark Crispin Miller (1997) on the decline of book publishing in the era of conglomeration.

Miller argues that, in spite of the seeming proliferation of books in the increasingly dominant chains (Borders, Barnes and Noble in the USA; Waterstones in the UK), things are very bad in book publishing. He contrasts book publishing in the mid-1990s with a previous era, before conglomeration, when publishing was not 'a profit-centered venture but a true labor of love' (113). The new focus on profits has, says Miller, led to a serious decline in quality. The common run of literature, he admits, has always been 'lousy' (114): 'Revisit any seeming "golden age" and read it all, and what you'll find is mostly dreck', he says, and he goes on to survey

---

5 The work of Bourdieu on 'restricted production' is important and useful in this context (see Bourdieu, 1993; and Hesmondhalgh, 1998 for discussion); but ultimately I find his approach towards small-scale production too haughty and cynical.

some of the golden ages. However: 'there's been no golden age – and yet books have gotten worse: worse in every way'.[6]

What evidence does Miller provide of this diminished quality? He tells the story of the decline in standards in three publishing companies (Little, Brown; Random House; Bantam Books) once they were taken over by conglomerates. Whereas once they published great novels and serious commentary, these corporations now sell various other books Miller objects to in a variety of different ways. These other books include: novels which may become films made by major studios (108); *romans-à-clef* about famous people (111); and books concerning stars and entertainment products distributed by other conglomerates (108). Miller seems to have a particularly violent objection to books about cooking, gardening and interior design (111). Miller also claims that standards of proofreading have slippped genrally (just kidding) and that many books lack indices and notes. Poor commissioning practice has resulted in many books that are poorly edited, overlong and badly argued, and he quotes reviews from *The New York Times Book Review* to prove this. In comparing the eras before and after conglomeration, Miller says that the previous lists of the major publishing houses contained nothing as 'half-baked, ill-informed, and crudely written as Newt Gingrich's *To Renew America*, or as prolix, muddled and me-me-me-me as Nancy Friday's *The Power of Beauty*' (116). Meanwhile, the Duchess of York's memoirs are 'empty and self-serving', and children's books contain nothing about 'boogers, farts, or puking' (116).

Miller seems to be making two arguments: that the overall quality of books is declining, and that this is associated with an unethical, excessive concern with making money on the part of conglomerates. The main evidence for this latter claim seems to be the first, that they publish bad books. Miller moves back and forth between an ethical condemnation of the overly commercial practices of the companies, and a denunciation of poor aesthetic standards. For example, his objections to lifestyle books seem primarily based on the fact that they allow 'synergies' with other wings of the same conglomerate: for example, cooking, gardening and interior design magazines. The old publishers

> . . . did their share of the eternal dreck; but for them it was a necessary evil – and that, finally, is the crucial difference between then and now. As book lovers and business-men, they did the high-yield trash in order to be able to afford the gems they loved (although the gems might also sell). (117)

---

6 Miller also offers copious examples of books that seem to have been developed in order to benefit from, or to cross-promote, texts and divisions from other parts of the same company. He seems to object to this on the grounds that it gives these firms an advantage in the marketplace, but he also strongly suggests that it results in poorer product.

Today, says Miller, 'crap is not a means but (as it were) the ends'. But his main evidence for this is that the companies which formerly fostered good writing now publish crap, alongside the good stuff. So the bottom line of his argument is aesthetic: that the resulting texts are poorer than they used to be.

The problem is that the argument for overall decline is impossible to substantiate in this way. To compare two different eras fully would be impossible: more books were published in 1950 than could be read in an individual's lifetime. More books were published in the year 2000 than a 12-strong research team could read in three decades. Any statistically significant sample would be too vast to handle in a realistic period. Miller is perhaps therefore entitled to engage in cultural criticism. Nevertheless, he might at least have made reference to the possibility that others might find the books published by the major companies pleasing or useful or beautiful. Instead, his argument rests on his own particular tastes for books.

The nature of Miller's tastes is quite clear: he likes highbrow literary fiction, and serious political and cultural commentary. His argument about declining quality (as opposed to the ethics of preferring commerce over creativity) therefore ultimately rests on his claim that highbrow literary fiction and other serious works, such as political commentary, are under-supplied by the book publishing industry. But his evidence for this amounts simply to showing that three companies which used to specialise in such books now publish other, more commercial books too. Miller hardly mentions the dozens of small publishing companies and university presses in the USA catering to the tastes of educated readers. To some extent, I share Miller's tastes for literary fiction. Speaking for myself, there are more novels available that I would like to read, than I could, even if I read a novel a week for the rest of my life and lived to be a hundred (about 3,500 novels). These novels are generally pretty cheap (my income is above the UK average, but my assets are below it). And this does not even include the other books I would like to read. I suspect the same would be true of most individuals who enjoy reading books.

I am sure that Miller's concern is not about whether his own tastes are being satisfied. Rather, he is worried that the most powerful companies in the market are encouraging others to read sub-standard books. This is a valid concern. The problem is that he cannot prove that this is happening, using evidence drawn principally from such brief references to his own personal tastes and from changes in three companies as they pass from independence to conglomerate divisions. He hints at important points about the lack of concern with the quality of the finished work within conglomerate organisations, but, beyond his suggestions that there are more typos in corporate books than there used to be, can only prove this through reference to the fact that he, and a few reviewers, find the books overblown, superficial or lacking in various other ways.

My close reading of Miller's analysis is intended to show the problems surrounding a critique of the cultural industries on the grounds of aesthetic quality. I have scrutinised this piece carefully, not because it is an example of bad writing. I suspect that it was intended as a polemic, rather than as a fully-argued piece. But it illustrates a problem typical of much work in the field of political economy. Arguments are often made which rest on an unacknowledged assumption that readers will share the aesthetic tastes of the writer. Of course, it is not always possible to forefront and examine problems concerning differences in tastes. Nevertheless, the limits to Miller's approach suggest that arguments based almost entirely on insufficiently scrutinised aesthetic criteria need to be treated with caution.

## Quality, independence and niche markets: US cinema

Let me deal with such issues of quality further by discussing another important cultural industry: cinema. As should be apparent, I am not saying that we should be complacent about the quality of product produced by the cultural industries; merely that bold statements about such quality tend to conceal important issues. The case of independent American cinema over the last 20 years offers a useful case study of the relations between the cultural industries and the resulting texts.

Many commentators feel that there has been a decline in the standards of mainstream US films since the 1970s, with the rise of special-effects blockbusters (e.g., Biskind, 1998). On the other hand, many young, urban, educated cinephiles would point to a richness in US film-making, especially US independent cinema, during the 1980s and 1990s. Especially in cinema and popular music, it is often felt that institutional 'independence' (as we shall see, the term is weighed down by problems of definition) can help foster better films. There are echoes of this view in popular music too – see Chapter 5. Independent cinema received huge coverage in the 1990s, as films such as *Reservoir Dogs* (1992) achieved cult status and huge admiration, while others such as *Pulp Fiction* (1994) and *The Blair Witch Project* (1999) were box-office hits. Independent film production boomed: in 1999, 1,716 films were submitted to the Sundance Festival, the main showcase for independent cinema. There was a strong tendency amongst audiences and film critics to associate independence with aesthetic adventurousness. In the words of one history of American independent cinema, independents were seen as 'celluloid mavericks' (Merritt, 2000). As Emanuel Levy (1999: 21) puts it, independent film-makers 'create alternative films that are different, challenging the status quo with visions that have been suppressed or ignored by the more conservative mainstream'.

In the 1960s, the Hollywood studios hit a crisis, based on declining audiences and profits. But in 1967, the huge success of *Bonnie and Clyde* (directed by Arthur Penn) amongst youth audiences around the world led Hollywood to believe that innovative films aimed at the youth audience might be their saviour, rather than the big-budget family spectaculars that they had relied on since the 1950s. This trend intensified following the unexpected success of *Easy Rider* (directed by Peter Fonda, 1969). Hollywood entered a period where young directors, producers and scriptwriters were given considerable creative autonomy within the studio system, through package deals with independent producers. With the success of *Jaws* (directed by Steven Spielberg, 1975) and *Star Wars* (directed by George Lucas, 1977) however – both made by young directors brought in to revitalise Hollywood – the studios began to turn back to big-budget special effects movies, aimed at the burgeoning teenage market. Fewer and fewer films were made aimed at older viewers in the late 1970s and early 1980s. With the mid-1980s success of films such as *Blue Velvet* (directed by David Lynch, 1987) and *She's Gotta Have It* (directed by Spike Lee, 1986) this began to change. *Sex, Lies and Videotape* (directed by Steven Soderbergh, 1989) is often cited as an important transition, because it crossed over from the independent and art cinema circuit in the USA into the multiplexes, showing a very high return on its low costs: production costs were US$1 million, profits US$25 million. It became apparent that there was significant money to be made from off-beat, small-scale films dealing with personal relationships, and appealing to an older audience. Levy describes 1992 as an *annus mirabilis* for indies, with films such as *Howard's End*, *The Crying Game*, *The Player* and *Bob Roberts* achieving critical plaudits, and considerable financial success. In 1994, the hip nihilism of *Pulp Fiction* (directed by Quentin Tarantino) achieved a crossover into the teen market drawn to horror films and 'sick' comedy.

Levy outlines a number of conditions that facilitated the emergence of the new American independent cinema as an alternative system.

- The need for self-expression on the part of young film-makers drawn to films which express personal visions rather than operate primarily within Hollywood genre conventions;
- Hollywood's increasing tendency to make big-budget blockbusters, rather than lower-budget, personal films left a gap in the market for indies to fill;
- There were increasing opportunities and capital for financing indies, partly because of internationalisation, which has meant the availability of foreign capital, but also because of the increasing demand for visual material, as channels proliferate;
- 'Supportive audiences', that is, older, more highly educated audiences looking for 'more mature themes';

- Decline of foreign-language films and the European art cinema;
- A proliferation of film schools in the USA, producing 'a large number of ambitious film makers eager to take advantage' of the new opportunities for making independent films;
- The Sundance Film Festival, now the second most important film festival in the world according to Levy, serves as an important showcase for independents; and there are numerous other festivals and associations such as the Independent Feature Project, and the Black Film-makers Foundation, which support independent film-making;
- The increasing commercial success of indies, and their increasing success at the Oscars.

Examining the issue of the 'supportive audiences' for independent cinema will allow us to explore further the issue of quality. Levy, without citing sources, describes the 'typical indie public' as being composed of:

- College students and college graduates
- Singles and childless couples
- Discriminating viewers seeking provocative entertainment
- Informed viewers with sharper sensibility and greater awareness of new film releases and new directors
- Frequent moviegoers who go to the movies at least once a month

All this basically translates into urban, highly-educated and relatively prosperous audiences. Levy clearly thinks that independent films are better than studio pictures. In his view, the major Hollywood studios redeem themselves with a few interesting pictures each year (1999: 500). For Levy, 1998 was an exceptionally good year for Hollywood in that it produced five 'great or near-great films': *Saving Private Ryan*, *The Truman Show*, *Bulworth*, *He Got Game*, and *Rushmore*. Levy does not stop to give a definition of greatness, but he clearly shares the aesthetic tastes of the higher-income, higher-educated audience for indie. There is a danger then that praise for the products of independent cinema is merely praise for films which correspond to the tastes of other highly educated people. These tastes change with time, but in recent years, these audiences have tended to favour thoughtful, sensitive pictures about human relationships; hip, energetic satire; and films full of reference to the codes of popular and high culture, reflecting the cultural omnivorousness of this kind of audience.

Perhaps it is too cynical to think of such high quality indie films as merely representing a kind of niche marketing to a wealthy, urban elite. Perhaps it is too pessimistic to think of tastes for such films as being confined to wealthier, more educated audiences. People are more able to enjoy different kinds of cultural experience than sociologists and market researchers sometimes give them credit for. It could be that the film industry assumes in advance that certain audiences will not be interested in certain kinds of product. The increasing credibility of market research, discussed in Chapter 5, would reinforce this tendency.

♦   ♦   ♦

In this chapter, I have attempted to assess changes in the texts produced by the cultural industries over the last 20 years. But the discussion has continually returned to the difficulties of providing evaluation on the kind of historical scale that I am dealing with here. Diversity is an elusive concept. Writers identify trends towards homogenisation, but provide little substantiation. Adequate transhistorical comparisons of quality may well be impossible. And sociological problems surrounding taste haunt textual evaluation: texts claimed as innovative and adventurous could just be aimed at the niche market to which the intellectual belongs. Clearly, my own analysis favours thinking about texts in terms of their role in promoting or inhibiting social justice. I have identified commercialisation as an important development in texts over the last 20 years (though not one of sufficient breadth and depth to merit the view that we have entered a new era of production of texts). However, this focus on issues of social justice marginalises the experiences that people are looking for in texts: various forms of aesthetic pleasure. Some people's solution is to reduce aesthetic experience to ethical questions concerning the stance of a particular film; but this will not do either. The solution may be to build bridges between the two; and to recognise how tenuous, indirect and contradictory some of the connections may be. But in reading for this book, one of the main conclusions I have come to is that the project of a sociologically-informed reflexive aesthetics is still in its infancy; and that the spectre of mass culture criticism haunts much political economy work that takes an aesthetic perspective. In this respect, I am aware that this chapter makes for something of an anticlimax. One of the reasons that the cultural industries are important is that they make texts. Yet critique of texts in historical terms is so difficult that I might seem to be suggesting that we abandon textual analysis altogether. I am not advocating this. Engagement with content remains the most difficult terrain in analysis of media and popular culture, then. But that does not mean that the task can be abandoned. Students and researchers of the cultural industries need to engage with issues of pleasure, interpretation and meaning.

## Further reading

Explicit treatments of textual change and continuity are rare indeed. But a number of books attempt to deal with the vital issue of the relationship between industrial/organisational dynamics and texts. Gripsrud (1995) is particularly impressive in its treatment of one text, *Dynasty*. Georgina Born's work (1993a; 1993b; 1995) has been very important for me in developing my thinking on these issues, as has Toynbee (2000). The formalist work of Bordwell, Staiger and Thompson (1985) and, more recently, Thompson (1999) explores these connections in a very different way. I have enthused elsewhere in this book about Gitlin's study of prime time television. I find Daniel Hallin's approach to journalism (1994, 2000) extremely useful. For a good collection of writing about news, including many treatments relevant to the issues raised in this book, see Tumber (1999).

# Conclusions: A New Era in Cultural Production?

I had three main aims in this book: to measure change in the cultural industries, to evaluate it, and to explain it.

## Measuring change/continuity

My treatment of change has gone beyond the historical time frame employed in most studies of the cultural industries. I borrowed from Raymond Williams work on changing social relations of cultural production across different periods of history in order to put recent changes in long-term historical context. Williams described how social relations based on patronage gave way in the nineteenth century to a system he dubbed 'market professional' and how this system in turn gave way in the twentieth century to the dominance of 'corporate professional' market relations. I modified Williams' term 'corporate professional' to 'complex professional' and used the term to refer to a whole matrix of conditions of cultural production and consumption, which emerged in the early part of the twentieth century, and which were thoroughly ensconced by the 1950s. These conditions centred on a particular set of relationships between primary creative personnel (symbol creators), other workers and the companies that commission and employ them. A crucial feature of these relations was a combination of loose control of creative input with much tighter control of the reproduction and circulation stages. The complex professional period, as I described it in Chapter 2, was also marked by other key features: a labour market in which some creative workers are vastly rewarded but most are underemployed and underpaid; the increasing presence of large corporations, often in the form of vertically-integrated conglomerates; significant internationalisation, dominated by the US cultural industries; and associated regimes of technology, consumption and policy. Much of the rest of the book has been concerned with assessing the degree to which these characteristics of cultural production, which developed in the mid-twentieth century, were still apparent in the 1980s and 1990s. This allows us now to confront more directly the question: did the 1980s and 1990s see a new era of cultural production, a new phase as markedly different from the complex professional era, as the complex professional was from the market professional era?

Chapter 4 assessed changes in government communications policy. Here there were considerable transformations, in that governments all across the world altered their policies in the direction of marketisation: the view that the production and exchange of cultural goods and services for profit is the best way to achieve efficiency and fairness in the production and consumption of texts. Various rationales for high degrees of state intervention were systematically attacked by a number of parties, including cultural-industry companies. The result was the privatisation of public telecommunications organisations and some public broadcasting institutions; the opening up of television systems to other terrestrial, commercial broadcasters and to cable and satellite companies; the tearing down of regulatory walls between different industries; plus significant changes in laws and rules on content, media ownership and subsidies. In Europe, public service broadcasting was attacked but was surprisingly successful in resisting the onslaught in some countries. In many societies, authoritarian-statist governments gave way to 'democratic' governments pursuing neoliberal economic policies. By the 1990s, neoliberalism was being further pursued by a number of important international bodies. All this added up to a vast transformation in the policy landscape; many of these changes were extremely important in driving other processes of upheaval and realignment.

Was this a new era in policy? The move towards neoliberalism was remarkable and the fact that neoliberalism was adopted in so many countries reflects the global interconnectedness of the late twentieth century. But I have argued that within the advanced industrial countries, ultimately this represents a shift of emphasis within a fairly stable policy system, whereby states regulate on the basis of tensions between the interests of citizens/voters and dominant business interests. In other countries, however, there was a different story. Countries such as India were making a transition from national protectionism to globalisation, from delinked national cultural-economic systems to participation in a new international system of cultural trade. This is part of a wider political-economic and sociocultural set of shifts, which may in retrospect be seen as the beginning of a new phase within these specific national societies. This in turn may help to bring about epochal changes in the advanced industrial countries. But we do not yet live in a 'global professional era' of cultural production. The nation state continues to be the main forum for cultural-industry activity.

Marketisation helped to create a context in which the cultural industries were seen as a good business investment. Chapter 5 showed the expansion of large cultural-industry corporations, a growth that may have reached a peak in the boom-bubble years of the late 1990s. These cultural-industry corporations have achieved an unprecedented international scope and level of revenue. However, such companies do not approach the size of the world's very largest corporations. Corporate growth in the cultural industries is an extension of a process that was already under way in the early part of the twentieth century, and is not sufficient to merit claims that the cultural industries are, or even look set to become, a new core in global business. Conglomeration fed into the growth of the corporations, but it is not a new thing in the cultural industries; it is a distinctive feature of the complex professional period as a whole. Conglomeration strategies vary over time, and we should be wary of analyses that present any particular strategy (such as hardware/software synergy) as representing the future. Vertical integration also supported the growth of large corporations; but again, vertical integration in the 1980s and 1990s was not of a qualitatively different kind from that which was present in earlier generations. Indeed, there has been some movement, in some industries, towards disintegration, and not only because of the actions of regulators, but also because some companies have found it more profitable to disintegrate. As with conglomeration, we should cast a sceptical eye on claims that see movements towards or away from integration as marking epochal shifts. Business fashions and strategies come, go and come again. Meanwhile, small companies continue to play an extremely important role in the cultural industries. Again, their proliferation represents an extension of processes already observable in the mid-twentieth century. But a key change is that large and small companies are increasingly interdependent, mutually entangled in complex networks of licensing, financing and distribution. This is a genuinely novel feature of the cultural industries in the 1980s and 1990s, as is the number of alliances between cultural-industry companies and computer and telecommunications companies in the late 1990s.

Chapter 5 then went on to examine changes and continuities in the distinctive organisational form of the cultural industries in the 1980s and 1990s, and in the terms and conditions of cultural work. Given my emphasis on the social relations of cultural production, this is clearly a key area for assessing change. Across the cultural industries as a whole, there are significant levels of continuity in that symbol creators continue to exercise relatively high levels of operational autonomy, and very low levels of power when it comes to the circulation of texts. Journalistic autonomy continues to be important in journalism, in spite of some important attacks on it. Although there were signs of a superficial loosening of control of creative work in some cultural industries, I argued that the prevailing trend was in the opposite direction, towards tighter (though still loose relative to other industries) control of creative work. This was manifested in the increasing importance of marketing and market research in the creative stages of cultural production. Even here, however, there is a mixture of trends, with some parts of some industries allowing for greater creative autonomy than before (e.g., advertisers), with others turning towards more rigid, bureaucratic forms of control (e.g., live theatre) and with trends elsewhere highly ambivalent.

Internationalisation of cultural-industry businesses and their texts is not new, but this process greatly accelerated in the 1980s and 1990s. The complex professional period saw a complicated mixture of geocultural markets develop across the world, with the USA generally but unevenly dominant, and with local or regional cultural products often just as popular as US ones, if not more so. This arrangement largely continued into the 1980s and 1990s, as I showed in Chapter 6. I assessed the growth of Latin American cultural-industry companies that based their operations on television. I also examined the huge growth of cross-border trans-missions (including 'diasporic television'). Both of these are significant and interesting developments, but they do not as yet remotely threaten the domination of the transnational corporations based mainly in North America, Europe and Asia. The power-geometry of international television remains largely intact. I showed the rise to further dominance of Holly-wood film in the 1980s and 1990s but examined the important film industries of Hong Kong and India, which had considerable success in the 1980s. Although these represent very different cinemas from the Holly-wood system, the presence of such domestic industries in global audio-visual markets is not a new phenomenon. The erosion of Hong Kong's industry should not be interpreted as signalling a greater level of domina-tion by Hollywood, whose hegemony rises and falls in cycles. Finally, in spite of some claims to the contrary, new genres such as world music and Euro-pop hardly represented significant disturbances to the geographical distribution of musical power that have been prevalent since the Second World War. The international distribution of cultural power was always more complex than the core/periphery models so effectively questioned by Sinclair et al. (1996). Nevertheless, there was significant inequality in access to global markets and international prestige and influence. That inequality remains.

Are the changes associated with digitalisation sufficient for us to speak of a new digital era in cultural production? Every era brings its innovations, but perhaps the last 20 years have seen a greater intensity of innovation than ever before. Even if this is the case, the production relations and business strategies of the complex professional era remain largely intact. New musical technologies have offered new opportunities for musicians, but have not radically democratised production, nor have they sig-nificantly reduced social music-making. Computer games are the basis of a new industry with many new texts and genres, but this industry is founded on the same principles of production as many of the cultural industries that already existed when it evolved. The internet is an important new medium, which has brought new cultural forms (such as the chat room) into the lives of the relatively wealthy and well-educated across much of the world. But it has supplemented the other cultural industries, rather than either replacing or transforming them. Cultural-industry companies have very quickly found ways of re-establishing control over circulation.

Perhaps the most radical changes brought about by digitalisation will involve convergence. Certainly, the expectation of convergence has helped to fuel the new tendency towards strategic alliances between telecommunications, computers and cultural-industry companies. But genuine convergence of cultural forms and communication systems is a long way from happening yet. Digital television may yet transform television completely, but that is still a matter for the future. It is likely that, for many years to come, it will provide an expanded version of what has been familiar in the past. Desktop publishing has destroyed entire crafts in the publishing industry, but the distinctive organisational form of the cultural industries is still apparent in the magazine industry, in a relatively unchanged form.

Digitalisation, then, should be seen as highly differentiated in its impacts, according to its very different manifestations; in fact, it hardly makes sense to speak of 'digital media' as one category at all. Digitalisation does what its designers ask of it, and that depends on so many other factors that the actual zeros-and-ones nature of its technological apparatus matters very little in terms of the social uses of the technology, other than allowing devices to be marketed as efficient and convenient. This suggests that terms such as the 'digital era' or 'being digital' (Negroponte, 1995) risk technological reductionism. But even if it were feasible to speak of all these different technologies as part of one, larger systemic change, the changes have not yet been sufficient as to merit the idea that we have moved into a new era of production, beyond the complex professional era.

The overall conclusion, in terms of measurement of change, has to be that there is sufficient continuity to undermine the suggestion that we have entered a new era of cultural production. Rather, we should think of the last 20 years as representing a new phase *within* the complex professional era, marked by greater competition, and a greater centrality for the cultural industries within advanced industrial economies as a whole. The fundamental features of the cultural industries established in the mid-twentieth century remain.

Some writers have suggested that other industries are becoming more like the cultural industries, in that there seems to have been a new emphasis on issues of aesthetics, design, information, planning and knowledge in all industries, most notably Lash and Urry (1994). Others (e.g., Padioleau, 1987) have suggested that the cultural industries are 'normalising', becoming less distinctive, and more like other industries. In fact, there have always been tensions between differentiation from, and the imitation of strategies in other industries, throughout the complex professional era. The cultural industries continue to be driven by the problems and solutions identified in the Introduction (see Box 0.2). But the view that the cultural industries are forming a new core to advanced industrial economies is premature, as can be seen from the figures presented in Chapter 5 on the relative size of cultural-industry companies, compared with other large corporations. There may have been a partial shift towards economies based on culture, information and symbols. But none of us yet live in a 'knowledge economy' or an 'information age'.

## Evaluating change/continuity

Chapter 2 (see Box 2.5) set up the main questions guiding my evaluation of change in the cultural industries. The continued and accelerated growth of the largest corporations is an obvious fact, and their increased scope and power (through such means as consolidation, various types of conglomeration, and either vertical integration or co-optation of contracting companies) carry significant implications. These corporations have the resources and expertise to pursue their interests, in a way that can do much to counteract the high-risk nature of the business they are in. Their main interest is the pursuit of profit. To achieve this, corporations will team up with other corporations that they normally compete with, with the aim of acting as advocates for their industry. Their efforts to pursue profits are often detrimental to the interests of people as citizens, even if they give us more choice and control over our leisure time as consumers. They also, in my view, tend to support political and economic stasis, often opposing attempts to achieve social justice. They provide a model for how cultural business should be carried out, a model which is not always a positive one. Whether they support such interests in texts is still controversial, but they certainly pursue such interests as lobbyists and in their business strategies. The internet has not posed any substantial threat to the power and reach of these corporations, though amongst certain social groups it has enabled and enhanced communication between people. Digital television looks unlikely to achieve any progressive transformation of the social relations of cultural production. The rhetoric of expanded choice surrounding its marketing is deeply dubious.

There has been little improvement in the rewards and working conditions of creative workers. Symbol creators remain underpaid and underemployed for the most part, while rewards for superstars continue to rise to disgraceful levels. There has been some movement towards greater awareness on the part of new entrants to cultural production about the dangers they face in undertaking creative work, and there have been some improvements in contracts. Control of creative work by cultural-industry companies remains relatively loose, but the increasing prominence and prestige of marketing personnel in the cultural industries, particularly in the creative conception stage, represents a potential erosion of some of that creative autonomy. Journalistic autonomy is also threatened, in many contexts, by the commercial imperatives of owners, but remains resilient as a professional ethos and as a defence against the demands of executives. New technologies such as MIDI and desktop publishing have not fundamentally altered the level of creative autonomy available to symbol creators.

Chapter 6 examined internationalisation, and found that there were still very few opportunities for producers from outside the 'core' areas of cultural production to gain access to networks of circulation. The geographical concentration of power remains remarkable, though it is not as marked as 'cultural imperialism' writers would sometimes have us believe. In spite of the claims of many commentators, digital media have not created a new world of access, where barriers between production and consumption are breaking down. The internet offered extremely interesting new subcultural uses of communication technologies, but professionalisation, commercialisation and strategies for controlling knowledge about websites, as well as perennial but important questions of access, mean that the radical potential of the internet will only be realised by a few. Digital television is far more likely than the internet to be the basis of any possible future move towards convergence. And digital television has helped advance commercialisation in that key medium, further threatening public service broadcasters, and reinforcing the power of some of the largest corporations.

My analysis of changes in texts highlighted the problems of making rashly optimistic or pessimistic claims about textual transformation. Chapter 8 began by noting a marked feature of cultural production over the last 20 years: a huge proliferation of texts. But is there greater diversity? Attempts to provide objective measures of diversity in liberal-pluralist communication studies have foundered. Equally, cultural commentary often descends into unsubstantiated assumptions about homogenisation. Diversity remains an elusive and difficult concept. Much clearer are changes concerning the commercialisation of texts. Advertising and promotional materials have all increased: in my view, to the detriment of the societies that we live in. Advertising messages encourage the view that buying objects and experiences are the primary means of achieving happiness. Of course the objects and experiences we purchase can enhance our lives in many ways. But such commercial messages encourage us to accumulate wealth and money in order to acquire and this leads to stress, misery, alienation, pollution and conflict. Hidden promotional messages relegate symbolic creativity to the needs of accumulation. Beyond this, however, it is difficult to say that texts have become more likely to favour the interests of the powerful than they were before. Compliance, conservatism and complacency coexist with scepticism, anger and utopianism. Popular culture continues to be riddled with contradiction. Although some see a decline in news standards, here too there is ambivalence, as the pompousness of some styles of serious journalism is displaced both by triviality and by efforts to speak to important private and emotional concerns. Meanwhile, the speeding up of the tendency among audiences to shift across different cultural experiences means that symbol creators can no longer rely on the guaranteed attentiveness of audiences (if indeed they ever could). But this restlessness also encourages a certain scepticism about the authority of the media. Historical comparisons of quality across the whole range of a cultural industry's output are so difficult as to be almost meaningless. Simple stories of transformation in texts are often to be found, but rarely stand up to scrutiny.

Overall, any assessment of the cultural industries must register the complexity, ambivalence and contradiction noted by Miège (1989) as features of capitalist cultural production. The growth of the large corporations is significant, but they work in more subtle and complicated ways than the jeremiads of some political economy accounts suggest. To make such an argument does not represent a compromise with corporate capitalism. Rather, it is the outcome of a clear-headed analysis of the very real complexities involved in making capital out of culture. As Toynbee (2000: 2) puts it, also employing Raymond Williams' historical sociology of culture to support his analysis, while much of 'culture belongs to capitalism, there is something antithetical to capitalism in it'.

## Explaining change/continuity

Here, we overlap into explanation. If the 'fundamentally irrational' process of symbolic creativity 'conflicts with the calculating, accumulative logic of modern capitalism' (Ryan 1992: 104), this helps to explain the very tangled and contradictory dynamics we have observed throughout this book. The irrationality of culture played an important part in the account of the specific dynamics of the cultural industries outlined in the Introduction. These shadowed our narrative throughout the book. Cultural-industry companies pursue profit and they use recurring strategies to do so. However, the internal dynamics of the cultural industries are by no means sufficient to explain change and continuity in them. Chapter 3 outlined the major *external* contexts for understanding change. Avoiding reduction, I identified four types of factor driving change and continuity in the cultural industries during the period under consideration: political-economic change, in the form of the neoliberal reaction to the Long Downturn; changing business strategies, in the form of shifts in investment towards service industries, internationalisation and organisational innovations; sociocultural changes; and technological change, particularly the development of the computer and various consumer electronics devices. As will have been apparent, I am suspicious of explanations that privilege the role of the latter factor, technology. Although technologies are important and have real effects, technological reductionism is a real danger in the present climate. I hope I have shown that there are many reasons to avoid it. Instead, I have shown how entangled the various types of determinant are. If the actions of cultural-industry companies have been privileged above other dynamics, this is because I believe their intentions have a great effect on cultural, economic and political processes. And after all, this is a book about the cultural industries.

## Implications for future study

This book has insisted on **the importance of thinking about the cultural industries as producers of texts**. The cultural industries are those industries most directly involved in the production of social meaning, because they make and circulate texts, artefacts that are primarily intended to inform and/or entertain. This is the key to understanding the particular role of the cultural industries in relationship to economic, political, social and cultural power. The study of the cultural industries has to incorporate the consideration of texts; and the study of texts has to take seriously analysis of the cultural industries. The best critical political economy and sociological approaches recognise the importance of meaning, but very few writers have achieved a sustained engagement with textual meaning in relation to cultural production (I would suggest Gitlin, 1983 and Gripsrud, 1995 are two of the most impressive attempts to do this, and my aim has been to build upon their achievements, though in a somewhat different manner). By incorporating textual change into my assessment and explanation of change/continuity in the cultural industries, I hope to re-emphasise the centrality, in the study of media, popular culture and mass communication, of the relationship between symbolic artefacts and the financing and organisation of their production.

My use of the concepts of diversity, quality and pursuit of interests represents a way of thinking about texts that focuses on the functions of texts in people's everyday lives in contemporary society. By trying to think carefully about the evaluative criteria people bring to texts, we can overcome the sweeping generalisations that debilitate various forms of cultural criticism. It should be clear that I have no time for fatuous dismissals of entire swathes of cultural production on the part of high-minded analysts. Equally, however, it must be apparent that I do not think that the cultural industries play an altogether progressive role in the contemporary world. There is no question of complacently celebrating popular culture. There are plenty of unimaginative, uninformative, uninteresting texts around, and they need to be questioned, probed and even lambasted. In other words, to repeat the formula I borrowed from Bernard Miège very early on in this book, we need to recognise the complexity, ambivalence and contestedness of culture. (Miège is hardly interested in texts, however.) What I am arguing for is **an open-minded attitude towards the kinds of uses and pleasures that people might take from texts**. By open-minded, I simply mean an attitude that does not judge or assume in advance that any text plays a negative role in society. Audience research on how and why people value texts is therefore an absolutely vital corollary of the approach I have taken here. There has been no space for such audience analysis on my part here: researching 50 years of cultural production has been enough of a task in itself.

One of the main achievements of radical studies of the media and popular culture has been to argue effectively for the importance of ethical questions regarding questions of power and social justice in relation to cultural production. I have attempted to build on this by emphasising the advantages of a **historically-informed analysis of contemporary culture**. The reasons for this are obvious enough to anyone who values historical study. Good historical analysis can help to undermine casual assumptions about the present, and the near future. It can help to put our own situation into perspective. And it can help us understand how things came to be the way that they are and therefore how they might be changed for the better. By using Williams' historical sociology of culture, I have tried to bring a long-term perspective to bear on recent issues. Media and cultural studies have generally taken a very shallow attitude towards history (with notable exceptions, mainly in studies of film and broadcasting, many of which are referred to above). In fact, this book was constructed around historical questions concerning change and continuity. This was because the question 'how much have things really changed?' kept cropping up time and again in my experience of teaching, and in general discussions with friends (and indeed strangers) about the cultural industries. Many people have an interest in exaggerating change in order to draw attention to themselves – and no doubt this has helped put the question of social and cultural change on the agenda. It seems to me that one useful function of academic work is to scrutinise carefully such exaggerated claims. In disciplines that tend to be heavily focused on primarily synchronic research methods such as ethnography and interviews, the question of change is one that might encourage more historical thinking. Finally, it seems to me that another valuable task of academic writers is to explain why they think things have happened in the way that they have: hence the emphasis on explanation in this book.

One of the most important aspects of my approach, borrowed from the cultural industries approach, but also to some extent from empirical sociology of culture, has been to **focus on symbol creators**. I commented in Chapters 1 and 2 on the surprising neglect of these cultural workers in studies of the cultural industries. This has not been a book about symbol creators, but I hope the considerable attention I have paid to creative personnel can help to revivify studies of cultural production. A focus on symbol creators and other workers in the cultural industries may encourage the formation of partnerships with organisations representing the interests of often exploited staff, and build bridges between the goals of university researchers and non-university activists. Concentrating on issues of symbolic creativity may also help save the study of cultural production from the reputation it currently (and unjustly) has amongst some students, as the dreary analysis of big corporations. Most students enter universities to study the media and popular culture because they want to be part of an environment where symbolic creativity is paramount. To forefront this issue represents a means of making connections between everyday desires and aspirations to be creative, and the world of business, economics and politics. Who has not wanted, at some time in their life, to play music, to perform on a stage, to capture a feeling or to express a viewpoint, in writing or in photography or in some other medium? I hope this book has made a contribution to restoring a focus on these aspects of life to studies of the cultural industries.

# References

References to articles from newspapers, magazines and trade journals are given in the main text, not here. Where two dates are given, the first date refers to the publication of the particular book, chapter or article cited, the second refers to the original date of publication. My apologies to authors for leaving out their precious sub-titles. I did it for reasons of space.

Adorno, Theodor and Max Horkheimer (1977/1944) 'The culture industry: enlightenment as mass deception', in James Curran, Michael Gurevitch and Janet Wollacott (eds), *Mass Communication and Society*. London: Edward Arnold. pp. 349–83.

Aksoy, Asu and Kevin Robins (1992) 'Hollywood for the 21st century: global competition for critical mass in image markets', *Cambridge Journal of Economics*, 16: 1–22.

Allen, Rod (1998) 'This is not television . . .', in Jeanette Steemers (ed.), *Changing Channels*. Luton: University of Luton Press. pp. 59–71.

Amin, Hussein (1996) 'Egypt and the Arab world in the satellite age', in John Sinclair, Elizabeth Jacka and Stuart Cunningham (eds), *New Patterns in Global Television*. Oxford: Oxford University Press. pp. 101–25.

Andersen, Robin (2000) 'Introduction', in Robin Andersen and Lance Strate (eds), *Critical Studies in Media Commercialism*. Oxford: Oxford University Press. pp. 1–21.

Anderson, Ben, Annabel McWilliam, Hazel Lacohee, Eileen Clucas and Jonathan Gershuny (1999) 'Family life in the digital home – domestic telecommunications at the end of the 20th century', *BT Technology Journal*, 17,1: 85–99.

Ang, Ien (1985) *Watching Dallas*. London and New York: Methuen.

Ang, Ien (1991) *Desperately Seeking the Audience*. London: Routledge.

Armstrong, Philip, Andrew Glyn and John Harrison (1991) *Capitalism Since 1945*. Oxford: Basil Blackwell.

Aufderheide, Patricia (1999) *Communications Policy and the Public Interest*. New York and London: The Guilford Press.

Aufderheide, Patricia, Erik Barnouw, Richard M. Cohen, Thomas Frank, Todd Gitlin, David Lieberman, Mark Crispin Miller, Gene Roberts and Thomas Schatz (1997) *Conglomerates and the Media*. New York: The New Press.

Augarten, Stan (1984) *Bit by Bit*. London: Unwin.

Auletta, Ken (1997) 'American keiretsu', *The New Yorker*, 20 and 27 October, pp. 225–7.

Bagdikian, Ben H. (2000) *The Media Monopoly* (6th edn). Boston: Beacon Press.

Barker, Chris (1997) *Global Television*. Oxford: Blackwell.

Baumol, William J. and William G. Bowen (1966) *Performing Arts – The Economic Dilemma*. New York: Twentieth Century Fund.

Becker, Howard S. (1982) *Art Worlds*. Berkeley and London: University of California Press.

Bell, Daniel (1974) *The Coming of Post-industrial Society*. London: Heinemann.

Berwanger, Dietrich (1998) 'The Third World', in Anthony Smith with Richard Paterson (eds), *Television: An International History* (2nd edn). Oxford: Oxford University Press. pp. 188–200.

Bettig, Ronald V. (1996) *Copyrighting Culture*. Boulder, Colorado: Westview Press.

Biskind, Peter (1998) *Easy Riders, Raging Bulls*. London: Bloomsbury.

Bloom, Allan (1987) *The Closing of the American Mind*. New York: Simon and Schuster.

Blumler, Jay G. (1992) *Television and the Public Interest*. London: Sage, in association with the Broadcasting Standards Council.

Blumler, Jay G. and Michael Gurevitch (1995) *The Crisis of Public Communication*. London: Routledge.

Bordwell, David, Janet Staiger and Kristin Thompson (1985) *The Classical Hollywood Cinema*. London, Melbourne and Henley: Routledge and Kegan Paul.

Bordwell, David (2000) *Planet Hong Kong*. Cambridge, Massachusetts: Harvard University Press.

Born, Georgina (1993a) 'Against negation, for a politics of cultural production: Adorno, aesthetics, the social', *Screen* 34,3: 223–42.

Born, Georgina (1993b) 'Afterword: music policy, aesthetic and social difference', in Tony Bennett, Simon Frith, Lawrence Grossberg, John Shepherd and Graeme Turner (eds), *Rock and Popular Music*. London and New York: Routledge. pp. 266–92.

Born, Georgina (1995) *Rationalizing Culture*. Berkeley, Los Angeles and London: University of California Press.

Bourdieu, Pierre (1984) *Distinction*. Cambridge, Massachusetts: Harvard University Press.

Bourdieu, Pierre (1993) *The Field of Cultural Production*. Cambridge: Polity.

Boyd, Douglas (1998) 'The Arab world', in Anthony Smith with Richard Paterson (eds), *Television: An International History* (2nd edn). Oxford: Oxford University Press. pp. 182–7.

Brants, Kees and Karen Siune (1992) 'Public broadcasting in a state of flux', in Karen Siune and Wolfgang Truetzschler (eds), *Dynamics of Media Politics*. London: Sage. pp. 101–15.

Brenner, Robert (1998) 'Uneven development and the Long Downturn: the advanced capitalist economies from boom to stagnation, 1950–1998', *New Left Review*, I 229: 1–267.

Brenner, Robert (2000) 'The boom and the bubble', *New Left Review*, II 6: 5–43.

Burnett, Robert (1992) 'The implications of ownership changes for concentration and diversity in the phonogram industry', *Communication Research* 19,6: 749–69.

Burnett, Robert (1995) *The Global Jukebox*. London: Routledge.

Burston, Jonathan (1999) 'Spectacle, synergy and megamusicals: the global-industrialisation of the live-entertainment economy', in James Curran (ed.), *Media Organizations in Society*. London: Arnold/New York: Oxford University Press. pp. 69–83.

Cairncross, Frances (1997) *The Death of Distance*. London: Orion.

Canclini, Nestor García (1995) *Hybrid Cultures*. Minneapolis: University of Minnesota Press.

Carroll, Noël (1998) *A Philosophy of Mass Art*. Oxford: Clarendon Press.

Carter, Bill (1998) 'ABC shelves report on parent Disney', *The New York Times*, A24, 15 October.

Castells, Manuel (1989) *The Informational City.* Oxford: Blackwell.

Castells, Manuel (1996) *The Rise of the Network Society.* Oxford: Blackwell.

Caves, Richard E. (2000) *Creative Industries.* Cambridge, Massachusetts: Harvard University Press.

Chambers, Iain (1994) *Migrancy, Culture, Identity.* London: Routledge.

Christianen, Michael (1995) 'Cycles in symbol production? a new model to explain concentration, diversity and innovation in the music industry', *Popular Music,* 14,1: 55–94.

Christopherson, Susan and Michael Storper (1986) 'The city as studio, the world as back lot: the impact of vertical disintegration on the location of the motion picture industry', *Environment and Planning D: Society and Space,* 4: 305–20.

Christopherson, Susan and Michael Storper (1989) 'The effects of flexible specialisation on industrial politics and the labor market: the motion picture industry', *Industrial and Labor Relations Review,* 42: 331–47.

Clark, Kenneth (1969) *Civilisation.* London: BBC.

Clifford, James (1988) *The Predicament of Culture.* Cambridge, Massachusetts: Harvard University Press.

Coffey, Steve and Horst Stipp (1997) 'The interactions between computer and television research', *Journal of Advertising Research,* 37,2: 61–7.

Cohn, Nik (1989/1969) 'Awopbopaloobop Alopbamboom', in *Ball the Wall.* London: Picador. pp. 49–139.

Collins, Richard (1998) *From Satellite to Single Market.* London: Routledge.

Collins, Richard and Cristina Murroni (1996) *New Media, New Policies.* Cambridge: Polity Press.

Commission of the European Communities (1984) *Television Without Frontiers. Green Paper on the Establishment of the Common Market for Broadcasting Especially by Satellite and Cable.* Brussels: COM (92) 480 final.

Commission of the European Communities (1994) *Europe and the Global Information Society: Recommendations to the EC* (The Bangemann Report). Brussels: European Commission, 25 May.

Compaine, Benjamin (1982) *Who Owns the Media?* White Plains, New York: Knowledge Industry Publications.

Congdon, Tim, Andrew Graham, Damian Green and Bill Robinson (eds) (1995) *The Cross Media Revolution.* London: John Libbey.

Corner, John (2000) ' "Influence": the contested core of media research', in James Curran and Michael Gurevitch (eds), *Mass Media and Society* (3rd edn). London: Arnold/New York: Oxford University Press. pp. 376–97.

Coser, Lewis A., Charles Kadushin and Walter W. Powell (1982) *Books.* New York: Basic Books, Inc.

Couldry, Nick (2000a) *The Place of Media Power.* London and New York: Routledge.

Couldry, Nick (2000b) *Inside Culture.* London: Sage.

Couldry, Nick (n.d.) 'Does disbelief have a future?' unpublished paper.

Council of the European Communities (1989) *Directive of the Coordination of Certain Provisions Laid Down by Law, Regulation or Administrative Action in Member States Concerning the Pursuit of Television Broadcasting Activities,* 89/552/EEC, *Official Journal of the European Communities,* L298/23, 17 October.

Croteau, David and William Hoynes (1997) *Media/Society.* Thousand Oaks, California and London: Pine Forge.

Curran, James (1986) 'The Impact of Advertising on the British Mass Media', in Richard Collins, James Curran, Nicholas Garnham, Paddy Scannell, Philip Schlesinger and Colin Sparks (eds), *Media, Culture and Society.* London: Sage.

Curran, James (1990) 'Culturalist perspectives of news organizations', in Marjorie Ferguson (ed.), *Public Communication: The New Imperatives*. London: Sage. pp. 114–34.

Curran, James (1996) 'Rethinking mass communications', in James Curran, David Morley and Valerie Walkerdine (eds), *Cultural Studies and Communications*. London: Arnold. pp. 119–65.

Curran, James (1998) 'Newspapers: beyond political economy', in Adam Briggs and Paul Cobley (eds), *The Media: An Introduction*. Harlow: Addison Wesley Longman. pp. 81–96.

Curran, James (2000) 'Rethinking media and democracy', in James Curran and Michael Gurevitch (eds), *Mass Media and Society* (3rd edn). London: Arnold/ New York: Oxford University Press. pp. 120–54.

Curran, James and Jean Seaton (1991) *Power Without Responsibility* (4th edn). London: Routledge.

Curran, James and Myung-Jin Park (eds) (2000) *De-westernizing Media Studies*. London and New York: Routledge.

Curtin, Michael (1999) 'Feminine desire in the age of satellite television', *Journal of Communication*, 49,1: 55–70.

Dale, Martin (1997) *The Movie Game*. London and New York: Cassell.

Daly, Charles P., Patrick Henry and Ellen Ryder (1997) *The Magazine Publishing Industry*. Boston: Allyn Bacon.

Davis, Howard and Richard Scase (2000) *Managing Creativity*. Buckingham and Philadelphia: Open University Press.

Dayan, Daniel and Elihu Katz (1992) *Media Events*. Cambridge, Massachusetts: Harvard University Press.

De Sola Pool, Ithiel (1983) *Technologies of Freedom*. Cambridge, Massachusetts: Harvard University Press.

DiMaggio, Paul (1977) 'Market structure, the creative process and popular culture: towards an organizational reinterpretation of mass-culture theory', *Journal of Popular Culture*, 11: 436–52.

Downey, John (1998) 'XS 4 all? "Information society" policy and practice in the European Union', in John Downey and Jim McGuigan (eds), *Technocities*. London: Sage. pp. 121–38.

Driver, Stephen and Andrew Gillespie (1992) 'The diffusion of digital technologies in magazine print publishing: organizational change and strategic choices', *Journal of Information Technology*, 7,3: 149–59.

Driver, Stephen and Andrew Gillespie (1993) 'Structural change in the cultural industries: British magazine publishing in the 1980s', *Media, Culture and Society*, 15: 183–201.

Du Gay, Paul, Stuart Hall, Linda Janes, Hugh Mackay and Keith Negus (1997) *Doing Cultural Studies*. Milton Keynes: The Open University/Sage.

Durant, Alan (1990) 'A new day for music? Digital technologies in contemporary music-making', in Philip Hayward (ed.), *Culture, Technology and Creativity in the Late Twentieth Century*. London: John Libbey. pp. 175–96.

During, Simon (1993) *The Cultural Studies Reader*. London and New York: Routledge.

Dyer, Richard (1981) 'Entertainment and utopia', in Rick Altman (ed.), *Genre: A Reader*. London: Routledge and Kegan Paul. pp. 175–89.

Euromedia Research Group (1997) *The Media in Western Europe*. London: Sage.

European Commission (1997) *Green Paper on the Regulatory Implications of the Telecommunications, Media and Information Technology Sectors: Towards a Common Approach to Information Society Services* (DGXIII). Brussels: European Commission.

European Commission (1998) *Culture, The Cultural Industries and Employment.* Brussels: European Commission (SEC (98)837).

Fairclough, Norman (1995) *Media Discourse.* London: Arnold.

Featherstone, Mike (1991) *Consumer Culture and Postmodernism.* London: Sage.

Fejes, Fred (1981) 'Media imperialism: an assessment', *Media, Culture and Society,* 3,3: 281–9.

Feld, Steven (1994) 'From schizophonia to schismogenesis: on the discourses and commodification practices of "world music" and "world beat" ', in Charles Keil and Steven Feld, *Music Grooves.* Chicago and London: University of Chicago Press. pp. 257–89.

Feldman, Tony (1998) *An Introduction to Digital Media.* London: Routledge.

Feuer, Jane (1984) 'MTM Enterprises: an overview', in Jane Feuer et al., pp. 1–31.

Jane Feuer, Paul Kerr and Tise Vahimagi (eds) (1984) *MTM 'Quality Television'.* London: British Film Institute.

Fine, Ben (1999) 'A question of economics: is it colonizing the social sciences?', *Economy and Society,* 28,3: 403–25.

Fiske, John (1990) *Introduction to Communication Studies* (2nd edn). London: Routledge.

Flichy, Patrice (1980) *Les industries de l'imaginaire.* Grenoble: Presse Universitaires de Grenoble.

Flichy, Patrice (1999) 'The construction of new digital media', *New Media and Society,* 1,1: 33–8.

Fligstein, Neil (1990) *The Transformation of Corporate Control.* Cambridge, Massachusetts: Harvard University Press.

Forester, Tom (ed.) (1985) *The Information Technology Revolution.* Oxford: Blackwell.

Forester, Tom (1987) *High-tech Society.* Oxford: Blackwell.

Fraser, Nancy (1997) *Justice Interruptus.* New York and London: Routledge.

Frith, Simon (1986) 'Art versus technology: the strange case of popular music', *Media, Culture and Society,* 8: 263–79.

Frith, Simon (1991) 'Anglo-America and its discontents', *Cultural Studies,* 5,3: 263–9.

Frith, Simon (1996) *Performing Rites.* Oxford: Oxford University Press.

Galperin, Hernan (1999) 'Cultural industries in the age of free-trade agreements', *Canadian Journal of Communication,* 24,1: 49–77.

Gamson, Joshua (1994) *Claims to Fame.* Berkeley and Los Angeles: University of California Press.

Gandy, Oscar H., Jnr (2000) 'Race, ethnicity and the segmentation of media markets', in James Curran and Michael Gurevitch (eds), *Mass Media and Society* (3rd edn). London: Arnold/New York: Oxford University Press. pp. 44–69.

Gans, Herbert J. (1979) *Deciding What's News.* New York: Vintage Press.

Garfield, Simon (1986) *Expensive Habits.* London: Faber and Faber.

Garnham, Nicholas (1990) *Capitalism and Communication.* London: Sage.

Garnham, Nicholas (1996) 'Convergence between telecommunications and audio-visual: consequences for the rules governing the information market: regulatory issues', Brussels: European Commission, Legal Advisory Board.

Garnham, Nicholas (1998) 'Media policy', in Adam Briggs and Paul Cobley (eds), *The Media: An Introduction.* Harlow: Addison Wesley Longman. pp. 210–23.

Garnham, Nicholas (2000) *Emancipation, the Media, and Modernity.* Oxford: Oxford University Press.

Garofalo, Reebee (1993) 'Whose world, what beat: the transnational music industry, identity, and cultural imperialism', in *The World of Music,* 35,2: 16–32.

Gates, Bill, Nathan Myhrvold and Peter Rinearson (1996) *The Road Ahead.* New York: Penguin.

Gates, Henry Louis, Jnr (1988) *The Signifying Monkey*. New York and Oxford: Oxford University Press.

Geraghty, Christine (1991) *Women and Soap Opera*. Cambridge: Polity Press.

Ghemawat, Pankaj and Ghadar, Fariborz (2000) 'The dubious logic of global megamergers', *Harvard Business Review*, July–August: 65–71.

Giddens, Anthony (1990) *The Consequences of Modernity*. Stanford: Stanford University Press.

Gilder, George (1993) 'The death of telephony', *The Economist*, 11 September.

Gillespie, Marie (1995) *Television, Ethnicity and Cultural Change*. London: Routledge.

Gillett, Charlie (1971) *The Sound of the City*. London: Sphere.

Gilroy, Paul (1993) *The Black Atlantic*. London:Verso.

Gitlin, Todd (1983) *Inside Prime Time*. New York: Pantheon Books.

Gitlin, Todd (1997) 'Introduction', in Patricia Aufderheide et al., pp. 7–13.

Gitlin, Todd (1998) 'The anti-political populism of cultural studies', in Marjorie Ferguson and Peter Golding (eds), *Cultural Studies in Question*. London: Sage. pp. 25–38.

Glasgow Media Group (1976) *Bad News*. London: Routledge and Kegan Paul.

Goldberg, David, Tony Prosser and Stefaan Verhulst (eds) (1998) *Regulating the Changing Media*. Oxford: Clarendon Press.

Golding, Peter (2000) 'Forthcoming features: information and communications technologies and the sociology of the future', *Sociology*, 34,1: 165–84.

Golding, Peter and Graham Murdock (2000) 'Culture, communications and political economy', in James Curran and Michael Gurevitch (eds), *Mass Media and Society* (3$^{rd}$ edn). London: Arnold/New York: Oxford University Press. pp. 70–92.

Gomery, Douglas (1986) *The Hollywood Studio System*. Basingstoke: Macmillan/ British Film Institute.

Goodwin, Andrew and Joe Gore (1990) 'World beat and the cultural imperialism debate', *Socialist Review*, 20,3: 63–80.

Gray, John (1998) *False Dawn*. London: Granta Books.

Greco, Albert N. (1995) 'Mergers and acquistions in the US book industry, 1960–89', in Philip G. Altbach and Edith S. Hoshino (eds), *International Book Publishing: An Encyclopedia*. New York and London: Garland Publishing. pp. 229–42.

Greco, Albert N. (1996) 'Shaping the future: mergers, acquisitions, and the U.S. publishing, communications, and mass media industries, 1990–1995', in *Publishing Research Quarterly*, 12,3: 5–16.

Greenfield, Steve and Guy Osborn (1994) 'Sympathy for the devil? contractual constraint and artistic autonomy in the entertainment industry', *Media Law and Practice*, 15: 117–27.

Gripsrud, Jostein (1995) *The Dynasty Years*. London and New York: Routledge.

Gronow, Pekka (1998) *An International History of the Recording Industry*. London: Cassell.

Grossberg, Lawrence (1995) 'Cultural studies vs. political economy: is anybody else bored with this debate?' *Critical Studies in Mass Communications*, 12,1: 72–81.

Guback, Thomas H. (1969) *The International Film Industry*. Bloomington and London: Indiana University Press.

Guback, Thomas H. (1985) 'Hollywood's international market', in Tino Balio (ed.), *The American Film Industry*. Wisconsin: University of Wisconsin Press. pp. 463–86.

Hafner, Katie and Matthew Lyon (1996) *Where Wizards Stay Up Late*. New York: Simon and Schuster.

Hall, Stuart (1992) 'Cultural studies and its theoretical legacies', in Lawrence Grossberg, Cary Nelson and Paula Treichler (eds), *Cultural Studies*. New York and London: Routledge. pp. 286–94.

Hall, Stuart (1994) 'Cultural identity and diaspora', in Patrick Williams and Laura Chrisman (eds), *Colonial Discourse and Post-colonial Theory*. Hemel Hempstead: Harvester Wheatsheaf. pp. 392–403.

Hall, Stuart (1997) 'The centrality of culture: notes on the cultural revolutions of our time', in Kenneth Thompson (ed.), *Media and Cultural Regulation*. London: Sage. pp. 207–38.

Hall, Stuart and Martin Jacques (eds) (1990) *New Times*. London: Lawrence and Wishart.

Hallin, Daniel C. (1994) *We Keep America on Top of the World*. New York and London: Routledge.

Hallin, Daniel C. (2000) 'Commercialism and professionalism in the American news media', in James Curran and Michael Gurevitch (eds), *Mass Media and Society* (3rd edn). London: Arnold/New York: Oxford University Press. pp. 218–37.

Hamelink, Cees (1983) *Cultural Autonomy in Global Communications*. New York: Longmans.

Harrison, Bennett (1994) *Lean and Mean*. New York: Basic Books.

Harvey, David (1989) *The Condition of Postmodernity*. Oxford: Blackwell.

Hatch, Martin (1989) 'Popular music in Indonesia', in Simon Frith (ed.), *World Music, Politics and Social Change*. Manchester: Manchester University Press. pp. 47–67.

Held, David and Anthony McGrew, David Goldblatt and Jonathan Perraton (1999) *Global Transformations*. Cambridge: Polity Press.

Herman, Edward S. and Robert W. McChesney (1997) *The Global Media*. London: Cassell.

Hermes, Joke (1995) *Reading Women's Magazines*. Cambridge: Polity Press.

Hesmondhalgh, David (1996) 'Flexibility, post-Fordism and the music industries', in *Media, Culture and Society*, 15,3: 469–88.

Hesmondhalgh, David (1997) 'Post-punk's attempt to democratise the music industry: the success and failure of Rough Trade', *Popular Music*, 16,3: 255–74.

Hesmondhalgh, David (1998) 'The British dance music industry: a case study in independent cultural production', *The British Journal of Sociology*, 49,2: 234–51.

Hesmondhalgh, David (1999) 'Indie: the aesthetics and institutional politics of a popular music genre', *Cultural Studies*, 13,1: 34–61.

Hesmondhalgh, David (2000) 'International times: fusions, exoticism and anti-racism in electronic dance music', in Georgina Born and David Hesmondhalgh (eds), *Western Music and its Others: Difference, Representation and Appropriation in Music*. Berkeley, Los Angeles and London: University of California Press. pp. 280–304.

Hirsch, Paul M. (1990/1972) 'Processing fads and fashions: an organization-set analysis of cultural industry systems', in Simon Frith and Andrew Goodwin (eds), *On Record*. New York: Pantheon. pp. 127–39.

Hobsbawm, Eric (1995) *Age of Extremes*. London: Abacus.

Hoffman-Reim, Wolfgang (1996) *Regulating Media*. New York and London: The Guilford Press.

Hoskins, Colin, Stuart McFadyen and Adam Finn (1997) *Global Television and Film*. Oxford: Oxford University Press.

Hotelling, Harold (1929) 'Stability in competition', *Economic Journal*, 34: 41–57.

Howard, Toby (1998) 'Survey of European advertising expenditure 1980–1996', *International Journal of Advertising*, 17,1: 115–24.

Huet, Armel, Jacques Ion, Alain Lefebvre and Bernard Miège (1978) *Capitalisme et industries culturelles*. Grenoble: Presses Universitaires de Grenoble.

Humphreys, Peter J. (1996) *Mass Media and Media Policy in Western Europe*. Manchester: Manchester University Press.

IJOA (1998a) 'Africa and the Middle East – focus on the smaller adspend regions', *International Journal of Advertising*, 17,4: 515–20.

IJOA (1998b) 'Adspend in the Americas – a tale of two regions', *International Journal of Advertising*, 17,3: 393–8.

IJOA (2000) 'World advertising expenditure', *International Journal of Advertising*, 19,1: 139–144.

Introna, Lucas D. and Helen Nissenbaum (2000) 'Shaping the web: why the politics of search engines matters', *The Information Society*, 16: 169–85.

Iosifides, Petros (1997) 'Methods of measuring media concentration', *Media, Culture and Society*, 19: 643–63.

Jenkins, Henry (2000) 'Art form for the digital age', *Technology Review*, 103,5: 117–19.

Johnson, Richard (1986/7) 'What is cultural studies anyway?' *Social Text*, 6: 38–90.

Jordan, Tim (1998) *Cyberpower*. London and New York: Routledge.

Kealy, Edward R. (1990/1974) 'From craft to art: the case of sound mixers and popular music', in Simon Frith and Andrew Goodwin (eds), *On Record*. New York: Pantheon. pp. 207–20.

Keane, John (1991) *The Media and Democracy*. Cambridge: Polity Press.

Keat, Russell and Nicholas Abercrombie (eds) (1991) *Enterprise Culture*. London: Routledge.

Keil, Charles and Steven Feld (1994) *Music Grooves*. Chicago and London: University of Chicago Press.

Kit-wai Ma, Eric (2000) 'Rethinking media studies: the case of China', in James Curran and Myung-Jin Park (eds), *De-Westernizing Media Studies*. London and New York: Routledge.

Kleinsteuber, Hans J. (1998) 'The digital future', in Denis McQuail and Karen Siune (eds), *Media Policy*. London: Sage. pp. 60–74.

Laing, Dave (1985) *One Chord Wonders*. Buckingham: Open University Press.

Laing, Dave (1986) 'The music industry and the "cultural imperialism" thesis', *Media, Culture and Society*, 8,3: 331–41.

Laing, Dave (1992) ' "Sadeness", scorpions and single markets: national and transnational trends in European popular music', *Popular Music*, 11,2: 127–40.

Lash, Scott and John Urry (1994) *Economies of Signs and Space*. London: Sage.

Lent, John A. (1990) *The Asian Film Industry*. London: Christopher Helm.

Lent, John A. (1998) 'The animation industry and its offshore factories', in Gerald Sussman and John A. Lent (eds), *Global Productions*. Cresskill, New Jersey: Hampton Press Inc. pp. 239–54.

Lerner, Preston (1999) 'Shadow force', *Los Angeles Times Magazine*, 7 November.

Levy, Emanuel (1999) *Cinema of Outsiders*. New York and London: New York University Press.

Liebes, Tamar and Elihu Katz (1993) *The Export of Meaning*. Cambridge: Polity.

Lomax, Alan (1978/1968) *Folk Song Style and Structure*. New Brunswick: Transaction Books.

Lopes, Paul D. (1992) 'Innovation and diversity in the popular music industry, 1969–1990', *American Sociological Review*, 57,1: 56–71.

Lowery, Shearon and Melvin L. DeFleur (1995) *Milestones in Mass Communication Research* (3rd edn). New York: Longman.

Lyotard, Jean-François (1984) *The Postmodern Condition*. Minneapolis: University of Minnesota Press.

MacDonald, Dwight (1963) *Against the American Grain*. London: Victor Gollancz.

Magder, Ted and Jonathan Burston (2002) 'Whose Hollywood? Changing forms and relations inside the North American entertainment economy', in Vincent Mosco and Dan Schiller (eds), *Continental Integration for Cybercapitalism*. New York: Rowan and Littlefield.

Mancini, Paolo and Daniel Hallin (2001) 'Italy's television, Italy's democracy', *OpenDemocracy*. www.opendemocracy.net, posted 19 July.

Mankekar, Purnima (1999) *Screening Culture, Viewing Politics*. Durham, North Carolina: Duke University Press.

Mansell, Robin (1993) *The New Telecommunications*. London: Sage.

Marglin, Stephen A. and Juliet B. Schor (eds) (1992) *The Golden Age of Capitalism*. Oxford: Clarendon.

Mattelart, Armand (1991) *Advertising International*. London: Routledge/Comedia.

Mattelart, Armand and Michèle Mattelart (1990) *The Carnival of Images*. New York: Bergin & Garvey.

Mattelart, Armand and Michèle Mattelart (1998) *Theories of Communication*. London: Sage.

Mazzoleni, Giuseppe (1995) 'Towards a videocracy: Italian political communication at a turning point', *European Journal of Communication*, 10,3: 291–319.

McAllister, Matthew P. (2000) 'From flick to flack: the increased emphasis on marketing by media entertainment corporations', in Robin Andersen and Lance Strate (eds), *Critical Studies in Media Commercialism*. Oxford: Oxford University Press. pp. 101–22.

McChesney, Robert W. (1993) *Telecommunications, Mass Media and Democracy*. New York and Oxford: Oxford University Press.

McChesney, Robert W. (1999) *Rich Media, Poor Democracy*. Urbana and Chicago, Illinois: University of Illinois Press.

McGuigan, Jim (1992) *Cultural Populism*. London: Routledge.

McGuigan, Jim (1998) 'What price the public sphere?', in Daya Thussu (ed.), *Electronic Empires*. London: Arnold. pp. 91–107.

McQuail, Denis (1992) *Media Performance*. London: Sage.

McQuail, Denis (2000) *McQuail's Mass Communication Theory*. London: Sage.

McQuail, Denis and Karen Siune (eds) (1998) *Media Policy*. London: Sage.

McRobbie, Angela (1998) *British Fashion Design*. London: Routledge.

Meehan, Eileen (1991) ' "Holy commodity fetish, Batman!" The political economy of a commercial intertext', in Roberta E. Pearson and William Urrichio (eds), *The Many Lives of the Batman*. London: BFI Publishing/New York: Routledge, Chapman and Hall. pp. 47–65.

Meier, Werner A. and Josef Trappel (1998) 'Media concentration and the public interest', in Denis McQuail and Karen Siune (eds), *Media Policy*. London: Sage. pp. 38–59.

Merritt, Greg (2000) *Celluloid Mavericks*. New York: Thunder's Mouth Press.

Miège, Bernard (1979) 'The cultural commodity', *Media, Culture and Society*, 1: 297–311.

Miège, Bernard (1987) 'The logics at work in the new cultural industries', *Media, Culture and Society*, 9: 273–89.

Miège, Bernard (1989) *The Capitalization of Cultural Production*. New York: International General.

Miller, David (1998) 'Promotional strategies and media power', in Adam Briggs and Paul Cobley (eds), *The Media: An Introduction.* Harlow: Addison Wesley Longman. pp. 65–80.

Miller, David and Greg Philo (2000) 'Cultural compliance and critical media studies', *Media, Culture and Society,* 22,6: 831–9.

Miller, Mark Crispin (1997) 'The publishing industry', in Aufderheide et al., pp. 107–34.

Mitchell, Tony (ed.) (2001) *Global Noise.* Hanover, New Hampshire and London: Wesleyan University Press.

Montgomery, Sarah S. and Michael D. Robinson (1993) 'Visual artists in New York: what's special about person and place?' *Journal of Cultural Economics,* 17: 17–39.

Moran, Joe (1997) 'The role of multimedia conglomerates in American trade book publishing', *Media, Culture and Society,* 19: 441–55.

Morin, Edgar (1962) *L'esprit du temps.* Paris: Bernard Grasset.

Morley, David (1986) *Family Television.* London: Comedia.

Morley, David and Kuan-Hsing Chen (eds) (1996) *Stuart Hall.* London and New York: Routledge.

Morris, Meaghan (1992) 'The man in the mirror: David Harvey's "condition" of postmodernity', *Theory, Culture and Society,* 9: 253–79.

Mosco, Vincent (1995) *The Political Economy of Communication.* London: Sage.

Murdock, Graham (1982) 'Large corporations and the control of the communications industries', in Michael Gurevitch et al. (eds), *Culture, Society and the Media.* London: Methuen. pp. 118–50.

Murdock, Graham (1990) 'Redrawing the map of the communications industries: concentration and ownership in the era of privatization', in Marjorie Ferguson (ed.), *Public Communication: The New Imperatives.* London: Sage. pp. 1–15.

Murdock, Graham (2000) 'Digital futures: European television in the age of convergence', in Jan Wieten, Graham Murdock and Peter Dahlgren (eds), *Television Across Europe.* London: Sage. pp. 35–57.

Murdock, Graham and Peter Golding (1974) 'Towards a political economy of the media', in Ralph Miliband (ed.), *Socialist Register 1974.*

Murdock, Graham and Peter Golding (1977) 'Capitalism, communication and class relations', in James Curran, Michael Gurevitch and Janet Wollacott (eds), *Mass Communication and Society.* London: Edward Arnold, in association with The Open University Press. pp. 12–43.

Murdock, Graham and Peter Golding (1999) 'Common markets: corporate ambitions and communication trends in the UK and Europe', *The Journal of Media Economics,* 12,2: 117–32.

Naficy, Hamid (1993) *The Making of Exile Cultures.* Minneapolis: University of Minnesota Press.

Negroponte, Nicholas (1995) *Being Digital.* London: Hodder & Stoughton.

Negus, Keith (1992) *Producing Pop.* London: Edward Arnold.

Negus, Keith (1997) 'The production of culture', in Paul du Gay (ed.), *Production of Culture/Cultures of Production.* Milton Keynes: The Open University/Sage. pp. 67–118.

Negus, Keith (1999) *Music Genres and Corporate Cultures.* London and New York: Routledge.

Neuman, W. Russell (1991) *The Future of the Mass Audience.* Cambridge: Cambridge University Press.

Nixon, Sean (1997) 'Circulating culture', in Paul du Gay (ed.), *Production of Culture/ Cultures of Production.* Milton Keynes: The Open University/Sage. pp. 177–234.

Ong, Aihwa (1999) *Flexible Citizenship*. Durham, North Carolina and London: Duke University Press.

Østergaard, Bernt Stubbe (1998) 'Convergence: legislative dilemmas', in Denis McQuail and Karen Siune (eds), *Media Policy*. London: Sage. pp. 95–106.

Padioleau, Jean G. (1987) 'The management of communications', *Media, Culture and Society*, 9: 291–300.

Patelis, Korinna (1999) 'The political economy of the Internet', in James Curran (ed.), *Media Organizations in Society*. London: Arnold. pp. 84–106.

Paterson, Richard (1998) 'Drama and entertainment', in Anthony Smith with Richard Paterson (eds), *Television: An International History*. Oxford: Oxford University Press. pp. 57–68.

Peacock Report (1986) *The Report of the Committee on Financing the BBC*. London: HMSO.

Pendakur, Manjunath (1990) 'India', in John A. Lent, *The Asian Film Industry*. London: Christopher Helm. pp. 229–52.

Peterson, Richard A. (1976) 'The production of culture: a prolegomenon', in Richard A. Peterson (ed.), *The Production of Culture*. Beverley Hills, CA: Sage. pp. 7–22.

Peterson, Richard A. (1997) *Creating Country Music*. Chicago and London: University of Chicago Press.

Peterson, Richard A. and David G. Berger (1971) 'Entrepreneurship in organizations: evidence from the popular music industry', *Administrative Science Quarterly*, 16: 97–107.

Peterson, Richard A. and David G. Berger (1990/1975) 'Cycles in symbol production: the case of popular music', in Simon Frith and Andrew Goodwin (eds), *On Record*. New York: Pantheon. pp. 140–59.

Peterson, Richard A. and Roger M. Kern (1996) 'Changing highbrow taste: from snob to omnivore', *American Sociological Review*, 61: 900–7.

Piore, Michael and Charles Sabel (1984) *The Second Industrial Divide*. New York: Basic Books.

Poole, Steven (2000) *Trigger Happy*. London: Fourth Estate

Porcello, Thomas (1991) 'The ethics of digital audio-sampling', *Popular Music*, 10,1: 69–84.

Prindle, David F. (1993) *Risky Business*. Boulder, Colorado: Westview Press.

Raboy, Marc (ed.) (1997) *Public Broadcasting for the 21st Century*. Luton: University of Luton Press.

Raphael, Chad (2001) 'Untangling the web', in Richard Maxwell (ed.), *Culture Works*. Minneapolis, Minnesota: University of Minnesota Press.

Raphael, Chad (n.d.) 'From *Red Lion* to *Food Lion*: privatizing US broadcast news regulation', unpublished paper, University of Santa Clara, California.

Reynolds, Simon and Joy Press (1995) *The Sex Revolts*. London: Serpent's Tail.

Rheingold, Howard (1992) *Virtual Reality*. London: Mandarin.

Rigby, S.H. (1998) *Marxism and History* (2nd edn). Manchester and New York: Manchester University Press.

Robertson, Roland (1990) 'Mapping the global condition: globalization as the central concept', in Mike Featherstone (ed.), *Global Culture*. London: Sage. pp. 15–30.

Robins, Kevin (1997) 'What in the world's going on?' in Paul du Gay (ed.), *Production of Culture/Cultures of Production*. Milton Keynes: The Open University/Sage. pp. 11–66.

Robins, Kevin and James Cornford (1992) 'What is "flexible" about independent producers?', *Screen*, 33,2: 190–200.

Ross, Andrew (1989) *No Respect*. London: Routledge.

Ross, Andrew (ed.) (1998) *No Sweat*. New York and London: Verso.

Ryan, Bill (1992) *Making Capital from Culture*. Berlin and New York: Walter de Gruyter.

Sadler, David (1997) 'The global music business as an information industry: reinterpreting economies of culture', *Environment and Planning A*, 29: 1919–36.

Said, Edward W. (1994) *Culture and Imperialism*. London: Vintage.

Sánchez-Tabernero, Alfonso, Alison Denton, Pierre-Yves Lochon, Philippe Mounier and Runar Woldt (1993) *Media Concentration in Europe*. Dusseldorf: The European Institute for the Media.

Sassen, Saskia (1998) *Globalization and its Discontents*. New York: New Press.

Sassen, Saskia (2000) 'Digital networks and the state', *Theory, Culture and Society*, 17,4: 19–33.

Schiller, Dan (1997) *Theorizing Communication*. New York and Oxford: Oxford University Press.

Schiller, Dan (1999) *Digital Capitalism*. Cambridge, Massachusetts: Harvard University Press.

Schiller, Herbert I. (1969) *Mass Communication and American Empire*. Boston: Beacon Press.

Schiller, Herbert I. (1976) *Communication and Cultural Domination*. White Plains, New York: International Arts and Sciences Press.

Schiller, Herbert I. (1981) *Who Knows*. Norwood, New Jersey: Ablex.

Schiller, Herbert I. (1989) *Culture, Inc*. New York and Oxford: Oxford University Press.

Schiller, Herbert I. (1998) 'Striving for communication dominance: a half century review', in Daya Thussu (ed.), *Electronic Empires*. London: Arnold. pp. 17–26.

Schlesinger, Philip (1978) *Putting 'Reality' Together*. London: Methuen.

Schlesinger, Philip and Howard Tumber (1994) *Reporting Crime*. Oxford: Clarendon Press.

Schumacher, Thomas (1995) ' "This is a sampling sport": digital sampling, rap music and the law in cultural production', *Media, Culture and Society*, 17,2: 253–73.

Scott, John (1995) *Corporate Business and Capitalist Classes*. Oxford: Oxford University Press.

Segrave, Kerry (1997) *American Films Abroad*. Jefferson, North Carolina: McFarland & Company.

Sinclair, John (1996) 'Mexico, Brazil and the Latin world', in John Sinclair, Elizabeth Jacka and Stuart Cunningham (eds), *New Patterns in Global Television*. Oxford: Oxford University Press. pp. 33–66.

Sinclair, John, Elizabeth Jacka and Stuart Cunningham (1996) 'Peripheral vision', in John Sinclair, Elizabeth Jacka and Stuart Cunningham (eds), *New Patterns in Global Television*. Oxford: Oxford University Press. pp. 1–32.

Singelmann, Joachim (1978) *From Agriculture to Services*. Beverley Hills: Sage.

Sinha, Nikhil (1997) 'India: television and national politics', in Marc Raboy (ed.), *Public Broadcasting for the 21st Century*. Luton: University of Luton Press. pp. 212–29.

Siune, Karen and Olof Hultén (1998) 'Does public broadcasting have a future?', in Denis McQuail and Karen Siune (eds), *Media Policy*. London: Sage. pp. 23–37.

Smith, Anthony with Richard Paterson (eds) (1998) *Television: An International History*. Oxford: Oxford University Press.

Sparks, Colin (2000) 'Media theory after the fall of European communism: why the old models from East and West won't do anymore', in James Curran and

Myung-Jin Park (eds), *De-westernizing Media Studies*. London and New York: Routledge.

Spivak, Gayatri Chakravorty (1988) *In Other Worlds*. New York and London: Routledge.

Sreberny, Annabelle (1997) 'The many cultural faces of imperialism', in Peter Golding and Phil Harris (eds), *Beyond Cultural Imperialism*. London: Sage. pp. 49–68.

Steemers, Jeanette (ed.) (1998) *Changing Channels*. Luton: University of Luton Press.

Sterling, Christopher H. and John M. Kittross (1990) *Stay Tuned*. Belmont, California: Wadsworth Publishing Company.

Stevenson, Nick (1999) *The Transformation of the Media*. Harlow: Addison Wesley Longman.

Stokes, Lisa Oldham and Michael Hoover (1999) *City on Fire*. London: Verso.

Straw, Will (1990) *Popular Music as Cultural Commodity: The American Recorded Music Industries 1976–1985*. Unpublished doctoral thesis, Graduate Program in Communications, McGill University, Montreal.

Tasker, Yvonne (1996) 'Approaches to the new Hollywood', in James Curran, David Morley and Valerie Walkerdine (eds), *Cultural Studies and Communications*. London: Arnold. pp. 213–28.

Teo, Stephen (2000) 'Hong Kong cinema', in John Hill and Pamela Church Gibson (eds), *World Cinema: Critical Approaches*. Oxford: Oxford University Press. pp. 166–72.

Théberge, Paul (1989) 'The "sound" of music: technological rationalisation and the production of popular music', *New Formations*, 8: 99–111.

Théberge, Paul (1997) *Any Sound You Can Imagine*. Hanover, New Hampshire and London: Wesleyan University Press.

Thomas, Pradip N. (1998) 'South Asia', in Anthony Smith and Richard Paterson (eds), *Television: An International History*. Oxford: Oxford University Press. pp. 201–7.

Thomas, Rosie (1985) 'Indian cinema: pleasures and popularity', *Screen*, 26,3–4: 116–31.

Thompson, John B. (1995) *The Media and Modernity*. Cambridge: Polity Press.

Thompson, Kristin (1999) *Storytelling in the New Hollywood*. Cambridge, Massachusetts: Harvard University Press.

Thussu, Daya Kishan (1999) 'Privatizing the airwaves: the impact of globalization on broadcasting in India', *Media, Culture and Society*, 21,1: 125–31.

Tomlinson, John (1991) *Cultural Imperialism*. London: Pinter.

Tomlinson, John (1997) 'Internationalism, globalization and cultural imperialism', in Kenneth Thompson (ed.), *Media and Cultural Regulation*. London: Sage/The Open University. pp. 119–53.

Tomlinson, John (1999) *Globalization and Culture*. Cambridge: Polity.

Towse, Ruth (ed.) (1997) *Cultural Economics*. Cheltenham: Edward Elgar.

Toynbee, Jason (2000) *Making Popular Music*. London: Arnold.

Toynbee, Jason (2001) 'Creating problems: social authorship, copyright and the production of culture', Pavis Papers in Social and Cultural Research 3. Milton Keynes: The Pavis Centre for Social and Cultural Research, The Open University.

Tracey, Michael (1998) *The Decline and Fall of Public Service Broadcasting*. Oxford and New York: Oxford University Press.

Tuchman, Gaye (1978) *Making News*. New York: Free Press.

Tumber, Howard (ed.) (1999) *News: A Reader*. Oxford: Oxford University Press.

Tunstall, Jeremy (1971) *Journalists at Work*. London: Constable.

Tunstall, Jeremy (1986) *Communications Deregulation*. Oxford: Blackwell.

Tunstall, Jeremy (1993) *Television Producers*. London: Routledge.

Tunstall, Jeremy (1994) *The Media are American* (2nd edn). London: Constable.

Tunstall, Jeremy (1997) 'The United Kingdom', in Euromedia Research Group/ Bernt Stubbe Østergaard (ed.), *The Media in Western Europe*. London: Sage. pp. 244–59.

Tunstall, Jeremy and David Machin (1999) *The Anglo-American Media Connection*. Oxford: Oxford University Press.

Tunstall, Jeremy and Michael Palmer (1990) *Liberating Communications*. Oxford, UK and Cambridge, Massachusetts: Basil Blackwell.

UNESCO (1980) *Many Voices, One World*. Paris: UNESCO.

UNESCO (1982) *The Cultural Industries*. Paris: UNESCO.

Van Leeuwen, Theo (1999) *Music, Speech and Sound*. Basingstoke: Macmillan.

Varis, Tapio and Kaarle Nordenstreng (1985) *International Flow of Television Programmes*. Paris: UNESCO.

Vink, Nico (1988) *The Telenovela and Emancipation*. Amsterdam: Royal Tropical Institute.

Vogel, Harold L. (1998) *Entertainment Industry Economics* (4th edn). Cambridge, UK and New York: Cambridge University Press.

Waisbord, Silvio (1998) 'Latin America', in Anthony Smith with Richard Paterson (eds), *Television: An International History* (2nd edn). Oxford: Oxford University Press. pp. 254–63.

Walser, Robert (1993) *Running with the Devil*. Hanover, New Hampshire: Wesleyan University Press.

Wasko, Janet (1994) *Hollywood in the Information Age*. Cambridge: Polity Press.

Waterman, Christopher Alan (1990) *Jùjú*. Chicago: University of Chicago Press.

Webster, Frank (1995) *Theories of the Information Society*. London: Routledge.

Webster, James G. and Patricia F. Phalen (1997) *The Mass Audience*. Mahwah, New Jersey: Lawrence Erlbaum.

Wells, Alan (1972) *Picture Tube Imperialism?* Maryknoll, New York: Orbis.

Whale, John (1977) *The Politics of the Media*. London: Fontana.

Wicke, Peter (1990) *Rock Music*. Cambridge: Cambridge University Press.

Willens, Michelle (2000) 'Putting films to the test', *New York Times*, Section 2, 25 June.

Williams, Raymond (1958) *Culture and Society*. London: Chatto and Windus.

Williams, Raymond (1961) *The Long Revolution*. London: Chatto and Windus.

Williams, Raymond (1974) *Television: Technology and Cultural Form*. London: Fontana.

Williams, Raymond (1977) *Marxism and Literature*. Oxford: Oxford University Press.

Williams, Raymond (1981) *Culture*. London: Fontana.

Willis, Paul (1990) *Common Culture*. Buckingham: Open University Press.

Winston, Brian (1998) *Media Technology and Society*. London and New York: Routledge.

Wolf, Michael J. (1999) *The Entertainment Economy*. London: Penguin Books.

Wolff, Janet (1993) *The Social Production of Art* (2nd edn). Basingstoke: Macmillan.

Wyatt, Justin (1994) *High Concept*. Austin: University of Texas Press.

# Index

For reasons of space, I haven't indexed the following categories: names of texts, unless they are the subject of prolonged discussion or are used as sources; company names, unless they have direct interests in the cultural industries; countries and geographical regions, except where the subject of sections; stars and celebrities, unless part of a substantive discussion.

policy, cultural, media and communications 2, 9, 64–6, 130, 145, 171, 173, 174, 207, 221, 257
 international bodies 130
Polish, badly-dubbed 186
political-economic change, as a context for change/continuity in the cultural industries 87–8, 264
political economy approaches to culture 29, 30–5, 37, 38, 39, 41, 43, 48, 67, 70, 82, 84, 145, 172, 197, 221–2, 248, 254, 263, 264
PolyGram 136, 141, 195
Poole, Steven 211, 212, 230
popular culture 23–4, 39, 60, 175, 192, 196, 263
popular music studies 233
Porcello, Thomas 207
pornography 119, 226
portal sites 219
post-Fordism 94, 144, 156
post-industrial societies 7
post-modernity 7
power 23, 36, 38, 40, 172, 200, 214, 229, 238, 241, 262, 265
Press, Joy 43
press, the; *see* newspapers
Prindle, David 17
product placement 78, 238–9
production of culture perspective 35–6, 38; *see* sociology of culture approach
production versus reproduction costs 18–19
production, relations between consumption and 34, 42
professionalisation, of internet 202, 262
profits 87, 92, 94, 155, 173, 208, 221, 241, 248
promotion 169, 232, 247
PTTs (postal, telegraph and telephone authorities) 110–11, 113, 122
public goods, cultural commodities as 19, 28, 58
public interest 114, 117–18, 131, 140, 143
public relations 122, 163
public service 114, 118; *see also* public interest
public service broadcasting 112–33 passim, 143, 161–2, 225, 228–9, 243, 245
public spending 87
public sphere 244–6
public utility, telecommunications as 110–11, 113, 118
public versus private 31
publicity 55, 71, 232
publishing industries 12, 110; *see also* book publishing, magazine publishing, newspapers
punk 23, 170

quality 11, 76–7, 142, 179, 193, 212, 231, 246–55, 263
quotas, cultural trade 130

Raboy, Marc 120

radical media sociology, as an approach to culture 36, 38, 41, 42
radio (as medium and technology) 12, 50, 59, 142, 184, 199, 201, 213, 222, 232; *see also* broadcasting
radio industry 146, 148
Random House 249
rap, *see* hip hop
Raphael, Chad 117, 130, 215, 219
rave 241
RCA (Radio Corporation of America) 59, 116, 141
Reagan, Ronald 88, 117
recording industry; *see* music industries
reductionism 45, 81–3
regulation, cultural, media and communications 2, 108–33 passim, 236; *see also* policy, cultural, media and communications
repertoire, cultural 19–20, 63
reproduction, stage in process of cultural production 21, 55, 72 MORE
re-regulation 109; *see* deregulation; policy
research and development 99
restructuring, organisational 94–6
Reuters 62, 200
rewards for cultural work, *see* symbol creators
Reynolds, Simon 43
Rheingold, Howard 213
Rigby, S. H. 46
RKO (Radio-Keith-Orpheum, Hollywood film studio) 61–2
Robertson, Roland 174
Robins, Kevin 33, 144, 152, 156
Robinson, Michael 168
rock and roll (phew) 194
Ross, Andrew 34, 76, 166
Royalties 50, 56, 168–70
Ryan, Bill 21, 22, 33, 34, 52–5, 79, 156–7, 167, 263

Sabel, Charles 94
Sadler, David 14
Said, Edward 39
samplers/sampling 203–4, 206, 229
Samuelson, Paul 85
Sanchez-Tabernero, Alfonso 91, 138, 142, 148, 172, 233
Sassen, Saskia 217, 218
satellite television 12, 113, 114, 123, 124, 125, 128, 129, 140, 142, 181, 185–7, 198–9, 222, 224–6, 228, 232, 236, 257
scarcity, artificial 21, 102
Scase, Richard 154, 161–2
Schiller, Dan 47–8, 217
Schiller, Herbert 32, 63, 73, 178, 197, 200
Schiller–McChesney tradition in the political economy of culture 33–6, 47, 150
Schlesinger, Philip 37, 163, 172
Schor, Juliet 85